Red Hat® Linux® "X" For Dummies

D0886250

vi Commands

The following list of commands contains the most useful and commonly-used commands to control the vi text editor. In fact, this author has been using vi since 1981 and has never learned to use many more commands than these. This proves that one can be lazy and stil get work done.

You enter these commands from a Shell prompt. See Chapter 4 for more details.

`vi filename`	Open *filename* in `vi`
`i`	Enter insert mode, inserting before the current position
Shift+`I`	Enter insert mode, inserting at the beginning of the current line
`a`	Enter insert mode, inserting after the current position
Shift+`A`	Enter insert mode, inserting at the end of the current line
`esc`	Return from insert mode to command mode
`a`	Delete a character while in command mode
`cw`	Delete the word to the left of the cursor and put the editor in input mode
`:w`	Write the file out
`:q`	Quit with no additional writes to the disk
`:wq`	Write back the file, and then quit
Shift+`ZZ`	Write back the file, and then quit
`:q!`	Quit the file with impending changes unwritten
`/string`	Search forward through the file for *string*
`?string`	Search backward through the file for *string*
`n`	Find the next string (either forward or backward)
`u`	Undo the last command

System Administration's

We list several commonly used Linux system commands below that help you to manage disks, shut down your computer, and gather information about it.

You enter these commands from a Shell prompt. Please consult Chapter 4 for more information about how to enter commands.

`mount [options] device file_system`	Mount a file system
`umount [option] file_system`	Unmount a file system
`fsck [options] file_system`	Check the structure and integrity of a specified file system
`mkfs [options] file_system`	Put a directory structure on a low-level formatted disk
`shutdown`	Shut the system down now instead of waiting for a message to be sent (Ctrl+Del does the same thing)
`vmstat [options]`	Look at the virtual memory performance
`procinfo`	Gather information about processes

File Permissions

The following examples show different file permission combinations. Please consult Chapter 15 for more information about file permissions.

`-rwxrwxrwx`	Read, write, and execute permissions for user, group, and other (the world) (mode 777)
`drwxr-xr--`	A directory that is completely open to its owner and that can be read and searched by the group and read (but not searched) by the world (mode 754)
`crw-r--r--`	A character special file that the owner can read or write to but that the group and the world can only read (mode 644)
`brw-------`	A block special file; only the owner can read or write to it (mode 600)

Red Hat® Linux® "X" For Dummies®

Cheat Sheet

A Few Good Commands

Some commonly-used and useful commands are listed below. You enter these commands from a Shell prompt. Please consult Chapter 4.

Command	Description
cd *directory*	Change the current directory to *directory*
ls	*[options] [directory]* List the current directory's contents
ls -l	List the current directory's contents, along with sizes, permissions, ownerships, and dates of files
ls -a	List all files, including invisible files (files whose names begin with a period)
pwd *[option]*	Print the working directory (the one you are in)
rm *[options] filename*	Remove *filename*
mkdir *[options] directory_name*	Make a new (empty) directory
rmdir *[options] directory_name*	Remove an empty directory
cp *[options] src_filename dst_filename*	Copy a file
mv *[options] src_filename dst_filename(s)*	Move (or rename) a file
cat *[options] filename*	Concatenate a file to the standard output (that means display the file)
more *[options] filename*	Paginate a file
less *[options] filename*	Paginate a file
touch *[option] filename*	Make a new (empty) file, changing the access date of an existing file
chown *[options] filename*	Change the owner of a file or a directory
chgrp *[options] filename*	Change the group of a file or a directory
chmod *[options] filename*	Change the permissions of a file or a directory
sort *[options] filename*	Sort a file in a particular order (depending on the option)
echo *[options] text string*	Echo on-screen what is typed after the command
date *[options] text string*	Read the date and time (without an argument); set the date and time (with an argument)
cut *[options] filename*	Break a wide file into multiple narrow files
sed *[options] filename*	Stream editor for large files or real-time editing
ln *[options] source_filename/directory target_filename/directory*	Link a filename to another file
grep *[options] filename*	Searching program that uses general regular expressions to find data, and then prints it to its output

Hungry Minds™

For Dummies: Bestselling Book Series for Beginners

Red Hat® Linux® 7.3 FOR DUMMIES®

by Jon "maddog" Hall and Paul G. Sery

Hungry Minds™

Best-Selling Books • Digital Downloads • e-Books • Answer Networks • e-Newsletters • Branded Web Sites • e-Learning

New York, NY ◆ Cleveland, OH ◆ Indianapolis, IN

Red Hat® Linux® 7.3 For Dummies®

Published by
Hungry Minds, Inc.
909 Third Avenue
New York, NY 10022
www.hungryminds.com
www.dummies.com

Library of Congress Control Number: 2002103293

ISBN: 0-7645-1545-4

Printed in the United States of America

10 9 8 7 6 5 4 3 2 1

1B/QX/QW/QS/IN

Distributed in the United States by Hungry Minds, Inc.

Distributed by CDG Books Canada Inc. for Canada; by Transworld Publishers Limited in the United Kingdom; by IDG Norge Books for Norway; by IDG Sweden Books for Sweden; by IDG Books Australia Publishing Corporation Pty. Ltd. for Australia and New Zealand; by TransQuest Publishers Pte Ltd. for Singapore, Malaysia, Thailand, Indonesia, and Hong Kong; by Gotop Information Inc. for Taiwan; by ICG Muse, Inc. for Japan; by Intersoft for South Africa; by Eyrolles for France; by International Thomson Publishing for Germany, Austria and Switzerland; by Distribuidora Cuspide for Argentina; by LR International for Brazil; by Galileo Libros for Chile; by Ediciones ZETA S.C.R. Ltda. for Peru; by WS Computer Publishing Corporation, Inc., for the Philippines; by Contemporanea de Ediciones for Venezuela; by Express Computer Distributors for the Caribbean and West Indies; by Micronesia Media Distributor, Inc. for Micronesia; by Chips Computadoras S.A. de C.V. for Mexico; by Editorial Norma de Panama S.A. for Panama; by American Bookshops for Finland.

For general information on Hungry Minds' products and services please contact our Customer Care Department within the U.S. at 800-762-2974, outside the U.S. at 317-572-3993 or fax 317-572-4002.

For sales inquiries and reseller information, including discounts, premium and bulk quantity sales, and foreign-language translations, please contact our Customer Care Department at 800-434-3422, fax 317-572-4002, or write to Hungry Minds, Inc., Attn: Customer Care Department, 10475 Crosspoint Boulevard, Indianapolis, IN 46256.

For information on licensing foreign or domestic rights, please contact our Sub-Rights Customer Care Department at 212-884-5000.

For information on using Hungry Minds' products and services in the classroom or for ordering examination copies, please contact our Educational Sales Department at 800-434-2086 or fax 317-572-4005.

For press review copies, author interviews, or other publicity information, please contact our Public Relations Department at 317-572-3168 or fax 317-572-4168.

For authorization to photocopy items for corporate, personal, or educational use, please contact Copyright Clearance Center, 222 Rosewood Drive, Danvers, MA 01923, or fax 978-750-4470.

Hungry Minds™ is a trademark of Hungry Minds, Inc.

About the Authors

Jon "maddog" Hall is the Executive Director of Linux International, a vendor organization dedicated to promoting the use of the Linux Operating System. He has been in the computer industry for over a quarter of a century (somehow that sounds more impressive than just "25 years"), the past 18 years of which have been spent using, programming, and admiring the UNIX Operating System. Currently, Jon works for Compaq Computer Corporation, where he is helping to shape Compaq's strategy with respect to Linux. Previously, Jon was the Department Head of Computer Science at Hartford State Technical College, where his students lovingly (he hopes) gave him the nickname "maddog" as he tried to teach them operating system design, compiler theory, and how to live an honorable life.

While working for Digital Equipment Corporation in May of 1994, maddog met Linus Torvalds, and was intelligent enough (his critics say maddog was just lucky) to recognize the potential of the Linux Operating System. Linux changed his life, mostly by providing him with 22-hour workdays. Since maddog has started working with Linux, however, he has also started meeting more girls (in particular, his two godchildren). You can usually find Jon speaking at various Linux conferences and events (maddog just barks), and he has also been known to travel long distances to speak to local Linux user groups.

Paul G. Sery is a Computer Systems Engineer employed by Sandia National Laboratories in Albuquerque, NM, USA. He is a member of the Computer Support Unit, Special Projects, which specializes in managing and troubleshooting UNIX and Linux systems.

When he is not beating his head against systems administration problems, he and his wife Lidia enjoy riding their tandem through the Rio Grande valley. They also enjoy traveling throughout Mexico. Paul is the author of *LINUX Network Toolkit,* Hungry Minds, 2000, and the co-author of several other books. He has a bachelor's degree in Electrical Engineering from the University of New Mexico.

Dedication

Jon "maddog" Hall: To Mom & Pop (TM), whose aversion to things electronic is well known, and who can still call their son Jon rather than maddog.

Paul G. Sery: To my wife Lidia Maura Vazquez de Sery.

Acknowledgments

I want to thank my wife, Lidia, for her patience, support, and good advice that made writing this book possible. Without her, I would still be the pocket protector inserted into shirt, busted-eyeglass-fixed-with-tape wearing, Star Trek watching, wrinkled shirt suffering, spaghetti-in-the-pot-over-the-sink eating, Saturday night hacking sorry sack sorta guy. Well I never was into Star Trek and am pecking at this keyboard on Saturday night, but my wonderful and beautiful wife sure has made me a better man.

I would also like to thank Laura Lewin, who gave me the chance to help write this book. She showed great confidence and patience in me. I am very grateful and wish her success in her new ventures.

And, of course, I'd like to thank the staff at Hungry Minds, who provided considerable and essential help too. Tiffany Franklin and Nicole Haims provided constant and essential assistance. Their patience with me was truly vital.

I'd also like to acknowledge a total lack of assistance in writing this book from my dog, the infamous Oso Maloso; eater of many things that should have ended his long career early, including but not limited to: ant poison, Advil, many pounds of tootsie rolls one Halloween, several bags of chicken bones one party, beer, and other assorted items; escaper of many fences and gates; and friend of the late, great Paunchy (whose name you'll see throughout this book).

How useful was Oso? Well, one night while working on this book I got a phone call. Leaving my apple pie behind next to the keyboard, I went downstairs to take the call and passed him on his way up. I should have known something was up because he had a cell phone with him and no one answered when I picked up to take the call. I went up the stairs while he went down. The apple pie was gone. Oso 1, human 0.

— *Paul G. Sery*

Publisher's Acknowledgments

We're proud of this book; please send us your comments through our Hungry Minds Online Registration Form located at www.dummies.com.

Some of the people who helped bring this book to market include the following:

Acquisitions, Editorial, and Media Development

Senior Project Editor: Nicole Haims

Acquisitions Editor: Tiffany Franklin

Copy Editors: Rebecca Huehls, Jean Rogers, Rebecca Senninger

Technical Editor: Matt Hayden

Editorial Manager: Leah Cameron

Permissions Editor: Laura Moss

Media Development Specialist: Gregory Stephens

Media Development Manager: Laura VanWinkle

Media Development Supervisor: Richard Graves

Editorial Assistant: Amanda Foxworth

Production

Project Coordinator: Erin Smith

Layout and Graphics: Stephanie Jumper, Barry Offringa, Jacque Schneider, Betty Schulte, Julie Trippetti, Jeremey Unger, Mary J. Virgin

Proofreaders: Angel Perez, Carl Pierce, Charles Spencer

Indexer: TECHBOOKS Production Services

General and Administrative

Hungry Minds Technology Publishing Group: Richard Swadley, Vice President and Executive Group Publisher; Bob Ipsen, Vice President and Group Publisher; Joseph Wikert, Vice President and Publisher; Barry Pruett, Vice President and Publisher; Mary Bednarek, Editorial Director; Mary C. Corder, Editorial Director; Andy Cummings, Editorial Director

Hungry Minds Manufacturing: Ivor Parker, Vice President, Manufacturing

Hungry Minds Marketing: John Helmus, Assistant Vice President, Director of Marketing

Hungry Minds Production for Branded Press: Debbie Stailey, Production Director

Hungry Minds Sales: Michael Violano, Vice President, International Sales and Sub Rights

Contents at a Glance

Introduction *1*

Part 1: Installing Red Hat Linux *9*

Chapter 1: And in the Opposite Corner . . . a Penguin? 11
Chapter 2: Preparing Your Hard Drive for Red Hat Linux 17
Chapter 3: Ready, Set, Install! 31
Chapter 4: Getting to Know Red Hat Linux 51

Part 11: Got Net? *61*

Chapter 5: Connecting to the Internet with a Dial-up Modem 63
Chapter 6: Broadband Rocks! 77
Chapter 7: Connect Locally, Browse Globally: Connecting to a
Local Area Network (LAN) 97
Chapter 8: Fire, Fire, Heh, Heh, Firewalls Are Cool 115
Chapter 9: Surfing the Web and Managing E-Mail with Mozilla 127

Part 111: Linux, Huh! What Is It Good For?
Absolutely Everything! *139*

Chapter 10: Gnowing GNOME 141
Chapter 11: Gnowing More Applications 157
Chapter 12: Configuring Your Red Hat Linux Sound System 169
Chapter 13: Using Streaming Media and RealPlayer 183
Chapter 14: Using Desktop Productivity Tools 199

Part 1V: Revenge of the Nerds *215*

Chapter 15: Bashing Your Shell 217
Chapter 16: Filing Your Life Away 235
Chapter 17: Becoming a Suit: Managing the Red Hat Linux File System 253
Chapter 18: Revving Up RPM 263
Chapter 19: Bringing In the Red Hat Repairman:
Troubleshooting Your Network 281
Chapter 20: Configuring X 295

Part V: The Part of Tens *307*

Chapter 21: Ten Sources of Help 309
Chapter 22: Ten Problem Areas and Solutions 317
Chapter 23: Ten Security Vulnerabilities 325

Part VI: The Appendixes 333

Appendix A: Discovering Your Hardware 335
Appendix B: Installing Red Hat Linux in Text Mode (The Ugly Way) 349
Appendix C: vi Me 361
Appendix D: Diggin' Them Linux Man Pages 369
Appendix E: About the CD-ROMs 383

Index 387

GNU License Agreement...405

Installation Instructions..........................Back of Book

Cartoons at a Glance

By Rich Tennant

"Drive carefully, remember your lunch, and always make a backup of your directory tree before modifying your hard disk partition file."

page 333

"When we started the company, we weren't going to call it 'Red Hat'. But eventually we decided it sounded better than 'Beard of Bees Linux'."

page 307

page 9

"Think of our relationship as a version of Red Hat Linux — I will not share a directory on the love-branch of your life."

page 215

page 61

"It's called 'Linux Poker.' Everyone gets to see everyone elses cards, everything's wild, you can play off your opponents hands, and everyone wins except Bill Gates, whose face appears on the Jokers."

page 139

Cartoon Information:
Fax: 978-546-7747
E-Mail: richtennant@the5thwave.com
World Wide Web: www.the5thwave.com

Table of Contents

Introduction *1*

About This Book 1
Foolish Assumptions 2
Conventions Used in This Book 2
　Typing code 2
　Keystrokes and such 3
How This Book Is Organized 4
　Part I: Installing Red Hat Linux 4
　Part II: Got Net? 4
　Part III: Linux, Huh! What Is It Good For?
　　Absolutely Everything! 4
　Part IV: Revenge of the Nerds 5
　Part V: The Part of Tens 6
　Part VI: Appendixes 6
What You're Not to Read 6
Icons in This Book 6
Where to Go from Here 7

Part I: Installing Red Hat Linux *9*

Chapter 1: And in the Opposite Corner . . . a Penguin? **11**

History of the World (err, Linux) Part 2 11
Knowing What You Can Do with Red Hat Linux 13
　Boosting your personal workstation 14
　Accessing intranets and the Internet 15

Chapter 2: Preparing Your Hard Drive for Red Hat Linux **17**

Preparing Your Hard Drive for Red Hat Linux 18
Finding Out If Your Computer Can Boot from CD-ROM 18
Creating a Red Hat Linux Boot Disk with Windows or MS-DOS 20
Making a Boot Disk with Linux 21
Move Over Windows, Here Comes Johnny 22
Nondestructive Repartitioning with fips:
　Can't We All Just Get Along? 23
　Defragmenting your hard drive 24
　Resizing with fips 26

Chapter 3: Ready, Set, Install! **31**

Installation Stage 1: Starting the Install 32
Installation Stage 2: Slicing and Dicing the Pie 36
Installation Stage 3: Configuring Your Network 40

Installation Stage 4: Configuring Your System 44
Installation Stage 5: The Point of No Return! 47
Installation Stage 6: X Marks the Spot 48

Chapter 4: Getting to Know Red Hat Linux 51

Introducing the Linux File System Tree 51
Giving Linux the Boot 52
Logging In 54
The Command-Line Interface (CLI) versus the
    Graphical User Interface (GUI) 55
Creating User Accounts with Red Hat's User Manager 56
Creating an Account without X 59
Ending Your First Session 59

Part II: Got Net? *61*

Chapter 5: Connecting to the Internet with a Dial-up Modem 63

Desperately Seeking an ISP 64
Configuring Your Internet Connection 66
    Locating your modem with Linux 71
    Getting desperate with dip 72
    Locating your modem with Windows 73
Setting Up DNS 73
Firing Up Your Internet Connection 75

Chapter 6: Broadband Rocks! 77

Introducing DSL and Cable Connections: The Proof Is in the Wiring 78
The Cable Modem Option 79
    Finding an Internet cable provider 80
    Dealing with the hardware 81
    Setting up Internet protocols 82
    Registering your modem with your ICP 86
The DSL Option 86
    Facing DSL-configuration woes head on 87
    Finding a DSL provider 88
    Connecting a Cisco 675 or 678 DSL modem 89
    Connecting your Cisco modem to your Linux computer 89
    Configuring the Cisco 675 or 678 DSL modem 93

**Chapter 7: Connect Locally, Browse Globally:
Connecting to a Local Area Network (LAN) 97**

Going Local 98
Configuring Your NIC with Red Hat's Network Druid 99
    Preparing to configure your wireless NIC 99
    Choosing between ad-hoc and infrastructure 100
    Configuring your Ethernet or wireless NIC 102

Configuring your host name 110
Configuring DNS service 111
Manually starting and stopping your network 112

Chapter 8: Fire, Fire, Heh, Heh, Firewalls Are Cool 115

Understanding Why You Need a Firewall in the First Place 116
Building an Effective Firewall the iptables Way 117
Setting Up an iptables-Based Firewall 118
Firing Up Your Firewall (And Dousing the Flames) 121
Saving your filtering rules to a script 121
Turning your firewall off and on 122
Displaying Your Firewall Rules 124
Testing Your Firewall 125

Chapter 9: Surfing the Web and Managing E-Mail with Mozilla .. 127

Setting Up Mozilla As You Like It 128
Picking a home page and history settings 128
Configuring your e-mail browser 130
Navigating the Net with Mozilla 133
Working with E-Mail 135
Getting your e-mail 135
Sending e-mail and attachments 136

Part III: Linux, Huh! What Is It Good For? Absolutely Everything! 139

Chapter 10: Gnowing GNOME 141

Introducing the Amazing X Window System 142
Comprehending window managers 143
Going old-school with the terminal emulators 144
Waxing vague with general applications 145
Getting Earthy with GNOME 145
Mucking about with basic window manipulation 146
Playing with the Panel 149
Working on your virtual desktop 152
Getting out of GNOME or X 154
Tinkering with GNOME 154

Chapter 11: Gnowing More Applications 157

Navigating with the Nautilus File/Internet Integration Manager 157
Waking up the little guy 158
Putting him through his paces 158
Navigating the Net with Nautilus 162

Checking Out Some Handy Linux Programs 163
  Going graphical with the Gimp 163
  Making spreadsheets with Gnumeric 163
  Reading PDF files 164
The Ximian Evolution Revolution 165

Chapter 12: Configuring Your Red Hat Linux Sound System 169

Playing CDs and MP3s 169
  Playing CDs and MP3s with xmms 170
  Playing MP3 files 171
  GMIX Mixer: Sounds for the rest of us 171
Setting Up and Testing Your Sound System 173
Ripping CDs 177
Entering the Ring of Fire: Burning CDs 178
  Installing the CD-ROM writing utility 179
  Burn, baby, burn: Saving files to a CD 179

Chapter 13: Using Streaming Media and RealPlayer 183

Configuring Your Red Hat Box 183
  Downloading and installing RealPlayer 8 184
  Launching RealPlayer from the Panel 188
  Finding radio stations 189
  Using RealPlayer 190
MP3 on the Net 191
Going Hollywood with RealPlayer Video 192
  Finding video at Real.com 192
  Finding streaming video from other sources 194
Punching through Firewalls 194
  Getting RealPlayer through your firewall 194
  Audio by proxy (Using RealPlayer with your firewall) ...196

Chapter 14: Using Desktop Productivity Tools 199

A StarOffice Is Born 200
  Getting StarOffice 201
  Installing StarOffice 203
  Getting to know StarOffice 206
The Word Is AbiWord 213

Part IV: Revenge of the Nerds 215

Chapter 15: Bashing Your Shell 217

Bashing Ahead! 217
Commanding Linux with bash 220
  Using commands without having to say please 221
  Getting in the pipeline 224
  Deleting text from the Linux command line 225

Getting less for more 225
Regular expressions: Wildcards and one-eyed jacks 226
Tweaking Linux Commands with Options 228
Letting bash's Memory Make Your Life Easier 230
Editing commands at the command line 230
Bang-bang! 231
Going back to the future 232
Recalling filenames 232

Chapter 16: Filing Your Life Away **235**

Getting Linux File Facts Straight 235
Storing files 236
Sorting through file types 236
Understanding files and directories 237
Moving Around the File System with pwd and cd 239
Figuring out where you are 239
Specifying the directory path 240
Changing your working directory 241
Going home 241
Creating and Adding to Files with cat 242
Making Sure the cat Command Works 243
Manipulating Files and Directories 244
Creating directories 245
Moving and copying files and directories 246
Removing files 247
Removing directories 248
Owning Files and Granting Permissions 249
Making Your Own Rules 251

**Chapter 17: Becoming a Suit: Managing the Red Hat Linux
File System** **253**

Mounting and Unmounting 253
Mounting Windows files from a floppy disk 254
Unmounting file systems 255
Sending Corrupted File Systems to Reform School 256
Increasing Drive Space 258
Creating a drive partition 259
Adding and configuring a hard drive 260
Installing a drive 260
Partitioning a drive 261
Making the file system 262

Chapter 18: Revving Up RPM **263**

Introducing RPM 263
Taking a Look at What RPM Does 264

Using GNOME RPM 265
   Starting GNOME RPM 265
   Installing an RPM package from a CD-ROM 267
   Installing an RPM package from the Internet 268
   Removing an RPM package 270
   Getting information about an RPM package 272
   Verifying RPM packages 273
   Modifying GNOME RPM defaults 275

Chapter 19: Bringing In the Red Hat Repairman:
Troubleshooting Your Network **281**
   It's the Tree's Fault, Not Mine! 281
   The Fix Is In: Troubleshooting Your Network 283
   Ticking through Your Linux Networking Checklist 284
      Is the power turned on? Check 284
      Is your network cable broken? Nope 285
      Is your Ethernet hub or switch working? Check 285
      Is your Ethernet adapter inserted correctly? Yup 286
      Is your network adapter configured correctly? Roger ...286
      Is there another computer or device to talk to? Uh-huh 292

Chapter 20: Configuring X **295**
   Discovering Your Hardware's True Identity 295
   Running SuperProbe 297
   Running Xconfigurator 297
   Starting Your Xengine 304
   Xterminating X 306

Part V: The Part of Tens *307*

Chapter 21: Ten Sources of Help **309**
   Books and More Books 309
   Linux HOWTOs 310
   School Days 310
   In the News 310
   User Groups 311
   Bring in the Cavalry 311
   Commercial Applications 312
   Visit Web Sites 313
   Attend Conferences 314
      Linux Kongress 314
      Linux Expo 314
      USENIX/FREENIX 315
      CeBIT 315
      Comdex 315
      IDG's Linux World 315
   Try to Help Others 315

Chapter 22: Ten Problem Areas and Solutions **317**

I Can't Boot Red Hat Linux Anymore 317
My Hard Drive Numbers Have Changed Since Installation 318
My CD-ROM Isn't Detected 319
I Don't Know How to Remove LILO and Restore My MBR 320
I Can't Use LILO to Boot 320
The ls Command Doesn't Show Files in Color 321
Linux Can't Find a Shell Script (Or a Program) 321
When I Start X Window System, I See a Gray Screen 322
I Don't Know How to Make the X Window System
    Start at Boot Time 323
I Never Seem to Have the Correct Time 323

Chapter 23: Ten Security Vulnerabilities **325**

How Many Daemons Can Dance on the
    Head of the Linux Process Table? 326
Open the Encrypt 327
Aaha, No Firewall. Very, Very Good. 327
Keeping Up with the Joneses 328
Backups? I Don't Need No Stinking Backups! 328
My Buffer Overflow-ith 329
Social Engineering 1010101010 330
Bad Passwords 330
Scan Me 331
I Know Where You Logged in Last Summer 331

Part VI: The Appendixes *333*

Appendix A: Discovering Your Hardware **335**

Knowing if Your Hardware Can Handle Red Hat Linux 335
Finding Out What You Have 336
Talking to Your Computer (And Knowing What You Should Ask) 337
    Hard drive controllers 338
    Introducing hard drives 340
Getting Information from Windows 341
Getting Information from MS-DOS 344
Leaving a Trail of Bread Crumbs 347

**Appendix B: Installing Red Hat Linux in Text Mode
(The Ugly Way)** **349**

Stage 1: Starting the Installation 349
Stage 2: Configuring Your Network 353
Stage 3: Entering the Point of No Return 355
Configuring X 356
Restarting Your System 359

Appendix C: vi Me **361**

   Comprehending Text Editors 361

   Getting Friendly with vi 362

      Moving around in a file 364

      Deleting and moving text in vi 364

      Controlling your editing environment 365

      Checking out common vi commands 366

Appendix D: Diggin' Them Linux Man Pages **369**

   Checking Out How the Man Pages Are Organized 369

   Using the Man Command 371

   Checking Out Topics in the Man Pages 372

      Name 372

      Synopsis 372

      Description 374

      Options 374

      Environmental variables 374

      Diagnostics 376

      Bugs/deficiencies 376

      Compatibility issues 376

      Caveats 377

      Disclaimers 377

      Authors 377

      Acknowledgments 377

      Debugging options 377

      Configuration files 377

      Copyrights 378

      Copying permissions/distribution policy 378

      POSIX compatibility/standards conformance 379

      Files 380

      Future work 380

      See also/related software 380

   Finding the Right Man Page 381

Appendix E: About the CD-ROMs **383**

   System Requirements 383

   Using the CDs 384

   What You'll Find 384

   If You Have Problems (Of the CD Kind) 385

Index *387*

GNU License Agreement *405*

Installation Instructions .... *Back of Book*

Introduction

*R*ed Hat Linux 7.3 For Dummies is designed to help you get Red Hat Linux working quickly and efficiently. This book shows you how to do fun and interesting — to say nothing of useful — things with Red Hat Linux. The book is also designed to be an effective doorstop or coffee cup coaster. Whatever you use it for, we hope that you have fun.

About This Book

This book is designed to be a helping-hands tutorial. It provides a place to turn to for help and solace in those moments when, after two hours of trying to get your network connection working, your 5-year-old tells you that you need to use the eth0 and not the eth1 Ethernet interface.

We tried our hardest to fill up this book with the things you need to know about, such as:

- Installing Red Hat Linux
- Getting connected to the Internet
- Getting connected to your local network
- Building a simple firewall
- Using Red Hat Linux to do useful things, such as playing CDs, MP3s, and listening to the world's radio stations
- Understanding the GNOME desktop environment
- Using useful and usable applications, such as the StarOffice desktop productivity suite from Sun Microsystems, Inc. and RealPlayer from RealAudio, Inc.
- Working with the StarOffice desktop productivity suite to satisfy your word processing, calculating, and presentation needs
- Knowing where to go for help
- Managing your Red Hat Linux workstation

You'll see troubleshooting tips throughout the book (Chapter 19 is devoted to the subject). It's not that Red Hat Linux is all that much trouble, but we want you to be prepared in case you run into bad luck.

Foolish Assumptions

You know what they say about people who make assumptions, but this book would never have been written if we didn't make a few. This book is for you if:

- You want to use the Linux operating system to build your personal workstation. Surprise, the CD-ROMs included with this book contain the Red Hat Linux distribution.
- You have a computer.
- You want to put the Red Hat Linux operating system and the computer together, and using duct tape hasn't worked.
- You don't want to become a Red Hat Linux guru — at least not yet.

Conventions Used in This Book

At computer conventions, thousands of computer people get together and talk about deep technical issues such as:

- What is the best hardware for running Red Hat Linux?
- Is Coke better than Pepsi?
- Could Superman beat Batman?

But these aren't the types of conventions we're talking about here. Our conventions are shorthand ways of designating specific information, such as what is and isn't a command or the meaning of certain funny looking symbols.

Typing code

Commands in the text are shown like this. Commands not shown in the text, but set off on lines by themselves, look like this:

```
[lidia@veracruz lidia]$pwd
/home/lidia
```

See the [lidia@veracruz lidia] in the preceding? You won't necessarily see that on your system, unless you're happen to be my wife's mirror image who also likes Veracruz, Mexico very much. But you will see something similar depending on what your computer and username are. The first name — lidia — is replaced by whatever your user name is. The second name is your computer name. The final one is the directory that you are working from, which in this case is lidia's home directory. Therefore, if your user name is zoot and computer name is wishbone, then your prompt is

```
[zoot@wishbone zoot]$.
```

When you see stuff in boldface, it means it's something you should type. For example:

Type **man chown** at the command prompt and press Enter.

If we tell you to type something in a bolded step, the text you type won't be bold. As in

1. **Type** man chown **at the command prompt and press Enter.**

Here's a rundown of the command syntax in Linux:

- ✔ Text *not* surrounded by [ ] or { } brackets must be typed exactly as shown.
- ✔ Text inside brackets [ ] is optional.
- ✔ Text in *italics* must be replaced with appropriate text.
- ✔ Text inside braces { } indicates that you must choose one of the values that are inside the braces and separated by the | sign.
- ✔ An ellipsis (. . .) means *and so on* or to repeat the preceding command line as needed.

Don't concern yourself with this too much now. For most of the book, you don't need to know these particulars. And when you do need to know something about a particular syntax, come back here for a refresher course.

Keystrokes and such

Keystrokes are shown with a plus sign between the keys. For example, Ctrl+Alt+Delete means you should press the Ctrl key, Alt key, and Delete key all at the same time. (No, we don't make you press any more than three keys at the same time.)

Most of the applications and utilities that we describe in this book use graphical user interfaces (GUI) such as GNOME, which allow you to control your computer by pointing and clicking with your mouse. Occasionally, however, we give non-graphical instructions that require pressing keys on your keyboard. In those situations, we often simplify the instructions by saying, "select OK". That generally means that you press the Tab key, which moves the cursor to the OK button, and then press the Enter key. That two-step process is equivalent to clicking an OK button in a GUI.

How This Book Is Organized

Like all proper *For Dummies* books, this book is organized into independent parts. You can read the parts in any order. Heck, try reading them backwards for a real challenge. This book is not meant to be read from front cover to back; rather, it was meant to be a reference book that helps you find what you're looking for when you're looking for it. Between the Contents at a Glance page, the Table of Contents, and the Index, you should have no problem finding what you need.

If you do read the book in order, you encounter the useful and interesting things first and the more technical items last. For instance, after installing Red Hat Linux in Part I, you may want to immediately proceed to Part II to see how to connect Linux to the Internet or your local network. From there, you can use your new workstation to surf the Internet and use e-mail.

The following sections describe each part.

Part I: Installing Red Hat Linux

In Part I, you find out what Linux is and how to prepare your computer to install Red Hat Linux. We then walk you through installation and show you the basics of working with Red Hat Linux.

Part II: Got Net?

In Part II, you find out about connecting to the Internet and local networks. You see how to jump on the Internet with your everyday modem or high-speed (broadband) DSL or cable modem. We also show you how to connect to an existing network. If that local network has a high-speed Internet connection, then you can use it as your portal to the wonderful world of surfing. The Internet can be dangerous, so we include instructions on creating your own firewall. Finally, we show you how to use Mozilla to satisfy your browsing and e-mail needs.

Part III: Linux, Huh! What Is It Good For? Absolutely Everything!

Part III guides you through the glorious particulars of actually doing something with Red Hat Linux. You're introduced to the GNOME desktop window environment. You're taken through its paces by moving, resizing, hiding, closing windows, using the file manager, and much more. Two chapters are devoted to using the Red Hat Linux multimedia capabilities. You can listen to CDs and MP3s, as well as rip and record them. The world's radio stations are now available to you with streaming media technology. The full-featured StarOffice desktop productivity suite is described in some detail. You can use StarOffice with your Red Hat Linux machine to do all your writing and other work-related functions. You can even write a book with it! Finally, you see how to get organized with Red Hat Linux.

Part IV: Revenge of the Nerds

In Part IV, you're guided through the processes necessary to care for and feed your new Linux computer. It's real nerd city but fun in its own way. Topics such as file management are introduced. We also introduce the software package management system — called RPM. We also devote an entire chapter to the art of troubleshooting and take you through the process of configuring the X Window System, which is the basis for all Linux graphics.

Martha Stewart we're not: Other uses for CD-ROMs

Where computers abound, so do CD-ROMs. Eventually these CD-ROMs become obsolete or are never installed — that's the case with software products that arrive as unwanted advertising. What can ecologically minded people do with these CDs so that they don't fill up landfills?

- Use those defunct CDs as coasters for drinks.

- Make pretty mobiles out of castaway CDs. (The sun shining off the CD-ROMs makes wonderful rainbows on the wall.)

- Make CD-ROM clocks and give them to all your friends at the holidays. Just purchase inexpensive quartz crystal clock motors (complete with hands) and use the CD-ROM as the face of the clock. I have four of these clocks made out of Windows NT CD-ROMs — hey, can you imagine a better use for them?

- Make a nice flowerpot. Just use a high heat to melt a CD-ROM around the base of a water tumbler, or, plug the hole and make an ashtray. Of course, if you try this at work you could cause some consternation among management, particularly after they find out that one of the more expensive programs they've purchased has ended up at the bottom of a flowerpot.

For now, please keep your *Red Hat Linux 7.3 For Dummies* CD-ROMs in a safe place, such as the sleeve in the back of the book, when you're not using it.

Part V: The Part of Tens

A *For Dummies* book just isn't complete without The Part of Tens, where you can find ten all-important resources and answers to the ten most bothersome questions people have after installing Red Hat Linux. (The folks at Red Hat Software provided these questions.)

Part VI: Appendixes

Finally, the appendixes. Appendix A describes how to find out about the details of your computer's individual pieces of hardware; this is sometimes helpful when installing Red Hat Linux. Appendix B revisits the Red Hat Linux installation system using the *Text* mode. The nongraphical installation system — known as the Text mode — is described there in case the installation system can't use your graphics driver. In Appendix C, instructions are given for using the de facto Linux text editor vi. In Appendix D, you find out all you need to know about the Linux man pages. Appendix E finishes by describing what you can find on the companion CD-ROMs.

What You're Not to Read

Heck, you don't have to read any of the book if you don't want to, but why did you buy it? (Not that we're complaining.) Part I has background information. If you don't want it, don't read it. Also, text in sidebars is optional, although often helpful. If you're on the fast track to using Linux, you could skip the sidebars and the text with a technical stuff icon. But we suggest instead that you slow down a bit and enjoy the experience.

Icons in This Book

 Nifty little shortcuts and timesavers. Red Hat Linux is a powerful operating system, and you can save unbelievable amounts of time and energy by utilizing its tools and programs. We hope our tips show you how.

 Don't let this happen to you! We hope that our experiences with Red Hat Linux will help you avoid the mistakes we made.

Recall information that is given here for later use.

 This is particularly nerdy, technical information. You may skip it, but you may find it interesting if you're of a geekier bent.

 This icon flags discussions that relate to the CD-ROMs. The CD-ROMs contain a copy of the latest Red Hat Linux distribution available at publishing time.

Where to Go from Here

You're about to join the legions of people who have been using and developing Linux. We've been using Unix for more than 20 years, Linux for more than 10 years, and Red Hat Linux for 8 years. We've found Red Hat Linux to be a flexible, powerful operating system, capable of solving most problems even without a large set of commercial software. The future of the Linux, and Red Hat Linux in particular, operating system is bright. The time and energy you expend in becoming familiar with it will be worthwhile. Carpe Linuxum.

Part I

Installing
Red Hat Linux

The 5th Wave   By Rich Tennant

WANDA HAD THE DISTINCT FEELING HER HUSBAND'S NEW
SOFTWARE PROGRAM WAS ABOUT TO BECOME INTERACTIVE.

In this part . . .

You're about to embark on a journey through the Red Hat Linux installation program. Perhaps you know nothing about setting up the operating system on your computer. That's okay. The Red Hat Linux installation system is savvy and helpful. Plus, we guide you through the installation.

In Chapter 1, you begin to discover what Red Hat Linux is all about and what it can do for you. Chapter 2 helps you to get ready to install Red Hat Linux. The real fun begins in Chapter 3 when you install your own Penguin. (Linus Torvalds — the inventor of Linux — loves penguins and they've been adopted as Linux's mascot.) Finally, Chapter 4 gives you a brief, but important, introduction to working with Red Hat Linux.

Chapter 1

And in the Opposite Corner . . . a Penguin?

. . . .

In This Chapter

▶ Napping through a bit of Linux history

▶ Finding out what Red Hat Linux can do

▶ Checking out how you can use Red Hat Linux

. . . .

*W*e see a penguin in your future. He's an unassuming fellow who's taking on a rather big foe — that other operating system — in the battle for the hearts, minds, and desktops of computer users. Red Hat Linux, with its splashy brand name and notorious logo, is undeniably one of the driving forces behind the Linux revolution.

This chapter introduces you to the latest and greatest Red Hat release: Red Hat Linux 7.3. This book covers all the bases — well, a good number of bases at least — about how to use Red Hat Linux as a desktop productivity tool, Internet portal, and multimedia workstation. You can do lots of things with Red Hat Linux, and this chapter gives you a good overview of the possibilities, as well as a brief look at the history of Linux.

History of the World (err, Linux) Part 2

In the beginning of computerdom (said in a booming, thunderous voice), the world was filled with hulking mainframes. These slothful beasts lumbered through large corporations; required a special species of ultra-nerds to keep them happy; and ate up huge chunks of space, power, and money. Then came the IBM PC and Windows, and the world changed. Power to the people — sort of.

In 1991, a student at the University of Helsinki named Linus Torvalds found himself dissatisfied with his current operating system. Torvalds thought that the Unix operating system might be better suited to help him accomplish his task. Unix was expensive, however, so he began writing his own version of Unix. After formulating the basic parts himself, Torvalds recruited a team of talented programmers, and together they created a new operating system, or *kernel,* now called Linux.

One of the most important decisions that Torvalds made in the early days of Linux was to freely distribute the Linux kernel code for anyone to do with as they wished. These free Linux distributions were and still are available in several forms — mainly online.

The only restriction that Linus imposed to the free distribution of his creation: No version of the software can be made *proprietary.* (Proprietary software is software that is owned and developed under wraps by private companies. *Open source* code is for the people — anyone can develop it without breaking the law.) You can modify the heck out of it and distribute it for fun (and for profit, if you wish). What you can't do is stop anyone else from using, modifying, and distributing even your modified version of the software — freely or for profit.

The lack of proprietary restrictions has led to drastic improvements in the technology. We can't overstress how important it's been to the Linux operating system that its source code is freely available; the Linux operating system continues to improve rapidly — even organically — because it is constantly being tweaked by a lot of really smart people. (In contrast, operating systems like Microsoft Windows are tweaked every once in awhile by a smaller group of smart people.)

By the early spring of 1994, the first real version of Linux (Version 1.0) was available for public use. Even then it was an impressive operating system that ran smartly on computers with less than 2MB of RAM and a simple 386 microprocessor. Linux 1.0 also included free features that other operating systems charged hundreds of dollars for. Nowadays, tens of millions of users enjoy Linux at home and work.

By the way, if you're wondering about the whole penguin thing, the answer is actually disappointingly simple. The reason the friendly penguin (whose name is Tux, by the way) symbolizes All Things Linux is because Linus Torvalds, the inventor of the Linux operating system, loves penguins. Some mystery, eh?

Knowing What You Can Do with Red Hat Linux

Linux is freely available software. The source code for Linux, which is the heart and soul of the operating system, is also publicly available. Red Hat Linux is an *integrated product,* meaning that Red Hat, Inc. combines the basic Linux operating system with software (some made by others, some made by Red Hat) to produce a package whose value is greater than the sum of its parts. That combination is known as a *distribution* of Linux.

So that you can get up and running with Red Hat Linux 7.3 as quickly as possible, we've been sweet enough to include the Publisher's edition operating system on the CDs that comes with this book. See Chapters 2 and 3 if you're chomping at the bit to install the new version.

Initially the sole domain of business and university servers, Red Hat Linux is now used by businesses, individuals, and governments to cut costs, improve performance, and just plain get work done. You can use Red Hat Linux as a desktop workstation, a server system, an Internet gateway, a firewall, the basis of an embedded system (such as a smart VCR or a robot), or even as a supercomputer. And thanks to the thousands of people working on different parts of Linux, Red Hat Linux becomes more flexible and capable with each release.

The following list includes some of the cooler features of Red Hat Linux:

- **Fully protected multitasking:** That's a nerdy mouth-full. This is just a way of saying that Linux processes (when you run an e-mail client, for instance, you are running a process) are automatically prevented from interfering with each other. That means that more than one application can be run safely at the same time without your system crashing every five minutes. This feature prevents problems such as the dreaded *Blue Screen of Death* (where Windows tells you it's messed up and that you have no choice but to reboot and like it). Fully protected multitasking also means that a slew of people can access a Red Hat Linux computer at one time.

- **Large file support:** Red Hat Linux can handle large files and programs. In fact, the Intel Pentium processor can handle files as large as 2GB. That's big. If you work with large databases, for example, you can store them on your own workstation if you have a large enough hard drive.

- **Graphical user interface (GUI):** Red Hat Linux includes a sophisticated interface called the X Window System, also known as X, and the GNOME desktop manager (and even K Desktop Environment, or KDE, if you want to use it instead of or in addition to GNOME). Together, X and GNOME give you a powerful and very stable graphical workstation.

✔ **File sharing:** Red Hat Linux can share files with Windows, OS/2, Macintosh, most other distributions of Linux, and of course Unix computers. Its file sharing capabilities give your network flexibility. For example, if you run both Red Hat Linux and Windows on the same computer, you can retrieve Microsoft Word files from your Windows partition so that you can read them with StarOffice and Abiware.

Boosting your personal workstation

With Red Hat Linux, you can easily create your own inexpensive, flexible, and powerful personal workstation. Linux provides the platform for most of the applications that you need to get your work done. Many applications come bundled with Red Hat Linux, from address books and text editors to checkbook balancers and Web browsers.

You can also download products such as Sun Microsystems' StarOffice office productivity suite (which is Office 97/2000 compatible) to satisfy your word-processing, spreadsheet-editing, and other desktop publishing needs.

The following list describes just a few of the major categories of free software that are available for Linux, along with some examples of popular programs.

Linux is everywhere

The Linux operating system has been *ported* (or converted) from the 32-bit Intel architecture to a number of other architectures, including Alpha, MIPS, PowerPC, and SPARC. This conversion gives users a choice of hardware manufacturers and keeps the Linux kernel flexible for new processors. Linux now handles *symmetric multiprocessing* (more than one CPU or mathematical and logical programming unit per system box). In addition, projects are in the works to provide sophisticated processing capabilities, such as:

✔ **Real-time programming:** Controlling machinery or testing equipment

✔ **High availability:** Running a reliable computer all the time

✔ **Journaled file systems:** Linux uses journaled file systems that can "heal" much more quickly and reliably than nonjournaled ones

✔ **Scalability:** Boosting computer power by adding more system boxes rather than faster CPUs

This last capability, known as Extreme Linux systems, and Beowulf clusters enable research organizations to create machines with supercomputer capabilities at a fraction of the price of supercomputers. In certain cases, Extreme Linux systems have been made from obsolete PCs, costing the organizations that make them nothing in material costs.

- ✔ **Office suites:** Complete desktop productivity suites, such as StarOffice and Applixware, include advanced word processors that can read and write Microsoft Word files (as can the open source AbiWord word processor), HTML editors, spreadsheet editors, and graphics editors. For simple, no-frills word processing, you can use the well-known AbiWord word processor. For more information on office productivity applications, see Chapter 14.

- ✔ **Streaming multimedia players:** You can download products like Real Network's RealPlayer to listen to radio stations across the world and watch video streams. The open source xmms MP3 player lets you listen to CDs and other multimedia on your computer and the Internet. The Internet is going multimedia, and streaming players let you get in on the action.

- ✔ **Freely distributable and freeware programs:** These are programs that you can download from the Internet and use without paying to register the product. Literally dozens of software packages are available on the CDs that come with this book, including (but by no means limited to) the `pine` text-based e-mail reader, the zip data-compression program (which compresses files using the same format as WinZip), the Gimp graphics manipulation program, the Mozilla Web browser, and the AbiWord word processor.

- ✔ **Web browsers:** The familiar Netscape Communicator 4.78 and its open source brother, Mozilla are included with Red Hat Linux 7.3. Red Hat Linux also provides the `lynx` and `links` text-based Web browsers, which do not show graphics but are otherwise fully functional Web browsers. The text-based Web browsers come in handy when using an older, slower modem because they don't require as much speed as Mozilla does. For more info on Mozilla, see Chapter 9.

Not all the software in the preceding list is included on the CDs with this book. StarOffice and Netscape Communicator, for instance, are only available for download over the Internet or on CD.

Accessing intranets and the Internet

Unix systems are at the forefront of the Web development projects that are making all kinds of networks (from the Internet to private networks and intranets) so flexible and functional. Of course, Linux shares many benefits of its Unix heritage. Both the Internet and intranets require similar services, such as the following:

✔ **FTP (File Transfer Protocol) clients:** FTP enables you to transfer files to/ from FTP servers. You can download Red Hat software from their FTP server at `ftp:/ftp.redhat.com` (URLs for FTP sites all start with `ftp:/.`)

✔ **OpenSSH:** The open source version of Secure Shell enables you to securely communicate across the Internet. Secure Shell is much safer than Telnet because Secure Shell encrypts your communication when you log in (even when you log in to other computers), making the chance that others can discover your passwords and other sensitive information much slimmer. OpenSSH also provides other authentication and security features and lets you securely copy files from machine to machine. With OpenSSH, you can prevent people from listening to your communication. (You can download a great SSH client that works on Windows system from `www.chiark.greenend.org.uk/~sgtatham/putty/`. Putty works great!)

✔ **Internet accessing utilities:** Red Hat Linux provides several configuration utilities that help you connect to the Internet. The utilities help you to configure DSL, cable modems, and plain old telephone modems to connect to the Internet. They also help you to connect to local area networks (LAN) using Ethernet adapters.

✔ **Firewalls:** A *firewall* is a system that controls access to your private network from any outside network (in this case, the Internet) and to control access from your private network to the outside world. To keep the bad guys out, Red Hat Linux provides protection by giving you the tools to build your own firewall. Red Hat Linux is very flexible in this regard and many software packages are available, including the popular and simple to use `Netfilter/iptables` filtering software, which is included on the accompanying CD-ROMs. We discuss how to build a firewall in Chapter 8.

Chapter 2

Preparing Your Hard Drive for Red Hat Linux

***

In This Chapter

▶ Finding out what you need to install Red Hat Linux

▶ Creating a boot disk if you can't boot from CD

▶ Repartitioning with `fips` so that Red Hat Linux can bunk with Windows

***

*U*nless you have a brand-spanking-new hard drive with nothing on it, you must get your hard drive prepared before you can install Red Hat Linux. This process is pretty straightforward when you have an entire hard drive to use for the installation, but the harsh reality (or Windows), unfortunately, is that you may not have that luxury. But all is not lost! With the caveat that your hard drive needs to have enough free space to accommodate both operating systems, Red Hat Linux can happily coexist with other operating systems such as Windows; you just choose one operating system or the other when you start the computer.

This chapter shows you how to properly tenderize and marinate your hard drive so that you have an easy time installing Red Hat Linux. We describe how to create a boot floppy disk that might be necessary to get the installation process started on some older computers. We also describe how to configure your hard drive to coexist (dual-boot) with Windows.

If you're a one-OS kind of person, Chapter 3 describes how to install Red Hat Linux as your computer's *only* operating system. It also describes the basic dual-boot installation process.

Preparing Your Hard Drive for Red Hat Linux

Before you install Red Hat Linux on your hard drive, you need to get your hard drive ready, especially if you intend to have Windows (or another operating system) installed on the same hard drive as Linux.

The following list describes the process you need to follow to prepare your hard drive for Red Hat Linux:

1. **Put on a red fedora hat (and have a mirror nearby so that you can see how cool you look!).**

2. **Make room on your computer's hard drive for Red Hat Linux if you want to install it alongside Windows (or another operating system).**

   This step, which generally involves deleting files and uninstalling application software, is totally unnecessary if you don't want Red Hat Linux to coexist with another operating system.

3. **Determine if your computer can boot from CD-ROM.**

   In the following section, we show you how to test your computer to see if it can boot from CD-ROM.

   If you can boot from the CD-ROM and don't have another operating system you want to keep, you can safely skip this entire chapter and just move on to the actual installation in Chapter 3 (lucky you!). If you can boot from the CD-ROM and do have another operating system that you want to keep, such as Windows, you don't need to haggle with the silly boot disk business in this section and can skip to the "Move Over Windows, Here Comes Johnny" section later in this chapter.

4. **Create a boot disk if your computer is not able to boot directly from CD-ROM.**

   We show you how to create a boot disk using Windows, MS-DOS, or Linux later in this chapter.

Finding Out If Your Computer Can Boot from CD-ROM

To start the Red Hat Linux installation process, you need some sort of boot disk (or disc), be it the *Red Hat Linux 7.3 For Dummies* CD1 that comes with this book (the easy way) or a boot floppy disk, which you have to create (the only slightly more complicated way).

If you have a computer that was manufactured around 1997 or later, then you can probably boot directly from the CD-ROM. Woo hoo!

Testing whether or not your computer can boot from CD-ROM is easy:

1. **Place CD1 that comes with this book into your computer's CD-ROM drive.**

2. **Turn on your computer.**

   If Red Hat Linux starts its preinstallation process, you're golden.

   If nothing happens, your computer isn't set to boot from CD-ROM by default. Or your computer isn't capable of booting from the CD-ROM at all.

If your computer doesn't boot, that doesn't necessarily mean that it's unable to boot from CD; you may not have the option selected.

You can try these general steps to find out if your computer is capable of booting from CD-ROM and just needs to have its settings tweaked. (Just about every BIOS is different from the next, so it's impossible for us to make these steps anything but general.)

1. **Boot (that is, turn on) your computer.**

   During the initial start phase, you should see some simple text displayed. While this is going on, you should see an instruction telling you what key to press to gain access to the menu that allows you to modify your computer's BIOS. For example, typical instructions are `Press <F1> to Enter Setup` or `Press <DEL> to Enter Setup`.

   BIOS stands for Basic Input/Output Settings. The BIOS controls the most basic functions of your computer that don't require an operating system, such as Red Hat Linux or Windows, to work. For example, the BIOS controls what devices your computer uses to boot from.

2. **Press the correct key to enter the BIOS.**

   A BIOS setup menu is displayed. Most of the time, you need to press a function key (F1, F2, and so on) to enter the various submenus and then identify the submenu that controls your computer's boot sequence.

3. **When you see the menu that includes your computer's boot sequence, press the appropriate function key to enter the menu.**

   This may take a bit of sniffing around, because some of the menus may have fairly techie-sounding names. Feel free to enter menus; just be very careful not to change anything. If you do accidentally change something and you're not sure how to fix it, exit the BIOS making sure to choose *not* to save changes when the BIOS asks you whether you want to save upon exit!

When you're in the boot sequence menu, it should be obvious whether your computer can boot from CD-ROM or not. When you toggle through the list of options, you see a reference to a CD-ROM alongside references to your floppy drive and your actual hard drive.

4a. If you find a CD-ROM listing, follow these steps:

1. Select the CD-ROM option (or equivalent) as the first device in your computer's boot sequence.

2. Press the Esc key to exit from the menu.

3. Make sure to save the changes you made when your BIOS asks if you want to save.

4. Reboot your computer from the CD-ROM.

4b. If you *don't* see any way to make your computer boot from CD-ROM, exit your BIOS without saving changes and skip to one of the next two sections to create your boot disk from either Windows (or MS-DOS) or Linux.

Creating a Red Hat Linux Boot Disk with Windows or MS-DOS

If you have an MS-DOS, Windows 9*x*/ME or a Windows NT/2000 system, then you can use your system to read the accompanying CD-ROM as well as create your boot disk. The CD includes a program called `rawrite.exe` that you can use to make the disks while you're running Windows.

If you need to use a PCMCIA card for a CD-ROM or floppy drive to install Linux (you have a Toshiba Libretto laptop, for instance), you have to create the PCMCIA version of the boot disk, which is also on CD1. In that case, substitute the `pcmcia.img` file for the `boot.img` file in the following instructions. If you need to install Red Hat Linux over a network — for example, if your PC or notebook does not have a CD-ROM drive but another computer on the network does — you need to create a network boot disk. In this case, substitute the `bootnet.img` file for the `boot.img` file in the following instructions.

In the following instructions, I assume that your CD-ROM is drive D: and your floppy drive is A:. If your drive letter designations are different, substitute the appropriate letters for *D* and *A* in the following instructions.

To create a boot disk, follow these steps:

1. **On a Windows computer, open a command prompt by clicking the Start button and choosing Programs⇨MS-DOS Prompt (or Programs⇨ Command Prompt on a Windows NT/2000 machine).**

   If you're running MS-DOS, you're already at a command prompt, which should look similar to C:\>.

2. **Insert an MS-DOS formatted, high-density (1.44MB) 3½-inch floppy into the floppy drive.**

3. **Insert CD1 that came with this book into your CD-ROM drive.**

4. **Type** d: **at the command prompt and press Enter.**

5. **Type** cd \dosutils **at the command prompt and press Enter.**

6. **Type** rawrite **at the command prompt and press Enter.**

   rawrite opens and asks you to type the disk image source filename.

7. **Type** d:\images\boot.img **at the command prompt and press Enter.**

   rawrite asks you to enter the location of the target disk drive where you want to create the boot disk.

8. **Type** a: **at the command prompt and press Enter.**

   rawrite tells you to insert a formatted disk into your A: drive and press Enter.

9. **Verify that you have a formatted disk in your A: drive and press Enter.**

   rawrite copies the boot image to the floppy disk, which can now *boot* (start up) your computer and begin the Red Hat Linux installation process.

   Wait until the floppy disk drive light is out before you remove the disk.

10. **Remove the boot disk and label it something ridiculously obvious like "Boot Disk" so that you know what it is later.**

Making a Boot Disk with Linux

If you don't have access to a Windows computer but do have access to another Linux system, this section is for you. To make a boot disk in Linux, you must log in as a user with permission to write to the 3½-inch floppy drive, which Linux refers to as /dev/fd0.

To create the boot disk and supplemental disk, follow these steps:

1. **Insert a blank, formatted floppy into your floppy drive and insert CD1 that came with this book into your CD-ROM drive.**

2. **Type** mount /mnt/cdrom **at the command prompt and press Enter.**

   Mounting means making the CD visible to the rest of the file system. You've just mounted the CD. Congratulations.

3. **Change to the images directory by typing** cd /mnt/cdrom/images **at the command prompt and pressing Enter.**

4. **Type** dd if=boot.img of=/dev/fd0 **at the command prompt and press Enter.**

   Linux copies the boot image to your floppy disk.

5. **Dismount the CD-ROM by typing** cd / **and pressing Enter and then typing** umount /mnt/cdrom **and pressing Enter.**

   Dismounting means removing the CD from the rest of the file system.

   Wait until the floppy disk drive light is out before removing the disk.

6. **Remove the boot disk from your disk drive and label it something obvious like "Boot Disk" so that you know what it is later.**

Move Over Windows, Here Comes Johnny

Before you install Red Hat Linux on your hard drive, you need to make room for it. Some people find space by getting rid of Windows and installing Red Hat Linux by itself, but you may not want to make such drastic changes. Perhaps you prefer to have Red Hat Linux and another operating system coexist peacefully. The former configuration is referred to as a *standalone system* and the latter as a *dual-boot system.*

Chapter 3 shows you how to install and use a standalone Red Hat Linux system, and all discussions and examples in the following chapters assume you have a standalone system. Because many people find dual-boot systems to be desirable, we describe how to create one here by using partitions.

A *partition* is a section of space on a drive used to organize files and directories. For example, the famous C: drive in MS-DOS and Windows is installed on its own partition on your hard drive. Most people wouldn't need to know this little tidbit, because most systems come with only one large partition that hogs up the entire hard drive.

We strongly suggest backing up any important files on your hard drive before performing any major work on repartitioning it. You don't want to lose any data or programs that you worked hard to install. Refer to your system's owners' manual to find out how to back up your system and how to restore the data if necessary.

You can reconfigure an existing Windows partition so that you can install Red Hat Linux on the same disk using one of two methods:

- **Destructive repartitioning:** This method involves shrinking the DOS partition, which wipes out all the data on the hard drive.

- **Nondestructive repartitioning:** This method moves and confines existing data on the hard drive safely into its own partition, leaving the rest of your hard drive for Linux.

Microsoft's NTFS file system (Windows NT/2000 and XP typically use NTFS but can also use FAT32) cannot be altered with the tools provided by Red Hat Linux. You can purchase commercial tools such as Norton's Ghost to modify NTFS. If you don't want to pay for the tools, you can still install Linux along with Windows if your NTFS-based computer has more than one partition, then you can use one of the partitions to install Red Hat Linux. You have to be willing, of course, to lose whatever is installed on that partition to do so.

Nondestructive Repartitioning with fips: Can't We All Just Get Along?

If you can't add another hard drive to your system, then your only choices are either destructive or nondestructive repartitioning. Nondestructive partitioning is definitely the better choice if you want to retain existing data or another operating system on the same computer as Red Hat Linux. (You still should back up your system, just in case you have to restore it afterward.) Destructive partitioning wipes out everything on your disk and makes installing a new operating system straightforward.

The fips utility works by dividing the drive into two partitions. The first partition includes your initial operating system, such as Windows. The second partition, which begins at the end of the space used by Windows and encompassing the rest of the drive space, is the non-DOS partition where you install Red Hat Linux.

The `fips` utility works only on FAT or FAT32 partitions. `fips` can't repartition NTFS file systems. You can purchase Norton Ghost 2001, which is a commercial system capable of repartitioning both FIPS and NTFS file systems. Go to www.norton.com for more information.

If you decide to create a dual-boot Linux and Windows system, keep Windows as the first partition. Windows likes to be first, but Linux is happy to be flexible and make your life easier.

The next two sections contain steps for defragmenting your hard drive and using `fips` to carve the drive into partitions.

Defragmenting your hard drive

Defragmenting a hard drive consolidates all the data on your hard drive within one partition, leaving the empty space behind for Linux. This is a necessary task because Windows is a slob as operating systems go, throwing data all over the hard drive rather than in any sort of logical order.

Follow the steps in one of the following two sections to defragment your hard drive while running Windows.

Defragmenting in Windows 9x/ME or Windows NT/2000

The following steps show you how to defrag your hard drive in Windows 9*x*/ME or Windows NT/2000:

1. **Close all programs and windows on your system, leaving just the desktop and icon bar.**

2. **Double-click the My Computer icon on the desktop.**

3. **Select your C: drive by clicking it and choosing File⇨Properties⇨ Tools.**

4. **Click Defragment Now.**

   The defragmentation program looks at the drive to determine whether it needs defragmentation.

   You may get a message telling you that you don't need to defragment because your hard drive is not very fragmented, but don't believe it. Under ordinary circumstances this may be true. But repartitioning isn't an ordinary occurrence; defragmenting your hard drive is necessary because you're going to move the end of the partition file system and make the partition smaller, erasing any data outside that barrier.

5. Click Start.

The defragmentation window appears and the defrag process begins.

Defragmenting can take a long time (even taking days if you have a very large disk with lots of errors!), depending on the size of your hard drive and the number of errors that need to be corrected.

By clicking the Show Details button, you can scroll up and down the large window to watch the defrag process in action, as shown in Figure 2-1. The colored blocks represent programs and data, and the white space represents free space on your hard drive that `fips` can allocate to the Linux file system. The movement of the blocks around the screen shows that the data is being moved forward on the drive. Expect to see white space appear toward the bottom of the window, which represents the end of your drive. At the end of the defragmentation process, no colored blocks appear at the bottom of the window, and all the blocks are compressed toward the top of the window.

After what may seem like a long time, defragmentation finishes. All useful blocks of information are now at the beginning of the drive, making it ready for the `fips` program in the "Resizing with `fips`" section later in this chapter.

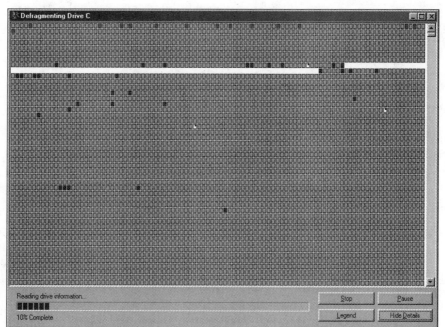

Figure 2-1:
The defrag program in progress.

Defragmenting in Windows

Follow these steps to defragment your hard drive in Windows 3.*x* or MS-DOS:

1. **Close all programs and windows on your system.**

2. **If you're running Windows, exit from Windows into MS-DOS by choosing File⇨Exit Windows.**

3. **Type** cd \dos **at the command prompt and press Enter.**

4. **Type** defrag **at the command prompt and press Enter.**

   The defrag program asks you which drive to defragment.

5. **Use the letter keys on your keyboard to select the drive you want to defragment.**

   The defragmentation program looks at the drive to determine whether it needs defragmentation.

   You may see a message telling you that you don't need to defragment because your hard drive is not very fragmented, but don't believe it. Defragmenting your hard drive is necessary because you're going to move the end of the partition file system and make the partition smaller, erasing any data outside of that barrier.

6. **Defragment the drive even if the program says the drive doesn't need defragmenting.**

   A long time passes and finally, defragmentation is completed. All useful blocks of information are now at the beginning of the drive, making it ready for the fips program in the next section.

Resizing with fips

The MS-DOS fips utility is used to nondestructively resize your MS-DOS and/or Windows partitions. Newer versions of Windows (including Windows ME) use a 32-bit file allocation table (called FAT32) and drive management that provide for single-drive configurations larger than 2GB. Older versions of Windows 95 used a 16-bit FAT (called FAT16, oddly enough); to use the space above 2GB, the drive had to be partitioned into logical drives of 2GB or less. Newer computers often have drives larger than the old 2GB limit. If the drive is repartitioned, the large drive management system is disabled, and DOS and Windows partitions are once again limited to 2GB.

To use fips, you must first exit your Windows interface and get to the MS-DOS prompt. To do so with Windows 9*x*, follow these steps (in Windows ME or Windows NT/2000, you need to reboot with an MS-DOS boot disk that includes the fips utility):

1. **Click the Start button.**

2. **Click the Shut Down button.**

3. **Select the Restart the Computer in MS-DOS Mode option.**

   If your computer can't boot into MS-DOS mode (such as with Windows ME), then you have one other option: Obtain an MS-DOS boot floppy (one that has CD-ROM drivers configured on it) and boot from it; the CD-ROM drivers are necessary because you have to access the `fips` program on CD1.

4. **Copy the `fips.exe` program from CD1 to your boot disk.**

   For MS-DOS and earlier versions of Windows 95, you need to use the FAT16 version of `fips.exe`, which is stored in the `\dosutils\fips15c\` directory. For later versions of Windows 9*x*/ME, the FAT32 version of `fips.exe` is found in `\dosutils\fips20\` directory. You can find documentation on both versions in the `fips.doc` file, which can be found in the `\dosutils\fips15c\` (for the FAT16 version) and `\dosutils\fips20\` (for the FAT32 version) directories on CD1.

5. **Boot your computer from the floppy.**

   The computer restarts in MS-DOS mode.

6. **Type** cd a: **at the DOS prompt and press Enter.**

7. **Type** fips **at the prompt and press Enter.**

   Some messages appear and flash by, but you can ignore them all except the last one, which asks you to press any key.

8. **When you see the** Press any key **message, do so.**

   You see all the existing partitions on the hard drive.

9. **When you see the** Press any key **message, do so again.**

   You're getting pretty good at this! A description of the drive and a series of messages flash by. Then `fips` finds the free space in the first partition.

10. **When asked whether you want to make a backup copy of sectors, type** y **for yes.**

    The screen asks whether a floppy disk is in your A: drive.

11. **Place a formatted floppy disk into your A: drive and then press** y.

    A message similar to Writing file a:\rootboot.000 appears, followed by other messages and then the message Use cursor key to choose the cylinder, enter to continue.

Three columns appear on the screen: Old Partition, Cylinder, and New Partition. The Old Partition number is the number of megabytes in the main partition of your hard drive. The New Partition number is the number of megabytes in the new partition you're making for the Linux operating system.

12. **Use the left- and right-arrow keys to change the numbers in the Old Partition and New Partition fields to give you the space you need for both the Windows operating system and Linux (see Figure 2-2).**

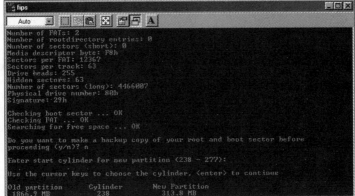

Figure 2-2:
The fips
program
carving up a
hard drive.

A minimum Linux system, without the X Window System graphical environment, requires about 40MB of hard drive space. A minimal graphical system requires about 150MB of hard drive space. The full distribution, along with all the programs and compilers on the hard drive, requires around 2,000MB (or 2 gigabytes - GB) of drive space. Then you have the amount of data space you need for your own files. The amount of data space that you divide between the Linux and Microsoft operating systems is up to you.

13. **When you have the correct amount of hard drive space in each field, press the Enter key.**

fips displays the partition table again, showing you the new partition that has been created for the Linux operating system. This new partition will probably be partition 2; your C: drive is probably partition 1.

You also see a message at the bottom of the screen asking whether you want to continue or reedit.

14. **If you are satisfied with the size of your partitions, type c to continue (if you are *not* satisfied type r, which takes you back to Step 12).**

Many more messages about your hard drive flash by. A message then appears, stating that the system is ready to write the new partition scheme to disk and asking whether you want to proceed.

15. **Type** y **to make** fips **write the new partition information to the hard drive.**

   If you type **n**, fips exits without changing anything on your hard drive, leaving your hard drive exactly the way it was after you defragmented it.

16. **To test that nondestructive partitioning worked properly, reboot your system by pressing Ctrl+Alt+Delete.**

17. **Allow Windows to start and then run ScanDisk by clicking the Start button and choosing Programs➪Accessories➪System Tools➪ScanDisk.**

   ScanDisk indicates whether you have all the files and folders you started with and whether anything was lost. Even if everything is found to be okay, consider keeping any backup files around for a while to be on the safe side.

Now you're ready to install the Linux operating system, which we explain how to do in Chapter 3.

Chapter 3

Ready, Set, Install!

In This Chapter

▶ Starting the Red Hat Linux installation

▶ Letting Red Hat Linux partition your hard drive for you

▶ Installing software

▶ Configuring your new installation

*I*nstalling Red Hat Linux isn't rocket science — it's more like nuclear science. No, no, just kidding! Don't run! Just relax, sit down, grab your favorite drink, and contemplate the excitement about to unfold: the installation and configuration of Red Hat Linux. After you're done, you'll have a powerful computer capable of performing most, if not all, of your daily chores — all for the cost of this book! That's pretty amazing when you think about it: For a few bucks, you get the same amount of operating power that cost mega bucks just a few years ago.

This chapter walks you through the Workstation installation of Red Hat Linux on your PC. If you're installing Red Hat Linux on a laptop, choose Laptop instead of Workstation. The steps are exactly the same, although the Laptop installation adds some extra software to help Linux work with your laptop.

The Workstation Laptop installation automates otherwise horrifically complicated decisions that no sane person would want to haggle with, such as partitioning your hard drive and selecting software. The Workstation installation includes the GNOME graphical user interface (GUI) and all the tools that an average computer user (that's you) needs to survive. If you want software that the installation doesn't provide, you can always add packages later.

Before you install Red Hat Linux, you need to boot or reboot (*boot* means to start, *reboot* means to restart) your computer with the CD that comes with this book in your CD-ROM drive. See Chapter 2 to find out whether or not you can boot from the CD-ROM. If you can't, you can make a boot floppy disk and reboot from your main floppy drive instead. Be sure before you proceed that you have the following system information at the ready: any information that you'll need to connect to your ISP (telephone number, user login name, password, and such); if you're connecting to a LAN administered by someone else — for instance, you're connecting your computer to your work LAN — you'll need information such as your IP address (you'll have to obtain that information from the administrator).

Installation Stage 1: Starting the Install

This section gets you started with the Red Hat Linux installation process. These initial steps start the installation and perform some basic configuration steps.

Before getting started you should know that you can easily change your configuration choices. If you realize you've made a mistake, you can hit the Back button to retrace your steps and redo your choices. And if you ever want to stop the installation process altogether, you can simply reboot your computer.

For installation masochists and text snobs only

You can run the Red Hat Linux installation system from a graphical interface or from a text-based interface. The graphical method is the default, and that's what we discuss in this chapter. In addition to the ease of using a mouse to point and click, the graphical method also groups similar configuration choices together. For example, the keyboard and mouse selection is presented within one window, not two, as in the text-based installation.

Here are some reasons why you might have to use the text-based installation:

✔ You really, really want to use the text-based install because you have some sick twisted prejudice against pointing and clicking.

✔ The Red Hat Linux installation system can't use your graphics adapter. You will figure this out when the graphical installation window doesn't appear and you see a text-based window appear; the text-based system uses the keyboard to enter information and the cursor (arrow) keys to move from step to step. This doesn't happen very often any more because Red Hat has done its homework and refined the installation process.

If you're one of those lucky readers who has to do a text-based installation, the instructions in this chapter are best used to line your birdcage. We show you how to install Red Hat Linux the ugly way in Appendix B.

The point of no return comes at the very end of the process when the configuration is written to disk (see "Installation Stage 5: The Point of No Return") and the installation software starts to partition your hard drive and write Linux to it. If you stop at that point, you need to reinstall an operating system before you use the computer again.

1. **Insert CD1 that came with this book (or a boot disk if you are using one) and boot or reboot your computer.**

   After your computer thinks for a while, the first installation screen appears displaying the `boot:` prompt, as shown in Figure 3-1.

2. **Press Enter.**

   A series of messages scrolls by, indicating whether the Linux kernel detects your hardware. Most of the time — particularly with newer systems — Linux detects all the basic hardware and then a welcome message appears.

3. **If you don't see a welcome message within a few seconds, reboot your system and manually locate the hardware for Linux at the `boot:` prompt:**

   ```
   boot: linux hdc=cdrom
   ```

   This example attempts to force your system to use your CD-ROM drive.

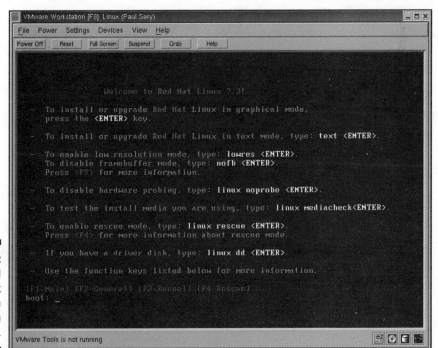

Figure 3-1:
The first Red
Hat Linux
installation
system
screen.

4. **When Linux has made friends with your hardware, the Red Hat installation process gets started and the Welcome message is displayed on-
screen. Click the Next button to proceed to the next window.**

   If you continue to have problems, you can get more installation information from Red Hat's online installation manual (if you can get access to a
   working computer, that is!) in HTML format located on CD1 in the `/mnt/
   cdrom/doc/rhmanual/manual` directory. You can mount the CD-ROM
   on another Linux or Windows system and view the document with
   Netscape.

   After you leave the Welcome message screen, the Language Selection
   window appears, as shown in Figure 3-2.

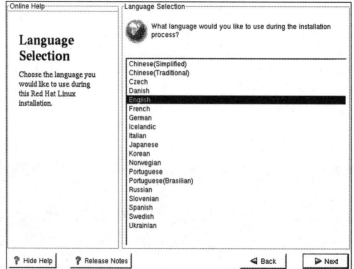

Figure 3-2:
Selecting
your
language.

5. **Select a language and click Next.**

   You have a choice to use several languages, so choose the language that
   you speak, or, if you're feeling adventurous, one that you don't (not
   recommended).

   The Keyboard Configuration window appears, as shown in Figure 3-3.

6. **Select the keyboard model and layout that you want to use and then
   click Next.**

   The Mouse Configuration window appears, as shown in Figure 3-4.

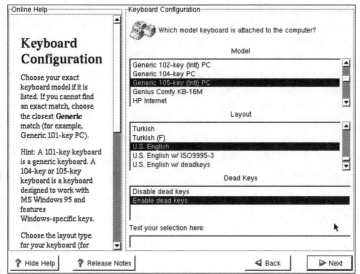

Figure 3-3:
Configuring
your
keyboard
layout.

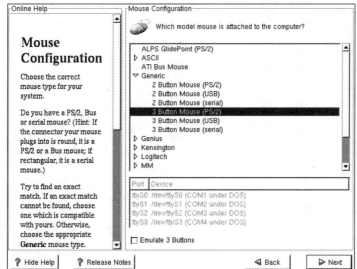

Figure 3-4:
Configuring
your mouse.

7. Select your mouse (squeak!) and click Next.

Red Hat provides a slew of mice to choose from. If you have a PS/2 mouse, all you have to do is select the manufacturer and number of buttons. If you have the older style of mouse that connects via a serial port, you have to select the manufacturer, number of buttons, and the serial port that it is connected to; you have only four serial ports to select from, and in many cases, it will be either `ttyS0` or `ttyS1` (or the equivalent `cua0` or `cua1`).

If you have a two-button mouse (either serial or PS/2), you can choose to have it emulate three buttons by clicking the Emulate 3 Buttons option. You emulate the third (middle) button by pressing both outside mouse buttons at once.

The Welcome to Red Hat Linux introduction window appears after you complete the initial configuration steps.

8. Click Next.

The Install Options window appears, as shown in Figure 3-5.

See "Installation Stage 2: Slicing and Dicing the Pie" to choose an installation option and continue.

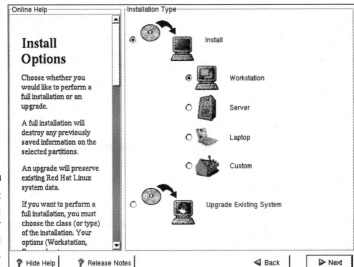

Figure 3-5: Choosing your installation type.

Installation Stage 2: Slicing and Dicing the Pie

Red Hat Linux gives you several installation types to choose from. The standard *Workstation, Laptop, Server* and, *Custom System* installations can preselect your partitions and software for you based on whether you expect to use your computer as a personal workstation or a general server; the Upgrade option leaves your partitions alone and, as you might guess, upgrades your software.

We're describing how to build a personal workstation or laptop so we don't discuss the Server or Custom installations or the Upgrade option here. We focus on using the Workstation or Laptop installations. They create essentially the same Red Hat Linux computer but the Laptop installs extra software to deal with the particulars of laptop computers. For instance, the Laptop installs software so you can use your PCMCIA cards.

Picking up from Step 8 in the preceding section, follow these steps to continue the installation:

1. **Select the Workstation or Laptop option in the Installation Type window and click the Next button.**

   The Disk Partitioning Setup window appears, as shown in Figure 3-6. The Red Hat Linux installation system must partition your hard drive in order to install its software. Partitions divide a disk into one or more parts. The divisions are used to organize the software and data (for instance, user files) that comprise the operating system.

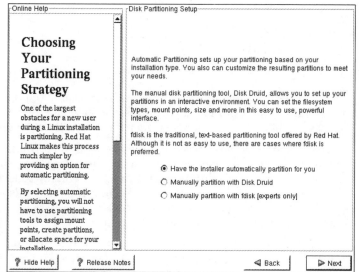

Figure 3-6:
The Disk
Partitioning
Setup
window.

Red Hat provides three partitioning methods: automatic, manual using Red Hat's Disk Druid, and manual using fdisk. The latter two manual methods require you to have some experience and so we use the first, automatic method. The automatic method is the easiest to use and we recommend it unless you're feeling lucky (or want to experiment or have experience). Select the Have the Installer Automatically Partition for You option.

2. **The Automatic Partitioning window, shown in Figure 3-7, appears. Select the option you need depending on the operating system (for instance, Windows) that's installed on your computer.**

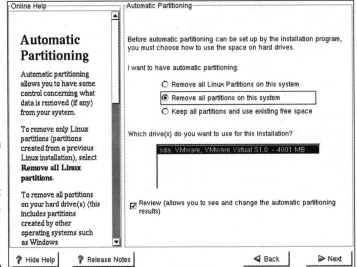

Figure 3-7: Choose to let Red Hat Linux partition automatically.

Select the Remove All Linux Partitions on This System option if you are re-installing Linux; your Linux partitions, and any data they contain will be erased while any existing Windows partitions will not be touched.

Use the Remove All Partitions on This System option if you are installing Linux over an existing Windows (or Linux) installation. Use extreme caution when choosing the option: It destroys your Windows installation and all the software and data that it uses. You would use this option, for instance, if your computer came with Windows pre-installed and you want to convert it to a Linux-only workstation.

Use the Keep All Partitions and Use Existing Free Space option if you want to install Red Hat Linux on extra, unused space on your hard drive (for instance, you have shrunk an existing Windows FAT or FAT32 partition as described in Chapter 2).

This book assumes that you're using Red Hat Linux as your only operating system. This chapter and the rest of the book are oriented around using a dedicated Red Hat Linux workstation. Therefore, we suggest that you select the second option that removes all partitions on your computer. That will erase any existing Windows or Linux installations and allow you to use the entire hard drive for Red Hat Linux.

Confidential for Windows users

If you are running Windows NT (or Windows 2000) and choose the Workstation installation, then your NT boot record is overwritten and you won't be able to boot Windows NT. Your NT partition won't be erased; it's just rendered unbootable. (An NT *boot record* is what enables a Windows NT system to start automatically when you start your computer.)

You can install Red Hat Linux 7.3 without overwriting the NT boot partition if you choose the Custom installation method and manually configure the Linux Loader (LILO). It is beyond the scope of this book to describe that process. For more information on the Custom installation, see the Red Hat Linux installation guide at Red Hat's Web site:

`www.redhat.com/docs`

You can roll your own Red Hat Linux system by selecting the *Custom System* installation. We don't discuss this option in this book because it's really not for the faint of heart. Finally, if you already have Red Hat Linux installed, you can choose the *Upgrade* option and the newer software installs over the older software without changing your current partitions or user software (for this chapter, though, we assume that you're installing fresh).

3. **A warning screen appears. Take a deep breath and make sure that you want to continue. Click on Yes to continue with the installation or No to return to the partitioning window.**

4. **The Disk Setup window appears.**

   Select the automatic partitioning option to allow the Red Hat installation process divide the available space on your hard drive into three partitions (the available space is determined by what option you selected in Step 2). The partitions created are *root* (/), *boot* (/boot), and *swap*. (Swap is used internally by Linux and isn't accessible to you like the other partitions.)

   At this point, you can click the edit, delete, and add options if you want to modify the default disk partitions. You should only do this if you're an experienced Unix or Linux user and understand the concept of using multiple partitions, but we recommend that, unless you feel really lucky or are very experienced, you let Red Hat do the work here.

5. **Click the Next button.**

   The Boot Loader Configuration window appears. The boot loader configures your computer to load one operating system or another when it starts. GRUB is the powerful and complicated new boot loader that Linux techies love. However, most people will never use its features. The traditional LILO is simpler and just fine for most of us (including us). Select the Use LILO As the Boot Loader option and click the Next button.

The partitioning process takes some time, but if you have a network card installed, the Network Configuration window eventually appears, as shown in Figure 3-8.

In "Installation Stage 3: Configuring Your Network," we show you how to configure your network for Linux use. If you don't have a network or just don't want to haggle with it right now, click Next and skip to "Installation Stage 4: Configuring Your System."

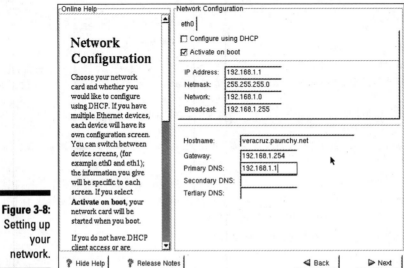

Figure 3-8:
Setting up
your
network.

Installation Stage 3: Configuring Your Network

If you're ready to configure your network, and your computer has an Ethernet adapter, then enter the appropriate information as described in the following steps. If you have a network adapter, but don't have a network to connect to, you should still enter a host name in Step 3. Entering a host name will make life easier if and when you connect to a network.

As you fill in the text boxes, you may find that Red Hat Linux guesses what information is needed and fills in some sections automatically. If Linux is right, pat it on the head and offer it a little treat. If Linux guesses incorrectly, simply change the information.

Picking up from the end of the last section, the Network Configuration window appears (refer to Figure 3-8). Follow these steps to configure your system for a network:

1. **Click the Activate on Boot radio button or, if you're connecting to a network that uses the *Dynamic Host Configuration Protocol* (DHCP), select the Configure Using DHCP option, click Next, and skip to Step 3.**

   Selecting this option ensures that your network starts when you boot your computer.

   If you selected the Configure Using DHCP option, you can skip Step 2 because with DHCP your computer obtains its IP address, netmask, default gateway, and nameserver information from the DHCP server on your network. You'll have to consult with your LAN's administrator to find out if it uses DHCP or not. If you constructed your own LAN and don't know if you're running DHCP then you're not. (You have to install the DHCP server and configure it.)

2. **Type your IP Address, Netmask, Gateway (IP), and Primary DNS into the appropriate text boxes.**

   The following list gives a brief description of the four parameters, which your Internet service provider should give you (if you're not using DHCP).

   - **IP address:** This is the numeric network address of your Linux computer and is the address your computer is known as on your local network and — in many cases — the Internet. If you haven't registered your private network's (also known as local networks or LANs) address space with the InterNic (the organization that is in charge of distributing IP addresses), then you can use the public address space that goes from 192.168.1.1 to 192.168.254.254.

     If you're connecting to an existing LAN, then consult the administrator to get an IP address that is not already being used. You'll have to keep track of unused IP addresses if you're running your own LAN.

   - **Netmask:** Private networks based on the Internet Protocol (IP) are divided into subnetworks. The netmask determines how the network is divided. For IP addresses such as the one in the preceding bullet (192.168.1.1), the most common netmask is 255.255.255.0.

   - **Gateway:** This is the numeric IP address of the computer that connects your private network to the Internet (or another private network). Red Hat Linux guesses the address of 192.168.1.254, for example, if you choose an address of 192.168.1.{1-254} for the IP address. You can accept this address, but leaving it blank is a better option, unless that address is your actual gateway. Chapter 5 describes how to configure your Linux computer to connect to the Internet via a telephone connection. If you do that, then setting a default route now can interfere with your connection.

- **Primary DNS:** The Internet Protocol uses a system called Domain Name Service (DNS) to convert names such as `www.redhat.com` into numeric IPs. A computer that acts as a DNS is called a *nameserver*. Red Hat Linux again makes a guess based on the IP address and netmask that you use. We suggest leaving this box blank, however, unless you are on a private network with a nameserver or will be connected to the Internet (your ISP will supply a DNS). When you designate a nonexistent nameserver, then many networking programs work very slowly as they wait in vain for the absent server.

3. **Type your computer's host name, including the network name (domain) in the Hostname text box.**

   For example, if you want to name your computer `veracruz` and your network name is `paunchy.net`, then you type **veracruz.paunchy.net**.

   If you do not give your computer a name and domain name during the network configuration process, then it is referred to as *localhost. localdomain*. Otherwise, the welcome screen refers to whatever name you gave it. For example, in the preceding example you would see `Welcome to veracruz.paunchy.net`.

4. **If you are connecting to the Internet directly through a modem, then leave the Gateway address blank, or, if you are on a LAN that has a gateway to the Internet, enter its address in the Gateway text box.**

   If you're connecting to someone else's LAN — if you're at work, for instance — then you should obtain this address from your system administrator. If you're connecting to your own LAN at home, then consult yourself, because you're probably the administrator.

5. **Type the primary DNS address in the Primary DNS text box.**

   DNS means Domain Name Server and is used by geeks and cool folk everywhere to change human names into Internet addresses. If you are connected to an ISP, they provide you with the DNS address. Otherwise, consult your friendly local system administrator (some Linux geek like your friendly authors if you're at work) for that information.

6. **If you have access to secondary and tertiary nameservers (IPs), type their IP addresses in the appropriate text boxes.**

   Your ISP will provide you with that information if you're connecting directly to the Internet. Otherwise, if you're connecting to a LAN run by someone else — for instance at work — then your system administrator will provide that information.

   Secondary and *tertiary* nameservers provide backup service to the primary nameserver. These are the IP addresses of the second and third DNS servers that your computer will use.

7. **When you complete the form, click the Next button to continue.**

8. **Select the No Firewall option and click the Next button.**

   Red Hat will create a firewall; however, we construct a better firewall in Chapter 8.

9. **The Additional Language Support window provides extra linguistic options. Make your selection (although most anyone in the U.S. will not have to make any) and click the Next button.**

   The Time Zone Selection window appears, as shown in Figure 3-9.

   The next section shows you how to configure your Red Hat Linux system.

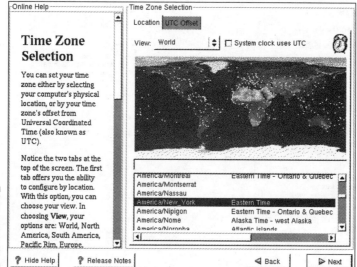

Figure 3-9:
Selecting
your time
zone.

Installation Stage 4: Configuring Your System

This section covers basic configuration for Red Hat Linux, at which time you set your time zone as well as the root user password. You can also add regular users and set their passwords. The following steps describe how to perform these basic tasks from the Time Zone Selection window (refer to Figure 3-9).

1. **Click the dot representing a city closest to where you live to select your time zone.**

   You can use the map to point and click your way to your time zone bliss. When you click one of the thousand points of light, the represented city and its time zone appear in the subwindow below the map. You can also click the slider bar at the bottom of the screen to locate the name of your city/time zone. After you find it, click the text to select your time zone.

2. **Click Next.**

   The Account Configuration window appears, as shown in Figure 3-10.

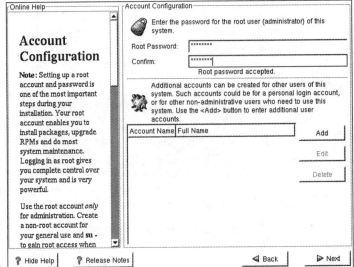

Figure 3-10:
Entering
your root
password.

3. **Type your root password into both the Root Password and Confirm text boxes.**

   The password is for the root user, also known as the *superuser,* who has access to the entire system and can do almost anything — good and bad.

   It's best to log in as the root user only to do system maintenance or administrative tasks. The root user is the only user with access to critical system files. To avoid making unwanted changes or deletions to these important files, add another user for yourself as described in Step 4 and use the root account only when you need to.

Knowing your password etiquette

Your password must be at least six characters long, but it's better to use at least eight. The more characters that you use, the harder the password is to break. If you're concerned about security at all, we recommend that you use a combination of uppercase and lowercase letters, symbols, and numbers to make your password as difficult to compromise as possible. In addition, don't choose anything that would be found in a dictionary or names or items that are easy to associate with you. In other words, your name, your name spelled backwards, your birthday, your dog's name, any word in any language, and so on are all poor choices. Beer, for example, is a poor selection for Jon's password, even though it has both uppercase and lowercase letters, because Jon and beer are usually seen in close proximity with each other.

A good way to come up with a good password is to select a phrase and destroy it. For example, take "I am not a number" and make it into something like "imN0tun#". Even though the end result does not spell out the phrase in any real way, it gives you all the cues to remember the essentially random characters ("I am" = "im", "not" = "N0t", "a" = "un", and number = "#"). Other common substitutions are 3 for e, 4 for a, 9 for g, 1 for l, 8 for b, 5 for s, and so on. Thus you can create passwords like s0uthb4y (southbay) and 14mn0t4g33k (iamnotageek).

Also, be sure to write your password down where it won't get lost and can't be easily found or stolen. For example, save your work passwords at home or else store them in a locked desk or safe. And don't write your password on a sticky note attached to your computer monitor, please!

You have to type the password two times to make sure that you typed it correctly. The password appears on-screen as asterisks when you type it in. Holy breach of security, Batman! You wouldn't want someone to be able to look over your shoulder and get your password, now would you?

4. **(Optional) You can create user accounts in the bottom half of the screen by entering an account name, entering the password for the account into both the Password and Password (confirm) text boxes, and then clicking Add.**

Your new user account name is displayed in the Account Name box. You can go on to add, delete, and edit new or old users until the cows come home. Enter any or all of the people who will log in to your Red Hat Linux computer.

You don't have to add every user possible at this point. You can add (as well as modify or remove existing accounts) at any time after you've successfully installed Red Hat Linux by running the LinuxConf application (which we describe in Chapter 4).

5. Click Next.

The Selecting Package Groups window appears, as shown in Figure 3-11.

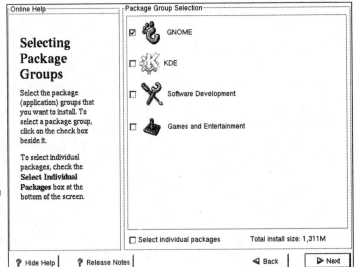

Figure 3-11:
Selecting
package
groups.

The final step of this section requires you to select the graphical window manager. If you intend to use graphics, you can choose either the GNOME or KDE system. GNOME is the default for Red Hat Linux and that's what we use throughout the rest of the book. KDE, however, is an excellent choice and many people prefer it.

6. Select GNOME and click Next.

The X Configuration window appears, as shown in Figure 13-12.

The next section shows you how to configure X Windows.

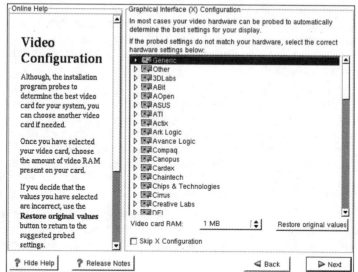

Figure 3-12:
The X
Configuration
window.

Installation Stage 5: The Point of No Return!

Until this point, no permanent changes have been made to your computer. The partitions you selected earlier have not been made permanent. No Red Hat Linux packages have been written to your hard drive. You can either stop completely or go back one or more steps by clicking the Back button.

If you want to stop the installation process completely, reboot your computer now. You will have to start the installation process all over again, but if you have a good reason to start over, by all means don't let us stop you.

You can reboot by pressing the reset button or by pressing the Ctrl+Alt+Del keys simultaneously. If you leave the Red Hat Linux installation CD-ROM in the drive, the computer restarts the installation process automatically when it reboots. If you remove the CD-ROM, then the previously installed operating system (if any) boots instead.

From the X Configuration window (refer to Figure 3-12), follow these steps:

1. **After you suck in your breath and decide to take the plunge, click Next.**

Your disk partitions are created and formatted and then the Red Hat Linux distribution is written to it. Yikes! The Installing Packages window tells you which package is currently being installed, as well as how many have been installed, how many remain to be installed, and the estimated time remaining.

The installer then asks if you want to create a boot disk. This is a good option, just in case something happens to the boot partition on your disk. Microsoft products, for example, have a bad habit of overwriting the Master Boot Record (MBR) — and therefore your Linux booting system — when they are installed or even updated. Hard drive boot failures can also happen for any number of reasons — aliens and gremlins are well known for wreaking havoc. The boot disk is a great tool for foiling these dastardly mischief-makers.

This boot disk is different from the one that you use to start the Red Hat Linux installation. This boot disk can start your Red Hat Linux computer in case the Linux boot information stored on your hard drive ever becomes corrupted.

2. **(Optional) Insert a blank disk into your main floppy drive, select the Create Boot Floppy option, and click Next to create a boot disk.**

Before the system reboots, remove the CD and any floppy disks in your drives. Otherwise you'll be faced with going through the entire installation process again. If that happens, there's no need to groan — you can always re-reboot and remove the pesky critters.

Your system reboots. Move on to the next section to finish installation.

Installation Stage 6: X Marks the Spot

Phew. You're almost at the finish line. Really!

One of the last things that you need to do is install X Server so that you can use the X Window System and a graphical user interface (or GUI), such as GNOME, to interact with Linux. To configure an X Server, you need to specify the video card and monitor for your system (if Red Hat didn't detect them automatically), including how much video memory the video card has, what speed it runs at, and a series of other options.

Picking up from the end of the last section, follow these steps to install the X Server:

1. **Select a monitor from the X Configuration window.**

   If your monitor is not included in the list, then you can select from within the Custom or Generic Monitor choices.

   Older monitors can't handle resolution rates and scan frequencies higher than what they were designed for. A monitor designed for a 640 x 480 resolution (and a low scan frequency) can't display a 2,048 x 1,024 resolution (and a high scan frequency), for example. If you try to make the monitor display a higher frequency than it's capable of displaying, the monitor may burst into flames. (We didn't believe this either until we saw a monitor smoking. Hey, but at least you get a new monitor out of it. Welcome to the 21st Century.)

   Modern monitors, called *multiscanning monitors,* can automatically match themselves to a series of scan frequencies and resolutions. Some of these monitors are even smart enough to turn themselves off instead of bursting into flames if the frequencies become too high. Finding the documentation and matching your vertical and horizontal frequencies properly is the best way to go (particularly with older monitors). Lacking this information, try a lower resolution (VGA or SVGA) first, just to get X Window System running.

2. **The installation process usually detects the video driver and configures the parameters for you. You can also specify the amount of memory on your video card.**

   This memory is different than the amount of system memory. Most modern cards have 1, 2, 4, or 8MB of video memory. Use your arrow keys to move down the list.

   If you are an expert, you can also select the `Customize X option` and configure it manually.

   If you don't know how much video memory your card has, try 1MB (the 1 Meg option). Although this setting limits the resolution of your screen, you will probably be able to get X Window System going. Later, you can experiment with the Xconfigurator program (which we describe in Chapter 20) to figure out the best values for how much video memory you have, if the probe did not work properly.

3. **Click the Test This Configuration button.**

4. **If you configured X correctly, this message appears:** `Can you see this message?`**. You have 10 seconds to either click the Yes button with your mouse or press the Enter key.**

5. **If you want to start X automatically at boot time, choose Yes. Otherwise, choose No.**

This book assumes that you answer yes to this option so that your Red Hat Linux computer starts X Windows and the GNOME window manager (if that's your default manager) every time you boot. If you choose no, whenever Linux boots, you're faced with the unexciting command prompt where, after logging in, you have to enter the `startx` command at the prompt to start X and your GUI.

If you choose No, then your system always starts up in character-cell or text mode. You can always manually start X with the aptly named `startx` command or modify the `/etc/inittab` to automatically start X. Change the line `id:3:initdefault` to `id:5:initdefault` in the `inittab` file to do that.

After you make your choice, a screen appears to inform you where you can find the configuration file. You're also pointed to the `X README. Config` file for more information.

6. **Click the Next button.**

If you have a problem with your X configuration, you see an on-screen message that regretfully informs you about the situation. You can quit or go back and start over. If you're game, go back and try, try again.

The About to Install window appears. At last you've reached the do-or-die stage — the point at which it's either go on and finalize the install (by writing to your hard drive) or to give it up with a whimper.

That's it! You now have built yourself a Red Hat Linux computer. Your computer will reboot itself and you can then use it as your personal workstation. The following chapters describe how to do just that. Have fun!

Chapter 4

Getting to Know Red Hat Linux

- -

In This Chapter

▶ Checking out the Linux file system

▶ Comprehending logins and the root user

▶ Adding a regular user

▶ Stopping Linux

- -

*B*efore you can use Red Hat Linux, you need to check out a few of the basics. This chapter covers enough of the Linux fundamentals to get you started, including topics such as starting and stopping Linux and understanding the difference between graphical and nongraphical applications.

Linux is a multiuser system, so you — and every other user — need an individual name and password to protect your information and keep your tasks separate from other people's tasks.

Introducing the Linux File System Tree

Linux, like Unix, refers to everything as a file, giving each device, file, and directory a *file address* by which it can be identified. Linux refers to drives and drive partitions by using a system of letters and numbers; for example, /dev/hda could be the name of the first IDE hard drive, and /dev/sdb could be the name of the second SCSI hard drive.

You can compare the Linux file system to a tree turned upside down, as shown in Figure 4-1, which shows three *subdirectories* (a directory within a directory) of root. The top of the upside-down tree is represented by a / (slash) and is called the *root directory,* or just root. A series of limbs, branches, and leaves extend below the root: Limbs are mount points, the branches that extend from the limbs are directories, and the leaves on those branches are your files.

Each *mount point* is a drive partition or remote file system (such as your CD-ROM drive) that is *mounted,* or made visible to, a directory of the limb above it. When a disk partition or remote file system is mounted on the directory branch, it turns that branch into another limb, allowing even more branches to be positioned and attached below the mount point.

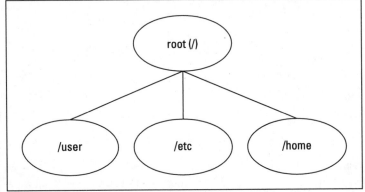

Figure 4-1:
The Linux file system is like an upside-down tree.

Linux needs at least a root partition in your directory structure (the upside-down tree) and a swap space partition. The root partition is used to store all your personal and system files and directories, and Linux uses *swap space,* the Hamburger Helper of the computer world, to extend your memory beyond the limit of your random access memory (RAM). If you have 64MB of RAM and 64MB of swap, for example, you can run programs that use up 128MB of memory.

The Workstation installation method we walk you through in Chapter 3 automatically sets up your root and swap partitions, as well as an additional boot partition that is used for storing the Red Hat Linux kernel and other files used for booting your computer.

Giving Linux the Boot

To *boot* a computer means simply to start it (and to *reboot* means to restart it). Follow these steps to boot your Red Hat Linux system for the first time:

1. **Make sure that your computer is turned off.**

2. **Turn on the power to the monitor if it's separate from the main system.**

3. Turn on the computer's main power switch.

After a short time, the Red Hat boot menu appears on your screen, as shown in Figure 4-2. If you have only Red Hat Linux installed on your computer, then you are given only one choice of operating systems to boot: `Linux`.

The default operating system is the one at the top of the list. If you have installed Red Hat Linux along with another operating system, you can change the one that boots by default.

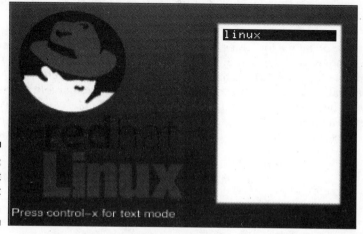

Figure 4-2:
The Red Hat
Linux boot
window.

You can exit from the Red Hat Linux graphical boot menu by pressing Ctrl+X. This places you at the — old style — LILO boot prompt. LILO's sole purpose in life (LILO stands for Linux loader, by the way) is to boot your Linux system and keep track of any other bootable systems on your machine. When the `LILO boot:` prompt appears, you can press the Tab key to see all the names for booting various operating systems or versions of operating systems.

4. Use the up or down arrow to highlight the word `Linux` **(if it's not high-lighted already) and press Enter.**

If you are running more than one operating system — for example, Red Hat Linux and Windows — you can select any of the listed operating systems to boot, but we assume here that you choose Linux.

After you press Enter, Red Hat Linux boots your system. During this process, a lot of information is displayed on your screen. Red Hat Linux gleans this information as it probes your computer in order to determine what hardware — disk drives, printers, and so on — it has.

If you don't press anything, the default operating system (Linux sets itself as default when you install it) starts automatically after a five-second delay.

Logging In

When you use Linux, you must log in as a particular user with a distinct login name. Why? Linux is a multiuser system, and as such, it uses different accounts to keep people from looking at other people's secret files, erasing necessary files from the system, and otherwise doing bad things.

The use of unique identities helps to keep the actions of one person from affecting the actions of another because many people may be using the same computer system at the same time (for instance, over a network). A benefit of this strategy is that Linux systems are essentially invulnerable to viruses, simply because each user's files and directories can't be used to corrupt the system as a whole. (Not that we're keeping score or anything, but Windows systems can be destroyed by viruses because they don't have this capability.)

As Red Hat Linux boots, you see all sorts of messages scrolling by on the screen. After the scrolling stops, the login screen shown in Figure 4-3 appears.

Figure 4-3:
The GNOME
login
screen.

During installation, if you chose not to have X start automatically when you boot your system, then you see the simple `login:` prompt.

If you make a mistake while typing the password or your login, the system asks you to retype it.

We strongly recommend that you do most of your experimentation with Linux as a nonprivileged user and log in as the root user only when necessary. By operating as root, you run the risk of corrupting your system, having to reinstall again, or losing data, because you can delete or change anything you want. When you are logged in as a regular user, you can accidentally erase your own files and data but you can't erase someone else's files or system files. Please look at Chapter 16 for information about how file permissions work and how you can modify them.

The Command-Line Interface (CLI) versus the Graphical User Interface (GUI)

Red Hat Linux installs the X Window System by default. You can perform most of the administrative tasks with the GUI-based tools (GUI stands for *graphical user interface*) that Red Hat provides. Most of the how-to instructions in this book use the X-based applications and utilities. We do that because they are generally easier to use and this is not a systems-administration–oriented book.

Occasionally, a utility or program doesn't run graphically, and other times using nongraphical methods and systems is just more interesting or convenient. Believe it or not, some geekier Linux users actually prefer to use a text-based, command-line interface, or what most call a *shell*. If you're not familiar with some basic administrative tasks with the shell we don't recommend using the command-line interface just to prove that you can. It's okay to be less of a geek. We'll still like you. On the other hand, it makes good sense to know some basics just in case a need arises for you to have to wing it with the text-based interface.

Text-based systems are generally run from a *shell,* which acts as a text-based interface between the Linux operating system and you. The bash shell, which Red Hat Linux uses by default, displays a prompt like [lidia@veracruz lidia]$. You enter commands at the shell prompt, and that's where the term *command-line interface* (or CLI) comes from.

You can start a shell from within the GNOME interface by starting a terminal session (also known as the GNOME terminal emulator). The GNOME system comes preconfigured with an icon on the GNOME Panel (the Panel is the bar at the bottom of your screen) that looks like a computer monitor. Clicking this icon starts a terminal session that you can use within GNOME, as shown in Figure 4-4. You can crack open more shell info in Chapter 15.

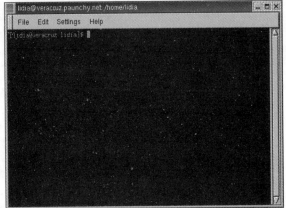

Figure 4-4:
A GNOME
terminal
session.

Creating User Accounts with Red Hat's User Manager

If you have cause to add new users (say if you have a home network), or you forgot to create a non-root user during installation, this section shows you how. Red Hat offers several systems administration tools for your convenience. The Red Hat User Manager is an excellent administration tool that can make your life easier.

The following instructions assume that you're using the GNOME window system, which is the Red Hat default. But the User Manager works the same under the KDE window system as with GNOME. KDE comes bundled with Red Hat Linux and can be selected during the installation process.

Use the User Manager to create a new account by following these steps:

1. **Open the User Manager by clicking on the GNOME Main Menu button and then choosing Programs⊏>System⊏>User Manager.**

   If you are not logged in as the root user, you are prompted to enter the root password.

2. **Click the GNOME Main Menu button and choose Programs⊏>System⊏>User Manager.**

   The Main Menu button looks like a footprint and is located on the toolbar in the lower-left corner of your desktop and works in a similar fashion to the Windows Start button.

   The User Manager help window appears, as shown in Figure 4-5.

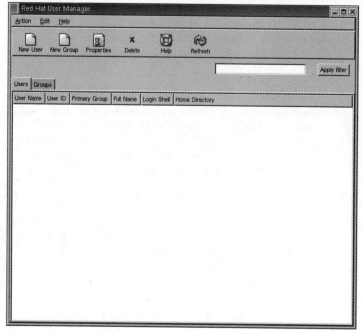

Figure 4-5:
The User
Manager
adminis-
tration tool.

3. **Click the New User button at the upper-left corner of the screen.**

   The Create New User window appears, as shown in Figure 4-6.

Figure 4-6:
The User
account
creation
form.

4. **Enter your user name, real-life name and the password twice (to confirm its correctness); accept the Login Shell default of bash. The User Manager will also create a home directory by default.**

   Most of these items are self-explanatory, but here are some additional explanations:

   • Your User Name (also known as a login name) is also the name that you will use to send and receive e-mail, so choose the name carefully. Make your login name short and use all lowercase letters. Names that seem cute or appropriate now may not be later. And avoid choosing a name that is too long, because you may have to type it several times a day. You may also have to give your e-mail address over the telephone, so a login name such as *phool* will result in missent messages, leaving you feeling very phoolish.

   • You can enter your full name if you want. That information is saved in the /etc/passwd file, which anyone with an account on your system can read. This information is generally useful to system administrators because it allows them to connect a person with each account. It's probably superfluous if you're configuring your personal system.

   • The new password should be different from the one you use for root.

     As you type the password, little asterisks, rather than the actual password, appear on-screen in case someone is looking over your shoulder as you type (Linux is showing its paranoid side here). The exception is in text mode — you won't get any feedback (asterisks or other characters).

   • Among your many choices for a default shell, /bin/bash is a good choice (bash is a popular shell that is the default for Red Hat Linux). For more on shells, check out Chapter 15.

5. **Click OK.**

   The account is created, and the Changing Password window appears.

   Red Hat Linux uses the Pluggable Authentication Module (PAM) that prevents you from entering trivial or otherwise dangerous passwords, but don't use that as assurance that your new password is a good one. A good password can't be found in any dictionary, because password crackers have programs that automatically try all dictionary words to crack your password. Avoid birthdays and anniversaries — or anything someone could associate with you. For ideas about good passwords, check out Chapter 3. Just don't forget it, or write it on a sticky note and put it on your computer monitor!

6. **Click the Quit button.**

   If everything is all right, the User Manager window has an entry for your new account.

7. **Click the Action⇨Exit buttons to leave the User Manager.**

You can use the User Manager to modify and delete existing user accounts. Click the user name and then the Properties or Delete button. If you select Properties, you see a screen similar to that of the new user account and can modify any of the fields. You are asked to confirm the deletion of an account.

Creating an Account without X

If X isn't working or if you want to work from a terminal emulator, you can still add the nonprivileged user account that we advise you to add earlier in the chapter. To do so, follow these steps:

1. **Type** useradd *name* **at the command prompt, where** *name* **is the login name for the new login account.**

2. **Type** passwd *name* **at the command prompt and press Enter.**

   This changes the password of the new account, which had a default password assigned to it by the useradd command in Step 1. What good is a password if you use the default one?

   See Chapter 3 for hints on creating a good password.

   As you type the password, little asterisks, instead of the actual password, appear on-screen in case someone is looking over your shoulder.

3. **Type in your password again.**

   Linux asks you to retype your new password to ensure that the password you typed is the one you thought you typed. If you don't retype the password exactly as you did the first time (which is easy to do because it doesn't appear on the screen), you have to repeat the process.

4. **Type in a password for the new login.**

   Linux updates the password for the new login.

Ending Your First Session

Logging off of the system and restarting the login process is simplicity itself. To do so, click the GNOME Main Menu button (which looks like a big foot in the lower-left corner) and choose Log out. The Really log out? window appears and you're asked to confirm that you want to log out. If you do — do you really? — then click the Yes button and you're outta there. Click No if you change your mind and want to play around with your new operating system for a little while longer.

You can also choose to reboot or halt your computer from this window by clicking either the Halt or Reboot button and then clicking Yes to confirm your decision. Depending on which you choose, your system proceeds to stop completely or reboot. You can also press the Ctrl+Alt+Backspace keys to shut down your current session. This method is less graceful but still effective, especially in case some renegade process freezes your X session.

Part II
Got Net?

In this part . . .

After you've created your own Red Hat Linux workstation, it's time to hit the great outdoors. This part shows three different ways to connect to the Internet: via the traditional and slow modem; or through a fast broadband DSL or cable modem; you can also connect your Red Hat computer to an existing Local Area Network (LAN) that itself is connected to the Internet.

Chapter 5 concentrates on telephone-based modems. Modems are very much like an old, reliable pick-up truck that may not be the fastest way of getting somewhere but will get you there. In fact, they provide the most simple, economical, and effective Internet connection available.

Chapter 6 introduces broadband Internet connections. Telephone, cable, and independent companies provide broadband service to many communities today. For not altogether unreasonable prices you can get high-speed, always-on service.

Many people have access to existing computer local networks (called LANs) at work, school, and home. Chapter 7 shows how to connect your computer to a LAN, and, if your LAN has an Internet connection, you can find out how to configure your workstation to use it.

Your computer becomes vulnerable after you connect to the Internet. This is especially true if you use a service, such as DSL, that is constantly connected. It's like the difference between living on a quiet versus a busy street. You're more vulnerable on the busy street. That's why we show how to configure a firewall in Chapter 8.

After you've connected to the Net and set up your firewall, you're ready to journey into the great uncharted territory of the World Wide Web. Chapter 9 shows how to surf the Net with Mozilla. Mozilla actually provides the core of Netscape. However, it's fully Open Source and the preferred Red Hat browser.

Okay, now that you're out in the wilds of computerdom, how will you communicate? Smoke signals? Yodeling? E-mail? That's the ticket, and you find out how to send and receive e-mail in Chapter 9 as well.

Chapter 5

Connecting to the Internet with a Dial-up Modem

In This Chapter

▶ Finding an Internet service provider (ISP)

▶ Configuring your modem

▶ Configuring your Internet connection with LinuxConf

▶ Setting up DNS

▶ Connecting to your ISP

Surfing the Internet is a lot of fun and a surprisingly useful activity. Come on, admit it: You know you want to tie up your phone line for hours in order to annoy your family or roommates, browse sites with ridiculous addresses such as www.theonion.com, and chat chummily with people you'd never dream of speaking to in person. The catch is that before you join the fray of the new online universe, you've gotta have access to the Internet.

This chapter describes how to use a modem to connect to an Internet service provider (or ISP), and create your bridge to the Internet. After you're hooked up to the Internet, you too can go to a party and drop the casual phrase, "I found this while surfing the Net this afternoon . . . on my Red Hat Linux system." If you've never been the life of the party in the past, this will certainly make you immediately more popular.

This chapter assumes you're connecting to the Internet using a standard dial-up modem. We describe how to configure your Red Hat Linux computer to use faster connection technologies, referred to as *broadband connections,* in Chapter 6, which describes how to use cable modems and DSL modems.

Many people have access to Internet connected networks at work and school. (Or maybe your 5-year-old has constructed an Internet connected home network.) Chapter 7 describes how to connect your Red Hat Linux computer to an existing private network and gain access to the Internet through its connection. You can then surf until the cows come home at light speeds compared to a dial-up modem.

Desperately Seeking an ISP

To get connected using a dial-up modem, you have to successfully hook up a modem to your computer and then find a good Internet service provider (ISP) to dial in to. Odds are that you have an internal modem that came installed with your computer. If you don't, you may want to consider upgrading. Check out *Upgrading & Fixing PCs For Dummies,* 5th Edition, by Andy Rathbone (Hungry Minds, Inc.).

The best way to find a good ISP is by word of mouth. Ask your friends and acquaintances who live nearby (if they live far away, their opinions won't mean much) which ISPs they use and whether they're satisfied with those ISPs. Getting personal recommendations is a good way to find out both the good and bad points of an ISP that you can't find from reading advertisements.

If you don't have any friends and your acquaintances won't speak to you, then try finding a local Linux User Group (LUG) to ask. You can look up LUGs at Red Hat's community Web page at www.redhat.com/apps/community.

Before you sign on with an ISP, make sure that the company supports Linux.

Table 5-1 shows a sample of national/worldwide ISPs that support Linux.

Table 5-1	ISPs That Support Linux	
ISP	*Toll-free Phone Number (U.S. Only)*	*Web Address*
AT&T WorldNet	800-967-5363	www.att.net
CompuServe	800-336-6823	www.compuserve.com
Earthlink	800-EARTHLINK	www.earthlink.net
Prism Access	888-930-1030	www.prism.net
SprintLink	800-473-7983	www.sprint.net
CompuglobalHypermega	555-867-5309	www.compuglobalhypermega.net

Be sure to ask your potential new ISP if it offers a dial-up PPP service — even if the company handles Linux. PPP (which stands for *point-to-point protocol*) is what Linux uses to connect to the Internet. If the person you talk to gives you the verbal equivalent of a blank stare, you may have troubles. If there appears to be some kind of a hitch, be warned. The ISP's tech staff probably isn't going to be able to walk you through procedures. You're on your own.

If you're buying a modem

Modems are an old technology but still the most common method for making personal or small business Internet connections. This may not be true for much longer as the number of users with broadband connections is rising fast, and most large businesses also use broadband services.

An *internal modem* plugs into a PCI or ISA slot on your computer's motherboard and receives its power from the computer. An *external modem* comes in its own case, requires its own power supply, and connects to the computer via a serial (RS232) connection. Both types of modems use your phone jack to connect to the Internet.

Internal modems are generally less expensive than external ones, but external modems have several advantages. You can easily turn them on and off, you can connect them to a computer without opening the computer case, and if your telephone line is struck by lightning, the charge passing through the modem won't damage your computer. On the other hand, internal modems are cheaper and require fewer external cables. Also, internal modems need only a telephone line cable, whereas external modems require a telephone line, a serial connection, and power supply cables.

A third type of serial line modem is a *PCMCIA card* (sometimes called a PC card). These cards are used most often with laptop computers. Most laptops come with internal modems already installed.

Avoid WinModems like the plague, because these modems are designed for Windows computers only. They're cheaper than regular modems because they're lazy (or smart depending on how you look at it) and depend on the Windows operating system to do much of their work for them. Linux drivers are only now beginning to appear for such modems.

Now is a good time to verify that your own telephone service is billed at a flat rate and not metered; you should make sure that the dial-up number you use isn't a toll call either. If you have metered service or end up making a long-distance toll call, you'll run up huge phone bills while spending hours chatting about lone gunmen and interdimensional space travelers.

After you choose your Internet service provider and arrange payment, the ISP provides you with certain pieces of information, including the following:

- ✔ Telephone access numbers
- ✔ A username (usually the one you want)
- ✔ A password (usually the one you supply)
- ✔ An e-mail address, which is typically your username added to the ISP's domain name
- ✔ A primary Domain Name Server (DNS) number, which is a large number separated by periods into four groups of digits

- A secondary Domain Name Server (DNS) number, which is another large number separated by periods into four groups of digits

- An SMTP (mail) server name

- An NNTP (news) server name

- A POP3 or IMAP4 server name, which is used to download e-mail from the ISP's server to your machine

Configuring Your Internet Connection

You need to configure your modem so that Red Hat Linux can use it to connect to your ISP. The Red Hat Dialup Configuration utility does a good job at detecting and then configuring your modem and a dial-up account to connect your computer to your ISP and thus to the Internet.

1. **Click the Main Menu button and choose Programs➪Internet➪Dialup Configuration.**

   The GNOME Main Menu Button is the icon that looks like a big foot in the bottom-left corner of your screen. If you are not logged in as root, you are prompted for the root password in the Input dialog box.

   Two windows open up simultaneously the first time you start the Dialup Configuration tool. The Internet Connections window, shown in Figure 5-1, displays the modems and PPP accounts that the tool knows about. The window has a blank screen if no Internet connections have been configured yet. The Create a New Internet Connection window, shown in Figure 5-2, is used to find the modems and create the PPP accounts.

2. **In the Create a New Internet Connection window, click Next.**

   The Select Modem window appears.

3. **Click Next again.**

   The Searching for Modems dialog box appears. The Dialup Configuration Tool scans your computer for modems. When it finds one, the Enter a Modem window, shown in Figure 5-3, appears (although the information displayed may differ). If Linux doesn't find a modem, or you click the Cancel button, it guesses that a modem is attached to your first serial port — /dev/ttyS0.

You can modify the modem settings, if you wish, in the Enter a Modem window. (Please see the following sections — "Locating your modem with Windows" and "Locating your modem with Linux" — for instructions on how to get information about your modem.)

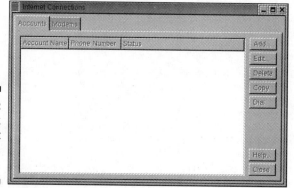

Figure 5-1:
The blank
Internet
Connections
window.

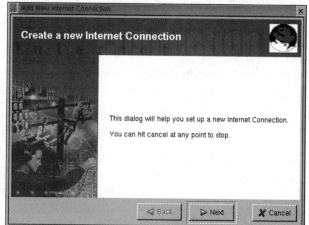

Figure 5-2:
The Create
a New
Internet
Connection
window.

4. Click Next yet again.

The Phone Number and Name window appears.

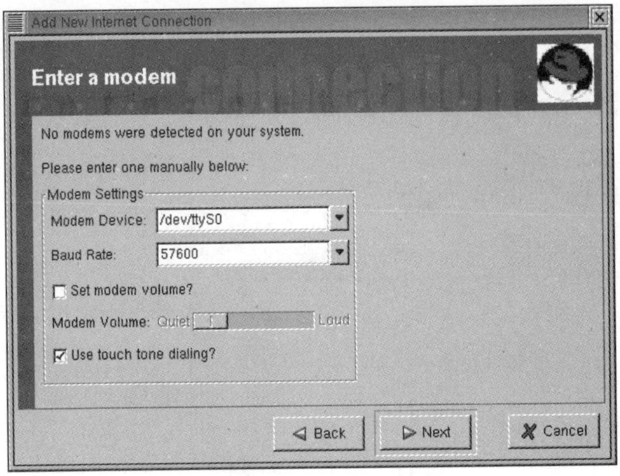

Add New Internet Connection

Enter a modem

No modems were detected on your system.

Please enter one manually below:

Modem Settings

Modem Device: /dev/ttyS0

Baud Rate: 57600

☐ Set modem volume?

Modem Volume: Quiet ▢▭▭▭▭ Loud

☑ Use touch tone dialing?

◁ Back | ▷ Next | ✗ Cancel

Figure 5-3:
The Enter a
Modem
window.

5. **Enter a name for your new connection in the Account Name text box and your ISP's phone number in the Phone Number text box.**

   You can choose any name that you want for the account name. You should also enter your ISP's prefix and area or country code if necessary in the appropriate text boxes.

6. **Click Next when you're finished filling in the info.**

   The User Name and Password window appears, as shown in Figure 5-4.

7. **Enter your PPP account name in the User Name text box and your password in the Password text box and then click Next.**

   Your PPP account name and password are often different than your login account and password. You need to be authenticated by your ISP when you dial up and attempt to establish a PPP connection. You have to supply the information for your PPP account when you do this, and it may be different than your user account. Talk to your ISP for more information about what information to supply here.

   The Other Options window appears, as shown in Figure 5-5.

8. **Select the Normal ISP option and then click Next if your ISP is not AT&T Global Network Services (if you use AT&T, click the selection for it and the Next button).**

   Your account information is stored, and the Create the Account window appears displaying your information, similar to Figure 5-6.

9. **Click Finish.**

   The Internet Connections window, which is grayed out (as in Figure 5-1) if there are no accounts to show, comes to life and displays your new account, as shown in Figure 5-7. If you click the Modems tab, you see the information about your modem, as shown in Figure 5-8.

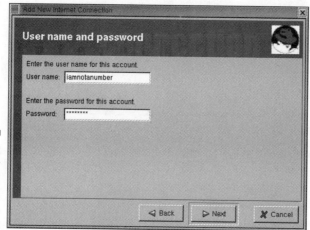

Figure 5-4:
The User
Name and
Password
window.

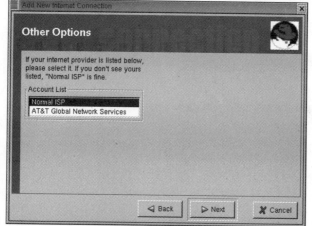

Figure 5-5:
The Other
Options
window.

Figure 5-6:
The Create
the Account
window.

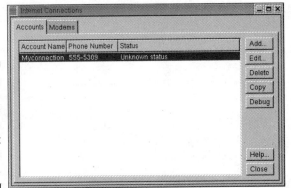

Figure 5-7:
The
Accounts
tab of the
Internet
Connections
window.

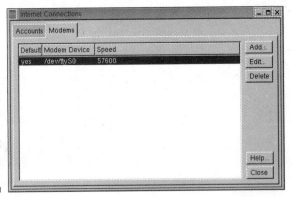

Figure 5-8:
The
Modems
tab of the
Internet
Connections
window.

Locating your modem with Linux

Linux uses device files to communicate with peripherals. Device files occupy the `/dev` directory and are equivalent to Windows drivers — you need them so that your hardware works.

Your modem can connect to one of four serial ports available on your PC. A *serial port* is the mechanism that your computer uses to communicate with a device, such as a modem. An external modem is generally connected to port `/dev/ttyS0` or `/dev/ttyS1`, although configuring it as `/dev/ttyS2` or `/dev/ttyS3` is possible. If you have an internal modem, then it can be any one of the `tty` devices.

During the boot process, Red Hat Linux provides a utility called `kudzu` that automatically tries to locate new devices when you boot your system. `kudzu` is good at detecting equipment like modems (both internal and external). When `kudzu` detects a new device, it prompts you to configure the device, and you should let it do so. `kudzu`'s one hard-workin' little guy. Make note of what device it is attached to.

If `kudzu` is unable to find your modem, then finding it by process of elimination is a crude but effective method. The following two numbered lists describe how to find your modem. The first method is for an external modem and involves sending a string of characters to the modem and looking for the light-emitting diodes (LEDs) to light up. The second method is for internal modems, which don't have LEDs and use the hideous screeching sound of your modem to track it down.

1. **If you have an external modem, then you can find it by running the following command from a command prompt:**

   ```
   echo "anything" > /dev/ttyS0
   ```

   Honestly, it doesn't matter what you put between the quote marks in the preceding commands. It just has to be some text — *any* text.

   If your modem is connected to the target serial port, you see the send/receive LEDs (sometimes marked as RX/TX) light up in a short burst.

2. **If your modem isn't found, try sending the string to** `/dev/ttyS1`, `/dev/ttyS2` **and finally** `/dev/ttyS3` **by altering the number at the end of the command in Step 1 to match the port you're targeting.**

Life is a bit harder if you have an internal modem because you don't have a visual response. You can, however, listen to the modem's speaker to find out what's going on. To do so, follow these steps:

1. **If you have an internal modem, enter the following command at a command prompt:**

   ```
   echo "atdt5555309" > /dev/ttyS0
   ```

If you hear the modem pick up and dial, you've won the game of hide-and-go-seek and know what device the modem is connected to. You can then skip to Step 4.

2. **If you don't hear anything, then make sure that you have the speaker turned on by entering the following command and then retry Step 1:**

```
echo "atv" > /dev/ttyS0
```

If you hear the modem pick up and dial, you've found what device it is connected to and can skip to Step 4.

3. **If you still can't hear anything, then try using the other serial ports by substituting** ttyS1, ttyS2, **and finally** ttyS3 **in the command in Step 2 and trying it again until you find one that works.**

4. **After your modem is found, send the following command to the modem to kill the connection:**

```
echo "atz" > /dev/ttyS0
```

Getting desperate with dip

If your modem still isn't found after trying one of the two methods in the last section, you can use the dip dial-up program. You can use dip interactively; that is, dip allows you to enter a command and immediately see the result — a great advantage when experimenting or troubleshooting modems.

To use dip to find your modem, follow these steps:

1. **Type dip -t at the command prompt and press Enter.**

   The dip> prompt appears (surprise!).

2. **Enter the following commands at the dip> prompt and press Enter after each:**

```
DIP>port ttyS0
DIP>dial 555-5309
```

If the modem picks up and dials, you've won! You can go on to Step 3. If the modem doesn't pick up, then dip returns you to the command prompt, and you should skip to Step 4.

3. **If your modem is found, press the Enter key to immediately kill the connection.**

   If the modem picks up and dials, you're done! You can skip Step 4. If the modem doesn't pick up, then dip returns you to the command prompt, and you should go to Step 4.

4. **Quit** `dip` **and then restart the program so that you can try ports** `ttyS1`, `ttyS2`, **and** `ttyS3`.

   Just modify the first command in Step 1 to match the serial port you're targeting.

Locating your modem with Windows

If you're running a Windows 9x/ME or a Windows NT/2000 system, then you can see which port your modem is connected to by following these steps:

1. **E-mail Bill Gates and ask him for your configuration.**

   If he's in court all week, see Step 2.

2. **Choose Start➪Settings➪Control Panel.**

   The Control Panel window appears.

3. **Double-click the Modem icon.**

   The Modems Properties dialog box appears.

4. **Select the Diagnostics tab.**

   You see your modem listed with a COM line number beside it. This is the Windows designation for your modem's serial communications line. Thus, if the number 1 appears, that means Windows knows it as COM1; if it's a 2, then it's on COM2; and so on. These number designations translate directly to the matching number of `ttyS0`, `ttyS1`, `ttyS2`, and `ttyS3` in Red Hat Linux.

Setting Up DNS

Finding your way around the Internet would be nearly impossible if not for the Domain Name Service (DNS) system. This system converts the dot.com type of Internet name format into a numeric Internet Protocol (IP) address. An example of an IP address is 198.59.115.2. All the information that flows across the Internet (Web browsing, e-mail, and so on) is carried by IP packets that have source and destination IP addresses. So when you go to browse `www.redhat.com`, for example, that name is converted into a numeric IP address by DNS.

Unless you want to do all your browsing and e-mail by remembering numeric IP addresses, you must set-up your own DNS. Your ISP provides you with one or two DNS server addresses, such as 198.59.115.2. You need to tell Linux about the DNS servers before you can browse the Internet. To do so, follow these steps:

1. **Log in to Linux as root.**

   See Chapter 4 for information about logging onto a Linux computer.

2. **Start the network system administrative tool by clicking the Main Menu button and choosing Programs⇨System⇨Network Configuration.**

   The Red Hat Network Configuration window appears, as shown in Figure 5-9.

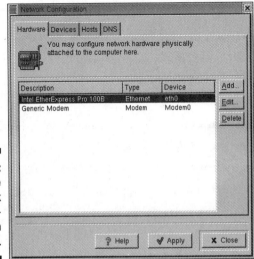

Figure 5-9:
The
Network
Configu-
ration
window.

3. **Click the DNS tab.**

   The DNS configuration window appears.

4. **Type the domain name of your ISP in the Primary DNS text box and press Enter.**

5. **Type the name server address in the IP of Secondary DNS text box.**

6. **(Optional) If you have a secondary name server, type it into the Tertiary DNS text box.**

   Figure 5-10 shows a completed DNS tab.

7. **Click the Apply button.**

8. **Click the Quit button.**

9. **Click the Activate the Changes button.**

   LinuxConf exits, and your settings are saved for future use.

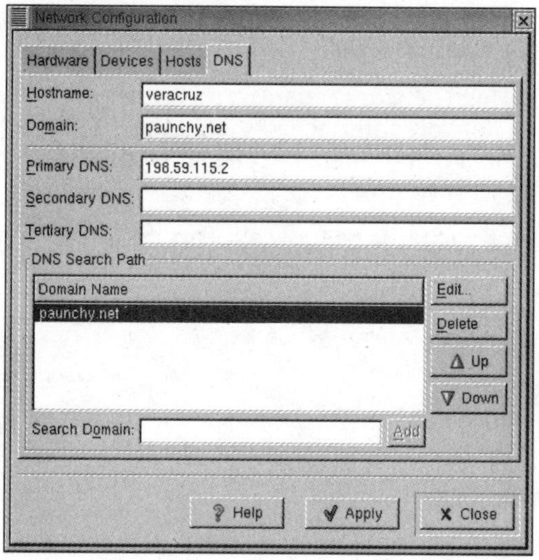

Figure 5-10:
The DNS
tab.

Firing Up Your Internet Connection

Red Hat Linux provides the Red Hat PPP dialer utility to help you establish a PPP connection. You establish this connection by using the PPP configuration that you set up with the Dialup Configuration Tool (which we described earlier in the "Configuring Your Internet Connection" section).

To connect to the Internet with the Red Hat PPP dialer, follow these steps:

1. **Log in to Linux as any user.**

2. **Click the Main Menu button and choose Programs➪Internet➪RH PPP Dialer.**

   The Choose window appears displaying all the network interfaces that you have, as shown in Figure 5-11.

Figure 5-11:
Choosing
your
connection
in the
Choose
window.

3. **Click the name of your connection interface, for instance Myconnection, and then click OK.**

If you have an Ethernet (network) adapter, then it shows up as `eth0`. Your internal Linux network interface — called the loopback (or `lo`) — also shows up. You can ignore them because they don't have anything to do with connecting with your modem.

The Change Connection Status window appears, as shown in Figure 5-12.

Figure 5-12:
Starting
your new
connection.

4. **Click Yes and the PPP dialer dials your modem and logs in to your ISP's PPP account.**

After your connection is established, the PPP connection status window (shown in Figure 5-13) graphically displays the amount of your modem's capacity that you're using.

Figure 5-13:
Your PPP
connection
status
window.

5. **When you're finished using the Internet, click the button (with a dot) in the PPP connection status window (refer to Figure 5-13).**

The Change Connection Status? dialog box reappears.

6. **To end your connection, click the Yes button.**

Your connection comes to an end. Go to Chapter 8 and construct a firewall before you use this connection again.

Linux is a multiuser and multitasking operating system, meaning that more than one task can be run at once, and that, unlike with Windows, more than one person can be logged in at once. This offers an attractive launching point for black hats. If someone can gain access to your Linux computer while it's on the Internet, then that person can use your machine to launch attacks against other machines, and you become the proxy that helps the bad guys hide their identities.

Chapter 6

Broadband Rocks!

· ·

In This Chapter

▶ Introducing DSL and Internet cable

▶ Finding an Internet cable provider

▶ Finding a DSL provider

▶ Connecting your cable modem

▶ Connecting your DSL modem

▶ Setting up your DSL router

▶ Setting up DNS

· ·

*Y*ou're probably familiar with the ubiquitous dial-up Internet connection: You log on to the Internet, hear that fax-like connection sound, a little static, and then presto-whammo — you're online. If you're lucky, the entire dial-up process takes about five minutes, but it can take longer; and then there's the fact that Web pages take just a *little* while to build on screen with a dial-up modem — especially when you compare dial-ups with high-speed connections (also called *broadband* connections).

The *broad* in broadband means that wires and cables that connect a modem to the Internet have a wide *bandwidth;* they can handle more data at faster speeds and with greater reliability. Plain old telephone service (POTS) was created for transferring analog voice data. Needless to say, POTS just won't do as well as broadband media when it comes to the Internet.

The two most popular broadband connections you can use to access the Internet are cable modems (which use your existing cable television lines to transfer data) and DSL (which use new, fancy-schmancy digital phone lines). Broadband connections work from roughly 500 thousand bits per second (Kbps) up to several million (Mbps). That is enough to transfer graphic rich Web pages in a few seconds; it is also enough to listen to several audio streams or a low-resolution video stream.

If you're ready to make the switch to a DSL or cable Internet connection, believe us when we tell you that you'll never go back to a dial-up modem. This chapter describes how to obtain and configure a broadband connection. We start out by describing how the systems work in general. We then describe how to use several different manufacturers systems.

We recommend avoiding ISDN, satellite, and mental telepathy Internet connections. ISDN is old technology that is rapidly being replaced by DSL. ISDN is difficult to configure and is not much faster than a modem connection. Satellite is just now being introduced and suffers from problems such as transmission delays that wreak havoc with your communications. Many say that mental telepathy works great but we're sure they don't mean for digital connection. Perhaps satellite systems will improve quickly, but until that happens, we recommend using a plain-old modem or, if you can, DSL or cable modem connections.

Introducing DSL and Cable Connections: The Proof Is in the Wiring

Although today's telephone network system is modern in many ways, it hasn't fundamentally changed since the early 20th Century. The network consists of pairs of copper wire that connect homes and businesses with a telephone company's central offices (CO). The phone company uses switches between its central offices to connect you to your destination when you make a call. The switches are designed to limit the range of frequencies — called bandwidth — that a phone call can use. The bandwidth is roughly 3,000 cycles per second (Hz), which is enough to recognize a voice, but not a whole lot more. Those limits prevent today's analog modems from pushing more than approximately 56,000 bits per second, or 56Kbs, through the telephone lines. (That 56Kbs speed varies, by the way, depending on the amount of Internet traffic your modem's competing with.)

What does all this mean to you? Improve your modem and the wiring, and you'll end up with faster Internet access. Two of the most commonly-used broadband alternatives are

✔ **Cable Television (CATV):** Although CATV companies do not provide service to as many residences and businesses that the telephone companies do, their fiber/coaxial cable networks can carry much more bandwidth than telephone wires can. CATV networks do not have the 3 to 4 mile limits that DSL has. Typically, you can get Internet cable through your CATV company if 1) they offer it and 2) they serve your neighborhood.

✔ **Digital Subscriber Lines (DSL):** Designed to skip the restrictions of the traditional telephone system by making an end-run around the voice switches, DSL rewires your existing telephone setup. Your local telephone company can connect you to new equipment that provides over 10 times the speed that a dial-up modem can.

The main limitation of DSL is that traditional copper wire can only carry a high-speed connection for a few miles. Connections between you and a CO are limited to 15,000 to 18,000 feet (roughly 3 to 4 miles). Your telephone company will tell you if they can provide you with service.

The Cable Modem Option

Cable modems provide fast and reliable Internet connections that are always turned on. Internet cable is simple to obtain and use if your cable TV company provides it. There are, of course, some down sides to consider:

✔ Unfortunately, not all cable companies have caught up with 21st-Century technology yet. Many companies may provide you with TV but not Internet service.

✔ Many people do not live in an area served by cable TV. Internet cable is also not a good medium to provide services such as Web pages out to the Internet.

✔ Most cable companies require that you connect to their ISP. Many people like to use a different ISP because it provides better service. Using your own ISP also makes it easier to set up your computer (or network) to provide services going out to the Internet. Cable companies can't prevent you from using a different local ISP, but they won't charge you less — so you end up paying for two services, one of which you're not using.

✔ Few cable companies support Linux. You're on your own if you need to troubleshoot problems, even problems that have nothing to do with Linux but which affect your machine. Don't worry, we're there for you.

DSL may give you an alternative if any of these problems are familiar to you. The "The DSL Option" section, later in this chapter, shows you how DSL works and how to use it.

If you decide that cable access is the right choice for your Internet access needs, here's an overview of the process for connecting your Red Hat Linux computer to the Internet via a cable modem:

1. **Do some research and subscribe.**

   Locate an Internet cable provider (ICP). Your ICP is usually your existing cable TV company and subscribe to the ICP service.

2. **Make a hardware commitment.**

   Purchase an Internet cable modem through your ICP or a third party distributor.

3. **Get registered.**

   Register the cable modem with your ICP.

4. **Set up the cable modem.**

   Cable modems have two connectors: a RG78 coaxial port and an RG45 connector. (The coaxial connector is the same type as used for cable TV. The RG45 looks like a large telephone cable connector.)

   • Connect a coaxial cable from the cable modem's coaxial port to your ICP just like you would a TV set.

   • Connect a network cable from the RG45 modem port to your Red Hat Linux computer. Normal network cables (referred to as category 5 cables) will not work if connected directly from the modem to your computer. You need to use a "cross-over" cable if you want to directly connect a computer to a cable modem. You can use normal category 5 cables if you connect the cable modem and your computer to an Ethernet hub or switch.

5. **Set up your Internet protocols.**

   Configure your computer to use DHCP on the network interface that connects to the modem. Restart your computer's network interface and you should be good to go.

The following sections take you through the process of finding a cable provider and setting up your access.

Finding an Internet cable provider

Finding an Internet Cable Provider (ICP) is as simple as calling your cable television company. Not all cable TV systems carry Internet traffic, but there are many who do. The ones that don't probably will in the future, and if they don't, these businesses may find staying in business to be difficult.

Locating a cable television company that provides broadband Internet connections is unfortunately quite easy. It's unfortunate because there is very little competition within the cable industry. Federal law effectively restricts competition within municipalities and creates the environment for monopoly-like companies. The end result, of course, is that prices remain higher than necessary. Oh well, at least many cable companies are offering Internet connections.

Your ICP will be your default Internet Service Provider (ISP). Most cable companies give you one or more e-mail addresses. However, cable companies don't in general provide login accounts like regular ISPs do. Login accounts are used for launching applications and storing information. They aren't essential, but they are useful. However, there's nothing to stop you from maintaining a regular ISP and using their login account. You'll have a high speed Internet connection that you can use to login to any account that you have.

We're not going to run you through the process of signing up for cable Internet service; we think the process is simple enough. A good portion of the sign-up process involves sitting on hold and listening to muzak. One suggestion, though — have pertinent information about your system, and be sure that the cable company knows you're using Red Hat Linux 7.3.

Dealing with the hardware

One of the great things about Internet cable is that you can buy the cable modems from your local electronics store or an Internet distributor. (DSL equipment is less readily available. At the time of this writing, we have not seen DSL modems for sale through retail stores; you have to purchase your DSL modem through your DSL service provider or from an Internet reseller.) Cable modems are generally priced the same whether you purchase through your provider, the Internet, or a brick and mortar store. But the convenience of running to a local store is great, especially if your cable modem breaks on a Saturday night and you just have to download the latest game patch.

Before you purchase a cable modem, make sure that you do the following:

- ✔ Ask your provider whether you have to buy your modem through them. If not, then you can shop around for the best price.

- ✔ Make sure the modem you buy is compatible with your service provider. The cable industry is converging on using the Data Over Cable Service Interface Specification (DOCSIS) as its Internet hookup standard. DOCSIS modems are quite easy to configure, so keep your fingers crossed that your service provider uses it.

- ✔ If your provider doesn't use DOCIS, then you likely will have to purchase your modem through your provider.

The instructions that we provide later in this chapter are designed for DOCSIS modems.

Setting up your cable modem is usually a straightforward process. Modern DOSCIS cable modems act as *network bridges*. A network bridge simply rebroadcasts network packets in both directions — incoming and outgoing. One side of the bridge connects to the cable TV company. The other side connects to your computer through your Ethernet NIC through a Cat 5 cross-over cable; you can also connect through a network switch or hub (LAN). If your modem is the bridge type, — we believe that the cable industry in the United States mostly uses that system — then it does not require any configuration.

Setting up Internet protocols

You do not have to configure your cable modem for it to work. What you *do* need to do, however, is tell your Red Hat Linux computer how to connect to the modem. This requires configuring the Ethernet adapter that connects to your cable modem to use the Dynamic Host Configuration Protocol (DHCP). Your cable modem sets the IP address of your Ethernet NIC by using DHCP. The following instructions show how to do that:

1. **Log in to your Red Hat Linux computer.**

2. **Click on the Gnome start button.**

   The button is in the lower, left hand of your screen and looks like a little footprint.

3. **Choose Programs⇨System⇨Network configuration buttons.**

   The Input screen, shown in Figure 6-1, pops up if you are not logged in as the root user.

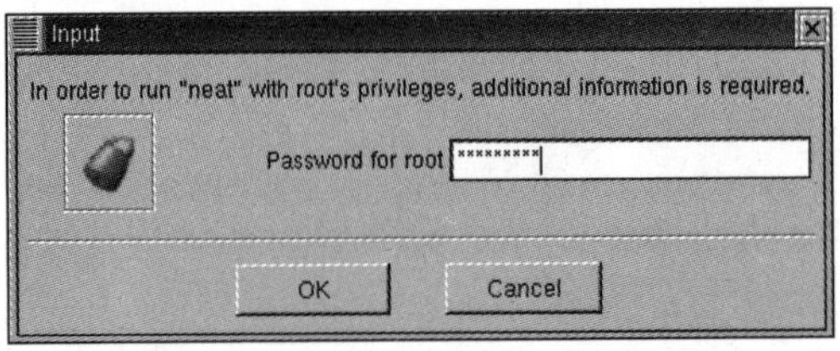

Figure 6-1:
Enter your
root
password.

4. **Enter the root password and click OK.**

5. **Click on the Devices tab and you'll see the device — eth0 — that the Ethernet device is configured as.**

   The Red Hat Network configuration screen appears (as shown in Figure 6-2). This example shows that our Ethernet adapter is an Intel EtherExpress device. You likely will see a different manufacturer's device.

   You may see a different number like eth1 if you have multiple network devices configured. For instance, you may have a wireless network adapter. Figure 6-3 shows an example display.

6. Click on the eth0 device and then on the Edit button.

The window shown in Figure 6-4 opens up. Click on the Activate Device When Computer Starts check box so that your network connection will automatically start up when you turn on your computer.

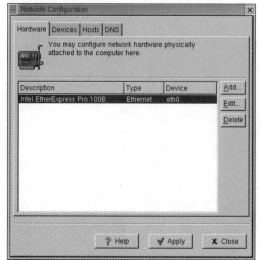

Figure 6-2:
The Network Configuration Hardware window.

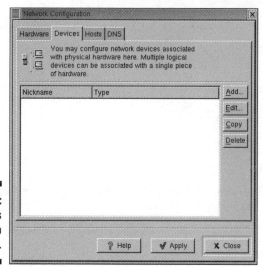

Figure 6-3:
The Devices screen check.

7. **Click on the Protocols tab and then on the Edit button as shown in Figure 6-5.**

   The TCP/IP Settings window allows you to set the Ethernet interface to use DHCP.

8. **Click on the Automatically Obtain IP Address Settings with: button as shown in Figure 6-6 (make sure that the dhcp option is selected).**

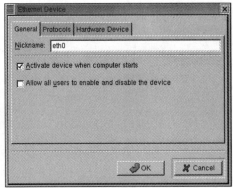

Figure 6-4: The Ethernet Device General window.

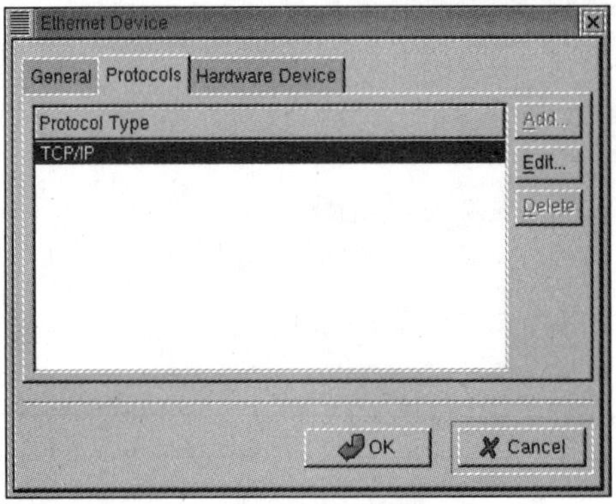

Figure 6-5: The Ethernet Device Protocol window.

9. **Next, click the Hostname tab to set the name of your Red Hat Linux workstation, as shown in Figure 6-7.**

10. **Click on OK until you arrive at the main Network Configuration window.**

    The system asks whether you want to save the information before exiting the configuration system.

11. **Select Yes.**

    You have saved the configuration necessary to use your cable modem. However, the settings won't activate until you reboot your computer or restart your computer's network interfaces.

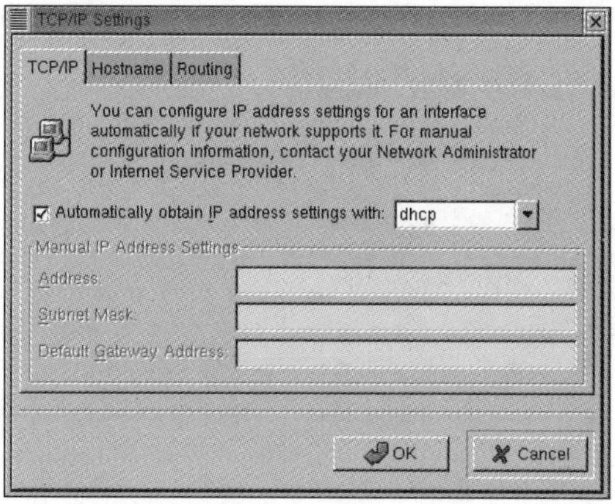

Figure 6-6:
The TCP/IP
Settings
window.

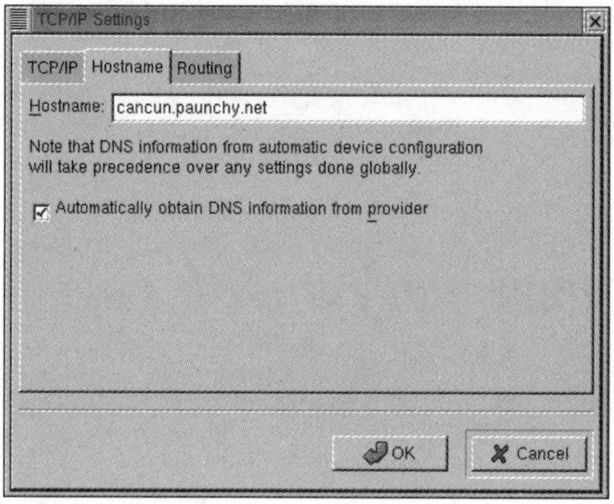

Figure 6-7:
Enter a host
name for
your
computer.

You can restart your network as follows:

1. **Click on the Gnome start button.**

2. **Choose Programs⇨System⇨Service Configuration buttons.**

   Scroll down the options until you see "network."

   Figure 6-7 shows that we have given a Hostname to our machine. We have also selected to use the Domain Name Service (DNS) from the ICP.

3. **Click on the Network tab.**

4. **Click on the Restart button at the upper right of the window.**

   Your network restarts and a window pops up, confirming the process.

Technical stuff

Modern cable modems do more than just transmit network packets of course. They transmit data packets by modulating and demodulating electrical signals over the cable TV wires — thus, the name MODEM (MOdulate/DEModulate). Today's cable modems use the industry standard Data Over Cable Service Interface Specification (DOCSIS) protocol to deliver the electrical signals across the cable network. The electrical signal carries the actual bits and bytes that comprise the network packets. A good analogy is an AM/FM radio system. The DOCSIS-based electrical signals carry data packets just like radio waves transmit speech or music.

---

5. **Check that you're connected to the Internet.**

   When you're satisfied, turn off your network connection by clicking on the Stop button.

Go to Chapter 8 to find out about building a firewall. After the firewall is working, you can restart your Internet connection and be reasonably safe from hackers.

Registering your modem with your ICP

You do have to register your modem with your ICP. During the registration process, your computer is assigned a network address to connect to the ICP. Network addresses are called Internet Protocol (IP) addresses.

You register your modem by giving your ICP the modem's machine address (MAC). The ICP generates an IP address by using the MAC address as its reference. You don't need to do anything to your cable modem. The registration process is all done by your ICP, and your modem automatically is assigned an IP address.

You're ready to use your Internet cable modem to connect to the Internet. Woo hoo! Blazing speed is yours now!

The DSL Option

The world is wired. Wired for telephones, that is. DSL takes advantage of this old but common technology to provide high-speed Internet connection to the consumers of the world. DSL uses special equipment to pump much more data through the POTS lines than the traditional analog modem do.

The telephone system is referred to as Plain Old Telephone System (POTS) in the Telecommunication industry.

DSL provides high-speed Internet connections by electronically converting your computer's digital information into a form that can be transmitted from your home or business to the telephone company. When your data finds its way to the telephone company, it's converted into another form and sent to your ISP.

DSL uses frequencies in the millions of cycles per second — the Megahertz (MHz) range — compared to traditional analog modems that work with signals in the thousands of cycles per second (KHz). You get much higher connection speeds when you use higher frequencies. The problem is, however, that the telephone system wasn't designed to work with higher frequencies.

Fortunately, the brainiacs of the world have figured out how to get high-speed DSL connections out of old, slow POTS wiring. They have designed new digital signal processing chips to overcome the POTS archaic architecture. The end result is that if you live close enough — roughly 3 to 4 miles — to your DSL provider's equipment, then you can use DSL to get connected to the Net.

Facing DSL-configuration woes head on

This section reviews the basic DSL modem configuration issues. We take the time to give you an overview because it's easy to get confused if you just concentrate on the details. Please check out the following list and get familiar with it. Getting your DSL modem working will be easier after you do so.

Today, most consumer DSL providers use the type of connection called asymmetrical DSL (ADSL). The following list describes the process for getting an ADSL connection working. (Please note that we use the generic acronym DSL interchangeably with ADSL. Most consumer DSL connections are really ADSL and that is the type of connection that we describe in this chapter.)

1. **Find a DSL provider.**

   You need to find out if you live or work close enough to the DSL provider's equipment to get a connection. DSL providers will check your address and tell you whether they can take your subscription.

2. **Connect your DSL modem to your telephone jack and your computer.**

   Your DSL modem acts as the intermediary between you and your DSL service provider. You must connect one side to the phone jack and the other to your computer's Ethernet NIC.

3. **Configure your Red Hat Linux to communicate with the DSL modem.**

   Your Linux computer connects to the DSL modem via an Ethernet NIC. You must configure your Ethernet NIC to work with the modem.

4. Set up the DSL modem user and administrative passwords.

DSL modems provide a reasonable level of security. You should take advantage of their security by assigning your own passwords to the modem. That will prevent hackers from breaking into your modem and causing you problems.

5. Set up the ISP/DSL connection account name and password.

You must authenticate your DSL modem to your ISP. DSL connections get logged on to your ISP just like traditional analog modems do. You configure your DSL modem with your ISP username and password.

6. Configure the DSL modem's internal (private) network interface.

Your DSL modem must be able to communicate with your Linux computer over an Ethernet connection. You must configure the DSL modem so that it uses the same network parameters as your computer.

7. Configure the modem's network address translation (NAT) settings.

The Internet was designed to send — route — information as quickly as possible to its destination. Internet Protocol (IP) addresses are used to designate where the information is coming from and where it's going. IP addresses can be routable or non-routable. Non-routable addresses can be reused — you can use the same non-routable addresses as your neighbor does without either of you interfering with each other.

NAT is used to convert non-routable IP addresses into routable ones. This is very useful when connecting your private network to the Internet by translating your internal IP addresses into one of your ISP's routable IP addresses. You need to configure your DSL modem to convert your computer's private — for instance 192.168.1.1 — and non-routable address into an address assigned to your DSL connection by your ISP.

8. Save the settings to non-volatile memory and reboot.

You need to save your DSL modem's settings after you've got them working. You don't want to enter the configuration every time you turn on the modem.

Finding a DSL provider

You must obtain both DSL and ISP services to make your broadband connection. Some companies, notably Regional Bells, can provide both services. However, in our case, we preferred our ISP to the ISP that was aligned with the DSL provider. We were fortunate enough to retain our existing ISP when we purchased our DSL service.

The DSL provider market is currently very fluid. Analyze the DSL service providers in your area carefully before choosing one, and remember that longevity is as important as price. For better or worse, the Regional Bells are more likely to provide long-term service than many of their competitors.

One advantage of DSL service is that you often don't have to sign a service contract, so you can reasonably switch providers if you're unsatisfied with the service.

You must select an ISP after you choose a DSL provider. Selecting an ISP is as much about personal preference as it is about price.

Connecting a Cisco 675 or 678 DSL modem

Writing explicit configuration examples is always problematic. The DSL world is still young and we're not convinced that any standards have emerged. Chances are that our instructions won't match your equipment.

But we're at least using fairly common equipment. The Baby Bells, such as Qwest, are the leaders in providing DSL circuits, so a significant percentage of DSL users use this equipment. Our Cisco 675 or 678 DSL modem/router is Qwest's recommended equipment.

Even if you're using different equipment, our instructions should still be useful in outlining the general process of configuring a DSL connection.

Connecting your Cisco modem to your Linux computer

You need to configure your Cisco modem in order to get your Internet connection working. Cisco and other manufacturer's DSL modems can be configured four different ways:

✔ By using Cisco's proprietary, Windows-based application. This system works well, but you need to run it on a Windows computer.

✔ By using Cisco's Web based (HTML) configuration system. This system also works well and is independent of any operating system because it works with any Web browser, such as Mozilla. However, you need to have the DSL modem successfully communicating on your network connection. After you have the DSL modem's network connection working, then simply enter the IP address of the DSL modem into your browser and you can configure the modem.

  ✔ By using Telnet and running Cisco's configuration commands. Cisco provides a command-line interface to enter configuration commands on. Unfortunately, you need to communicate with the DSL modem over its network connection to use Telnet.

  ✔ By connecting to the modem with a serial cable and running Cisco's configuration commands. This connection method uses the Cisco's command-line interface just like Telnet. However, no network is used and thus, no prior configuration must take place before using this method.

The many faces of DSL

Of the numerous types of consumer DSL service, the most common is Asymmetrical DSL (ADSL). The other types are more suited for business use. Most locales will only have access to two or three of these services. The following list describes the DSL variations.

✔ **ADSL (Asymmetrical DSL):** ADSL uses a single twisted-pair POTS line. ADSL's upstream and downstream speeds are different. Individual consumers use the Internet to browse the Web more than any other function. Browsing inherently involves downloading data far more often than uploading information. Therefore, the DSL provider can minimize its infrastructure and costs by taking advantage of the customers' usage patterns and provide them with lower-cost, but effectively high-speed, service.

The maximum ADSL speed is 8 Mbps, but it's usually limited to less due to the POTS infrastructure limitations.

✔ **G.Lite:** Also known as Universal DSL and splitterless ADSL, G.Lite is a low-speed version of ADSL that doesn't require filtering out the POTS signal. It provides up to 1.5 Mbps downstream and 512 Kbps upstream.

G.Lite is DMT incompatible, so it requires a modem different than the ADSL modems in use today.

✔ **HDSL (High bit-rate DSL):** HDSL is a symmetrical protocol with both upstream and downstream speeds being equal. You can use HDSL as a substitute for T1 connections because it provides the same data rates of 1.544 Mbps. (HDSL also provides the same rate of up to 2.048 Mbps as E1 connections do in Europe.) This technology uses two loops (4 wires) and works up to roughly 6,000 feet; it requires repeaters to go up to a maximum of 12,000 feet.

✔ **HDSL2 (High Bit-rate DSL 2):** HDSL2 provides the same specifications as HDSL but works over a single twisted-pair connection.

✔ **IDSL (ISDN Digital Subscriber Loop):** IDSL is the successor to the current ISDN technology. It uses the same line encoding (2B1Q) as ISDN and SDSL. Unlike ISDN, IDSL requires only a single line. IDSL is mostly used to provide DSL service in areas where the more popular forms, such as ADSL and SDSL, aren't available. IDSL is capable of providing upstream and downstream rates of 144 Kbps.

✔ **SDSL (Single-line DSL):** SDSL is commonly called *Symmetric DSL* because SDSL upstream and downstream speeds are the same. SDSL is a two-wire version of HDSL. Businesses use SDSL because they need to upload information for customers. SDSL uses only a single pair of copper wires. (Early DSL required two pairs.) SDSL supports T1/E1 up to 11,000 feet (3667 meters).

✔ **VDSL (Very high bit rate DSL):** VDSL provides up to 50 Mbps over distances up to 1500 meters on short loops, such as from fiber to the curb. In most cases, VDSL lines are served from neighborhood cabinets that link to a CO via optical fiber. VDSL is particularly useful for campus environments —

universities and business parks, for example. VDSL is currently being introduced in market trials to deliver video services over existing phone lines. You can also configure VDSL in symmetric mode.

✔ **xDSL:** xDSL is a generic term for all of the DSL flavors.

DSL types come in a rich variety. Most consumers will end up using ADSL because it offers inexpensive Internet connections at reasonably high speeds. ADSL will serve an individual computer user's Internet needs very well; it will even provide a small business with adequate service.

The first three methods require that you can communicate with the Cisco modem over a network connection. Getting the modem's network connection to work with your Linux computer (or your LAN if you're using one) can be tricky, so we recommend (and explain) the one sure method that uses a serial cable and terminal emulation-based connection:

1. **Connect the blue cable that come with the Cisco modem (the blue cable is a RS232 serial cable with a 9 pin DB9 female connector) between the computer and the Cisco 675 or 678 DSL modem.**

   You must be able to communicate with your DSL modem from your Linux computer. Unfortunately, your modem is not configured to speak to a Linux computer over its network connection until you configure it to do so. Therefore, you must use the serial cable to get its network connection running.

2. **Log in as root on your Red Hat Linux computer.**

3. **Open a terminal emulation window.**

   See Chapter 4 if you don't know how to open a terminal emulation window.

4. **Install the `minicom` terminal emulator package if it isn't already installed.**

   If `minicom` has not been installed, then insert the companion CD-ROM and mount it.

   ```
   mount /mnt/cdrom
   rpm -ivh /mnt/cdrom/dsl/minicom*
   ```

You can use any terminal emulator program that you want. For instance, you can use the old but tried-and-true seyon or dip terminal emulation programs if you wish.

5. Create the default minicom configuration file.

```
minicom -s
```

6. Run the program.

```
minicom
```

Don't worry about the warning you see about running minicom as root. We won't do anything dangerous.

The initial minicom screen is displayed.

```
Welcome to minicom 1.83.1

OPTIONS: History Buffer, F-key Macros, Search History
         Buffer, I18n
Compiled on Feb 23 2001, 07:31:40.

Press CTRL-A Z for help on special keys
```

7. Press Ctrl+A and then Z to enter the configuration menu.

Change the communication device from /dev/modem to /dev/ttyS0 (or whatever the serial device that is appropriate to your system (/dev/ttyS1, /dev/ttyS2, or /dev/ttyS3).

8. Change the communication parameters to a speed of 9600, 8 bits, and no parity.

Turn off hardware and software flow control too.

9. Connect to the Cisco DSL modem by pressing the enter key.

The first time that you connect to the modem you should see the following prompt:

```
User Access Verification
Password:
```

10. Set the DSL modem's password by pressing Enter.

You'll see the *Cisco Broadband Operating System* (cbos) prompt.

```
cbos>
```

You have successfully configured the serial connection to the Cisco DSL modem. The next steps involve setting up the Cisco 675 or 678 to access your ISP via its DSL connection.

Configuring the Cisco 675 or 678 DSL modem

The following steps describe how to configure a Cisco 675 or 768 DSL modem. We use a DSL modem here because it's the most common DSL device available today.

The following process involves setting up your authentication, routing, and NAT. You must first configure the DSL modem with its own passwords and other information. (See the "Connecting your Cisco modem to your Linux computer" section, earlier in this chapter.)

To configure your DSL modem so that it will work with Red Hat Linux, follow these steps:

1. **Only the enable account can be used to configure the modem, so type**

   ```
   enable
   ```

   You need to set the Cisco modem passwords. Cisco 675 or 678 modems use two passwords. One password is for the regular (non-privileged) password called *exec,* and the other works for the administrative account, called *enable.*

2. **No enable password is set, so press the Enter key when prompted for the password.**

   The cbos> prompt changes to cbos# with the pound sign (#) indicating that you're in enable mode.

3. **Enter the non-administrative *exec* password:**

   ```
   set password exec dslrocks!
   ```

   You should use your own password — not dslrocks! — of course.

4. **Set the administrative *enable* password:**

   ```
   set password enable dslisablast!
   ```

   Again, you should use your own password rather than our example password. That makes sense because our password is displayed in millions of books — well probably just three or four books, but we can be optimistic. Make sure you use a different password.

   Your DSL modem is very mellow because it uses non-volatile memory. Non-volatile memory is very good at remembering things like the passwords that you just set, but only if you tell it to remember these things.

5. **Save your changes by running the following command:**

```
write
```

The **show nvram** command shows what's in the DSL modem's memory. Run the command and you'll see something like the following:

```
[[ CBOS = Section Start ]]
NSOS Root Password = a_lsbgegr
NSOS Enable Password = a_lsbgegr
```

6. **Set up the DSL modem so that your Linux computer can connect to the Ethernet interface.**

```
set interface eth0 address 192.168.1.1 netmask
        255.255.255.0
```

7. **Configure the DSL modem's** wan0-0 **interface to authenticate with your ISP.**

```
set ppp wan0-0 login iwantdsl@myisp.com
set ppp wan0-0 password dslrocks!
```

Use the values that your ISP gives to you in place of our fictitious example.

8. **Set DSL modem default route.**

```
set ppp wan0-0 ipcp 0.0.0.0
```

9. **Set up the DSL modem's DNS.**

```
set ppp wan0-0 dns 0.0.0.0
set dhcp server disable
```

10. **You don't EVER allow Telnet connections to be established from the Internet, so just turn off all connections.**

```
set telnet disabled
```

11. **Finally, enable NAT.**

```
set nat enabled
```

The Cisco 675 or 678 DSL modem now automatically converts the source addresses and ports of outgoing connections to its external (wan0-0) interface.

12. **Save the changes to nvram again.**

```
write
```

13. **Reboot your DSL modem by entering the following command.**

```
reboot
```

The wide area network (WAN) LED indicator on the modem starts blinking after several seconds. The blinking LED indicates that the device is attempting to connect your ISP. When the connection is established and authenticated, then the light turns to a constant on state. If the connection isn't established, then consult the troubleshooting section at the end of this chapter.

14. **To see what you've done, run the command show nvram to examine your modem's configuration.**

```
[[ CBOS = Section Start ]]
NSOS Root Password = a_lsbgegr
NSOS Enable Password = a_lsbgegr
NSOS Remote Restart = enabled
[[ PPP Device Driver = Section Start ]]
PPP Port User Name = 00, iwantdsl@myisp.com
PPP Port User Password = 00, dslrocks!
PPP Port Option = 00, IPCP,IP Address,3,Auto,Negotiation
        Not Required,Negotiabl0
PPP Port Option = 00, IPCP,Primary DNS
        Server,129,Auto,Negotiation Not Required0
PPP Port Option = 00, IPCP,Secondary DNS
        Server,131,Auto,Negotiation Not Requir0
[[ IP Routing = Section Start ]]
IP Port Address = 00, 192.168.1.1
IP NAT = enabled
[[ DHCP = Section Start ]]
DHCP Server = enabled
DHCP Relay = disabled
[[ Telnet = Section Start ]]
Telnet = disabled
```

15. **Turn off your DSL modem and set up your firewall.**

    Chapter 8 shows you how to build a firewall.

Phew, that was easy! Wasn't it? Anyway, you should be connected to the Internet with a fat DSL pipe. Unfortunately, the great features that DSL gives you — high speed and a continuous connection — can also work against you. Hackers now have a fast and continuous connection to your computer. Oh no, Mister Bill!

Don't worry. If you build a good firewall, you'll be protected from most of the Internet's dangers. Make sure that your DSL modem is turned off. Go to Chapter 8 and build a firewall. Turn your modem back on when the firewall is working.

Chapter 7

Connect Locally, Browse Globally: Connecting to a Local Area Network (LAN)

In This Chapter

▶ Networking with an Ethernet or wireless NIC

▶ Using the Red Hat Network Configuration Druid

▶ Starting and stopping your local network connection

---

*T*his chapter shows you how to connect your Red Hat Linux computer to an existing local area network (LAN) or private network. This is different than connecting directly to the Internet with a modem or broadband connection as described in Chapters 5 and 6. In this case, you connect directly to a LAN with an Ethernet or wireless network adapter. If your LAN has an Internet gateway, then you can connect to the Internet, too.

We describe how to connect to an existing LAN because many people have access to them. You may be building your Red Hat Linux computer to use at work or at school. It doesn't matter what the venue is, you can use this chapter to connect your computer to an existing LAN. You'll be able to access the Internet if that LAN is connected to it.

In this book, the terms LAN and private network are used interchangeably.

If you configured your Ethernet card during the installation process we show you in Chapter 2, then great! You can skip this chapter or just browse through it. Otherwise, if you have a wireless adapter (not described in Chapter 2) or didn't configure your Ethernet adapter in Chapter 2, then use this chapter to configure your Ethernet adapter for the first time or reconfigure networking for your Red Hat Linux machine.

Although forming a private network isn't exactly rocket science, describing in detail how to network two or more computers is still beyond the scope of this book because there are so many possible network configurations. Many good books are available that explain how to do that, and you can consult the Linux documentation found in the /usr/doc/HOWTO directory of your Red Hat Linux installation. See the Ethernet-HOWTO, Networking-Overview-HOWTO, NET-3-HOWTO, and NET-3-4-HOWTO for more information on networking.

Going Local

The invention of Linux has revolutionized the use of networks. Creating a LAN prior to Linux was complicated and expensive. LANs were nearly the exclusive domain of big corporations, universities, and other such monstrous organizations.

But TCP/IP networking was built into Linux from the beginning. In the mid-1990s, if you could afford a couple of PCs, a cheap piece of coaxial cable, and a few 10 Mbps (megabits per second) or faster Ethernet adapters, a LAN was born! The Ethernet adapters, which are also commonly known as *network interface cards* (NICs), cost about $150 at the time. Prices fortunately have crashed since then, falling to earth like David Bowie: A 100 Mbps NIC now costs as low as $15, and you can buy an 11 Mbps wireless NIC for less than $100!

To get your Red Hat computer on a network, you have to configure only a handful of networking subsystems. Here's what needs to occur for your networking to work:

✔ Load your wireless or Ethernet NIC kernel module. Linux generally detects your hardware and loads the correct kernel modules.

✔ Configure your network interface card (NIC).

✔ Configure your domain name service (DNS), which converts Internet names into Internet Protocol (IP) addresses.

Wireless networking currently suffers from some security vulnerabilities. Please consult the sidebar, "Wireless network warning."

Performing these steps is pretty heavy lifting. The load is eased somewhat by using the graphical Network Configuration Druid system administration tool provided by Red Hat. (Red Hat likes to refer to its various configuration utilities as "Druids." Your guess about how programmers came up with that convention is as good as ours, but regardless of their name, Druids work very well.) You can also use individual commands to perform the same configuration. Both methods are described in this chapter. Have fun!

Configuring Your NIC with Red Hat's Network Druid

In order to use your Red Hat Linux computer with an existing local area network (LAN), you need a wireless or an Ethernet NIC installed on your computer and a network hub, or switch, to connect the NIC to. After you set up the hardware, you need to configure your Linux network settings.

If your LAN also has an Internet connection, you can set up your Linux computer to communicate with the Internet, too. A high-speed Internet connection is best, but it doesn't matter in terms of the network configuration.

Preparing to configure your wireless NIC

Before you can configure your wireless NIC, you need to figure out two things:

- ✔ What type of wireless NIC you have (or need)
- ✔ How your wireless NIC is going to connect to your network

Two main types of wireless electronics (chip sets) are in use today: Wavelan and Prism2. Intersil designed Prism2, and Lucent Technologies built Wavelan. The two types are configured differently. The following list shows the manufacturers of each type and can help you figure out what kind of chip set your device uses.

- ✔ **Wavelan:** Orinoco, Apple Airport Enterasys RoamAbout 802, Elsa AirlLancer 11, and Melco/Buffalo 802.11b.
- ✔ **Prism2:** D-Link DWL-650, LinkSys WPC11, and Compaq WL100. Others include Addtron AWP-100, Bromax Freeport, GemTek WL-211, Intalk/Nokia, SMC 2632W, YDI, Z-COM X1300, and Zoom Telephonics ZoomAir 4100.

Red Hat Linux comes packaged with software to enable the use of Wavelan products (such as the popular Orinoco PCMCIA cards), and a Wavelan wireless NIC is very easy to configure. Prism2 NICs are more difficult to configure, and we recommend using Wavelan-based systems. We describe how to configure Wavelan in this chapter, but not Prism2 NICs. If you want to use a Prism2, you can download the drivers for Prism2 from www.linux-wlan.org.

You need to figure out how your wireless NIC (or network adapter) is going to connect to your network. There are two ways for wireless NICs to connect to a LAN: adapter-to-adapter and adapter-to-wireless hub. The first type is referred to as an *ad-hoc* connection and is useful if you have two or more computers that you want to talk together and form their own exclusive network. The second type is called *infrastructure* and provides a single entrance — an *access point* — into a LAN. An access point allows one or more computers to

IEEE and wireless networks

The dominant wireless standard is based on the IEEE 802-11b (and the older 802-11a and the about-to-be-released 802-11g) standard; the 802-11b is also referred to as *WIFI*. If you hear people talking about a WIFI NIC, they're just talking about wireless NICs.

IEEE, pronounced *Eye-Triple-E,* stands for the Institute of Electrical and Electronic Engineers and is a worldwide professional society of nerds. (I have proudly been a member for 21 years. Woo-hoo, that and a buck-89 will buy me a coffee!) The IEEE is the triclops of wireless networking and concerns itself with things like what frequency networking devices should use. Fortunately, this group has devised this wonderful standard that now enables everyone who's interested to communicate without stringing wires between machines.

be connected to a network. However, unlike an ad-hoc network, the individual computers can connect to any access point that allows them to.

The wireless configuration instructions that we provide work with either the infrastructure or ad-hoc connection methods. Your wireless NIC can connect to either the access point or other computers (Linux and Windows) as long as you configure your Network ID (ESSID) and encryption key correctly.

Choosing between ad-hoc and infrastructure

There are several advantages to using ad-hoc mode, including lower costs, simpler configuration, and somewhat better security.

- ✔ **Lower costs:** You don't have to purchase an access point. Computers using wireless NICs running in ad-hoc mode communicate directly with each other.

- ✔ **Simpler configuration for the Linux user:** You generally configure an access point by using Windows-based software. You need to connect a Windows computer to the access point via an Ethernet network. That can be difficult if you don't run any Windows-based computers. (Good thing access points are beginning to use HTML-based configuration systems. You can use browsers like Mozilla to configure those devices.) If you're not using Windows-base software, you can use Red Hat's Network Configuration Druid to configure a wireless NIC. You can create a network of Linux computers by configuring each NIC with the same Network ID and encryption key.

✔ **Somewhat-better security:** Access points make life a little bit easier for hackers (the practice of discovering and breaking into wireless networks is referred to as war driving) because the access points tend to handle more network traffic than individual wireless NICs; for instance, if you have 10 wireless NICs communicating with an access point, then it handles 10 times the traffic that each NIC does. War driving software must examine a lot of network traffic in order to discover the encryption keys. So, because access points process more network traffic they provide war drivers with more raw material to work with.

Ad-hoc networks can provide a bit more security because they connect to other networks — and the Internet — via a network router. Access points work as network bridges. Routers examine IP addresses before transmitting network traffic from one network to another. Bridges automatically pass on all traffic. Ad-hoc networks can be configured to more tightly control network traffic than access point based ones. You can configure ad-hoc networks with a firewall more easily than one using an access point.

In the end, the IEEE is going to have to fix the wireless encryption scheme so we all can sleep at night.

We explain how to connect a wireless NIC (or WIFI NIC) to an access point using infrastructure mode. It's beyond the scope of this book to describe how to configure an access point in order to construct a wireless network. We assume that you already have access to an access point.

Wireless network warning

WIFI, the standard for wireless technology, uses an encryption system called wireless equivalent privacy (WEP) to provide security. WEP encrypts communication between wireless devices in order to prevent anyone with the right equipment from listening to and using your wireless network. But WEP is flawed and can be broken using tools available on the Internet (big surprise). If your WIFI is hacked, a hacker can read your communication. But your problems don't end there. A hacker can use your wireless network to connect to both your private network and also the Internet — you'll give the hacker a launch pad to Internet.

On the other hand, wireless networking is so useful that many people make accommodations for the risk. The thinking is, that if you assume that your wireless network has already been hacked, you don't have to worry about *when* it might be hacked in the future.

You should use Open Secure Shell (open SSH) and Secure Socket Layer (SSL) — both bundled with Red Hat Linux — to conduct all your internal and external communication. Please keep in mind that using SSH and SSL protects your information but doesn't prevent someone from connecting to your network. The next generation of WIFI — 802.11g — is supposed to fix the WEP weakness. Until WEP's problems are solved, be aware of the risks.

Configuring your Ethernet or wireless NIC

To get your Red Hat Linux computer working on a LAN, you must first configure its NIC. The NIC is the device that electrically connects your computer to your LAN. In order to work with the other computers on your network, your Ethernet or wireless adapter must be given a network address and a few other pieces of information.

We've divided the configuration instructions between Ethernet and wireless (or WIFI) NICs. The instructions start by explaining how to start Red Hat's Network Configuration Druid. We then devote a subsection each to describing the particulars of configuring Ethernet and wireless devices. After the device specifics are covered, we go back to describing general configuration issues. The overall configuration process is shown in the following list:

1. Start the Network Configuration Druid.

2. Configure your Ethernet or wireless device.

3. Configure your computer's host name.

4. Configure your computer's domain name service.

5. Restart your network.

Starting the Network Configuration Druid

Use the following steps to start the Network Configuration Druid:

1. **Log in as root.**

   See Chapter 4 for instructions about how to log in as root.

2. **Start the Network Configuration Druid by clicking the GNOME Main Menu button and choosing Programs⇨System⇨Network Configuration.**

   Figure 7-1 shows the initial configuration window. If you aren't logged in as root, then you are prompted to enter the root password before proceeding to the initial configuration window.

   The Hardware tab is active to start. It shows all of the network devices that Linux is aware of. Linux detects PCI devices (the standard PC adapter uses the PCI standard), such as Ethernet NICs. Figure 7-1 shows that Linux detects an Intel Ether Express Pro NIC.

   Linux doesn't detect PCMCIA network devices, such as wireless NICs. Linux detects that a PCMCIA card is installed but not what type of card it is. That job is performed by the wireless-tools package that is installed as part of the Red Hat Linux distribution.

3. **Click the Devices tab, which is shown in Figure 7-2.**

4. Click Add.

The Choose Hardware Device Type window appears, as shown in Figure 7-3. From the Device Type drop-down list, you can choose to use an Ethernet, XDSL, CIPE, or Wireless NIC.

5. Select the Ethernet or Wireless NIC.

The Ethernet or Wireless Device window opens, depending on your choice.

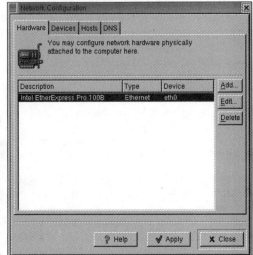

Figure 7-1:
The Hardware tab of the Network Configuration window.

Figure 7-2:
The Devices tab.

Figure 7-3:
Selecting an
Ethernet or
wireless
network
adapter.

What you do next depends on whether you're configuring an Ethernet NIC or a wireless NIC. The following two sections are devoted to the Ethernet and wireless NICs respectively.

Configuring an Ethernet NIC

If you're using an Ethernet NIC, use the steps in this section to configure the parameters for your NIC. (If you're using a wireless NIC, go to the next section, "Configuring a wireless NIC.")

1. **Follow the steps in the preceding section, "Starting the Network Configuration Druid."**

   When you choose Ethernet from the drop-down list in Step 5 of the preceding list, the Ethernet Device window shown in Figure 7-4 appears.

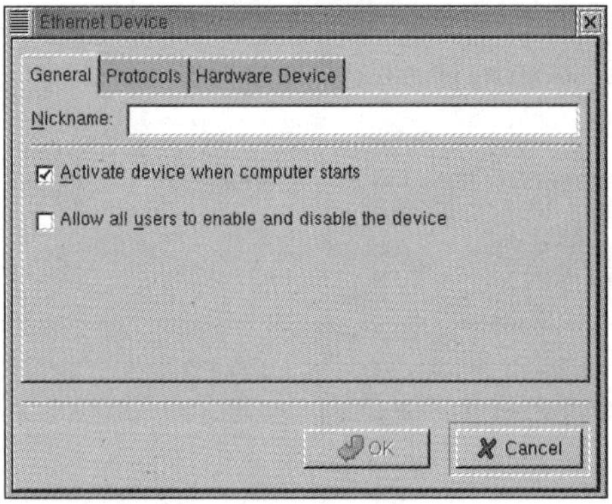

Figure 7-4:
The
Ethernet
Device
window.

2. **Type descriptive word such as** *Ethernet* **in the Nickname text box.**

3. **Click the Protocols tab.**

4. **The TCP/IP protocol is highlighted by default. Click Edit.**

   The TCP/IP Settings window appears, as shown in Figure 7-5.

5. **Configure your TCP/IP address settings.**

The Red Hat Network Configuration Druid selects DHCP (Dynamic Host Configuration Protocol) as the default method for determining your machine's IP address. If you're connecting to a network that provides DHCP service and the system administrator wants you to use it, then click OK. DHCP dynamically assigns an IP address to your Ethernet NIC, and you're finished configuring your NIC.

If your network doesn't use DHCP, then you need to manually configure your IP address. Click in the Automatically Obtain IP Address check box so the check mark disappears. You should ask your friendly local system administrator what system your network uses. You can now enter your IP address and other options as shown in Figure 7-5.

Life is made a bit more complicated if you have both a wireless and Ethernet NIC on your computer. You can run both devices at once, but the configuration becomes much more difficult. You can solve the problem by clicking in the Automatically Obtain IP Address check box so that the check mark disappears. This simple mouse click prevents the Ethernet NIC from starting automatically.

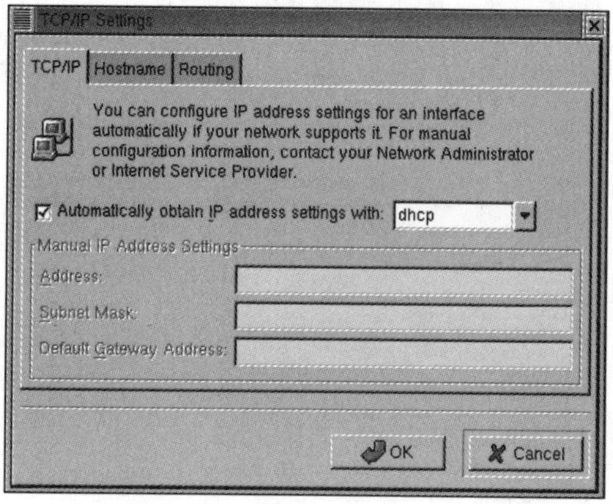

Figure 7-5:
The TCP/IP
Settings
window.

6. **Assign an IP address to your computer by typing it in the Address text box.**

IP addresses are analogous to street addresses; they provide a number that uniquely identifies your machine from all others. Public IP addresses don't require any registration with the powers that be — the InterNIC organization that distributes IP addresses. Public IP addresses aren't routed on the Internet and can be used on LANs for your own use.

If you're on a network with registered IP addresses, be sure to get an IP address from your system administrator. Otherwise, go ahead and use a private IP address. (Use any class C address between 192.168.1.1 and 192.168.254.254. For example, 192.168.128.5 or 192.168.1.20.) Private IP addresses in this range are designated for use by anyone on their private networks. By design, private IP addresses don't get routed (sent from one machine to another) through the Internet and — anyone can use them. Private IP addresses would wreck havoc on the Internet if they were routed.

7. **Type** 255.255.255.0 **or the netmask for your IP address in the Subnet Mask text box.**

The Internet Protocol (IP) defines only three network address classes: A, B, and C. Only class C addresses are assigned by the InterNIC. Use the 255.255.255.0 netmask for class C networks, 255.255.0.0 for class B, and 255.0.0.0 for class A. Class C netmasks are used almost universally now, and we use only class C addresses here. If you're not using a class C address, then you're probably experienced in the ways of TCP/IP and know what netmask to use. Otherwise, don't fool with Mother Nature, buddy: Use a class C address.

8. **In the Default Gateway Address text box, type the IP address of the Internet gateway for your LAN.**

The Internet gateway is the device (router or computer) that connects your network to your ISP and the Internet. Obtain the address from your system administrator if you're at work and have one. If you're a home user, a typical convention is to assign the highest address — 254 — of a class C subnetwork as the gateway. For example, type **192.168.1.254.**

Your TCP/IP Settings look similar to the screen shown in Figure 7-6.

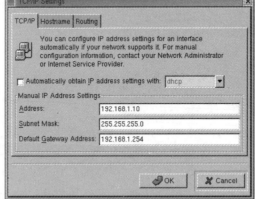

Figure 7-6:
Entering
your static
(non-DHCP)
IP address
settings.

This completes your Ethernet NIC configuration. You still need to configure your domain name service (DNS) if you aren't using DHCP. Proceed to the sections, "Configuring your host name" and "Configuring DNS service."

You won't have to enter information into the Kernel Module, IO Port (opt), or IRQ (opt) text boxes because Linux is good at detecting this information directly from the device.

Kernel modules are the Linux equivalent to Microsoft Windows device drivers. Usually, Red Hat Linux can detect your Ethernet adapter and automatically load the correct module, but if Red Hat can't find your Ethernet adapter, you probably won't be able to find the correct one from the supplied list. You can still go ahead and try; there's no harm in that.

Configuring a wireless NIC

This section describes how to configure the parameters for a wireless NIC, also called a WIFI NIC. (Skip this section if you don't have a wireless NIC.) If you haven't already done so, read the earlier section, "Preparing to configure your wireless NIC," to make sure that your NIC is a Wavelan and that you want to set up your network for infrastructure mode. Then, follow these steps:

1. **Follow the steps in the section, "Starting the Network Configuration Druid," earlier in this chapter.**

   When you choose Wireless from the drop-down list in Step 5 of the earlier list, the Wireless Device Configuration window shown in Figure 7-7 appears.

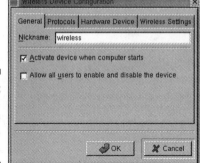

Figure 7-7: Choosing a nickname for the device.

2. **In the Nickname text box, type a name for the device, such as** Wireless, **or any name that you feel comfortable with.**

3. **Click the Protocol tab.**

4. **Click the Edit button.**

   The TCP/IP Settings screen opens, as shown in Figure 7-8.

5. **Configure your TCP/IP address settings.**

   The Red Hat Network Configuration Druid selects DHCP as the default method for determining your machine's IP address. If you're connecting to a network that provides DHCP service then click OK and skip to Step 7. (Contact the LAN system administrator if you're unsure whether it runs DHCP.)

If the network that you're connecting to doesn't have DHCP (you can find more information about DHCP by reading the README file in /usr/share/doc/dhcpcd-1.3.21p12 directory), click in the Automatically Obtain IP Address button to remove the check mark. You can now enter your IP address manually. If you're on a network with registered IP addresses, then get an IP address from your system administrator. Otherwise, go ahead and use any class C address between 192.168.1.1 and 192.168.254.254. For example, type **192.168.128.5** in the Address text box.

IP addresses are analogous to street addresses; they provide a number that uniquely identifies your machine from all others. Public IP addresses don't require any registration with the powers that be — the InterNIC organization that distributes IP addresses. Confusing? Not really. Public IP addresses aren't routed on the Internet and can be used on LANs for your own use.

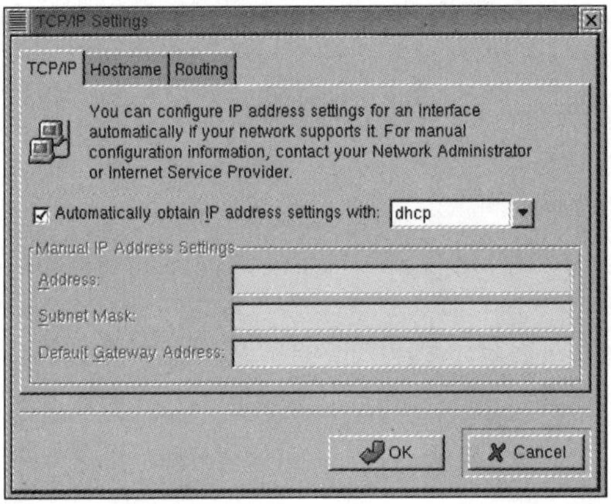

Figure 7-8:
The default
TCP/IP
Settings
window.

> TCP/IP Settings
>
> TCP/IP | Hostname | Routing
>
> You can configure IP address settings for an interface automatically if your network supports it. For manual configuration information, contact your Network Administrator or Internet Service Provider.
>
> ☑ Automatically obtain IP address settings with: dhcp
>
> Manual IP Address Settings
>
> Address:
>
> Subnet Mask:
>
> Default Gateway Address:
>
> ✓ OK   ✗ Cancel

6. **Type** 255.255.255.0 **or the netmask for your IP address in the Subnet Mask text box.**

The Internet Protocol (IP) defines only three network address classes: A, B, and C. Only class C addresses are assigned by the InterNIC. Class C netmasks (255.255.255.0) are used almost universally now, and we use only class C addresses here. (Netmasks divide IP addresses into network and host addresses. The three "255" in a class C netmask means that the first 3/4 of the address specifies the network address; the single "0" specifies the host address. The last quarter of the IP address translates into a total of 255 hosts.) If you're not using a class C address, then you're probably experienced in the ways of TCP/IP and know what netmask to use. Otherwise, don't fool with Mother Nature, buddy: Use a class C address.

7. **In the Default Gateway Address text box, type the IP address of the Internet gateway for your LAN.**

The Internet gateway is the device (router or computer) that connects your network to your ISP and the Internet. Obtain the address from your system administrator if you're at work and have one. If you're a home user, a typical convention is to assign the highest address — 254 — of a class C subnetwork as the gateway. For example, type **192.168.1.254**.

Your TCP/IP Settings should look similar to the screen shown in Figure 7-9.

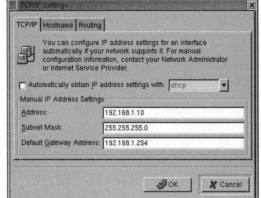

Figure 7-9:
Entering
your IP
address.

8. **Click OK.**

   You return to the Wireless Device Configuration window (refer to Figure 7-7).

9. **Click the Hardware Device tab.**

   If your computer already has an Ethernet NIC installed that you want to use along with your wireless NIC, then select eth1. Otherwise, select eth0.

   You probably don't want to run an Ethernet and wireless NIC simultaneously. (Your wireless connection loses much of its appeal if your computer remains connected to an Ethernet cable.) But you may run into a situation where you want to use one or the other — for instance, you use the Ethernet connection at work but the wireless at home. In that case you should disable one or the other by turning off the *Activate device when computer starts* option. To disable the Ethernet NIC, click on the *Activate device when computer starts* option box to remove the check mark and then click OK to save the configuration.

10. **Click the Wireless Settings tab.**

    The Wireless Settings window activates.

11. **Type any in the ESSID (Network ID) text box.**

    You must specify the Network ID and encryption key to connect to your network's access point or the other wireless computers running in ad-hoc mode.

12. Type the encryption key in the Key text box.

You can obtain the encryption key from your network administrator. If you're a home user, you should generate the key yourself. An encryption key is nothing more than a string of text similar to the password you used to protect your user and root accounts in Chapter 3. Think of a password that is different than from user password and type it into the text box. Figure 7-10 shows an example of the Wireless Settings window.

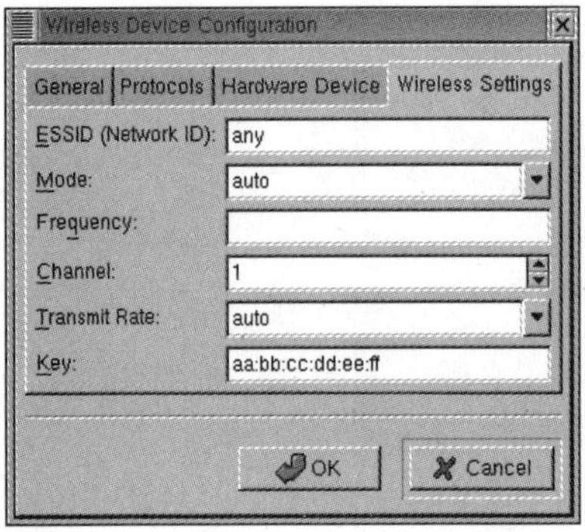

Figure 7-10:
Typical
wireless
NIC
configu-
ration.

13. Click OK.

The Network Configuration window appears on-screen again.

This completes your Wireless NIC configuration. You still need to configure your domain name service (DNS) if you aren't using DHCP. Proceed to the sections, "Configuring your host name" and " Configuring DNS service," if that is the case.

Configuring your host name

After you configure your Ethernet or your wireless NIC (see the preceding sections for details if you haven't done this yet), you're ready to configure the host name and DNS settings for your Red Hat Linux computer. This information is what your computer will be known as to the rest of your LAN.

You return to the Network Configuration window after configuring the Ethernet and/or wireless NIC. You still need to configure your machine's host name. The following steps describe the process:

1. Click the Hosts tab in the Network Configuration window.

2. Click the Add button.

3. Enter your computer's IP address in the Address: box.

4. **Type the combined host name and domain name of your computer in the Hostname: text box.**

   For example, our machine's host name is Veracruz, and its domain name is paunchy.net. The default DNS setting is to use Automatically obtain DNS information from provider. Leave this option turned on if you're using DHCP from a private network or cable modem. Otherwise, turn it off. Figure 7-11 shows our entries.

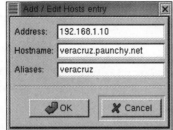

Figure 7-11:
The host name configuration.

5. **Enter the simple name of your computer in the Alias: text box.**

   If, for instance, you entered *veracruz.paunchy.net* in the Hostname: box, then your alias is *veracruz*.

6. **Click OK to return to the Network Configuration window.**

You may have configured your LAN settings during the Red Hat installation process described in Chapter 3. In that case, Red Hat folded your hostname, domain name, and alias into your localhost configuration. You should remove that information from the localhost configuration because you're adding the hostname, domain name, and alias as separate entities. Edit the localhost configuration and remove those items.

Configuring DNS service

You now need to configure your DNS information. This is the same process described in Chapter 5, but in this case, you're connecting to a LAN that may operate its own DNS server.

1. **Make sure that you're on the DNS tab of the Network Configuration window, which is where you left off in the preceding steps list.**

2. **Type the domain name of your network in the Domain text box.**

   A domain name is a two-part name separated by a period. For example, `paunchy.net` is a domain name. This is the domain name discussed in Step 5 of the preceding section. It's the network name of the example

LAN being constructed here. You should, of course, replace the `paunchy.net` domain name with the name of your LAN.

3. **Type the IP address of your DNS server in the Primary DNS text box.**

   IP addresses are made up of four sets of numbers separated by periods (192.168.1.254, for example). Your ISP provides you with an IP address when you subscribe.

   If your LAN provides a DNS server, then you can use it as your primary name server (DNS).

4. **If you have one, type the IP address of your secondary name server in the Secondary DNS text box.**

   Most ISPs provide a backup DNS server address. If your LAN has its own DNS server, you can specify your ISP server as your secondary DNS server if you wish.

5. **(Optional) If you are connected to a network that has multiple domain names, then you may want to provide additional search domain names in the DNS Search Path text box.**

   If, for instance, say you set up a domain name called `veracruz.paunchy.net` on your LAN. You should enter that name here. You can then use just the name of the machine you're looking for. For example, if you have a machine named `pumas.veracruz.paunchy.net`, then you can refer to it as simply `pumas`. Without the secondary domain name, you have to use the entire name — `pumas.veracruz.paunchy.net` — instead of just `pumas`.

6. **Click Apply.**

7. **Click Close.**

   The Network Configuration Druid asks you if you want to save your changes.

8. **Click Yes.**

   The Network Configuration Druid exits. Your settings are saved and will be activated the next time you reboot your computer. Proceed to the following section, "Manually starting and stopping your network," to activate your settings immediately.

Manually starting and stopping your network

Sometimes the Network Configuration Druid configures your network stuff but doesn't activate it. Why does this happen? Who knows — it may be because the Network Configuration Druid is still relatively young and will become better with age. In the meantime, you can start your networking systems another way.

1. **Click the Gnome Main Menu button and choose Programs⇨System⇨ Service Configuration menu.**

2. **Enter your root password if prompted.**

   The Service Configuration window appears, as shown in Figure 7-12. Scroll down until you find the Network option.

3. **Click Network and then click the Restart button.**

   The Information window opens and confirms that your network has been restarted. Your new network settings take effect.

4. **If you're using a wireless NIC and it's not communicating, you may have to restart your PCMCIA system. Here's how:**

   a. Locate and click the PCMCIA service in the Service Configuration Druid.

   b. Click the Restart button.

   c. Repeat Step 3 to restart your network.

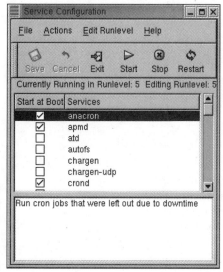

Figure 7-12:
The Service Configu-
ration Druid.

TIP

You can use the `/etc/rc.d/init.d/network` script to start and stop your networking system. To start your network modules, NIC, and routes, log in as root and run the following command: `/etc/rc.d/init.d/network restart`. All networking components are stopped and then started again. Alternatively, you can use `/etc/rc.d/init.d/network start` to simply start and configure your Ethernet NIC and routes. The `/etc/rc.d/init.d/network stop` command turns off all networking on your system.

Chapter 8

Fire, Fire, Heh, Heh, Firewalls Are Cool

- -

In This Chapter

▶ Introducing the `Netfilter/iptables` firewall system

▶ Designing filtering rules

▶ Automating your firewall

▶ Viewing your firewall filtering rules

▶ Testing your firewall

- -

*A*fter you connect to the Internet, you run the risk that the bad guys will try to rip off your computer. The bad guys that we speak about wear black hats just like in the movies (as opposed to red hats, which are a bit odd but still cool). You may also have heard them called hackers, crackers, and so on. Whatever their names and whatever their intentions, the Internet is getting more dangerous every day, and ya gotta protect yourself.

This chapter describes how to build a firewall to help protect your Red Hat Linux computer from the bad elements found on the Internet. First, in case you doubt that you actually need a firewall, we explain why firewalls are important. We introduce you to `iptables`, Linux's firewall system, and discuss two different ways to set up your firewall filtering rules. After you set up your firewall filters, you need to know how to run the firewall automatically. You do that by setting up a script — something else we explain in this chapter. And, of course, what good would your firewall be if it didn't work? So we show you how to do a simple test to make sure your firewall is burning brightly.

The firewalls described in this chapter enable you to make RealAudio connections, but you must follow the directions for getting RealPlayer through your firewall, which you can find in Chapter 13. There, we explain how to configure RealPlayer to use the HTTP protocol in place of its native RTSP (what?) and PNA (huh?) protocols — those acronyms are just technical jargon that we clear up in Chapter 13. RealPlayer works with the firewalls we discuss in this chapter because HTTP is allowed to pass through to the Internet.

Understanding Why You Need a Firewall in the First Place

You may think that there's safety in numbers. After all, literally millions of people, businesses, and organizations are connected to each other through networks and internetworks — including the Internet — at any given time. What do you — a simple person with a simple computer connected to the Internet — have to be concerned about? The bad guys are usually interested in big money or big publicity, right?

Well, that way of thinking is mostly true, and chances are that you'll never get hacked. In technical jargon, you're relying on security by obscurity.

Many hackers have tools that automatically scan and attack entire networks. The happy hacker doesn't have to work hard to find and exploit unprotected computers. You shouldn't risk getting *owned* — your computer broken into and controlled — by a hacker, especially when Linux provides effective tools for protecting yourself.

Using a firewall is a simple but most effective method for protecting yourself when you connect to the Internet. A firewall allows you to connect to the Internet while blocking unnecessary and unwanted connections from coming in.

Linux is a multiuser and multitasking operating system, meaning that more than one task can be run at the same time. Unlike Microsoft Windows, more than one person can be logged in at once. This flexibility comes at a price — it offers an attractive launching point for hackers. If someone can gain access to your Linux computer while it's on the Internet, then that person can use your machine to launch attacks against other machines, and you become the proxy that helps the bad guys hide their identities.

LAN-ho: Adding firewall protection to a network

Firewalls are especially important if you're connecting to the Internet via a local area network (LAN). Most Internet-connected LANs have a firewall that protects your computer from the worst aspects of the Internet. But a LAN's overall firewall technology may not protect your computer; there's always the danger of the insider threat — no, not from evil tobacco companies but from your fellow LAN users. Running a personal firewall gives you an added layer of protection. For instance, if you want to connect your computer to a university network, then you definitely want to use a firewall because such environments are very dangerous.

Building an Effective Firewall the iptables Way

Linux comes bundled with a simple but extremely effective firewall system called `Netfilter/iptables`. The `Netfilter` part refers to the firewall system that's built into the Linux operating system, and `iptables` is the interface that controls it. We refer to the overall system as `iptables` because that is the part that you'll be working with.

The `iptables` utility filters IP packets, which are the backbone of the Internet (IP stands for Internet Protocol, in fact). When you're connected to the Internet, all the information (graphics and text) that you send and receive is sent in the form of IP packets. All the information that enters and leaves your computer via the Internet is packaged in the form of IP packets. You can use `iptables` to accept or deny IP packets based on their destinations, source addresses, and ports.

`Iptables` is so effective because it uses stateful filtering. *Stateful filtering* means that the firewall is able to keep track of the state of each network connection. That's a technical way of saying `iptables` knows whether connections are valid. For instance, if you are browsing `www.dummies.com` through your firewall, then `iptables` is able to keep track of all the packets that belong to that connection. `Iptables` can deny packets that are trying to reach your computer but that don't belong to your connection, thus preventing any hackers from sneaking packets through your firewall.

Red Hat Linux installs the `ipchains` firewall by default. The installation system configures a medium level of protection during the installation process. Recall that we advised you not to use the default `ipchains` configuration in Chapter 3. `Ipchains` is not nearly as sophisticated or safe as the modern `iptables` firewall system. The Red Hat `ipchains` configuration also is not as comprehensive as the ones we set up in this chapter.

Ports are an essential part of the Internet Protocol. Ports are used to organize the communication between clients and servers. For instance, when you click on a Web page, your browser communicates with the Web server by using a port. That's, of course, a gross simplification but describes the basic idea. Suffice it to say that ports are used to control the internal workings of the Internet for such things as Web browsing.

Designing filtering rules:
Permissive and restrictive methods

Firewall filtering rules are like the bricks, or asbestos if you prefer, that build your firewall. Basically, the rules determine what network communication can come and go between your computer and the Internet.

When you design firewall filtering rules, you can take two directions: You can allow all connections or deny all connections by default. Allowing all connections takes the view that it's best to start by allowing all communication with your computer and then denying connections one by one. The danger with this method is that you unintentionally allow dangerous traffic to reach your machine. The alternative method is to start by denying *all* communication and then selectively allowing certain traffic. This is the best way to create a firewall from a security

standpoint, but it can also create problems because you may unintentionally prevent needed or wanted network traffic from reaching your computer.

We explain how to use the restrictive method in this chapter for two reasons:

✔ It's the safest method. The restrictive method is safer because it nearly completely prevents port scanning and other hacker attacks from accessing your computer.

✔ It's easier to configure. Iptables provides stateful filtering and requires only two rules to allow all outgoing network connections. You need to configure individual rules to block incoming communication when using the permissive model.

Setting Up an iptables-Based Firewall

So now you know that you need a firewall and want to create one. What's next? Well, the following sections explain how to set up an iptables-based firewall by using the restrictive model. This section describes how to manually create the firewall filtering rules. When you're done setting up your rules, proceed to the "Saving your filtering rules to a script" section so that you don't have to enter these rules every time you turn on your computer.

The rules you use for each method vary slightly depending on the type of Internet connection you have. In the following sections, we've made the bold assumption that you've set up your Internet connection by using one of the three methods we discuss elsewhere in this book. We cover dial-up connections in Chapter 5, broadband connections in Chapter 6, and LAN connections in Chapter 7.

In this section, you design an iptables-based firewall that turns off all incoming connections on your modem but still enables you to establish an outgoing connection to the Internet. You must follow all the steps in this list, or the firewall will likely prevent you from using the Internet:

1. **Log in to your computer as root.**

2. **Open a terminal emulation window by clicking the terminal icon on the GNOME Panel. Figure 8-1 shows the terminal emulation window.**

   The Panel is that big menu bar at the bottom of your screen. The terminal icon looks like a monitor. (Chapter 4 describes the function of a terminal emulation window.)

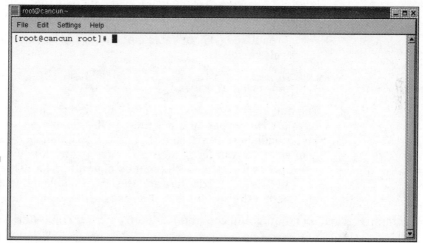

Figure 8-1: A terminal emulation window.

3. **Make sure that you're not already running a firewall by entering the following rules at the command prompt in the Terminal window:**

   ```
   iptables --flush
   iptables --flush -t nat
   ```

   The iptables entries remove all the general-purpose filtering and Network Address Translation (NAT) rules that may be in place. *NAT rules* masquerade your network address as another address, making your computer appear to be someone else; NAT is frequently used to make your computer appear to be coming from your ISP so that you don't have to register your computer for an official Internet Protocol (IP) address.

4. **Enter the following rules to allow network traffic to pass through the loopback device:**

   ```
   iptables -A OUTPUT -j ACCEPT -o lo
   iptables -A INPUT  -j ACCEPT -i lo
   ```

   Linux computers use an internal network called a *loopback interface*. The loopback is not an actual device, but the Linux operating system uses it for internal communications (a lot goes on behind the scenes on a Linux computer).

5. **Turn off all network communication to your computer via the modem (or whatever you're using) by entering the** `iptables` **rules that correspond to your connection type.**

   - For a dial-up modem connection, use these rules:

   ```
   iptables -A INPUT  -i ppp0 -j DROP
   iptables -A OUTPUT -o ppp0 -j DROP
   ```

   The modem uses the ppp0 interface, which is based on the Point-to-Point Protocol (PPP). Note that the first modem that you set up will use the ppp0 interface; the second modem uses ppp1, and so on.

   - For a broadband (DSL or cable modem) or LAN connection, use these rules instead:

   ```
   iptables --policy INPUT  -i eth0 DROP
   iptables --policy OUTPUT -i eth0 DROP
   ```

   The only difference between these rules and the dial-up modem rules is the network interface that the firewall blocks access to. The broadband rules assume that your broadband modem is connected to your first Ethernet device — eth0. Modify the rules as appropriate if you use a different configuration; for instance, if you have two Ethernet adapters and the DSL or cable modem is attached to the second one, then use eth1 instead of eth0.

6. **Turn on all outgoing communication from your computer:**

```
iptables -A OUTPUT -m state -state NEW,RELATED,
        ESTABLISHED -j ACCEPT
iptables -A INPUT -m state --state RELATED,ESTABLISHED -j
        ACCEPT
```

These rules don't specify any particular network interface. However, because the filter is stateful, these rules effectively work on your broadband or LAN interface.

The first filter rule permits all outgoing communication. The `--state NEW, RELATED, ESTABLISHED` option tells the firewall to allow packets of both new and already established connections to pass. (Packets are the basic part of all network communication.) Packets that are related to existing connections, such as FTP data transfers, are also permitted.

The second filter rule controls the packets coming back from outgoing connections. When you connect to a Web site, for instance, your browser sends out packets, and the Web server responds to them. You might click a button on the Web site, and a new display pops up. Clicking a button sends a packet out, and the Web server sends packets back. You've previously blocked packets from the Internet. This rule creates an exception that allows packets that belong to an existing connection — such as the connection that represents you clicking a button — to return to your computer through the firewall. Note that we don't allow new connections — `-state NEW` — to be established because that would defeat the purpose of this firewall.

7. **(Optional) Use the following rule to allow SSH connections to your Linux computer.**

```
iptables -A INPUT -p tcp -m state --state NEW,ESTABLISHED
        -j ACCEPT -d 0/0 -dport 22
```

This rule permits SSH connections on port 22 to enter into your computer. (You can install OpenSSH server by logging in as root, mounting your companion CD-ROM and running the following command: `rpm -ivh /mnt/cdrom/RedHat/RPMS/openssh-server*`. Start the OpenSSH server by running the following command: `/etc/init.d/sshd start`.)

You can modify this rule to allow other types of incoming connections to your computer. For instance, change port 22 to 80 and the firewall will pass HTTP packets to your computer. All you need to do is install the Apache Web server (included on the companion CD) and your workstation morphs into Web server.

You have now created a firewall that protects your computer from the big, bad Internet wolves ("They'll rip your heart out, Jim!"). Your firewall will be active until you reboot your computer, or if you're using a dial-up modem, when you drop your connection; please note, however, that the filtering rules will not disappear if you exit from the terminal emulation window. The next section describes how to save the rules that you just created so that they can be started automatically.

Firing Up Your Firewall (And Dousing the Flames)

The previous section described how to create your firewall. However, you do not want to manually enter these rules every time you reboot your computer. This section shows you how to automate your firewall. We show you how to make use of Red Hat's utilities that save the rules that you just created and start up the firewall whenever you boot your computer.

These instructions assume that you have configured the firewall described in the previous set of instructions, and that they are still in effect.

Saving your filtering rules to a script

You need to save your rule-set after you've created your firewall. Red Hat provides a utility for doing just that. The utility `iptables-save` reads your current firewall rules and converts them into script-compatible form. Red Hat also provides a script to start up your firewall when you start your computer. The `/etc/init.d/iptables` script is run whenever you start your computer and, thus, your firewall is started, too.

1. **Login as root.**

2. **Open a terminal emulator window (see Chapter 4).**

3. **Run the following command and your firewall rules are saved to a script.**

```
iptables-save > /etc/sysconfig/iptables
```

Turning your firewall off and on

Red Hat uses the `/etc/sysconfig/iptables` script to start `Netfilter/iptables` firewalls. The `/etc/init.d/iptables` script uses the filtering rules stored in the `/etc/sysconfig/iptables` file to implement the filtering rules.

You can start the `Netfilter/iptables` firewall by running the following `iptables` script:

```
/etc/init.d/iptables start
```

You must be logged in as root, of course. Note that you can turn off your firewall by replacing "start" with "stop."

You can also use the graphical Red Hat Service Configuration Druid. The following instructions show you how to use the Druid to start or stop your firewall.

1. **Click the GNOME Main Menu button and choose Programs⇨System⇨Service Configuration.**

2. **If you're not logged in as root, then the Input window pops up and you're asked to enter the root password.**

   Enter the root password that you set during the Red Hat installation process.

   The Service Configuration window appears, as shown in Figure 8-2. This window controls all the Linux daemons (processes that provide services).

3. **Scroll down the Service Configuration window until you find the `iptables` service. Click on the box so that a check mark appears, as shown in Figure 8-3.**

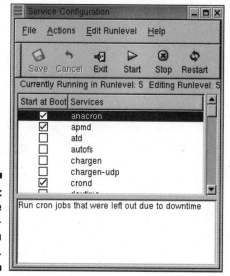

Figure 8-2:
The Service
Configu-
ration
window.

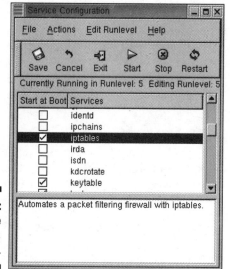

Figure 8-3:
Finding the
`iptables`
service.

4. Click the Restart button in the upper-left corner of the window.

You could click the Start button, but we advise you to use the Restart function. The Start and Restart buttons give you the same result, but restarting works if the service is already running. Using the Start function won't work if the service is already running.

Click on the Stop button to turn off your firewall.

After the service restarts, you see a confirmation message like the one shown in Figure 8-4.

5. Click OK.

Your firewall is restarted, and you can exit from the Service Configuration window.

Figure 8-4: Confirming that `iptables` has been restarted.

You can also prevent the `iptables` script from being automatically started when you boot the system. Click in the box immediately to the left of the service name to remove the check mark. Click the Save button, and the pointer (`/etc/rc.d/rc5.d/S08iptables`) to the startup script (`/etc/init.d/iptables`) is removed. You can restore the pointer by clicking in the box so that the check mark reappears.

Displaying Your Firewall Rules

After you configure your firewall, you'll naturally want to verify that the filtering rules are set up correctly. To display the firewall rules, follow these steps:

1. Open a Terminal window by clicking the terminal icon on the GNOME Panel.

The Panel is that big menu bar at the bottom of your screen. The terminal icon looks like a monitor.

2. If you're not already the root user, type su - **at the command prompt in the terminal window and press Enter to become root.**

3. Enter the root password.

4. Type in the following command to display the firewall rules.

```
iptables -L
```

You should see a list displayed in the terminal window, as follows:

```
Chain input (policy DENY):
target     prot opt    source       destination  ports
ACCEPT     all  ------  anywhere     anywhere     n/a
ACCEPT     all  ------  anywhere     anywhere     n/a
ACCEPT     tcp  !y----  anywhere     anywhere     any ->
           any
ACCEPT     udp  ------  anywhere     anywhere     domain ->
           any
Chain forward (policy DENY):
Chain output (policy DENY):
target     prot opt    source       destination  ports
ACCEPT     all  ------  anywhere     anywhere     n/a
ACCEPT     all  ------  anywhere     anywhere     n/a
ACCEPT     tcp  ------  anywhere     anywhere     any ->
           any
ACCEPT     udp  ------  anywhere     anywhere     any ->
           domain
```

The first *chain* (which is simply a set of rules used for a common purpose or function) is for incoming — or input — IP packets. You can see that the default policy is to deny all IP packets. The first two rules tell iptables to allow all internal packets on the logical loopback (lo) and Ethernet (eth0) interfaces. The next rule allows the return packets from outgoing connections to come back in. The last rule allows the incoming UDP domain packets, which are used for domain name service (DNS).

The next chain — forward — denies all packets from being forwarded through your Linux computer. Forwarding is only necessary if you use your computer for routing or other advanced networking functions.

The last chain — output — defines what IP packets are allowed out of your computer. The first two rules are for your lo and eth0 interfaces again and allow all internal traffic. The next rule allows any and all IP packets destined for the Internet to leave through the firewall. The last rule allows domain (DNS) packets to go out to the Internet.

You can make your iptables rules tighter by allowing only certain types of packets out to the Internet. You can specify certain ports and addresses that are allowable, for example. This makes your firewall incrementally safer but also more restrictive.

Testing Your Firewall

Your new firewall is no silver bullet, but it does provide a great deal more protection than if you didn't have one. Treat it for what it is — a good, sturdy lock. It's the beginning of your Internet security, but not the end. Don't trust it, however, without first making sure it works.

To test your firewall, follow these steps:

1. **Throw some gasoline on your computer and light a . . . no, no, just kidding. Don't do that, especially if you plan to sue.**

2. **Try to Telnet to your ISP or university account; any computer account that's external to your own computer will do.**

   Telnet is a network program that allows you to connect to a remote computer and interactively enter commands.

3. **If you don't know it already, find out what your temporary (dynamic) IP address is by entering the following command at the command prompt:**

   ```
   who | grep login
   ```

   where *login* is your, well, login name. This command shows an IP address in numeric form, similar to the following:

   ```
   iamme (192.168.32.254) ...
   ```

4. **Run a port scan against your Red Hat Linux computer by typing in the actual address that you received in Step 3 in place of *IP_address* in the following command:**

   ```
   nmap IP_address
   ```

   For instance, if your IP address is 192.168.32.254, then run the nmap as follows:

   ```
   nmap -P0 192.168.32.254
   ```

   Please note that the preceding IP address has been changed to protect the innocent. The address is what is known as a public address and will (should) never exist on the Internet anyway.

   If your firewall is set up correctly, then nmap should not be able to detect anything of interest about your computer. The wolves have been held at bay!

Congratulations, you've successfully set up your firewall. Your job as a security professional, however, has only just begun. In reality, there's no silver bullet where security is concerned. Education is your one true defense. For more information on firewalls and security, search the Internet for security-related topics. The SANS (www.sans.org), USENIX (www.usenix.org), Red Hat (www.redhat.com), and CERT (www.cert.org) Web sites are all good places to start. You should also consult Chapter 23 for the top 10 Linux security vulnerabilities.

Chapter 9

Surfing the Web and Managing E-Mail with Mozilla

- -

In This Chapter

▶ Introducing Mozilla

▶ Tailoring Mozilla to your liking

▶ Checkin' out da Web

▶ Receiving and reading e-mail

▶ Sending e-mail messages and attachments

- -

*O*nce upon a time, there was a company called Netscape that created a browser to surf the Internet. The browser was called Netscape Navigator and after that Netscape Communicator, and millions of people downloaded it from the Internet for free. Netscape put in the hands of millions of people — including us, your authors — the power to access the exploding number of Web servers. Netscape Navigator made history and changed the world because it changed the Internet from a medium that served scientists into a tool that anyone could use.

Even though Netscape Communicator is freely distributed to anyone who wants it, Netscape Communicator is not open source software in the same way that Linux is. Quite simply, Netscape Communicator is a money-making venture, and Netscape considers the way the software works to be proprietary.

On the other hand, Netscape recognizes the importance of the open source dynamic, which is why it released an open source version of Netscape called *Mozilla*. Now, countless numbers of people are developing and enhancing Mozilla, which is the default browser for Red Hat Linux computers.

Open source software uses a license that basically says, "You can use and modify this software in any way as long as you don't prevent anyone else from doing the same." The open source license has enabled Linux and many other software systems to grow and develop.

In this chapter, we show you how to set up Mozilla for your Red Hat Linux computer so that you can surf the Net and send and receive e-mail.

Our goal in this chapter is to describe how to use its basic features, but Mozilla can do far more than we describe here. For more information about Mozilla, check out the features available under the Help menu, such as the Reference Library or Help contents.

The *Red Hat Linux 7.3 For Dummies* companion CD-ROMs include Mozilla. Mozilla is the open source brother of Netscape and they are quite similar. They have slightly different look and feel but are more the same than not. If you're familiar with Netscape, you'll have no problem with Mozilla.

Setting Up Mozilla As You Like It

If you've ever browsed the Internet (and who hasn't, these days?), the first thing that you want to do is to tailor Mozilla to your preferences. You can do this *offline* (without connecting to the Internet). Use the steps in the following sections to customize Mozilla to your liking and set up Mozilla to be your e-mail client.

Picking a home page and history settings

When you connect to the Internet, you have the option to see a page that you want to see instead of looking at page that someone else wants you to see. And you may also want to tweak your history settings for whatever reason (but certainly not a paranoid one). These steps explain what you need to do:

1. **Start Mozilla by clicking the red Dinosaur icon on the GNOME Panel.**

   The Welcome to Red Hat Linux screen appears in Mozilla, as shown in Figure 9-1. You can use this page to find out more information about Red Hat and its products. We want to concentrate on configuring Mozilla and skip over all the Red Hat information; there's a lot of good information, however, so explore their world at your leisure.

2. **Choose Edit⇨Preferences.**

   The Preferences window appears, as shown in Figure 9-2.

   On the left side of the Preferences window is a list of categories, which you can think of as a map of where you are in the Preferences window.

Figure 9-1:
Mozilla
displaying
info about
Red Hat
Linux.

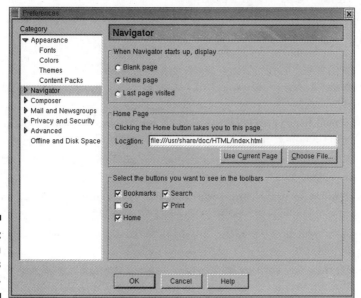

Figure 9-2:
The Mozilla
Preferences
window.

3. Click the arrow next to the Mozilla category to expand it.

Here is where you determine what Web page appears when you start
Mozilla and which Web page loads when you click the Home button on
the Navigation toolbar.

4. **In the Home Page area of the Preferences window, fill in the Location field with the URL of the Web page you'd like to be your home page.**

For instance, type **www.linuxworld.com**, and you see interesting information about Linux whenever you start up your browser.

Mozilla remembers where you have been and lets you select (and go to) a previous location. How long Mozilla remembers (and thus how big the list becomes) depends on how many days of history you choose. The History configuration option determines the length of time in days that the locations you visit are saved. If you're short on disk space, then choose a lower History number, such as 1 or 2 days. Otherwise, leave the default setting alone.

Configuring your e-mail browser

Mozilla gives you an e-mail client to read — amazingly — your e-mail. This section describes how to configure Mozilla to access your e-mail accounts.

1. **Choose Tasks➪Mail & Newsgroups.**

2. **When the Mozilla e-mail browser opens, choose Edit➪Mail & Newsgroups Account Settings.**

The Mail & Newsgroups Account Settings window appears.

3. **Click the Add Account button.**

The Account Wizard, shown in Figure 9-3, starts.

4. **Make sure the ISP or Email Provider radio button is selected and click Next.**

This option is for setting up an ISP e-mail account that you'll use to send and receive e-mail directly through your ISP.

After you click Next, the next page in the Account Wizard window opens, as shown in Figure 9-4.

5. **Type your name and e-mail address in the Your Name and Email Address text boxes respectively and click Next.**

After you click Next, the Incoming Server window appears, as shown in Figure 9-5.

6. **Click in the POP or IMAP radio button, depending on which one your ISP uses.**

IMAP is more powerful and secure than POP. Most ISPs use IMAP so you should not even have to make a choice. However, if you are given a choice, then select IMAP.

Your ISP or local system administrator supplies you with access to the machines that process your e-mail even when you are not connected to the Internet. When you do connect to the Internet, your computer tells the server to deliver the e-mail or send your messages.

7. Type the incoming and outgoing server names in the appropriate text boxes and click Next.

You can find out these names by contacting your ISP if you are connecting to the Internet via a dial-up, DSL, or cable modem. You need to contact your system administrator if connecting to a LAN.

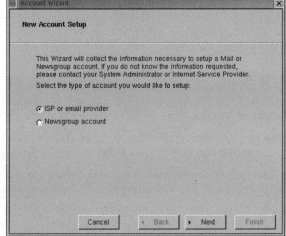

Figure 9-3:
Using the
Mozilla
e-mail
Account
Wizard.

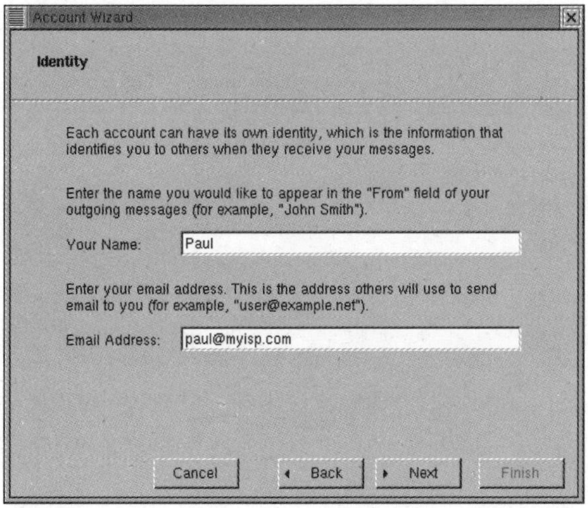

Figure 9-4:
Enter your
name and
Email
address in
the Account
Wizard.

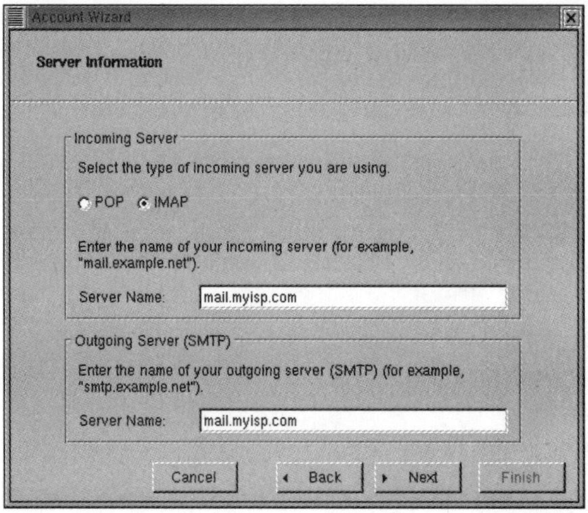

Figure 9-5:
Selecting
the e-mail
server type
and name.

8. **You see the User Name that you selected. Change the name if necessary and then click Next.**

9. **Your account name is displayed in the Account Name: text box. You can change it if necessary. Otherwise, leave it as is and click Next.**

10. **You see the final e-mail configuration window, shown in Figure 9-6. It summarizes the information you entered and also congratulates you on a job well done.**

   Your account information is displayed in the next window. Click on the Back button if you need to change any of the settings. Otherwise, click Finish and you return to the Mail & Newsgroups Account Settings window.

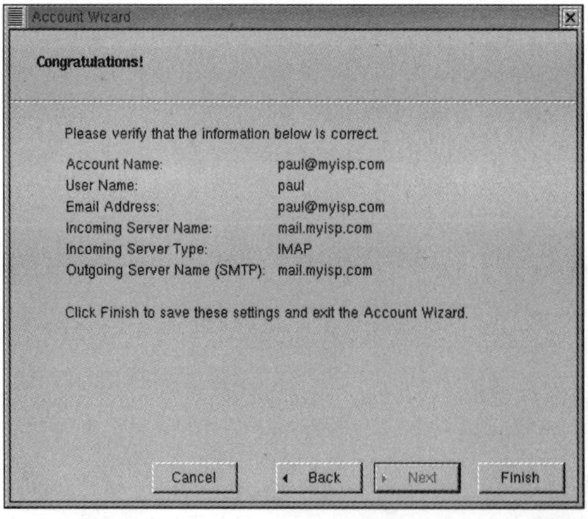

Figure 9-6:
Your e-mail
account
summary.

11. Click the OK button, and your job is done.

You can send and receive e-mail to your heart's content.

Navigating the Net with Mozilla

After you've configured your browser properly, you can connect to the Internet. If you need to configure your Internet connection with a modem, see Chapter 5; see Chapter 6 if you want to configure a broadband connection.

Like other common browsers, you can navigate the Web with Mozilla by typing a URL in the location text box.

You can type over a URL and press the Enter key to send the browser off to another Web page. And you can always click the Back button to return to where you were before, or click the Forward button to revisit a page you've just come from.

Here are a few interesting URLs related to Linux that you can try:

```
www.redhat.com
www.linuxworld.com
www.linuxtoday.com
www.linux.com
www.linux.org
www.linuxcare.com
www.li.org
www.slashdot.org
www.ssc.com
```

Another way of opening a new Web page is to choose File⇨Open Web Location. Mozilla displays the Open Page dialog box, shown in Figure 9-7, where you can type the new URL and then choose whether you want to open that URL in Mozilla.

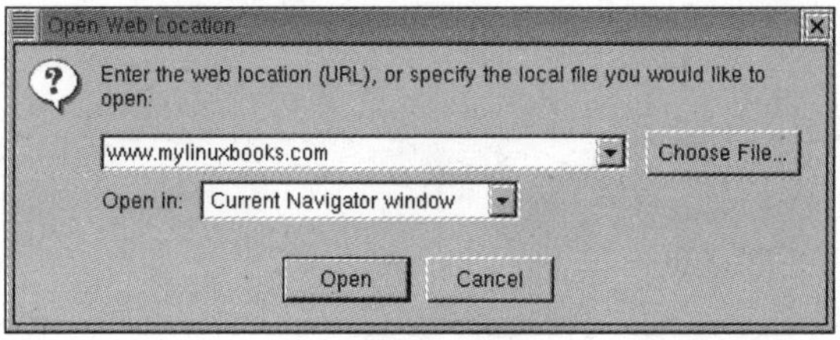

Figure 9-7:
The Open
Page dialog
box.

Open Web Location

Enter the web location (URL), or specify the local file you would like to open:

www.mylinuxbooks.com   Choose File...

Open in: Current Navigator window

Open   Cancel

If you dabble in Web page design or some other programming language (who, *moi?*) you can also use the Open Page dialog box to open a file of HTML or XML code that's on your system. If you decide to load a local file, click the Choose File button. The Open File dialog box, shown in Figure 9-8, springs up so that you can search the file system to find the file you want.

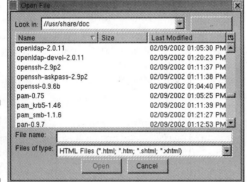

Figure 9-8: Navigating through local files.

Type **electriclichen.com/linuxbierwanderung** into the text box and see the cute penguin (the mascot of the Linux world) going off to drink a beer while working on his Linux notebook, as shown in Figure 9-9.

Figure 9-9: A penguin and his beer — you can send images through the Web.

You can even send sounds through the Web, although illustrating this capability is a little difficult for us to do through the pages of this book. (Sorry. Technology just hasn't caught up with us yet.) Sounds are transmitted over the Internet as files, and you can play them after they reach your browser, computer, and sound card.

Working with E-Mail

Besides its browsing and Web design capabilities, Mozilla can send and receive e-mail, too. This section describes how to send and receive messages with Mozilla's e-mail program. We show you how to set Mozilla up to be your e-mail client in the "Setting Up Mozilla" section earlier in this chapter.

Getting your e-mail

To get your e-mail, you first need to start Mozilla Messenger by choosing Tasks⇨Mail. The Mozilla INBOX appears, as shown in Figure 9-10.

To get your mail, simply click the Get Msg icon. This icon tells Mozilla to make contact with your mail server and see whether any e-mail messages are waiting for you. If you have no new e-mail, a message at the bottom of the screen tells you so. If you do have e-mail, the subject and sender appear in the center of the screen, and the e-mail message itself appears at the bottom of the screen, as shown in Figure 9-11.

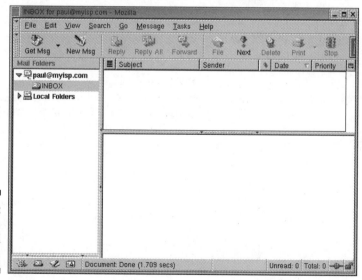

Figure 9-10: The Mozilla INBOX window.

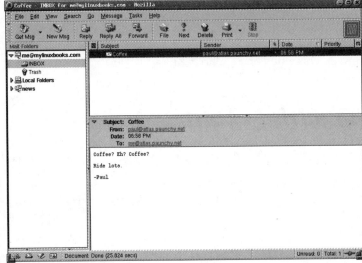

Figure 9-11:
Receiving
an e-mail
message.

You may reply to, forward, or delete a particular message by clicking its Subject line and then clicking the appropriate icon (Reply, Forward, or Delete).

Sending e-mail and attachments

To send an e-mail message, you need to know the recipient's e-mail address. For example, to send an e-mail to the President of CompuGlobalHyperMeganet, you address it to prez@compuglobalhypermeganet.com.

From the Mozilla INBOX window, click the Compose icon. The Compose window appears.

In the To: field, type the e-mail address of the person you're trying to reach. You can also attach a file, an image, or even a sound to your message and send it. To attach a file to your letter, simply click the Attach icon at the top of the Compose window. The Attach File dialog box appears, as shown in Figure 9-12, enabling you to search your hard drive for the file you want to send.

Getting a look at Mozilla's other communication tools

Mozilla provides more than just browsing and e-mail capability. Mozilla also helps you to organize your life a bit. Mozilla provides an address book and a Web composer. Mozilla can also be used to read Internet newsgroups.

The Address Book and Web composer functions can be reached by choosing Mozilla Tasks⇨ Address Book and Tasks⇨Composer menus.

The Address Book is simple to use. You create new entries by clicking on the New Card button and entering the address information. Addresses can be edited and deleted, of course. You can organize individual addresses into customized lists.

The Composer function provides a specialized service. You use the Composer to create Web pages. Because this book does not describe how to create Linux services, we don't describe how to use the Composer. However, if you're a Web page developer, then you'll find Composer to be a good product.

Figure 9-12:
The Attach File dialog box for selecting a file to attach to a message.

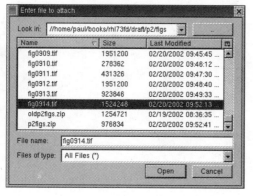

Part III
Linux, Huh! What Is It Good For? Absolutely Everything!

"It's called 'Linux Poker'. Everyone gets to see everyone elses cards, everythings wild, you can play off your opponents hands, and everyone wins except Bill Gates, whose face appears on the Jokers."

In this part . . .

You have finished your initial journey. Red Hat Linux is up an' running, and you've mastered the basics of the Internet and LANs. You've looked at the map enough to know where you are. Now, the big question is: What do you do with it?

Well, one thing that you can do with the computer is warm your feet while you watch the screen saver kick in. You can also confide to all your friends that you have a "Red Hat Linux box" at the next party you go to. Wow, that'll make you popular as they clamor to know when your stock options mature. Or you can actually use your new Red Hat Linux workstation to get things done.

Chapter 10 introduces you to the wonderful world of the GNOME windows environment. GNOME is a friendly li'l guy who likes to put a friendly face on Linux. With GNOME, you can set up the "look and feel" of Linux so that you feel comfortable and at home. Chapter 11 takes you a bit further and introduces some of the many cool things that you can do from GNOME.

Next, in Chapter 12, the serious fun starts. Can you say, "par–*tay*?" (Sorry.) Chapter 12 describes how you can listen to audio CDs and MP3 files. We also show you how to record the sound from CDs. Finally, you become your own recording studio by recording audio — and data if you're a nerd — to CD.

Finally, Chapter 13 takes the audio thing one step further. It shows how to use the commercial product RealPlayer to listen to streams. No, not water streams, but audio and video streams flowing from the Internet. You can listen to radio, audio clips, and watch video, too. RealAudio provides a free version of its player (that we use here), which you can download from the Net. We also use two of the CD/MP3 players — xmms and gtv — that come with Red Hat Linux to play MP3 audio and video. With this knowledge, you never have to leave your couch again. Now, that's living!

We finish Part III by describing how to get work done with StarOffice. Sorry, but reality bites and personal productivity suites — word processor, spreadsheet — are a necessary evil. Gotta make the donuts.

Chapter 10

Gnowing GNOME

• •

In This Chapter

▶ Introducing the X Window System

▶ Managing windows

▶ Closing and killing windows

▶ Understanding the virtual desktop

▶ Logging out of GNOME

▶ Stopping X

▶ Configuring GNOME

• •

The Linux operating system comes with two interfaces in one, a command-line interface (like that found in MS-DOS) and the graphical X Window System, also known as just X, with GNOME sitting on top of X. X itself is said to sit on top of the command-line operating system, allowing total access to the operating system through a graphical interface. (Some operating systems, such as Windows Me, provide you with only a graphical interface.)

GNOME is the default graphical user interface (GUI) for Red Hat Linux. You can also use the other Red Hat Linux GUI, K Desktop Environment (or KDE), if you want. KDE is a fine environment and many people swear that it's great. However, for the sake of brevity we describe how to use GNOME because it's the default.

In this chapter, you find out a little bit about X and the basics for working with GNOME. You also get to mess around with the GNOME Panel and desktop (the Panel is similar to the taskbar on a Windows computer). We also show you some cool but simple maneuvers to manage your windows (such as moving them, changing their size, bringing them to the front, and hiding them in the background). Find out here how to lock your screen, log out of GNOME, and stop X altogether.

Introducing the Amazing X Window System

The GNOME desktop environment provides Red Hat Linux's graphical interface by default (although you can use KDE if you want). GNOME and its Sawfish window manager run on top of the X Window System, also known simply as X, which is the software underneath GNOME that makes your Red Hat Linux computer able to display graphics.

Although the version of X that comes with Red Hat Linux 7.3 is quite sophisticated it's pretty simple to use. This was not always the case. It took a lot of natural — dare we say Darwinian — selection to arrive at the current arrangement of X, and the end result works well.

X has three main parts:

- A graphics server
- A set of graphics libraries
- A set of graphics applications that usually use the graphics libraries

The graphics server is a program that talks to a bunch of important hardware — the video card, keyboard, and mouse — on your system, and runs interference between this hardware and the other graphics software.

X's graphics server receives commands from the set of graphics libraries that are associated by default with specified programs. Sometimes these programs are executed directly on the same system where the graphics device resides; other times, these programs talk across a network to a graphics device on another system. Using X, you can run your program in one part of the world, and someone can see the output of it in another part of the world over the Internet.

For instance, say you're logged into a computer in Australia and want to see what time it is there. You could run the `date` command (from a command line) to see the date and time, but that would be boring. You could instead run the `xclock` program on the remote machine and see a graphical clock displayed on your local computer. You can then verify that the Aussies use clocks that run clockwise and have 24-hour days.

The server program, often called the *X Server,* is not part of the operating system, as it is in some other operating systems. Instead, X Server is a *user-level* program — a special and complex one.

Separation anxiety? Not Linux

Unlike in the Microsoft world, Linux is not defined by its graphical interface. Microsoft Windows includes both the operating system — the software that makes for a usable computer — and its familiar graphical interface. The two are closely intertwined and essentially inseparable. Linux and X, however, are completely separate animals.

So what? Well, for one, separating the two makes for a more reliable and robust workstation.

Without the burden of having to incorporate graphics into itself, the Linux operating system can remain a lean, mean fighting machine. The X Window System concentrates on providing graphics and does not interfere with the operating system. Separating the two also makes for varied and interesting development efforts.

The following sections discuss each of the three major types of programs in Red Hat Linux that interact with X:

- ✔ Window managers, which control the appearance of windows, dialog boxes, menus, and other on-screen objects that enable you to click and type to make choices and run programs. GNOME and KDE are the window managers that Red Hat gives you to use.

- ✔ Terminal emulators are programs that allow you to type in commands and see the results. Terminal emulators are often used to connect to other computers using communication programs like Open Secure Shell.

- ✔ General applications, such as xclock and Mozilla, provide the functionality that help you see the time and browse the Web.

Comprehending window managers

Window managers, like GNOME's Sawfish window manager, are programs that receive commands indirectly from the user through mouse clicks and keystrokes. The window manager passes those commands to a set of graphics libraries, which then communicate with the X server to manipulate windows on the graphics device (usually your monitor screen). All this happens *seamlessly,* behind the scenes. All you see are the windows and other objects on-screen.

Sawfish acts like a playground monitor; it's the central point of control for the major windows you see on the screen (and even some windows that you can't see). It blows a whistle when a window gets unruly. The window manager can also serve as a desktop, where you can use it to launch applications.

A window manager isn't necessary, but it would be difficult to use more than one or two applications at the same time without also using a window manager. (The applications themselves would need to be written to allow resizing, window positioning, and so on. What a drag that would be for a programmer!)

Among the many functions they perform, window managers may also maintain an *icon bar,* which keeps clickable icons easy to find and manage. But the most important thing to remember about window managers in X is that they are just user-level programs like any other — they are not part of the system. You have a choice of window managers, and each has different capabilities, although a discussion of window managers other than GNOME and their capabilities is outside the scope of this book.

The *Red Hat Linux 7.3 For Dummies* CD-ROMs contain several window managers including the GNOME Sawfish window manager, KDE, and the previous Linux standard Fvwm. GNOME Sawfish is the default for Red Hat Linux and so is the window manager used in this book. KDE is similar to GNOME in many ways. You can also use good old Fvwm to start applications (and stop them of course), move windows, shrink windows, expand windows, and do everything but wash windows. Just think, you can use your system without ever typing a command!

Going old-school with the terminal emulators

The second main type of program under X is the *terminal emulator,* shown in Figure 10-1, a program that emulates the old-style terminal from within the GUI. Back in the good old days, you could only type in text commands and see the results in text and you did that on a terminal. You may be wondering why you would want to simulate a dumb, inexpensive terminal when you paid a lot of money for a neat graphics monitor. Shouldn't every program be graphical?

Well, in the early days of X, few graphical programs were available. Most programs were written to run on nongraphical interfaces and did not include the libraries that create graphical programs on an X Server. That means that to run both graphical and nongraphical programs, the dumb terminal had to be emulated through software.

When you start a terminal emulator, the emulator usually executes a shell and gives you a command-line prompt. You type commands at this command prompt, and the results are output to the terminal emulator window. GNOME provides a terminal emulator called the *GNOME terminal.* You can start the GNOME terminal by clicking the icon that looks like a TV monitor with a footprint on it. You can find this icon on the GNOME main menu bar at the bottom of the screen.

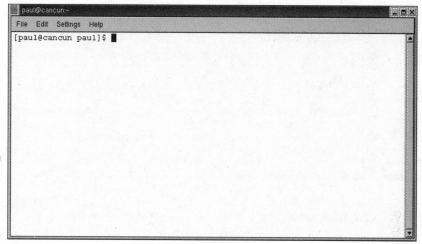

Figure 10-1:
A terminal
emulator
window.

Waxing vague with general applications

The third main type of program is the general application. A general application can materialize in various forms, including

- Text editors, such as xedit, which looks a lot like a terminal emulator but is much different
- Applications such as xfig, which manipulates images, and xpaint, which enables you to draw objects
- Games such as Doom

These programs would be impossible (or at least very hard) to run in a nongraphical interface. Can you imagine playing Doom with command-line prompts?

Getting Earthy with GNOME

To check out the GNOME interface, log in to your Linux computer. Unless you specified otherwise during installation, you see the GNOME window environment appear, as shown in Figure 10-2. By default, the GNOME Hint screen starts when you log in.

If X does not automatically start when you boot your computer, then you need to start X manually by typing the conveniently named startx command at a command prompt. If X fails to start, consult Chapter 20.

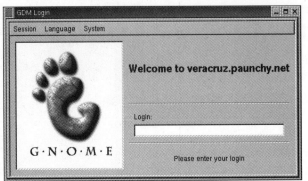

Figure 10-2:
The GNOME
login
window.

GNOME consists of the following three major elements:

- ✔ **The desktop:** Quite simply, the desktop is the space where you do your work. The desktop comes preconfigured with several icons that include links to your home directory, Red Hat's home page, the Dialup Configuration tool, your floppy disk, and the Trash bin.

  When you click the home directory or floppy disk icons, the GNOME File Manager (the Midnight Commander application) starts and displays the contents of those directories. The *File Manager* is a graphical system for working with files and directories in your home directory as well as the entire file system.

- ✔ **Standard applications:** Programs such as the Nautilus network and file system manager, the GNOME Help Browser, and so on.

  The GNOME Help Browser provides a comprehensive and easy-to-follow tutorial and takes you through all GNOME basics. The Help Browser also provides a good reference.

- ✔ **The Panel:** The menu bar that runs across the bottom edge of your GNOME screen.

Mucking about with basic window manipulation

GNOME performs all the basic graphical functions that you expect a GUI to do. You can move windows, resize them, minimize them, and so on. The following sections show you how to perform typical window manipulations in GNOME. Figure 10-3 shows a typical application — Mozilla — running in a window.

Figure 10-3:
A typical
window
(Mozilla)
running
inside
GNOME.

Getting focused

Before you can do anything to a window, you have to get its attention. When you have a window's attention, it's said to have *focus*. Depending on how you've set up GNOME, you can give a window focus with GNOME in several ways, including the following:

- ✔ Click the window's name in the Panel.
- ✔ Click the window's title bar, which is at the top of the window.
- ✔ Click a part of the window itself, which typically also makes the window the topmost one.
- ✔ If you're working in an office with a lot of people, then you can shout "Hey you, wake up!" While this tactic isn't likely to wake your window up, it sure is fun.

In this book, we stick with the Red Hat/GNOME default of clicking a window to focus it.

Moving day

To move a window, click anywhere on the window's title bar and hold down the left mouse button. As long as you continue to hold the left mouse button down, the window moves anywhere that you move your mouse. Release the button, and the window stays there.

Resizing windows to your heart's content

Sometimes a window is a little too big or a little too small, and you know life would be much easier if you could just nudge that window into shape. To do that, position the mouse cursor on either the lower-left or lower-right corner of a window until the cursor changes into a double-sided arrow. Click and drag the window's outline to your desired size. Release the mouse button and the window takes the new size.

Another way to resize a window is to click the far, upper-left corner. A menu appears. Click the Window Size submenu and you get another menu that allows you to toggle either the height, width, or entire window between its normal (default) size and the entire desktop.

Making a molehill out of a mountain

Now that you've put a lot of windows on the screen, how can you get rid of a few or all of them? Well, you can *minimize* (or *iconify*) a window by clicking the bold, underscore button towards the upper-right corner, which removes the window from the desktop and places it in a storage area on the right side of the Panel. If you're in a particularly devilish mood, you can be more drastic and *close* a window. Figure 10-4 shows the previously open Mozilla window minimzed — you can see its icon in the GNOME panel along the lower, central edge of the screen.

Here are a few ways to get rid of a window, starting with the least drastic and escalating to outright window death:

- ✔ Take advantage of any exit buttons or menu options that the window or application in the window give you. For example, many applications allow you to choose File⇨Exit or File⇨Quit to close the application.

- ✔ Click the X button in the upper-right corner of the window's title bar to close the window.

- ✔ Click the upper-left corner of the window or the title bar and then choose either the Close or Destroy option in the menu that appears. Close attempts to contact the application and ask it nicely to stop itself, whereas Destroy doesn't care what the application thinks and stops it immediately.

- ✔ You also have the option of completely closing the application by right-clicking its icon in the Panel and choosing either Close or Kill App in the menu that appears. The difference between the two is that Kill App closes the program if it does not respond to the Close command. Kill App isn't as nice as Close and potentially could cause problems if you are running a program like a database that is actively manipulating data.

You can return a minimized window to the desktop by clicking the icon that corresponds to the window on the Panel.

Figure 10-4:
Mozilla
minimized
inside
GNOME.

Mozilla minimized to icon status

Making a mountain out of a mole hill

To make a window fill up the entire screen, click the Maximize button in the upper-right corner of the window. If you check out those buttons to the right of the title bar of a typical window, the Maximize button is the one in the middle; it looks like a square and is similar in action to the Cascade button in Windows.

Playing with the Panel

The GNOME Panel is the menu bar along the bottom of the desktop. The Panel is similar to the taskbar in Windows, providing a location to place common menus and applets for easy starting or viewing. The Panel also gives you a view of the virtual desktop (described later in this chapter) and lets you keep track of minimized windows.

By default, Red Hat Linux places icons on the Panel for accessing the GNOME Help Browser, the Configuration tool, the GNOME terminal emulation program, and Mozilla. You can start any of these programs by clicking its icon. There is also a simple clock placed at the far right of the Panel.

Another important element of the Panel is the Main Menu button at the far left, which is used to access all the standard GNOME applications and configuration tools. Click the Main Menu button, shown in Figure 10-5, which looks like a small footprint located in the lower-left corner of the screen. You can choose from any of the menus displayed when you click the Main Menu button.

Configuration tool

GNOME terminal program

Clock

Figure 10-5:
The GNOME
Panel.

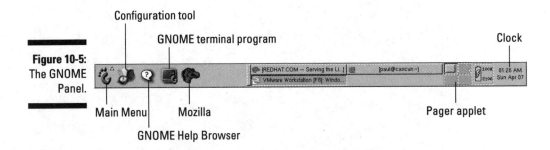

Main Menu | Mozilla

Pager applet

GNOME Help Browser

The Programs submenu is pretty much self-explanatory. For example, the System menu contains programs used to configure GNOME and other systems tied to GNOME and X. The Multimedia menu provides access to your CD player, while the Internet menu provides access to applications that help you connect to the Internet.

You can use the Panel submenu to modify the configuration and behavior of the Panel itself. For example, if you click the Main Menu button and choose Panel⇨Add to Panel⇨Applet⇨Amusements⇨gEyes, you get the nifty pair of eyes applet added to the Panel. The eyes follow your mouse around the screen — ohh, scary. gEyes demonstrates the great functionality that enters your life when you use Red Hat Linux. (You can remove the eyes by right-clicking its icon and selecting the Remove from Panel option.)

One of the other interesting functions of the Panel menu is the Add New Launcher function. Click the Main Menu button and choose Panel⇨Add to Panel⇨Launcher Buttons. The Create Launcher Applet window appears, as shown in Figure 10-6. By entering the pathname of an application, you can add a new applet to the Panel that *launches,* or starts, that application.

Give it a try. For example, if you download the StarOffice desktop productivity suite (which includes a full-fledged word processor, spreadsheet, and so on — we describe StarOffice in Chapter 12), you can add an applet for it to your Panel so that you don't have to haggle with menus to launch it. From the Create Launcher Applet window, add the name, any comments, and the command to launch the program. The instructions in Chapter 12 have you install StarOffice into your home directory — for example /home/*login*/office52/soffice — so if you want to add a StarOffice applet to your Panel, you type this pathname (switching *login* for your login name) into the Command text box. If you click the No Icon button, you are given a few pages of standard icons that you can use to distinguish your new applet from others on the Panel; in our case we chose the `gnome-tigert.png` as our icon mascot. Figure 10-7 shows the finished applet launcher window.

After you finish editing the Create Launcher Applet window, click OK. The icon is added to your Panel, as shown in Figure 10-8. You can create a launcher for any application on your Linux computer in the same way.

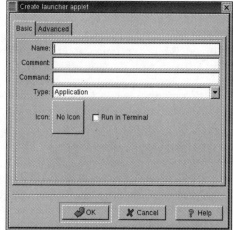

Figure 10-6:
The blank
Create
Launcher
Applet
window.

Figure 10-7:
The
StarOffice
launcher
applet is
born.

Figure 10-8:
The
StarOffice
launcher
applet icon
on the
Panel.

StarOffice launcher applet icon

You can create an icon on your desktop for any application found in the GNOME Main Menu. Just click the Main Menu button, find the menu item for the application that you want an icon for, and then left-click the application and hold the mouse button down. While continuing to hold down the button, drag the mouse cursor to any open area on the GNOME desktop. Release the mouse button and an icon for that application is placed on the desktop. You can then start the application by double-clicking the icon.

Working on your virtual desktop

After using GNOME for a while, you'll probably know that you can create lots and lots of windows on the screen. You may even lose windows behind other windows. Perhaps you wish that your monitor was larger just so you could open up more windows and do more things at one time, or maybe you just don't want to close down or minimize one application before going to another application.

Well, monitors are expensive, and a lot of systems can have only one graphics card, so you're probably stuck using a single monitor. But you don't have to be stuck with one *screen*. X, with the help of GNOME, can give you both virtual screens and virtual desktops.

A *virtual desktop* enables you to have more than one desktop screen to work on. It's like having four desks to spread out all your work in front of you. You have the option of organizing your work — terminal screens, window applications like Netscape, Mozilla, StarOffice, and such — on different desktops. The default for Red Hat Linux GNOME is four virtual desktops. The virtual desktop display icon — the *pager applet* — on the far-right side of the GNOME Panel controls the virtual desktops.

By clicking any of the four Desk Guide buttons, you are placed in the corresponding desktop. Click the lower-right one, and you go to that screen. Give it a try!

You can easily switch between desktops by turning on Edge Flipping. When active, Edge Flipping allows you to switch to an adjacent desktop by moving the mouse cursor to the edge of the screen. After a short delay, you are placed in the new desktop. Edge Flopping — er, Flipping — is turned off by default in Red Hat Linux's installation of GNOME. To turn it on:

1. **Click the Main Menu button and then choose the Start Here option at the top of the pop-up menu.**

   The Nautilus Start Here screen appears.

2. **Click the Preferences icon.**

3. **Click the Sawfish Window Manager and then click Workspaces.**

4. **Click the Edge Flipping tab.**

5. **From the window shown in Figure 10-9, click the Select the Next Desktop When the Pointer Hits Screen Edge option.**

6. **Click the Hitting the Screen Edge Selects the Next option and change it from Viewport to Workspace.**

7. **(Optional) You can also change the time you have to wait for the flip by changing the Milliseconds to Delay Before Flipping number.**

8. **Click OK to save the changes.**

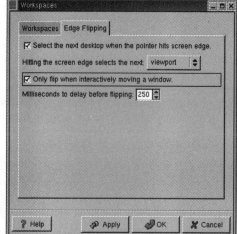

Figure 10-9:
Turning
on Edge
Flipping.

You may notice that the upper-left block in the pager applet (the virtual desktop display), shown back in Figure 10-5, seems to be colored or seems to contain smaller blocks. That upper-left block represents the virtual desktop you are in right now. The smaller rectangle within the upper-left block is a window (in this case, it's The Gimp, which is the graphical image manipulation tool used to create the figure).

Getting out of GNOME or X

If you want to leave your computer on but don't want to leave your computer open to anyone just walking along, you can save the time logging out of your GNOME desktop by using the screen lock. To do so, click the Main Menu button and choose Lock Screen. The screensaver is displayed. To return to productive life and your desktop, press any key or wiggle your mouse and enter your password in the X Screensaver window that appears.

Securing your computer while you step out

Locking your screen is actually one of the best security features that you can use. GNOME preconfigures an icon for locking your screen. You must enter your password to get your screen back after using this icon.

To use this icon, click the little padlock icon that sits almost all the way to the left of the GNOME Panel. Your screen locks up and you must enter your password to get back in. Locking your screen is a good idea when you're going to be away from it for even a minute or two.

Locking up the shop

When you've finished for the day and want to go home (or just upstairs), you need to log out. Click the Main Menu button and choose Log Out. The Really Log Out? screen appears. Click Yes to log out. You also have the options to *halt* (shut down) or reboot your computer.

eXterminating X

When you can't get your applications to respond to you, you can simply stop X, which kills all the programs running under it. To do so, press the Ctrl+Alt+Backspace keys all at once. If you started X manually, you can then log out of the account. If X is started automatically at boot time (as this book assumes), then you get the X login screen and you can log back in.

Tinkering with GNOME

You can start the GNOME Nautilus by clicking the Main Menu button and then clicking the Start Here option at the top of the pop-up menu. The Nautilus control utility — called Start Here — appears, as shown in Figure 10-10. Here you can modify all the basic properties of GNOME. Choose Desktop⇨ Background and you can set the color and other aspects of the desktop. Choose Desktop⇨Screensaver⇨Xjack and you switch from the default random screensaver to the "All work and no play makes Jack a dull boy" screensaver. Not a bad selection for those long winters spent at peaceful resorts with plenty of time to write Linux books!

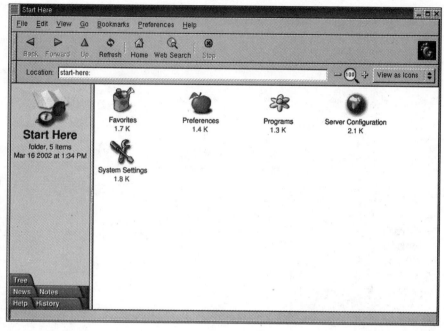

Figure 10-10:
The GNOME
Nautilus
control
utility —
Start
Here —
window.

The Nautilus also lets you configure things other than screensavers with maniacal rantings. We leave it to you to explore the wonderful world of setting your keyboard bell and such. This system gives you lots of flexibility.

You can reach the Sawfish window manager by clicking on the Preferences⇨Sawfish icons in the Start Here window. The Sawfish window is shown in Figure 10-11.

Focus Behavior and Appearance are the important menus here. The Focus Behavior menus let you change the style of how windows appear as they are moved and resized. More importantly, the Focus Behavior menus enable you to change how the movement of your mouse controls windows. This is called *keyboard focus.*

By default, you have to click a window to bring it to the surface. You can change this so that merely moving the mouse cursor to a window focuses it. The sloppy focus behavior works as a compromise by bringing focus to a window when you move the mouse there, but not raising it to the top of the screen until you click the mouse button.

The Appearance menu gives you the ability to change the window frame styles; a *frame style* is the way a window border looks. For example, click the Default Frame Style (Theme) and you get a selection of window borders. They're fun to play with and give you the ability to customize your windows to your taste.

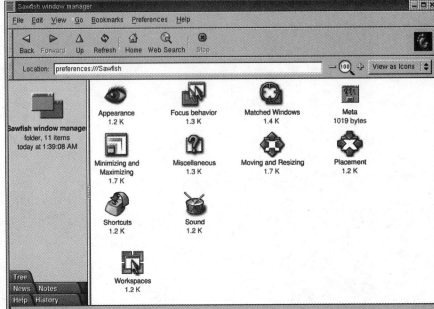

Figure 10-11:
The Sawfish
window
manager
window.

The Miscellaneous section provides control over settings, such as how long it takes for tooltips to appear and for keyboard focus to take effect. The other options provide control over the remaining look and feel of your desktop; for example, you can control the number of virtual windows displayed, your audio system (if you have one), and other such things. There are too many other menu options and combinations to describe here, so be adventurous and give the Sawfish window manager a cruise!

Chapter 11

Gnowing More Applications

In This Chapter

▶ Introducing Nautilus, the GNOME file, and integration manager

▶ Introducing more useful GNOME applications

▶ Introducing Ximian Evolution e-mail and personal organizer

*I*n this chapter, you find out how to use several of the most useful applications that are packaged with Red Hat Linux. The first one is called Nautilus and is an integral part of the GNOME desktop system; Nautilus provides the means for seamlessly navigating both your computer and the Internet. The second application is the new e-mail/organizer called Evolution. We also introduce several other useful applications. These applications help make your Red Hat Linux computer more useful for your everyday work.

Navigating with the Nautilus File/Internet Integration Manager

Being the boss doesn't make you a bad person. It's just a job. Right? Well that little GNOME guy is a good worker and doesn't get paid much. Just press a key here, click a button there, and you can boss him around like any worthy pointy head Dilbert manager. GNOME even comes with its own file and integration manager that saves you work and makes time for those long lunches.

Nautilus is GNOME's file and Internet navigator system. Nautilus follows in the tradition of all good file managers, graphically displaying the files and directories on your computer. You can copy, move, delete, and execute files by pointing and clicking; creating directories and viewing file details are a snap, too. But Nautilus goes a step further and can be used to configure your GNOME desktop. But that's not all! Nautilus can also navigate the Internet, access multimedia, and slice and dice! Not a bad deal, considering that it works for free.

Waking up the little guy

Red Hat Linux configures the Nautilus to start automatically when you log in. Nautilus appears toward the end of the login process, as shown in Figure 11-1, and works as a file manager showing the contents of your home directory. Should you want to start it manually — after you've closed it, for example — then click the Main Menu button and choose Programs⇨Applications⇨ Nautilus.

The main menu follows familiar menu formats (File, Edit, and so on) and does all the things that you would expect those menus to do. The toolbar immediately below the main menu enables you to quickly move up one directory (Up) and redo previous moves (Back and Forward). It also lets you rescan a directory, go to your home directory, and change the way that icons are displayed. The Rescan function, for example, is useful if you create a new file via a terminal screen. The file doesn't show up in the File Manager until you move to another directory and return, or else rescan.

Putting him through his paces

Most people use file managers to do the basics: copying, moving, and deleting files, and such. We introduce show how to use Nautilus to do those basic tasks and leave the rest (advanced functions) for you to explore on your own.

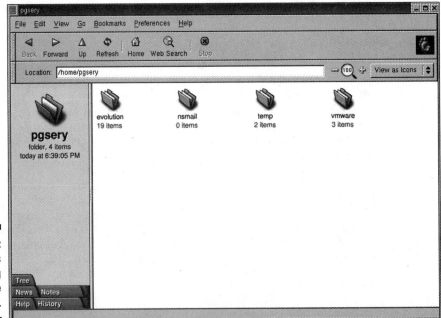

Figure 11-1:
Nautilus
working
as a file
manager.

Moving files and directories

Moving a file or directory is as simple as clicking and dragging the item you want to move to the directory that you want to move it to. Release the button and you have moved your file or directory.

You can move multiple files by clicking and dragging the mouse cursor over the files that you want. The mouse cursor creates a rectangular outline and highlights all the files within that box. Next, click anywhere within the highlighted box and drag the mouse cursor to the desired directory. Release the mouse button and the files move to the specified directory.

Copying files and directories

Copying a file or directory is a bit more complicated then moving one. Rather than simply clicking and dragging an icon someplace, you have to right-click the file or directory icon and choose Copy from the menu that appears, as shown in Figure 11-2. The menu lists all the options available from the File Manager. Choose Copy and another dialog box appears. Within that dialog box, you can manually enter the pathname of where you want to copy the file, or you can use the Browse function. If you click Browse, yet another dialog box appears, and you can click and search for the target directory.

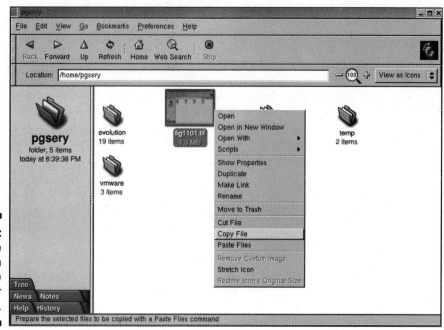

Figure 11-2:
Choose
Copy from
the File
Manager
menu.

You can copy multiple files and directories in the same manner that you move them (see the preceding section); you simply trace a box around the files that you want to copy by clicking and dragging the mouse cursor. Next, right-click any of the highlighted icon names (but not the white space around the icon and names themselves) to open a menu with three options: Copy, Move, and Delete. Choose Copy and follow the directions described in the last three sentences of the preceding section.

Deleting files and directories

Deleting files and directories is much the same process as copying them. You right-click the desired file or directory icon and choose Delete from the menu that appears. You're then prompted to verify that you really want to delete that file or directory. Exercise your normal caution and self-preservation skills before you click Yes.

Deleting directories is naturally a little more complicated. When you choose to delete an entire directory that isn't empty, you're prompted to delete it recursively, which means that any subdirectories will be deleted, too. Answer Yes and every file and directory within that directory is removed.

Finally, you can delete multiple files and directories. Again, you trace a box by clicking and dragging the mouse cursor. Right-click the icons or icon names (but not the white space around the icon and name). The simple menu, as described previously, appears. Choose Delete and then answer Yes in the confirmation window.

You can change the confirmation behavior of moving, copying, or deleting functions. Choose Settings⇨Preferences and select the Confirmation tab in the Preferences window. You can then toggle various options that control such behavior.

Creating directories

To create a new directory, choose File⇨New⇨Directory. The Create a New Directory dialog box appears in which you type the name of the new directory. Linux creates the directory in the current working directory, which is the directory that the File Manager currently shows.

Viewing files and directories

By default, files and directories display in iconic — symbolic — form. The only information that an icon shows is the name and whether an item is a file or directory. You can see more information by clicking the View as Icons, View as List, or View as ... buttons that appear when you click the View menu button at the top of the screen. Figure 11-3 shows the window after the View as List button is clicked.

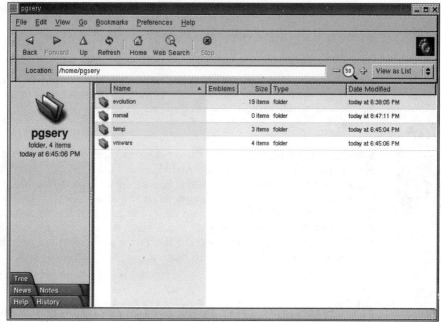

Figure 11-3:
Changing
the
Nautilus's
worldview.

The following list describes the differences between these views:

- ✔ **Icons view:** Displays the symbol (icon) and indicates whether an item is a file or directory. Regular file icons take several forms, but text and configuration files look like pieces of paper with a corner folded, and executable files look like pistons. Links, devices, and so on take other forms. Directories take the form of a partially open file folder. Icons are evenly placed across the entire File Manager screen. Icons tend to make distinguishing files and directories easier but take up more space on-screen.

- ✔ **List view:** Displays the size and time stamp of each file and directory, as well as their names.

- ✔ **Custom view:** Enables you to choose what file attributes to display. You can select the attributes by choosing Settings⇨Preferences and selecting the Custom View tab. From there, you can add and delete the attributes from a list of possible attributes.

Running programs and scripts

Nautilus is such a hard worker that it happily launches commands for you. Right-click the icon that you want to run to open a submenu, and then choose Open. For example, if you click the xclock icon in the /usr/bin/X11 directory, the xclock appears on your desktop. (Double-clicking the icon also works.)

Managers are generally not that smart. But Nautilus is, and it tells the manager what to do when it encounters various file types. If you open a nonexecutable file, such as a PDF file, the file manager knows what program to use in order to view it.

Nautilus recognizes various file types because it keeps a list — its own Rolodex of sorts. These file types are known as Multipurpose Internet Mail Extensions (MIME) types, and they define what type of information a file stores.

You can use Nautilus to create shortcut icons on your desktop that point to files or applications. In Nautilus, just click and drag any file or application to any blank part of the desktop and then release the mouse button. An icon is placed on the desktop. You can then start the application by double clicking its icon. If the icon points to a data file (such as a text file, for example) and Nautilus knows how to handle its MIME type, then Nautilus launches the appropriate application to open the file. Otherwise, Nautilus prompts you to tell it which application to use to open it.

Navigating the Net with Nautilus

Nautilus is more than just a file manager; it's a double and triple threat. You can use it as a browser to navigate the Internet. Nautilus is just full of surprises.

Nautilus is powerful, but it's not a full-featured Web browser. It's designed to extend your GNOME desktop from your Linux workstation's hard drive to the Internet. The idea is to minimize the number of applications and utilities that you need to do simple, everyday tasks.

Nautilus performs admirably to that end, but the GNOME people wisely didn't burden the slim Nautilus system with every function including the kitchen sink. That wouldn't be nearly as fun as providing a link to the kitchen sink. You choose between using Galeon (a lightweight browser), Mozilla, or Netscape when you view a Web page. Simply click the appropriate button, and the page opens in any of those browsers.

To view Web pages, simply type an address in the location bar just like you would with Mozilla. Nautilus opens and displays the Web page. It's just that simple.

You can search for files and directories by using Nautilus's search function. Click the Web Search button, and Nautilus opens a search engine. Nautilus knows what's what and uses Google to do its searches.

Nautilus provides the ability to bookmark your favorite Web sites. Nautilus's bookmarks work just like Mozilla's. Go to a Web page and choose Bookmark➪Add. You can then add the URL as a bookmark to a subfolder. You can also organize existing bookmarks by choosing Bookmarks➪Manage.

Checking Out Some Handy Linux Programs

GNOME not only does the work described in the previous sections of this chapter, but also works overtime. Many cool programs are bundled along with Red Hat Linux. A few of the particularly useful ones are described in the following sections.

Going graphical with the Gimp

The Gimp is more than just a graphics-viewing program — it's also a great graphical manipulator. Click the GNOME Main Menu button and choose Programs➪Graphics➪The Gimp to start The Gimp.

The Gimp opens up several screens, including a Tip window. If you choose File➪Open, you can open, view, and even modify your graphics files. You can also copy any window, or your entire screen by using The Gimp's Acquire function. Choose File➪Acquire➪Screen Shot. You can then save any images that you want. (This is how most of the figures in this book were obtained.)

Making spreadsheets with Gnumeric

GNOME includes a powerful spreadsheet program called Gnumeric (pronounced Gee-numeric), which is capable of creating and editing spreadsheets that do most of what any general-purpose user wants to do. It lacks some of the high-level functions that other commercial products have but is useful for doing everyday types of tasks.

To start Gnumeric, click the Main Menu button and then choose Programs➪Applications➪Gnumeric. You do your spreadsheet thing — calculate the millions of royalty dollars you plan to make, for instance — in the spreadsheet shown in Figure 11-4. To save your millions, choose File➪Save As.

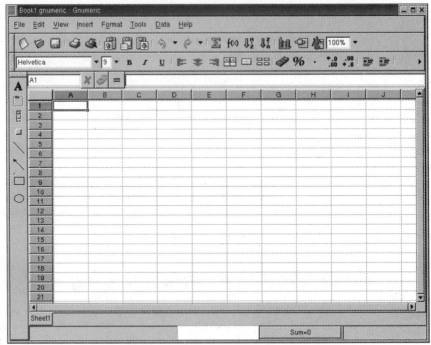

Reading PDF files

You can view portable document format (PDF) files with xpdf. PDF files are used to provide a lot of documentation on the Web. PDF files are nice because they enable you to page forward and backwards through a document rather than having to view the whole thing at once.

Start xpdf by logging in as any user, clicking the GNOME Main Menu button, and then choosing Programs⇨Applications⇨xpdf.

What you see isn't very interesting — just a blank page with some buttons pushed off to the bottom of the window. To open a file, you need to right-click your mouse button anywhere on the blank page and choose Open. The xpdf: Open window pops up.

Download or copy a PDF file of your choice and open it up. An example of a PDF document appears in Figure 11-5.

You can use the forward and backward buttons to page through the document. You can also use the Print button to print all or parts of a document. The binocular button is used to search for text. Have fun!

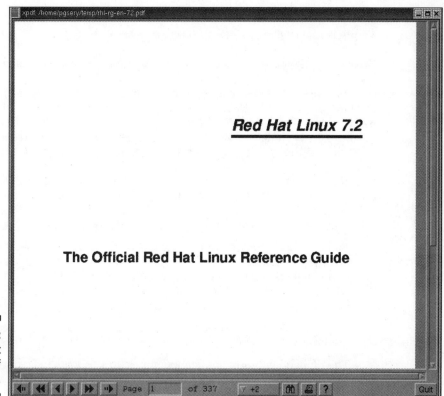

Red Hat Linux 7.2

The Official Red Hat Linux Reference Guide

Figure 11-5:
A document
in the xpdf
viewer.

You can see other applications by clicking the GNOME start button and choosing Programs⇨Applications. You'll see the menu of applications waiting to be used. New applications are constantly being added to the GNOME universe. Go to www.gnome.org/applist to see what's available.

The Ximian Evolution Revolution

Evolution is a workhorse. Evolution's calendar and related utilities provide the last significant desktop productivity tools that Linux has lacked. As Chapter 14 explains, StarOffice and other similar suites enable you to do word processing in Linux. The new Ximian Evolution provides the calendaring capability. Evolution provides the following:

- Calendar
- E-mail
- Task master (to-do list)

✔ Contact manager

✔ Personal Digital Assistant (PDA) manager

You can use Evolution's calendar, to-do manager, and contact manager with your PDA. In this section, we concentrate on using Evolution to back up your PDA, because that's one of more interesting and fun things you can do. You can find out more about using the calendar by reading Evolutions' online documentation (click on Help) and experimenting with it. Because the e-mail functionality is similar to Mozilla's, you can use the Mozilla instructions in Chapter 9 as your guide to configuring Evolution's e-mail functions.

One of the cool things that you can use Evolution's pilot-link utility for is to back up your PDA databases to your computer. To do so, follow these steps:

1. **Plug your Pilot cradle into your computer's serial port.**

   The cable attached to your cradle has a female 9-pin (called a DB9) plug attached to it. Most, if not all, modern computers have a 9-pin male plug that connects to serial port one, which is controlled by the /dev/ttyS0 Linux device. (In the DOS/Windows world, /dev/ttyS0 is equivalent to COM1, /dev/ttyS1 is COM2, and so on.)

2. **Click the GNOME start button and choose Programs⬧Applications⬧ Evolution.**

   The Ximian Evolution application starts up as shown in Figure 11-6.

Figure 11-6:
The Evolution e-mail and desktop organizer.

3. **Click the Contacts button.**

4. **Choose Tools⇨Pilot settings.**

   The Welcome to gnome-pilot wizard opens.

5. **Click Next and the window shown in Figure 11-7 appears.**

   You need to tell Evolution where to find your PDA. Click the Port menu and choose the serial device. The device is probably /dev/ttyS0 or /dev/ttyS1. There's no shame in trial and error, so choose each port in order until you find the right one.

   Don't worry about selecting the speed. The default value is adequate unless you have a very old computer.

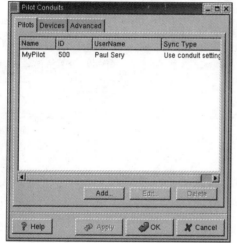

Figure 11-7:
Starting the
Evolution
configur-
ation
Wizard.

6. **Click the No, I've Never Used Sync Software with This Pilot Before button.**

7. **Type your login (any name will do) name in the User Name window. Click Next.**

8. **Press the synchronize (for instance, HotSync for a Palm Pilot) button on the PDA cradle and the calendar database is copied to your Red Hat Linux computer.**

   Evolution can also synchronize your contact list and address book. Pretty cool, eh?

Running a computer inside a computer

If you want to use applications like Microsoft Word, we have good news for you: You don't need to use a Windows computer. VMware, Inc. produces a truly great product called VMwareWorkstation, which offers a different solution. VMwareWorkstation creates a virtual PC inside your real one. The virtual computer "looks" just like a real computer to the operating system that you install on it. All you have to do is install VMwareWorkstation and then install Windows in the virtual machine. The virtual Windows machine runs in an X Window under Linux, and you get the best of both worlds.

We run virtual Windows computers on our Linux workstations to get those functions that aren't yet available under Linux. For instance, this book was written using StarOffice, which is a Linux application. However, StarOffice lacks the sophisticated collaboration tools that are essential during the editing process. Editors and authors trade a lot of information back and forth after the initial drafts are complete, and although StarOffice can perform those tasks, using Microsoft Word is easier.

The VMwareWorkstation license costs $100 for personal use — more if you use it professionally. You can also download a temporary 30-day license. The actual software doesn't cost anything, and you can download it or purchase it on CD-ROM. Go to www.vmware.com/download to get the temporary license and software. Of course, to install Windows on a virtual computer, you need a valid Windows license. (You can run Linux under VMware, too!)

Chapter 12

Configuring Your Red Hat Linux Sound System

In This Chapter

▶ Playing your CDs and MP3s

▶ Setting up your sound card

▶ Ripping your CDs

▶ Burning your own CDs

*I*magine that you're sitting alone, working at your computer. Feeling lonely? Want a little company? Well, we can't provide friends, but we can show you how your system can provide some tunes.

In this chapter, we show you how to have fun with your Red Hat Linux computer. Red Hat Linux provides all the tools that you need to make your workstation into a sound system, including all the necessary applications to play CDs and MP3s, several CD and MP3 players, and tools for connecting your PC to a sound card and speakers.

Playing CDs and MP3s

Everyone wants a little music in his or her life. That's why you bought a $1,000 computer instead of a $300 stereo system, right? No? Well even so, you can use your Red Hat Linux machine as a music system if you want. This section describes how to set up your computer to play music CDs and MP3s.

Playing CDs and MP3s with xmms

Several CD players are available to Linux users: gtcd, xplaycd, and xmms are the ones that ship with Red Hat Linux. We use the xmms application here because it has a slick interface — the most important thing you could want — and plays both CDs and MP3s. Well, actually we see the MP3 thing as the reason to use it, but it does have a nice look to it.

Log in as any user, click the GNOME Main Menu button, and choose Programs➪Multimedia➪XMMS. The xmms application appears, as shown in Figure 12-1.

Figure 12-1:
The xmms
main
screen.

The xmms program is installed by default as part of the Workstation installation. The xmms application is (surprise!) part of the xmms RPM package.

If you've used a CD player — that is, if you weren't raised by a family of wolves — most of the symbols in the xmms interface should be familiar (Paul's dog, Oso, often fiddles with xmms so that he can listen to his friends bark out "Jingle Bells" — really!). Anyway, xmms does have a few unfamiliar buttons and options, which we describe in the following list:

- ✔ If you click the PL button, a play list window pops up to the right. You can see what tracks are playing in this window. You can also select which tracks to play.

- ✔ Click the button immediately to the left of PL and the graphics equalizer shown in Figure 12-2 appears. What's the difference between a $300 equalizer you purchase in a store and xmms? About $300.

- ✔ The volume control slide is in the middle of the screen.

- ✔ The balance control slide is to the right of the volume control.

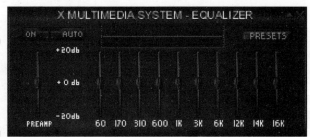

Figure 12-2: The xmms graphics equalizer window.

- ✔ You can open music files to play by right-clicking anywhere on the xmms window. From the pop-up window, choose File to open a dialog box. From there, you can browse the files that you want to open.

- ✔ Other options exist for how to change the look and feel of xmms and other miscellaneous features. Right-click the window and select options or any of the other features.

Playing MP3 files

Not much changes when you want to play an MP3 file. You simply obtain the MP3 files from the Internet — for example, from www.mp3.com. You can then use the multimedia players, such as xmms (described in the preceding section) to play MP3 files. (MP3 files have the .mp3 suffix.)

You can also play streaming MP3s from the Internet. Chapter 13 describes that process.

GMIX Mixer: Sounds for the rest of us

You can control your sound card volume and other features directly with the help of GMIX Mixer. You start GMIX Mixer by clicking the GNOME Main Menu Button and choosing Programs⇨Multimedia⇨Audio Mixer.

Figure 12-3 shows the GMIX Mixer window with all its buttons and slider bars. These controls may or may not match the capabilities of your sound card; the GMIX Mixer application is written for sound cards in general, not a specific sound card.

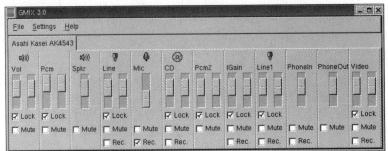

Figure 12-3:
The GMIX
Mixer
window.

For GMIX Mixer to work, you must have a sound card, a cable must attach the CD-ROM drive to the sound card, and the speakers or headphones must be plugged into the sound card (not the CD-ROM).

Most of the GMIX Mixer controls are labeled in Figure 12-3. Here's a little additional information:

- ✔ The Loudness control boosts the bass slightly for when you want low volume output (such as when your parents are home, the baby is asleep, or you have new batteries in your hearing aid).

- ✔ The Stereo Separation control is labeled with the red and black speaker connector wires and is for cards that try to convince you that they have stereo separation capabilities.

- ✔ Each slider is made up of two columns, one for the left channel and one for the right channel. Place the cursor directly over one of the columns and drag the slider to move the column up or down. Move the cursor between the two columns to move both columns at the same time.

Some find it easier to use the middle mouse button to grab the top of the column. To do so, move the cursor to the top of a column, click and hold down the middle mouse button, and then move the mouse to pull the column up or down. If your mouse has only two buttons but you requested three-button emulation when you installed your system, hold down both buttons at the same time to simulate the middle mouse button.

If you didn't ask for three-button emulation but want it now, follow these steps:

1. **Log in as root.**

2. **Type the following command at the command prompt and press Enter:**

   ```
   /usr/sbin/mouseconfig
   ```

3. **Press the Tab key until the cursor is over Emulate Three Buttons and then press the Spacebar.**

The Emulate Three Buttons radio button is located just above the OK, Cancel, and Help buttons.

4. **Select the OK button and then press Enter.**

   You have installed three-button emulation for your mouse.

5. **Press Ctrl+Alt+Backspace to restart X Server and enable the emulation.**

Setting Up and Testing Your Sound System

Red Hat Linux comes configured to use your computer's sound system. However, you may run into problems — especially on older computers — and so Red Hat provides the sndconfig utility. You can use the sndconfig utility to manually checks for problems with and configure your computer's audio capabilities. This section shows how to use the sndconfig system.

You can configure and test your sound card at the same time by following these steps:

1. **Log in to Linux as root (see Chapter 4).**

2. **Insert CD1 that came with this book into the CD-ROM drive.**

   GNOME automatically mounts the CD-ROM for you. If the CD-ROM fails to mount for any reason, please refer to Chapter 17 for instructions on mounting drives.

3. **Start a terminal session by clicking the GNOME terminal icon on the GNOME Panel.**

   The GNOME Panel is the menu bar along the bottom of your screen. The GNOME terminal icon looks like a computer monitor and is described in Chapter 10.

   Red Hat Linux uses the following packages to power the sound system: sox, awesfx, playmidi, and sndconfig. They are installed by default during the Workstation/Laptop installation process we describe in Chapter 3.

4. **Type the following command at the command prompt and press Enter:**

   ```
   sndconfig
   ```

   The Sound Configuration Introduction screen appears, as shown in Figure 12-4.

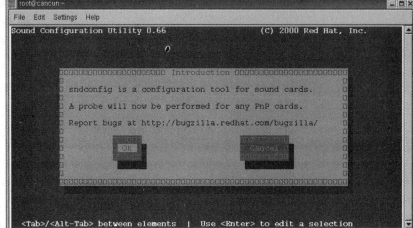

Figure 12-4:
The Sound
Configu-
ration
screen.

5. Read the information and press Enter.

If your sound card is Plug and Play (PnP), then `sndconfig` detects it and you can just press Enter and skip to Step 11. After your sound card is detected, the PCI Probe results window is displayed. Figure 12-5 shows the information that was detected about our sound card; your informa-tion will almost certainly be different. If your sound card isn't detected, continue to Step 6.

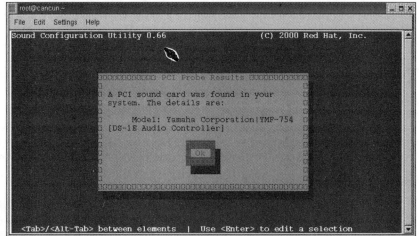

Figure 12-5:
The PCI
Probe
Results
dialog box.

6. If you know what your sound card is, highlight your sound card and skip to Step 10.

Use the up- and down-arrow keys. If you don't know, continue to Step 7.

7. **If you don't know what kind of sound card you have, look at the files in the** /proc **directory by typing the** ls /proc **command at the command prompt and press Enter.**

The proc file system doesn't correspond to an actual (physical) hard drive. proc is a virtual file system that exists only within the mind of the Linux kernel. It is designed to provide information about Linux processes and hardware. proc provides a window into the running Linux kernel (operating system). You can find out a lot of information about your equipment from it.

8. **Type** cat /proc/sound **at the command prompt and press Enter.**

After you determine the name of your sound, return to Step 6, or proceed to Step 9 if you can't find your sound card name.

The /proc/sound file contains information about your sound card. Our system shows the following sound card information, for example:

```
OSS/Free:3.8s2++-971130

Load type: Driver loaded as a module
Kernel: Linux veracruz.mp.sandia.gov 2.2.16-21 #1 Wed Aug
        9 11:45:35 EDT 2000 i686
Config options: 0
Installed drivers:
Card config:
Audio devices:
Synth devices:
Midi devices:
Timers:
0: System clock
1: Crystal audio controller (CS4236)
Mixers:
```

Note that towards the end it shows our CS4236 sound card. Yeah!

9. **If your** proc **file system doesn't contain information about your sound card, look at your computer's boot message log by entering the following command at the command prompt:**

```
more /var/log/dmesg
```

You can look at your computer's boot message log one page at a time by pressing the spacebar (press Q when you want to quit). Look for any information that may be sound-card related. For example, our CS4236-based sound card shows up as follows:

```
cs4232: set synthio and synthirq to use the wavefront
        facilities.
```

Look for words that suggest audio such as synthesizer, wave, and so on. After you determine your sound card name, return to Step 6.

If all else fails, power down your computer and look at the sound card with your analog eyes. If that doesn't work, go out and buy a $20 sound card.

10. Select the OK button and press Enter.

When we say, "Select the OK button" we mean to press the Tab key until the OK button is highlighted.

Appendix A describes some of the methods used to determine this information.

The Sound Card Test screen appears, as shown in Figure 12-6.

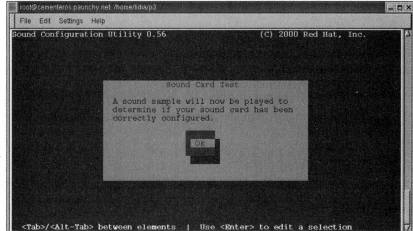

Figure 12-6:
Your sound system is about to be tested.

11. Press the Enter key to play the sound clip.

The sound clip is not just any sound clip: It's the voice of the big guy himself — Linus Torvalds, the inventor of Linux addressing the burning question of how you should pronounce the word Linux. (By the way, it's pronounced *Lin*–ux — with a short *i,* like in the word *tin.*)

After you hear The Man, you're asked if you heard the message.

12. If you heard the message, select Yes and press the Enter key.

The `sndconfig` program finishes, and you are returned to the GNOME terminal screen. Now that you have music in your life, you can enjoy blasting your neighbors' sensibilities late at night as you groove to your Red Hat Linux sound box. Have fun, but don't call us when the cops arrive.

If you didn't hear the message, then you're sad and should select the No button and press the Enter key. This returns you to the Card Type screen. Repeat Step 6.

If you didn't hear the sound test sample, make sure that you have compatible speakers or earphones plugged into your sound card output. Plugging into the wrong output is actually quite easy. If you're not sure, turn down your speakers to a low setting and try plugging into the different audio outputs.

If you're plugged in correctly, one of the following reasons may explain why you didn't hear the sound:

- You chose the wrong sound card.
- You entered the wrong parameters for the right sound card.
- Someone else's stereo is way too loud.

Ripping CDs

Are you paranoid? If not, do you want to be? Well, cdparanoia can help fulfill all your fears. Just kidding. Really, cdparanoia is used for ripping the audio information — music files — from CDs to your hard drive or to other CDs. Ripping refers to the process of copying audio from a CD into your computer.

The following steps show you how to use cdparanoia to copy music off a CD and into a Linux file:

1. **Insert your favorite CD, log in as any user, and type the following command:**

```
cdparanoia -Q
```

You should see output similar to the following for a three-song CD:

```
Cdparanoia III release 9.8 (March 23, 2001)
(c) 2001 Monty <monty@xiph.org> and Xiphophorus

Report bugs to paranoia@xiph.org
http://www.xiph.org/paranoia

Table of contents (audio tracks only):
track        length                    begin        copy pre
        ch
===============================================================
        ==
    1.    22157 [04:55.32]        0 [00:00.00]    no    no
        2
    2.    21100 [04:41.25]    22157 [04:55.32]    no    no
        2
    3.    20673 [04:35.48]    43257 [09:36.57]    no    no
        2
TOTAL    65020 [13:32.05]    (audio only)
```

This output displays information about your CD. The first column shows the length, in sectors, of each track and how many minutes and seconds long they are. The second column shows where each track begins. The last column shows the number of channels on each track — two channels equals stereo; does anyone have a quadraphonic CD? The last row shows the totals.

2. **Try ripping a CD by entering the following command (which copies the first 60 seconds of a file):**

```
cdparanoia "1[:0]-1[:60]"
```

The command rips the CD and stores the music in the cdda.wav file.

To show some more ways to use the cdparanoia, the following commands rip the first track, tracks one through three and tracks four and five respectively:

```
cdparanoia "1"

cdparanoia "1-3"

cdparanoia "4-5"
```

You can choose the name of the file where cdparanoia saves the music by specifying the filename as the last option. For example, if you want the filename to be tomwaits_o155.wav, then type in the following command (the file is stored to your current working directory):

```
cdparanoia "1[:0]-1[:60]" tomwaits_o155.wav
```

To copy the entire CD, use the 1– option. The 1 tells cdparanoia to start copying at track one, and the – option tells it to continue to the end.

```
cdparanoia "1-" tomwaits_o155.wav
```

After you create the music file, you can listen to it with any of the CD players mentioned earlier in this chapter.

Entering the Ring of Fire: Burning CDs

Back in the '80s, when vinyl melted away under the invasion of CDs, it cost millions to build a CD factory where the CDs where created. Today, for roughly the $100 that it costs to purchase a CD burner (to *burn* means to record to CD), you can build your own personal factory. Amazing.

If you don't have a CD burner (or writer), this section won't do you a bit of good.

A recordable CD is referred to as a CD-R; a rewritable CD is called a CD-RW (the difference is that CD-Rs can only be recorded on once). CD burners look like regular read-only drives and are connected with either an IDE or SCSI interface.

Installing the CD-ROM writing utility

Red Hat Linux comes preconfigured to record CD-ROMs. However, just in case the CD-ROM writing utility was not installed, you can do so by following the following steps.

1. **Log in as root.**

2. **Insert CD2 that came with this book into your CD-ROM drive.**

3. **Open a Terminal emulator.**

4. **Enter the following command to install the** cdrecord **package:**

```
rpm -ivh /mnt/cdrom/RedHat/RPMS/cdrecord*
```

The cdrecord package is installed. You can now use cdrecord to record your own CD-ROMs. The next section describes the process of making CDs.

Burn, baby, burn: Saving files to a CD

The following instructions describe how to create, or *burn,* a CD-ROM. You can copy either data or music to your CD-R. In this section, we switch gears to show how to back up your Linux home directory to a CD; however, you can also use these instructions to copy music. (The instructions are the same whether you have an IDE/ATAPI or SCSI CD-ROM drive.)

1. **Log in as root and insert a CD-R or CD-RW disc into your CD writer.**

   What can you burn? Well, the world's your oyster, and you can make a CD of anything you want — data, software, or music. A good place to start is backing up your /home directory on CD.

2. **Choose what you want to burn to CD.**

   To copy data to a CD, you first need to make an ISO image of the data using the mkisofs utility. The general mkisofs syntax is the following:

```
mkisofs -R -o filename filename or directory
```

The first *filename* is the name of the output file and the second *filename* is the path to the file or directory that you want to burn to CD.

For example, if you want to back up the */home/mydir* directory, you would enter the following command (make sure that you have enough space left on your disk):

```
mkisofs -R -o mydir-10apr02.raw /home/mydir
```

3. **Determine where your CD-ROM drive is by entering the following command:**

```
cdrecord --scanbus
```

The output shows information similar to the following code:

```
Cdrecord 1.8 (i686-pc-linux-gnu) Copyright (C) 1995-2000
        J!!rg Schilling

Using libscg version 'schily-0.1'
scsibus0:
    0,0,0    0) 'IDE-CD  ' 'R/RW 4x4x24      ' '1.04'
             Removable CD-ROM
    0,1,0    1) *
    0,2,0    2) *
    0,3,0    3) *
```

This is the output you see if you have an IDE/ATAPI CD-ROM drive. SCSI-based systems, however, may show up with other values depending on their configuration. You recognize SCSI drives by their controller, target, and slice numbers. *Slice numbers* correspond to the three numbers in the above output. For example, if you have a SCSI-based CD-ROM drive that's connected as the third target on the first controller, then it shows up as: 0,3,0 in the preceding code. (Slices are not used in this configuration and are always 0.) Whatever the numbers are, you simply need to use them in the dev= parameter described in the next step.

SCSI doesn't mean that it's a dirty (scuzzy) interface: This acronym stands for *Small Computer System Interface*. Most inexpensive to moderately priced computers use an IDE interface to control both the CD-ROM drive and hard drive. SCSI interfaces also control hard drives and CD-ROM drives. You find SCSI interfaces on high-end computers because they provide higher performance and are more expensive.

You can now write the file you chose (or created) in Step 2 to a CD.

The cdrecord utility is designed to interact with a SCSI-based CD-R drive. Red Hat Linux installs a kernel module called ide-scsi that allows cdrecord to interact with an IDE-based CD-R drive; most PCs use IDE devices. You may need to install the ide-scsi module if the cdrecord -scanbus command does not show a CD-R device. Run the command **modprobe ide-scsi** to insert the module.

4. **Take the** scsibus **values from Step 3 and use them with the** cdrecord **command by entering the following command:**

```
cdrecord -v speed=n dev=scsibus_values -isosize filename
```

Where *n* is the speed of your CD-ROM drive, *scsibus_values* are the virtual SCSI values obtained from Step 3. *-isosize* specifies that you are recording raw data, and *filename* is the name of the file that is created.

For example, if you have a 4X speed ATAPI/IDE CD-ROM drive and want to create a CD from the mydir-31aug00.raw file, you run the following command.

```
cdrecord -v speed=4 dev=0,0,0 -isosize mydir-31aug00.raw
```

The scsibus values from Step 3 — for example 0,0,0 — are used with the dev= parameter. The 0,0,0 value is combined with dev= to create the dev=0,0,0 parameter.

Please note that you need to set your speed according to what your CD-ROM drive can handle. You need to obtain the speed value from the documentation that came with your recordable CD-ROM drive in order to enter it as part of the speed parameter in the cdrecord command. Look for a value like *4X* or *8X*. Don't worry if you don't know them. If you set the speed too high, then your CD is just recorded at the lower level.

That's it! You computer writes the information to CD. Congratulations! You've created a new CD.

The process changes just a little bit if you want to burn music. First, you don't need to create an ISO image. Second, the following cdrecord command is used in place of the one shown in Step 3 of the preceding numbered list:

```
cdrecord -v speed=n dev=scsibus_values -audio filename
```

Where *n* is the speed of your CD-ROM drive, *scsibus_values* are the virtual SCSI values obtained from Step 3, *-audio* specifies that you are creating an audio disc, and *filename* is the name of the file that is created.

For example, if you have a 4X speed ATAPI/IDE CD-ROM drive and want to create a music CD from the tom_waits.raw file, you should run the following command:

```
cdrecord -v speed=4 dev=0,0,0 -audio tom_waits.wav
```

Chapter 13

Using Streaming Media and RealPlayer

In This Chapter

▶ Listening to live radio with RealPlayer

▶ Listening to broadcast MP3s

▶ Viewing video clips with RealPlayer

*O*ne of the coolest Internet innovations is streaming technology used for audio and video files. Streaming technology provides a continuous flow of sound and picture from a variety of sources in real time. Video streaming (movie, television, and so on) online is still somewhat limited, especially on slower connections, but the force of streaming media is certain to explode in the near future as broadband connections become more common.

This chapter describes how to use your Red Hat Linux machine as both a radio and a TV using the popular RealPlayer streaming audio/video client. After configuring your Internet connection, firewall, and Mozilla browser in earlier chapters of this book, you've done most of the heavy lifting. All you need to do is download RealPlayer 8 and configure it.

You can also play video and audio clips with the `gtv` player (although you can't play Real file formats in `gtv` — you need RealPlayer for that). The `gtv` program plays MPEG-formatted video files. It's installed by default on your Red Hat Linux machine. Click the GNOME Main Menu button and choose Programs⇨Multimedia⇨gtv.

Configuring Your Red Hat Box

You can think of your Red Hat Linux computer as a simple appliance. Even though it does all the usual, diverse computeresque things, it can also work like any old, garden-variety radio. Downloading Real Audio's free RealPlayer 8 software enables you to listen to radio stations — and any other streaming audio — from around the world, and to watch video (which we discuss towards the end of the chapter).

Being snubbed big-time by QuickTime

Okay, in regards to Apple and QuickTime, we have bad new and good news. Want the bad news first? Of course you do. The bad news is that Apple does not support Linux with its QuickTime player or plug-in, nor does Microsoft with its Windows Media Player — at least not yet. Unfortunately, this means that if you want to see streaming movies in these two formats, you can't view them through Linux. Many companies, however, make their video clips in multiple formats, and Real's plug-in currently has the greatest support in the streaming industry. So take heart; for every one QuickTime clip that you can't view through Linux, there are probably nine that you can view through RealPlayer. And

besides, Linux wouldn't be open source if Apple and Microsoft didn't snub it!

The guys and gals at Real could also stand to create some applications that support Linux better: RealJukebox by RealAudio is real good at converting CDs to MP3s and provides numerous ways to organize your MP3s. RealJukebox has all sorts of cool stuff that you can do, like change skins and themes, fade one track to another to create continuous music, add cover lyrics, cover art, and artist info to each track, and watch really nifty visualization effects. But you guessed it: RealJukebox has no Linux version yet. Come on, guys, get with the program!

Downloading and installing RealPlayer 8

To get and make use of RealPlayer, you need four things: a working Internet connection, Mozilla, and a working sound system (all three of which are described in Chapters 5, 6, 7, 9, and 12, respectively), and the RealPlayer 8 software. To get RealPlayer, follow these steps:

1. **Log in as root, connect to the Internet, and start Mozilla.**

   You can start Mozilla by clicking the Mozilla icon in the GNOME Panel at the bottom of the screen.

2. **Enter the following URL in the Mozilla location text box and press the Enter key:**

   ```
   www.real.com/player/8/index.html
   ```

   Mozilla displays Real's download page.

3. **Click the <u>RealPlayer 8 Basic - is our free player</u> link on the lower-left side of the page.**

   You are prompted to enter your e-mail address, country, operating system, and so on, but don't bother entering anything but information about your operating system.

4. **Don't enter any information in the text boxes, just click the Select OS drop-down list and choose UNIX.**

   The Select OS drop-down list doesn't include a Linux option. But by selecting UNIX, you go to the menu that does have a Linux option (Linux and Unix are fully compatible). The Community Supported RealPlayer Download Page appears, as shown in Figure 13-1.

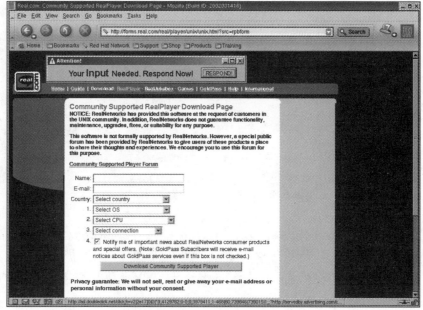

Figure 13-1: The Community Supported RealPlayer Download Page.

5. **Fill in the fields with the requested information. Make sure that you specify your computer's processor type — Pentium for PCs — and select Linux 2.x (libc6 -386) RPM as your operating system.**

   If you don't want to receive extra e-mails (and who does?), click the Notify Me of Important News check box to remove the check mark so that you don't get e-mail from Real.

6. **Click the Download Community Supported Player button.**

   The page shown in Figure 13-2 appears.

7. **Click the location to download from the available options, preferably from a location geographically close to you.**

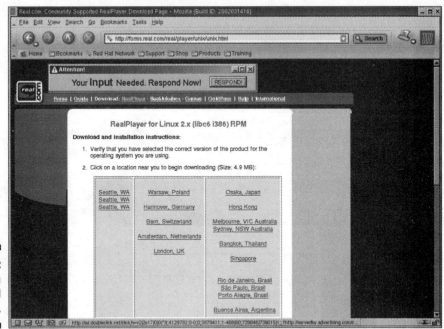

Figure 13-2:
Selecting a
download
site.

If the locations nearest you are busy, try one that is in a time zone where it's night or early morning (thus, less likely to be busy).

The Save As window appears, prompting you to download the file.

8. Click OK.

The Save As dialog box appears.

9. Choose a location to download the file to and then click the Save button.

The file is saved to the directory you chose, or to the default directory if you didn't choose anything. We suggest saving it to the `/usr/local/src` directory, as shown in Figure 13-3, which is a good general-purpose location for storing source files.

You can manually install the RealPlayer 8 RPM file by running the `rpm -ivh rp8*` command.

10. Open a GNOME Terminal Emulator window.

See Chapter 4 for instructions.

11. Install the RealPlayer 8 package by running the following command.

```
rpm -ivh rp8*
```

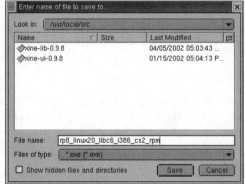

Figure 13-3:
Selecting
the
directory to
download
the
RealPlayer 8
installation
program.

12. **Click the Main Menu button and choose Applications⇨Nautilus.**

    Nautilus starts.

13. **Type** /usr/bin/X11 **in the Location box.**

    Figure 13-4 shows the RealPlayer 8 program displayed in Nautilus (look
    in the upper-right side of the screen).

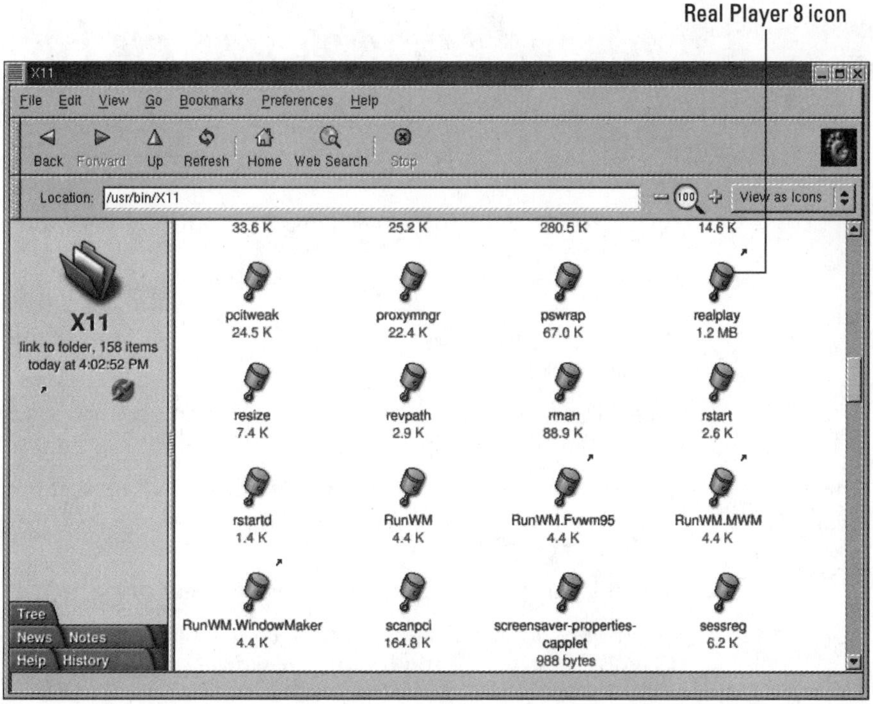

Real Player 8 icon

Figure 13-4:
The
RealPlayer 8
icon is
displayed in
Nautilus.

14. **Double-click the RealPlayer icon and RealPlayer 8 starts.**

15. **You're prompted to enter information such as your zip code and Internet connection type and speed. Enter the information and click Next.**

16. **Select your connection speed and click Finished.**

    RealPlayer plays its intro bump — a short piece of music, which you quickly learn by heart — and then waits to play you a tune (see Figure 13-5).

Figure 13-5: The RealPlayer 8 Welcome window.

Launching RealPlayer from the Panel

After you've installed RealPlayer, you need to be able to start it. GNOME provides just such a capability from its applet launcher. You can create an applet launcher (an icon to click) for RealPlayer on GNOME's Panel.

The Panel is the gray bar that rests along the bottom of your screen.

Follow these steps to create a launcher applet for RealPlayer:

1. **Click the GNOME Main Menu button and choose Panel⇨Add to Panel⇨ Launcher menus.**

2. **Type a name for the RealPlayer launcher icon (try something obvious, such as RealPlayer 8).**

    You can optionally enter a comment in the Comment text box. The text that you enter is displayed in a tooltip that appears over the icon when you hover the mouse cursor over it.

3. **Type realplay into the Command text box and press the Tab key.**

    RealPlayer supplies images that can be used as the applet icon on the GNOME Panel, which you can now pick from.

4. **Click the Icon button at the bottom of the Launcher window to pick an icon for the launcher.**

   A window appears that shows the default GNOME icons.

5. **Type** /usr/local/RealPlayer8/Help/realplay/pics/RealLogo.gif **in the text box and click the OK button.**

   The RealPlayer icon is displayed in the Launcher window, ready and waiting to launch RealPlayer.

6. **Click the OK button in the launcher window.**

   The new icon is inserted into the GNOME Panel, as shown in Figure 13-6.

Figure 13-6:
The
RealPlayer 8
launcher on
the GNOME
panel.

7. **Click the new RealPlayer launcher that you just created in the GNOME panel.**

   The RealPlayer window appears.

You can easily place the RealPlayer icon (or any icon) on your desktop. Click any icon in Nautilus and drag it to your desktop. Release the mouse button, and the icon remains on your desktop background. You can then right-click the desktop icon and choose Show Properties from the menu that pops up. The Show Properties menu enables you to modify the icon's look and feel.

Finding radio stations

"What can I play with this thing?" you may be asking, or more importantly, "How do I find stuff to play? Mom, I wanna play!" Well, you can find streaming radio content in several ways and places, including the following:

✔ Search with Mozilla Search (click Mozilla's Search button) to find individual stations and radio station databases and to see if they have a RealPlayer-supported streaming format.

✔ Stumble across RealPlayer files all around the Internet (look for the blue Real logo — you see them everywhere when you start looking).

✔ Mozilla, now a product owned by AOL, gives you access AOL's Spinner. com radio content (choose Mozilla⇨Radio). Mozilla Radio requires you to have the RealPlayer plug-in installed (the plug-in installs when you install RealPlayer).

✔ Browse Real's content lists by following these steps:

1. **Choose Content⇨Live Stations in the RealPlayer window.**

   RealPlayer starts Mozilla and the Real Audio Web page appears. The live station content list gives you access to Real Audio's content and enables you to search for other radio stations.

2. **Click the <u>Find a Station</u> link to search for radio stations based on various criteria, such as location or call letters.**

   As of this writing, the RealPlayer database contains over 2,500 stations.

3. **Find your station, go to that Web site, and start the tunes.**

You can access information about RealPlayer at www.real.com/help. The site supplies a frequently asked questions (FAQ) guide, a beginner's guide, and other useful information.

Real Audio, Inc. designs its own streaming audio/video formats (protocols). Microsoft, as you may guess, rolls its own, and some radio stations support only Microsoft's Windows Media Player, although many support both formats. You can differentiate Real Audio from Microsoft by the suffix that it appends to its files. RealAudio ends with ram, ra and rm, while Microsoft appends asx to its stuff. If you click the Windows Media button, you are asked whether you want to save the link as the file kbac.asx. That's because Mozilla knows how to handle Real Audio broadcasts but not Microsoft ones — it has no MIME helper (application) that it can run.

Using RealPlayer

Internet radio stations often play an introduction message and/or advertisement, called a *bump*, when you connect and before playing the live feed. This happens because the radio station's URL points to multiple streams.

If you right-click the station's URL and choose the Save Link As option, then the individual URLs are saved to a file.

You can manually open the streaming radio feed. In RealPlayer, choose File⇨ Open Location. The Open Location window appears, as shown in Figure 13-7.

Figure 13-7:
Opening a
radio
station's
audio feed.

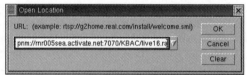

When you type a station URL into the window's text box, Mozilla starts RealPlayer, and you can listen to music, talk, and even static from around the world. For instance, go to WRTI's Web page at www.wrti.org (Temple University's fine radio station) and click the Listen Live icon in the upper middle of the page. RealPlayer starts, opens a connection to WRTI's Internet feed, buffers the audio stream, and starts playing a great selection of jazz (after 4 p.m. EST).

You can listen to an outstanding interview with The Man himself by opening the following URL from RealPlayer: rtsp://audio.npr.org/fa/20010604. fa.rm. Terri Gross conducted this interview during the summer of 2001 on her program Fresh Air. Linus discusses the development of Linux, his life in Silicon Valley, and other matters.

RealPlayer, of course, uses the standard controls to play, stop, pause, mute, and pump up the volume. You can also display information about the stream, if available. You can display statistics about your Internet connection by choosing View⇨Statistics; the player's audio stream speed is shown below the Clip Info subwindow.

MP3 on the Net

MP3 (MPEG audio layer 3) is a popular medium for storing music and other audio information. You can create incredible music libraries on your hard drive and then store big chunks of it on a CD-R disc. You can even stream MP3 just like RealAudio; however, streaming MP3 isn't nearly as popular as RealAudio so you don't find many streaming sources. That's not for lack of trying, though, and you can find sites where you can listen to streaming MP3 music or radio-like feeds.

A good place to start is the well-known www.mp3.com Web site. Once there, click the Stations link. (Channels provides similar service on a subscription basis.) Click one of the station types (music, sports, and so on) and then one of the individual items. For example, click Music and then click Space Radio.

You're prompted to play Space Radio on either a high-speed or low-speed link. (Ground control to Major Tom, you're out of tune.) Click the low-speed link if you're using a modem for your Internet connection or are on a heavily loaded high-speed connection — for example, if all your colleagues are listening to Space Radio, too. If you have a better-than-a-modem connection and no one is hogging your bandwidth listening to Art Bell, go crazy and click the high-speed connection link.

Mozilla uses the mpg123 MP3 player by default when it encounters an MP3 connection. Sometimes it's difficult to get the mpg123 player to work correctly. If that's the case, right-click the link and save the MP3 link as a file. The next time that you want to access that particular audio feed, you can open the file and access the stream directly from your application without going through a browser. (The file that points to the MP3 stream has an .m3u extension.)

.m3u files are metafiles similar to .ram files, containing information on the actual connections that are used to play the audio stream. Start the xmms MP3 player by clicking the GNOME Main Menu button and choosing Programs➪ Multimedia➪xmms. When xmms starts, it automatically opens the Load File window. Click the .m3u file and then the OK button. xmms starts playing the audio stream.

Going Hollywood with RealPlayer Video

RealPlayer 8 plays streaming video in addition to audio. You can connect to video streams in the same way you connect to audio streams. (This process, including installing and setting up RealPlayer, is described earlier in this chapter.)

RealPlayer — and streaming media in general — is undeniably an exciting technology that makes your Red Hat Linux system a television set as well as a radio! But what video can you play? The following two sections give you a good head start on finding streaming video content to check out.

Finding video at Real.com

A good place to start looking for video is Real's home page at www.real.com, where you can find a lot of cool features. The lower half of the page shows numerous links to content that it provides or gives access to. Here's some of the cool stuff you can find at Real.com:

✔ **Movie trailers:** There's always a link to a featured trailer on the Real Audio home page. You can click the <u>more trailers</u> link on the Real.com home page to see a list of the current trailers. Click a trailer, and you go to another Real Audio Web page that contains a link to the video stream as well as information about the movie.

Broadband and narrowband links are provided to the movie's video clips. Broadband refers to Internet connections that are very fast. Broadband connections can be classified as any connection faster than a 56 Kbps modem. Click the <u>Broadband</u> link if you're connected to a network with a fast connection (such as a DSL or cable modem connection); otherwise click the <u>Narrowband</u> link.

Mozilla fires up RealPlayer. Your RealPlayer then connects to the video stream for that clip, buffers several seconds of the clip, and starts playing it. It's a lot more fun to watch movie trailers all day than work! (As the warning goes, don't try this at work. We're professional, experienced slackers — er, hackers — and know what we're doing. You may get into trouble if you're not careful.)

✔ **Music videos:** Right below the movie trailers on the Real.com home page are links to music videos. There's always a link to a featured video displayed on the RealAudio home page. You can go look at other videos by clicking the <u>more music videos</u> link.

✔ **Video archives:** The archives that Real Audio provides are a lot more fun than the current list. You have the choice of viewing a large library of old or older movies. To find the archives, click the <u>more trailers</u> link on the Real.com home page. On the left side of the screen, a <u>Vintage</u> link takes you to the archive. You can select from many great pictures.

The movies listed on the Vintage page are all a year (or two or three years) old. You can have fun looking through all the movies that you did see — or didn't.

Another fun repository of video clips that you can use `gtv` to view is at the following URL, where you can even find video clips of everyone's favorite pals, Wallace and Grommet:

```
wwwzenger.informatik.tu-muenchen.de/persons/paula/mpeg/
                 index.html
```

✔ **News clips:** If you want topical information, you can get news clips from numerous news organizations. For example, from RealPlayer 8, choose File⇨Open Location. Enter the following URL into the text box:

```
channels.real.com/vram/single?programs=16
```

The current headlines from Fox News are then displayed in RealPlayer 8. You can access the news of the day as if you tuned into the five o'clock news on TV.

✔ **Cable programming:** Some cable TV channels — especially the fun ones — are starting to provide some of their programming on the Internet. For example, you can choose File⇨Open Location and enter a URL (like the one we list here) into the text box.

```
channels.real.com/vram/single?programs=44&&tcode
```

Press the Enter key and the video page you chose appears.

Finding streaming video from other sources

Other than Real.com and stumbling across content, probably the best way to find multimedia Web fun is to search the Internet for *video MPEG*. As of this writing, however, you're not going to find a whole lot of video content available on the Internet. But this dearth of content is bound to reverse itself as access to high-speed Internet access becomes widely available and as the big movie studios and television networks discover new ways to make money.

We think RealPlayer is a lot of fun and, more importantly, a preview of what you can expect to see more of. In the near future, there will be a wealth of programming available directly from the Web. No one knows who will be showing what and what the "what" will be. We can say with confidence that there will be a lot of it out there. Have fun!

Punching through Firewalls

Firewalls are often necessary to fight the evils that lurk on the Internet, but they can really put a kink in your listening pleasure. The following two sections describe how to fight your way out through a firewall into the fresh streams of audio — and video — air.

Getting RealPlayer through your firewall

If your Red Hat Linux workstation sits on a network with a filtering firewall (see Chapters 5 and 6), then you don't need to modify RealPlayer. A firewall is used to prevent unauthorized access from outside — in most cases the Internet — your computer and/or network. The key is that the filtering firewall allows all outgoing TCP/UDP connections (ports), such as either of the ones we show you how to construct in Chapters 5 and 6. But if your network uses a filtering firewall that allows only specific connections, then you may have to modify RealPlayer. In such a case, it's likely that RealPlayer can find its way through the firewall if you tell it to use the HTTP protocol in place of the specialized PNA and RTSP; PNA and RTSP are protocols that are used to access RealAudio streams.

To configure RealPlayer so that it's not blocked by the firewalls described in Chapters 5 and 6, follow these steps:

1. **Start RealPlayer and choose View⇨Preferences.**

   The Preferences window appears, as shown in Figure 13-8.

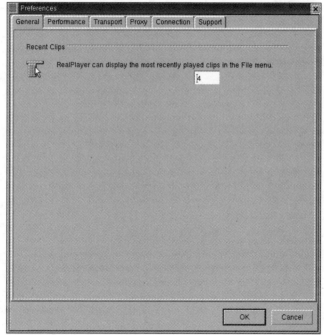

Figure 13-8:
The
RealPlayer
Preferences
window.

2. **Click the Transport tab and then click the RTSP Settings button.**

   The Specify Transport window appears. By default, RealPlayer uses the TCP transport protocol to make its connections. TCP is another Internet protocol used to transport information over the Internet. In order for TCP to work, your Internet gateway/firewall generally has to be specifically configured to allow it.

3. **Click the Use HTTP Only button and then click the OK button.**

   Specifying HTTP makes RealPlayer use that protocol for all its connections. HTTP is almost universally used for browsing the Web. RealPlayer can make connections more reliably with HTTP. Figure 13-9 shows the window with the HTTP Only button activated.

4. **Repeat Steps 2 and 3 but click the PNA settings button instead in Step 2.**

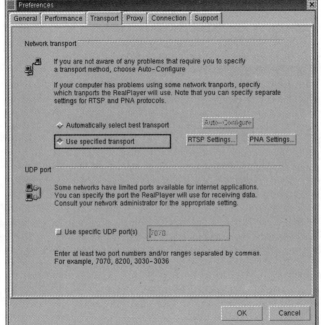

Audio by proxy (Using RealPlayer with your firewall)

If a proxying firewall protects your Red Hat Linux computer and/or network, then you need to tell RealPlayer about it. A *proxying firewall* is a system that is designed to protect your system from unauthorized outside access. To clue RealPlayer in about your proxying firewall, follow these steps:

1. **In RealPlayer, choose View⇨Preferences.**

2. **Click the Proxy tab.**

   From here, you can tell RealPlayer how to get through your firewall to the Internet. How you configure RealPlayer depends on your firewall. This subject is far too large to approach in depth here, but you can do a few simple things that should allow you to get out of your local network through the firewall.

   First you need to tell RealPlayer the location of your proxying firewall. Many proxys allow HTTP through the standard port 80. This is a good place to start.

3. **Click the Manually Configure HTTP Proxy option.**

   The Proxy Server text box appears.

4. **Type the network address of your proxy server in that window.**

   For example, if your proxy server address is `proxy.paunchy.net`, as shown in Figure 13-10, then that is what you type. If the proxy uses a port other than 80, then change the value; in most cases, this is not necessary.

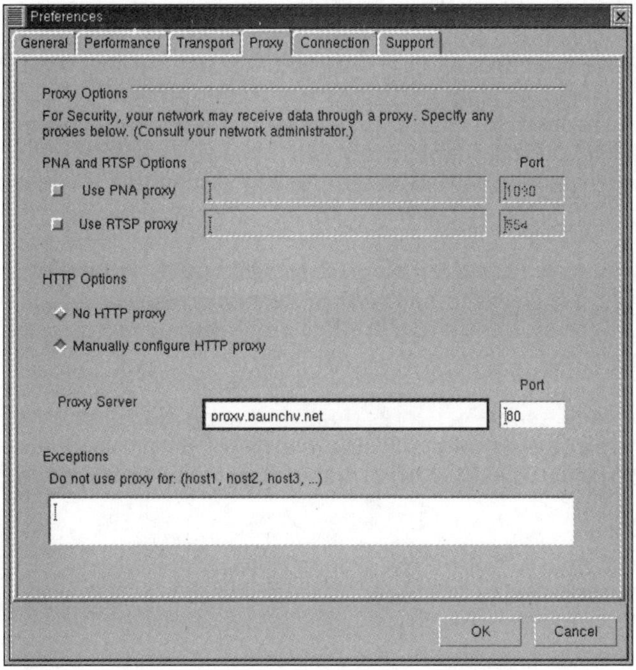

Figure 13-10: Configuring RealPlayer to use a proxy firewall.

Having a proxy firewall that provides proxys for the PNA and RTSP protocols is unusual. If you do have one, then you can type its address in the Use PNA Proxy and Use RTSP Proxy text boxes.

5. **Click OK and try to use RealPlayer.**

If you can't access an audio stream after modifying RealPlayer, then go back to the Preferences window and click the Transport tab. Click the RTSP button and the Specify Transport window appears. RealPlayer tries to use the TCP transport protocol to make its connections. Your firewall — either proxy or filtering — may not allow that, so you need to click the Use HTTP Only option.

Repeat the process for the PNA settings to tell Real Audio to use only the common HTTP protocol, not PNA and RTSP. HTTP is less efficient than PNA and RTSP, but is still better than nothing. Click OK to return to the Preferences window. Click OK again and try to make your connection.

If you still can't get the connection to work, go back to the Preferences window and click the Transport tab. Try to let RealPlayer figure things out for you. Click the Automatically Select Best Transport option and then click the Auto-Configure button. RealPlayer tries everything it can think of to get connected. If you're lucky, it figures out what to use. If not, then you must go back to the Proxy tab and make sure that you set the proxy server address correctly.

If you manage your firewall yourself, then consider turning it off. Whether you want to risk that is up to you. Assess your system and determine what you need to protect. If you're running a bank, then you don't want to turn off the firewall. If you're a simple home user, then you can probably turn off your firewall briefly; you may want to temporarily disconnect the rest of your network from your Internet gateway.

Turn off your firewall and try connecting again. With no firewall, everything should work. If it doesn't, then your problem lies elsewhere. If it works, then try to modify your firewall to allow Real Audio connections (this discussion is outside the scope of this book). Good luck!

Be forewarned — some networks (including some business networks) simply may not give you the option of using RealPlayer. Sorry. We're just the messengers. Talk to your friendly system administrator and try to figure things out.

Chapter 14

Using Desktop Productivity Tools

In This Chapter

▶ Obtaining and installing StarOffice

▶ Using StarOffice

▶ Taking a look at other Linux applications

*R*ed Hat Linux is a great distribution with a large base of applications. But Red Hat Linux also lacks a major desktop office suite, probably because full office suites provide you with word processing, spreadsheet, and other high-level capabilities all within one suite of applications. Some major desktop-productivity suites, such as StarOffice, Applixware, and WordPerfect Office, have taken Linux out of the back office and into the light of everyday use. Actually, there's a bunch of monstrous programs, and Red Hat wants to ship with less than 10 CD-ROMs (as do the publishers of this book), so you have to find these programs on your own. (Don't worry, we show you where to do your downloading.)

In this chapter, we discuss StarOffice, not Applixware, because StarOffice is free *and* was recently released as open source by Sun Microsystems! Which office suite is better is a question best left to personal taste and opinion. You can find a good comparison of Applixware and StarOffice in Issue 54 of the *Linux Journal* at www.linuxjournal.com/issue54/3080.html, by Fred Butzen, coauthor of *The LINUX Network* (Hungry Minds, Inc.).

If you're interested in Applixware, which supplies pretty much the same desktop productivity functions as StarOffice (with the exception of one grand feature I discuss in this chapter), it's available from VistaSource at www.vista source.com. Corel Corporation — the former king of DOS word processing with WordPerfect — also produces a full office suite similar to StarOffice or Applixware called WordPerfect Office 2000. For more information on this product, go to www.corel.com and click the <u>WordPerfect Office 2000</u> link. The word processor WordPerfect 8 is available alone for download from www.corel.com/download.

A StarOffice Is Born

StarOffice is a desktop productivity suite that does nearly everything that Microsoft Office does, but for less money. How much less? Well, 100 percent less because it's now 100 percent free. Sun Microsystems, Inc. purchased StarOffice and licenses it under the GPL/LGPL and SIISL licenses. What do all those letters mean? They mean F-R-E-E, and they also mean that Linux can integrate office productivity features from StarOffice now because the Linux and StarOffice share the GPL license. More information about the licenses can be found at the following URL:

```
www.openoffice.org/project/www/license.html
```

Not only is StarOffice free (did we mention that it's free?), but it is also powerful, providing the user with the following functions:

- **Writer:** A full-function *what-you-see-is-what-you-get* (WYSIWYG) word processor. StarOffice comes with many functions that you expect — formatting, cutting and pasting, graphics, spell check, and more. It can also read from and write to Microsoft Word 97/2000 files.

- **Calc:** A full-function spreadsheet program used by Wall Street brokers. If you're familiar with spreadsheet software, then Calc should be straightforward to use.

- **Impress:** A graphics program with all the bells and whistles for creating presentations. You can also import and export PowerPoint documents.

- **Draw:** Your personal graphics tools for creating anything from a novice drawing to a masterpiece. This program provides your creative side with a tool for creating graphics.

- **Schedule:** This program helps you to organize your time. If you're like Paul, it's increasingly difficult to schedule quality coffee time. Schedule helps find the time.

- **E-mail client:** This is a full-function e-mail client program that can read, write, and filter your e-mail for you. You probably want to stick with Mozilla if only to minimize the number of software packages that you use. Nothing is wrong with this tool, but if you're like us and run the Mozilla browser constantly, then you may as well use it for e-mail, too. Doing so provides you with fuller integration of your Web browsing and e-mail clients.

- **HTML editor:** StarOffice writer is also able to create HTML documents. HTML is the language of the Internet, and this function makes it easy to create Web pages. HTML editor works the same as the word processor, but the text that you enter is saved in an HTML-formatted document. Any HTML document that you save can be used as a Web page.

Okay, so StarOffice has a lot of great features. But how good are they? Can they get the job done? Well, the last edition of this book was written in Applixware Words and edited with Microsoft Office, and this one was written mostly in StarOffice. Applixware Words, you see, can't use the Microsoft Word Track Changes mechanism (also known as revision marks), which enable you to see who's done what to a document. (This feature makes it impossible to read all of your editor's many suggestions. As attractive as those suggestions may be on a Monday morning at 3 a.m. with a couple of hours to go before deadline, it's still necessary to be able to read those revision marks. Trust us. We know from experience, and so does our editor.) When StarOffice released its new version — 5.2 — with Track Changes and the ability to save files in Word 97/2000 format, there was no competition. That's why we decided to write and edit this book in StarOffice 5.2.

StarOffice also has the advantage of running nicely on less than top-of-the-line equipment, such as Paul's creaky old Cyrix P120 (equivalent to a Pentium I 90 – 120 MHz processor); that machine does have a decent video card, however, which really helps with applications like StarOffice that use heavy-duty graphics. Paul is definitely thrifty when it comes to buying computer equipment, and he appreciates not having to pay top dollar for a 1 GHz chip simply to write down a few words.

Getting StarOffice

StarOffice is freely available from Sun Microsystems, Inc. You can download it from Sun's Web site or purchase a copy on CD-ROM for $10. To download it from the Web site, follow these steps:

1. **Log in as a regular user and start Mozilla.**

   We recommend that you install StarOffice as a regular user, and that's what we show you how to do here. That's because you want to be able to use it without changing its file permissions and ownership. Using StarOffice as a regular user can be difficult if you install it as root.

2. **Go to** www.sun.com/staroffice/get.html.

3. **Under the heading Free Downloads! (see Figure 14-1), click the <u>StarOffice 5.2 software</u> link.**

   The StarOffice 5.2 Application Suite Web page appears.

4. **Click your language under the Linux (x86) column heading towards the top-left of the page.**

5. **Assuming this is your first time downloading StarOffice, click the Register button.**

Figure 14-1:
Sun Micro-
systems'
Get
StarOffice
page.

6. **Type in the username and password that you want to use; then give Sun the story of your life by entering your name, address, and so on. Then click the Register button.**

The next screen is for the lawyers.

7. **Click the Accept button and then click Continue.**

8. **The Sun Download window provides three different U.S. time zones from which to download: East, Central, and West.**

There are also European and Asian zones. Select the zone closest to you and click the Download StarOffice 5.2, Linux, English (97.62MB) button.

The Save As window dialog box appears.

97.62MB is a lot of megabytes. If you're using a 56K modem, it should take several hours to download. The people at Sun are nice — they let you download the file in pieces so that you don't have to download the whole monstrous file in one sitting. For this book, we assume you down-load the one big file, which is much less complicated to deal with. The time needed to download StarOffice is worth it. Just think: You get a fully fledged word processing, spreadsheet editing, database-ing, HTML-ing piece of software! If you're pressed for time and don't want to download StarOffice in pieces, remember, you can always buy the CD.

9. **Click the Save button.**

The StarOffice installation file is saved to your home directory. You can then exit Mozilla if you want.

If you haven't configured Linux to connect to the Internet yet, use Chapters 5, 6, and 7, which give you instructions for connecting to the Internet. After you connect, use the Mozilla browser to go to the Sun Web site and download the software as described in the preceding steps, or order StarOffice on CD from the following URL for $9.95 plus shipping:

```
www.sun.com/products/staroffice/5.2/buy.html#small
```

Installing StarOffice

After downloading StarOffice (the filename is `so-5_2-ga-bin-linux-en.bin`), you must install the program.

 These steps assume that you've got plenty of room in the file system where you want install StarOffice. So, don't take another step, buster, before you make sure that you have enough space — at least 100MB — on the file system of your choice. The steps that follow show you how to install StarOffice in the /home directory, so you'll need at least 100MB there. If you use the default Red Hat installation (see Chapter 3), you can find the /home directory in the Root (/) file system.

To install StarOffice in the /home directory, follow these steps:

1. **Log in as root.**

   StarOffice comes stored in a self-extracting file. But before you can extract it, you must turn on its Linux execution privileges.

2. **Start Nautilus by clicking the GNOME Main Menu button and choosing Programs⇨File Manager.**

3. **Go to the directory where you saved the** `so-5_2-ga-bin-linux-en.bin` **file.**

   Figure 14-2 shows the Nautilus window.

4. **Turn on the Linux execution flag by right-clicking the file and then choosing Properties from the pop-up menu that appears.**

5. **Click the Permissions tab in the Properties window (see Figure 14-3).**

6. **Click the User button in the Exec column and then click the OK button.**

   The file can now be executed by root.

 You can manually change the file permission to add execute (x) privilege by running the following command from a terminal session:

```
chmod +x /home/useraccount/so-5_2-ga-bin-linux-en.bin
```

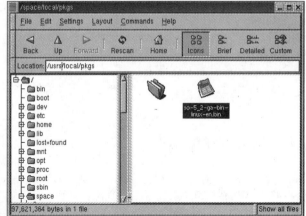

Figure 14-2:
The Nautilus
File
Manager.

Figure 14-3:
Making the
StarOffice
installation
script
executable.

The pathname that you supply depends on where you downloaded the software. The preceding instruction assumes that you downloaded Star Office to your home directory. If you put it someplace else, or have a CD-ROM copy, then make the appropriate adjustments.

7. **Start the installation process by double-clicking the** `so-5_2-ga-bin-linux-en.bin` **file icon in the File Manager window.**

StarOffice is powerful. It's also big. Depending on how fast your computer is, it may take a minute or two for the script to run and the installation process to begin. After it starts, the Welcome to the Installation window appears, as shown Figure 14-4.

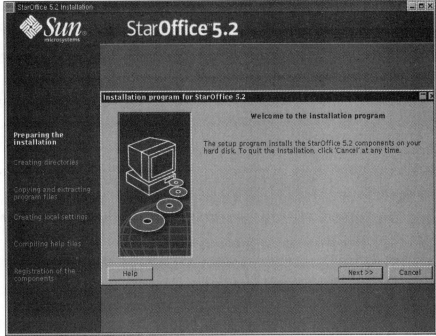

Figure 14-4:
The
StarOffice
installation
window.

8. **Click Next.**

   The Important Information screen appears.

9. **Read the oh-so-important information and click the Next button.**

   The next window takes care of the lawyers.

10. **Click Accept.**

11. **(Optional) Enter your life's history in the Enter User Data window that appears and click Next.**

   Your user information is included in all StarOffice documents that you create — so maybe you should edit your life history before you type it into this window.

   The Select Installation Type window appears.

   You have three installation types to choose from. The standard one includes most of the StarOffice features, but it takes over 265MB of hard drive space. If you want to roll your own installation, select the Custom option. You're prompted in further windows to select the features to install. If you're tight for space, then select the Minimal install. We assume that you select the Standard installation here.

12. **Click the Standard Installation option and then click Next.**

    The StarOffice setup program wants to install itself into your home directory. If you select the default, it creates the directory — for example, /home/lidia/Office52 — for you. We use the StarOffice default here.

13. **Click Next.**

    You are prompted to let the setup program create the /Office52 directory in your home directory for you.

14. **Click Yes.**

    A dialog box is opened that asks you if you want to run Java.

15. **You do not need to run Java, so click the Next button.**

    The Start Copying screen appears. As each StarOffice module — for example the word processor — is installed, you are given short explanations of what they do. You're also shown a progress meter that displays the estimated time to completion.

    When the installation process is finished, a window opens up thanking you for installing StarOffice.

16. **Say, "You're welcome," and click the Complete button.**

    StarOffice is installed to your Red Hat Linux computer.

17. **Click OK to continue.**

    Your software is installed. You may encounter messages that tell you that certain secondary elements can't be installed for one reason or another. They shouldn't cause any problems for you, so just click OK.

    The installation is finished, and you're shown the Installation Completed window.

18. **Click the Complete button.**

    You now have a great word processing system — and more.

StarOffice 6.0 is now being created, and we're hoping that it'll be in circulation by the time this book is published. StarOffice 6.0 is leaner and more powerful than 5.2. Version 5.2 bundles all the functions — word processing, spreadsheet, presentations, and so on — into one big program. Version 6.0 separates the functions into separate pieces making it easier to use, faster, and more reliable.

Getting to know StarOffice

If you're familiar with Microsoft Office, then you should be able to find your way around StarOffice. The look and feel is a little different, but the idea is the same. StarOffice is also morally superior to Office because it's free *and* open source. The following sections briefly describe some of the most common functions of StarOffice.

This section provides only a basic introduction to the things you can do with StarOffice. No, we're not lazy — it's just that it would take too much space to describe it all in detail. Please experiment with your own test documents and consult the online help for more information, or see *StarOffice For LINUX For Dummies* by Michael Meadhra (Hungry Minds, Inc.).

Firing up StarOffice

After you install StarOffice, you need to be able to start it. You can create a GNOME applet launcher that starts StarOffice with a click of a mouse. To do so, follow these steps:

1. **Click the GNOME Main Menu button and choose Panel⇨Add to Panel⇨ Launcher menus.**

   The Create Launcher Applet window appears, as shown in Figure 14-5.

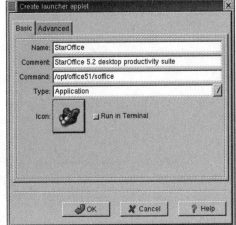

Figure 14-5: Creating an applet launcher window for StarOffice.

2. **Enter the name of the launcher icon in the Name text box.**

   For instance, type **StarOffice**.

3. **(Optional) You can enter a comment in the Comment text box.**

   The text that you enter is displayed over the icon when you place the mouse cursor over it.

4. **Enter the location of the StarOffice program in the Command text box.**

   For example, type **/home/lidia/Office52/soffice** if that's where you installed it.

   StarOffice supplies some images that can be used for the applet icon, but they're sorta wimpy. Instead, we use the normal GNOME icons; in this example, we select the GNOME tigrette.

5. **Click the OK button in the launcher window.**

   The new icon is inserted into the GNOME Panel (the bar along the bottom of your screen).

6. **Click the new StarOffice launcher that you just created in the GNOME panel.**

   After thinking about life for a while, the StarOffice window appears, as shown in Figure 14-6.

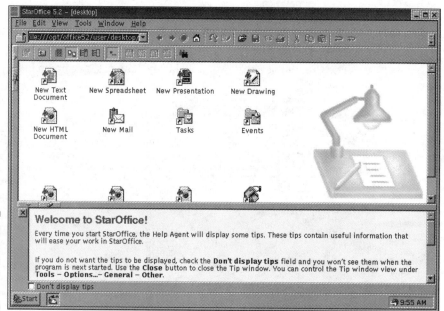

Figure 14-6:
The
StarOffice
desktop
window.

The first time that you start up StarOffice, it prompts you to decide if you want to use the Internet. If you click Yes, it tries to find information about how you connect to the Net. With the default Red Hat Linux installation, StarOffice should find that you have Mozilla. Click Mozilla and then click Next. If you use Mozilla to read e-mail from the Internet, click the Don't Use the Internet button.

Wandering around the desktop

The StarOffice window that is displayed in the previous section (refer to Figure 14-6) is the launching point for all the StarOffice components and is referred to as the *desktop*. StarOffice is technically also a window manager just like GNOME; it displays the individual applications that make up Star Office. You can also show files and directories in the desktop just like you do with GNOME or Windows.

The desktop is organized by default to show the applications available to you from StarOffice. You can click the New Text Document icon, for example, and StarOffice opens up the Writer word processor with a new document for you.

The desktop is really a file manager that you can access and use files and directories. The StarOffice desktop default directory is `Office52/user/desktop` (Office52 is installed in `/home/login` by default, where login is your login name, so the full pathname is `/home/login/Office52/user/desktop`). Therefore, it displays the applications stored in that directory. Those applications are actually URLs that point to the actual applications; you can view the information about the URLs by right-clicking any of them and then choosing Properties from the pop-up menu.

To demonstrate how the StarOffice desktop works as a file manager, click the Up One Level button near the top-left of the screen (it looks like a yellow folder with an up arrow on it). The desktop displays the next directory up — `/home/login/Office52/user`. This directory contains mostly directories and is displayed as such. Keep moving up by levels and you eventually go to the root (/) directory.

The desktop also has a menu bar displayed across the top of the screen. You can access all its functions through this menu. The following list introduces the main menu functions. You're probably familiar with the layout and operation of the menu if you're familiar with Microsoft Office:

✔ **File:** As you may expect, you can open, close, save, and otherwise manipulate StarOffice documents with the File menu. Writer files have the .sdw suffix. Other file formats, such as Microsoft Word and HTML, must be imported and exported.

✔ **Edit:** Provides all the functions that you need to modify documents. Functions such as cut, copy, paste, and delete are all provided here. The functions that are active at any time depend on whether you are editing a document, spreadsheet, or presentation. For example, the cut, copy, and paste options aren't active if you're not editing a document (like just after you start up StarOffice and have not opened any files).

You can also track changes just like with Microsoft Word. Go to Edit⇨ Changes, and you can track changes on a character-by-character basis. You can display the changes or keep them hidden from view. When you're satisfied with your edits, you can commit the changes and save only the finished document to disk. Pretty cool.

StarOffice also provides the Find and Replace function from the Edit menu. The Find and Replace feature enables you to find text strings and either replace them with another string or delete them. You can search forward or backward through a document. You can replace one instance or all instances.

✔ **View:** Displays or hides the various menu bars. You can display a document's formatting characters and also increase or decrease the size — zoom in or out — of the text displayed on the screen. The zoom function enables you to make smaller fonts more readable without changing the document.

✔ **Insert:** Lets you insert special characters, objects, files, and macros into your documents. Special characters include various symbols (accents and umlauts, for example) that aren't part of the everyday character set (unless you happen to use word like cafés a lot). Objects include graphics, symbols, and figures. (You can create your own figures with Draw.) You can also insert macros and hyperlinks into your documents.

You can insert tables into documents with any number of rows and columns. Words can automatically adjust the row height, or you can do it manually. Choose Insert⇨Tables and play around with it.

✔ **Tools:** Provides access to the spell checker, thesaurus, and similar functions. The spell checker and thesaurus are self-explanatory.

✔ **Window:** This menu provides control over how your desktop looks. It can modify and move windows as well as provide other manipulation capabilities.

✔ **Help:** StarOffice provides pretty good online help services. Many are context sensitive. If you are editing a text document, click the Help menu to get access to information related to the Writer module.

For example, choose Help⇨Help Agent, and the Help Agent window appears. The Help Agent provides assistance in several areas of interest to the new user, including the following:

- **Introduction to Writer:** Provides an introduction to the word processor.

- **Basics tips text documents:** All you ever want to know (and then some) about reading, writing, and printing text documents.

- **Advanced tips:** Extends the previous basic text document tip to more advanced subjects.

- **Menus:** Describes how all the StarOffice menus work together.

- **Toolbars:** Describes the toolbars that provide information and shortcuts.

- **Shortcuts:** Describes what key combinations can be used to perform various word processing functions.

- **New stuff:** Describes what's new since the last StarOffice version.

- **Support:** Displays brief information about getting support from Sun Microsystems.

Printing with StarOffice

Printing from StarOffice is a simple process after you have configured Red Hat Linux to use a printer. This section first describes how to configure a Red Hat Linux printer and then shows how to setup StarOffice to use that printer.

Configuring a printer that is attached to your Red Hat Linux computer is a simple process. All that you have to do is run the `printtool` configuration tool and enter the information about your printer. The following steps describe how to do it:

1. **Log in to your Red Hat Linux computer as root.**

2. **Attach a printer to your Linux computer's parallel (printer) port.**

   The parallel port is a 25-pin female connector on the back of your computer case. New computers usually label the parallel port with some kind of printer icon (although sometimes it's hard to imagine how they come up with the symbol). If yours isn't marked, there's no harm in plugging your printer into the appropriate port. If you choose a non-printer port, it's probably a serial port and nothing bad can happen other than not being able to print. In that case, use trial-and-error to find the correct port.

3. **Start the printer configuration tool by clicking the GNOME Main Menu Button and choosing Programs⇨System⇨Printtool.**

   If you haven't already configured a printer, `printtool` starts up with a blank screen.

4. **To add a printer, click the Add button.**

   The Add a Printer Entry window appears, as shown in Figure 14-7.

   If you're not on a network, you want to configure a local printer, which is the option selected by default.

Figure 14-7:
The Add a Printer Entry window.

5. **Click OK to install a local printer.**

   Because your printer is already connected, `printtool` detects and displays it.

6. **Click OK.**

The Edit Local Printer Entry window appears, as shown in Figure 14-8.

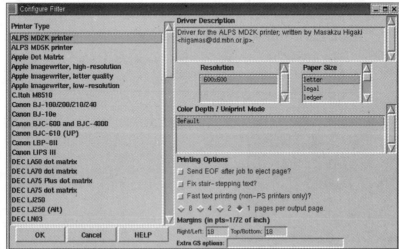

The default values for the printer name, spool directory, and file limit fields should all be acceptable. (You can choose any name for the printer that you want, but by convention, the default name is lp. You can assign multiple names to a single printer.)

7. **If your printer port is detected, it appears in the Printer Device field; if it doesn't, choose the port yourself and then click the Input Filter Select button.**

The Configure Filter window appears, as shown in Figure 14-9.

8. **Highlight and select the correct printer type and click OK.**

   The control will be sent back to the Edit Local Printer Entry window.

9. **Click OK.**

   You are sent back to the RHS Linux Printer System Manager window, where your new printer is displayed.

10. **To test your new printer setup, choose Tests⇨Print Postscript Test Page (you can also choose to print a plain text file).**

    The PostScript test file is printed.

Now that you have a printer connected to your Red Hat Linux computer, you can print from StarOffice without any further configuration. StarOffice uses the Red Hat Linux printer configuration by default. Open a file that you want to print. From the StarOffice desktop, choose File⇨Print. You can choose to print the entire document, individual pages, or ranges of pages. It's quick and easy.

Importing and exporting Office files

The File menu contains the Import and Export selections, from which you can import an office file from major office productivity suite formats, such as Microsoft Office and WordPerfect. To import a file, follow these steps:

1. **Choose File⇨Import.**

   The StarOffice File Manager window appears.

2. **Double-click any of the directories to browse the Red Hat Linux file system (directories are distinguished by orange file folder icons).**

3. **Click the file that you want to open.**

4. **Click the Open button. StarOffice imports the file and you can happily edit away.**

You can use the StarOffice export function to convert a file into another format. Exporting files is similar to the import process described before. Just select File⇨Export and select the format and then save the file.

The Word Is AbiWord

In addition to the StarOffice and Applixware software you can use, GNOME gives writers another excellent, lightweight word processor called AbiWord. AbiWord is capable of reading and writing Microsoft Word files. It also has its own native format. We use AbiWord to create and modify simple Word files.

Applications galore!

The list of Linux applications is growing by leaps and bounds. Red Hat maintains a Web page for information on Linux applications — both commercial and open source. The address of that page is www.redhat.com/appindex/index.html.

You can find programs for every major area of interest on this page. The list is constantly growing and is a good indication of the overall health and future direction of Linux.

You can 't use AbiWord to write whole books or for other complex word processing jobs, but it does quite well when all you need to do is write a memo or view a Word file. And AbiWord provides good fonts, spell checking, and other basic functions.

You can start AbiWord by logging in as any user, clicking the Main Menu Button, and choosing Programs⇨Applications⇨AbiWord. Figure 14-10 shows the AbiWord window with a simple sentence written in it.

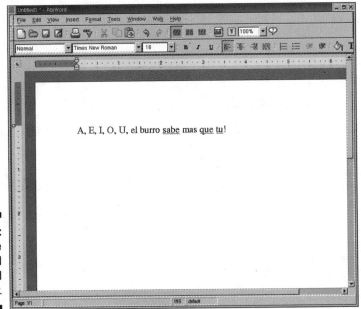

Figure 14-10:
Behold the
AbiWord
word
processor.

Part IV
Revenge of the Nerds

The 5th Wave
By Rich Tennant

"Think of our relationship as a version of Red Hat Linux – I will not share a directory on the love-branch of your life."

In this part . . .

In the great tradition of slackers and procrastinators, we've left the real work for last. In this part, you find out about the basics of running a Red Hat Linux computer. These chapters won't make you into a Linux guru capable of commanding six-figure consulting fees, but they will introduce you to the technical side of Linux.

We start by describing the standard Linux shell called bash in Chapter 15. Chapter 16 introduces the basics of Linux files and directories. We move on to teach you how to manage disks and partitions in Chapter 17.

If you're to manage a Red Hat Linux box, then some serious attention is warranted, and given, in Chapter 19. It provides some detailed help in fixing computer problems. Networking is used as the backdrop for your troubleshooting apprenticeship. We finish up your nerdy education by describing how to reconfigure your X display. When you're done with this part, you'll be wearing pocket protectors with the best of us!

Chapter 15

Bashing Your Shell

• •

In This Chapter

▶ Discovering the bash shell

▶ Experimenting with wildcards

▶ Using bash history to find files

▶ Banging around to find files

• •

*1*magine that you are in a foreign country, for instance New Mexico (Estados Unidos de Norte America), and you don't know the language (English and Español), so you hire an interpreter to accompany you. You tell the interpreter what you want to do and where you want to go. Assuming that nothing goes wrong with your flight, the interpreter then decides what steps to take (hire a taxi or take the subway, for example) and in what order. When you to talk to people, the interpreter translates your statements into that country's native language. Sorta simple in concept, but you need to do your homework first to make it work right.

Shells do much the same thing that your interpreter would do. They take the English-like commands that you type in, gather resources (such as filenames and memory), and supply lower-level statements to the computer to do what you want. Shells act as command line interpreters (CLI) — introduced in Chapter 4 — providing you with a platform to launch applications and Linux utilities.

Bashing Ahead!

In Red Hat Linux, bash is the default shell. The first thing that you need to do is to give bash a platform. You can do that by starting a terminal emulation program such as the GNOME terminal that is provided by the GNOME window environment. A *terminal emulator program* simulates the old-style terminals that were used for many years to interact with computers.

You can start the GNOME terminal emulator program by clicking the icon that looks like a computer screen on the GNOME main panel, as shown in Figure 15-1.

Figure 15-1:
The GNOME
terminal
icon in the
GNOME
main panel.

Terminal icon

The GNOME terminal emulation window appears, as shown in Figure 15-2 (terminal emulators are also referred to as *Xterms,* which is short for X terminal). You see the bash shell prompt in the GNOME terminal window. Your shell prompt looks something like this:

```
[lidia@veracruz lidia]$
```

The most important element of this *prompt* is the $ at the end of the line, which is the shell's method of saying, "Okay, I'm finished with the last thing, so give me something else to do." The information contained within the square brackets ([ ]) tells you who you are logged in as, the name of the computer that you are logged in to, and the last part of the directory that you are in; for instance, if you are in your home directory, /home/me, the *me* part of the directory is displayed.

If you are logged in as root or have become a superuser through the use of the su(1) command, the $ is replaced with a # sign, which indicates that the user is root or otherwise has become a superuser. You should be careful not to reset the superuser's # prompt to a $. The # prompt is a warning of sorts that tells you that you're running as the superuser. You need to be careful when running as the superuser because you can easily run commands that will hurt your computer — such as rm -rf /, which erases your entire disk.

To make sure that your default shell is the bash shell rather than one of the other shells, type the following:

```
[lidia@veracruz lidia]$ bash
```

After you press Enter, Red Hat Linux gives you one of two responses. If bash wasn't installed properly, you see the following:

```
command not found
```

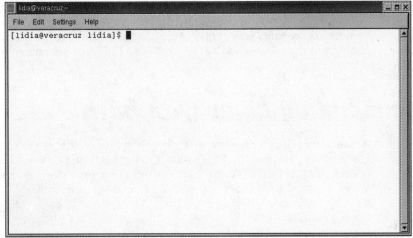

Figure 15-2:
The GNOME
terminal
emulation
window.

If you didn't install your own Linux system, you should find the person who did and give him a wedgie . . . no, no. You should find the person who installed your Linux system and kindly ask him to help you use the bash shell as your default shell.

You can find out where commands are located by using **which**. For instance, running **which bash** returns /bin/bash. That tells you that the bash program is in the /bin directory.

When you log in to a Red Hat Linux computer, you're assigned a shell to use. The shell is specified in the /etc/passwd file. The root user, for instance, has a line in the passwd file that looks like this: root:x:0:0:root:/root:/ bin/bash. The segment /bin/bash tells Red Hat Linux where to find the shell to use for the user.

If you're lucky, you see the following:

```
[lidia@veracruz lidia]$
```

Geez. Linux didn't seem to do much. It did, though. You're definitely in the bash shell and ready to see its power.

If you're logged in as superuser or root (a # appears at the end of your shell prompt), change over to a nonsuperuser account. No examples in this chapter require superuser privileges. And because you're experimenting with shells, limiting potential damage is a good idea. Remember, it's not called *superuser* for nothing. You should also alias commands like rm and mv to rm -i and mv -i respectively. The -i option forces rm and mv to ask you before deleting or moving files. Adding such protections makes it more difficult to delete or move files and directories unintentionally. The alias commands are **alias rm = 'rm -i'** and **alias mv = 'mv -i'** respectively. You should put those aliases in /etc/bashrc so they'll be set for every user.

Commanding Linux with bash

A *command* is just a program that you run in order to get something done. For instance, you use the ls command to list files and the mount command to make a floppy or CD-ROM drive accessible. Linux provides a rich and varied set of standard commands that you use to manage your system.

Issuing commands can be simple or complicated. That's because Red Hat Linux is a powerful operating system and can do just about anything that you want it to. We introduce some Red Hat Linux commands in this chapter.

Commands can contain one, two, or all three parts, but the first part — the command name — must always be present. Linux commands three major parts are:

✔ The command name

✔ Options to the command (telling the command how to change its actions for a specific execution)

✔ Input or output files, which supply data or give the command a place to put output data, respectively

A shell for all seasons

When Ken Thompson and Dennis Ritchie first started writing Unix, they wanted to investigate lots of new ideas in using computers. One of the ideas they explored was making the human interface to the computer changeable and adaptable to the specific needs of the application.

This human interface (or more specifically, what humans interact with most) is typically called a *command interpreter* because it looks at each command as it is typed and converts it into something the computer can follow as an instruction. Most computer systems back then had the command interpreter built into the operating system, which meant the user couldn't change it. (DOS is constructed this way.) The Unix developers wanted to separate the command interpreter from the rest of the operating system. Because the functionality desired was both a command interpreter and a complete environment, it was called a *shell*. The first command interpreter for Unix was called the Bourne shell, often abbreviated as sh.

Later, when Unix escaped from Bell Labs and fled to the University of California, Berkeley, the developers decided to extend the shell. They made it more of a programming language and included some features found in the C language. The resulting shell was the C shell, abbreviated csh (pronounced "sea shell," of course).

Both the Bourne shell and the C shell existed for many years. The Bourne shell version was available on both System V and Berkeley-based systems. The C shell was used only on Berkeley systems — AT&T was paranoid about having a shell on its system that was created by long-haired college students. The researchers at Bell Labs fought to add the C shell, and eventually it was ported to System V, too.

Next, enter GNU, a collection of software based on Unix and maintained by the Free Software Foundation. (GNU, by the way, stands for GNU's Not Unix.) The GNU project decided it needed a shell free of royalty restrictions. Unfortunately, at the time, the C shell was still under restrictions from AT&T. So the GNU folks decided to create their own royalty-free, GPLed shell. Their new shell would be compatible with the Bourne shell, incorporate some of the C shell ideas, and have some interesting new features. They called their shell bash, for Bourne Again SHell.

Meanwhile, innovation stirred at AT&T. David Korn, a researcher there, merged the best of the Bourne shell, C shell, and any other shells he could find, and made the resulting shell even better for programmers by implementing several programming features. The most notable addition was *functions* (which helps to divide large shells into smaller, easier-to-maintain ones). His shell was named the Korn shell (abbreviated ksh). Eventually, this shell also developed graphical features and was adopted by the Open Software Foundation folks as part of their Common Desktop Environment (dtksh).

As the price of computers dropped and freely distributable versions of Unix (netBSD, FreeBSD, and Linux) made their way across the Internet, new shells evolved from the old ones and other shells started to appear, such as

- ✔ **tcsh:** A C shell with filename completion and command-line editing

- ✔ **ash:** A System V–like shell

- ✔ **zsh:** Like ksh, but with built-in spelling correction on the command-line completion, among other useful features

- ✔ **pdksk:** A public domain re-implementation of the Korn shell

So why do we have all these shells (and shell-like languages)? They are examples of how separating the command interface from the operating system can allow the language to grow and improve. They are also examples of how specialized languages can be combined with other shells and programs to do really powerful work. If one shell existed under the control of one person or organization, innovation would probably take much longer.

Using commands without having to say please

To see how the three parts of a command work together, suppose you type the following Linux command at the shell prompt:

```
ls -l *
```

When bash looks at that line, it performs the following steps:

1. The bash shell creates a new environment for the ls command to be executed in and determines what should be *standard input* and *standard output* to the command. Standard input is normally the keyboard, and standard output is normally the video screen. (You find out more about environments in a moment.)

2. Then, bash expands * to match all the filenames in that particular directory. By *expanding* the filenames, we mean that certain special characters are used to indicate groups of filenames. When these characters are used, the computer sees what filenames match up with these special characters and supplies the filenames to the command, instead of the special characters.

    For example, suppose that you have the files ert, wert, uity, and opgt in your current directory. If you type

    ```
    ls -l *
    ```

    to the ls command, it looks like you typed

    ```
    ls -l ert opgt uity wert
    ```

    The shell puts the names in alphabetical order before giving them to the command.

3. Next, bash searches the PATH environmental variable looking for a command called ls. The PATH variable holds the names of directories that contain commands you may want to execute. If the command you want is not in the list, you have to explicitly tell the shell where it can find the command by typing either a complete or relative pathname to the command.

4. After bash finds ls, it executes the ls command in the new environment, passing to the command the -l argument and all the filenames it expanded, due to the use of the * character in the command.

5. After ls runs, bash returns to the current environment, throwing away all the side effects that occurred in the new environment, such as an environmental variable changing its value.

In Step 1, we mentioned the *environment*. A shell operates in an environment just like humans live and work in an environment. We expect to have and use certain things in our human environment. Suppose you leave your office for a few days, and someone else steps in to use it. At first, this newcomer uses your environment as you arranged it. The person probably appreciates the fact that the phone works, office supplies are in the desk, and so on. But after a while, the newcomer starts moving and changing things, and maybe even drinking decaffeinated coffee out of your coffee mug! When you come back from your trip, everything is changed. You can't find things easily, and green stuff is growing in the bottom of your mug. Wouldn't it have been nice if that person had left the office (your environment) exactly as you had arranged it?

The bash shell creates an environment for commands to operate in. When a new command is executed, bash creates a clean copy of the environment, executes the command in it, and then throws away that environment, returning to the environment it started with.

Now look at a more complex example than just the one command ls -l *:

```
cd /usr/lib
ls -l * | more
```

In this case:

1. The bash shell creates a new environment for the ls command to be executed in and determines what should be the input (called *standard input* in technical jargon) and the output (called *standard output* in nerd-speak) to the command. You can call this new environment child number 1; the old environment is its parent.

2. Next, bash creates another new environment for the more command to be executed in, called child number 2, and determines what should be input and output to the more command. Because the pipe | symbol is used between the ls -l * command and the more command, the output of the ls -l * command is sent to the input of the more command. The output of more is sent to the output of the parent bash shell. The parent shell is the one into which you have been typing commands and information, and the output of that original bash shell is the screen.

3. And then bash expands * to match all the filenames in that particular directory, as before.

4. Next, in the child 1 environment, bash searches the PATH environmental variable looking for a command called ls. The same process occurs for the more command in child number 2.

5. bash executes the ls command in the child number 1 environment, passing to the command the -l argument and all the filenames it expanded, due to the use of the * character in the command.

6. The more command sees the output of ls -l * as its input, and puts its output to the screen.

   The output of a command or application is sent to standard output (stdout); input comes from standard input (stdin). Linux (and UNIX too) uses the concept of stdout and stdin to — what else — standardize the location that input and output taken from and sent to. The terminal emulator window is stdout by default; your keyboard is stdin by default.

7. After ls runs, bash returns to the parent environment, throwing away all the side effects that occurred in the child number 1 environment.

8. The `more` command sees the end of its input from `ls`, puts the last of its data out to the screen, and terminates.

9. The `bash` shell returns to its parent environment, throwing away all the changes that `more` may have made to the child number 2 environment.

The original `bash` shell is called the *parent,* and the two new environments that `bash` created are called *children,* or *child number 1* and *child number 2.*

Putting the output of one into the standard input of the other, as demonstrated with the command

```
ls -l * | more
```

is called *piping.* The | symbol is called — you guessed it — the pipe symbol.

Getting in the pipeline

Many Linux commands generate a lot of output, and if it all went to standard output as output to the screen, without some type of control, it would scroll past. For example, type the following:

```
ls -al /etc
```

This command lists all the files in your /usr directory. Because this directory holds a truckload of files, the information scrolls down your screen faster than you — or any Evelyn Wood graduate — can read it. You can, however, correct this.

With a process called *piping,* Linux and UNIX can use the output from one command as the input for another. It's not as confusing as it sounds. In the previous section, we showed you what happens when you have too much information — or *output* — to fit on one lonely screen. You can take that information and put — or *input* — it into a program that divides the information into screen-sized pieces and then displays them. This all comes under the heading of input/output (I/O) redirection. Got it?

To get the piping process started, you use the `more` command, which is an appropriate name for this tool. You *pipe* the list command's output to the `more` command. But how do you pipe? You use the | character on your keyboard. We bet you were wondering what the heck that key was for. Type the command as follows:

```
ls -al /etc | more
```

Linux doesn't care if spaces surround the | character, but you may want to use them for clarity and to get in the habit of including spaces because they are important at other times.

When you press Enter, the information appears one screen at a time with the word *More* appearing at the bottom of each screen except the last one. To move to the next screen, press the spacebar. When you finish with the last screen, the more command takes you back to the Linux prompt. The more command can do even, well, more. When the screen halts with the word *More* appearing at the bottom, you can type some commands to the more program:

- ✔ **q** to get out of the more command without wading through all those screens
- ✔ **h** to see a list of all commands available in the more command

If you press Enter after one screen, Linux shows you the next entry in the list, not the next screen.

Some commands to the more program (such as the b command) don't work when you're piping input into the program, as opposed to using more with a file.

Deleting text from the Linux command line

Everyone makes mistakes. Everyone changes his or her mind from time to time. For those reasons, you need to know how to delete text from the Linux command line. If you want to start over, press Ctrl+U to remove everything you have typed on the command line — if you have not yet pressed Enter. The Backspace key erases one character at a time. The left- and right-arrow keys move the cursor along the line of characters without erasing; when you get to the place you want to change, use the Backspace key to erase mistakes and retype changes. In most cases, the up- and down-arrow keys jump the cursor back and forth through the last few commands.

Getting less for more

Linux sometimes uses a command called less, which duplicates the functionality of the more command. Originally, the less command was designed to be more robust than the more command, but the more command caught up and they are now almost the same. Some Linux systems display text with the less command instead of the more command, which most Unix programs use.

The less and more commands have two apparent differences. One, the less command requires a q command to get back to the Linux prompt, even when you're at the end of the last page. Two, the more command always says *More* at the bottom of a screen, whereas less has just a : character at the bottom of the screen to indicate that it's waiting for you to input the next command.

Regular expressions: Wildcards and one-eyed jacks

If you had to type every filename for every command, Linux would still be useful. But something that makes Linux more useful is the capability to use a few special characters — called *metacharacters, pattern-matching characters, wildcards*, or *regular expressions* — to supply filenames. Just as you can substitute wildcards for any card of your choice in a poker game, Linux pattern-matching characters can be substituted for filenames and directory names, much like DOS wildcards.

Three of these special pattern-matching characters follow:

- ✔ * (asterisk)
- ✔ ? (question mark)
- ✔ \ (backslash)

The asterisk matches at least one character in any filename. For example, * matches the following filenames:

> a
>
> acd
>
> bce
>
> moody

You'll probably use * the most in the command ls -l *.

The question mark matches any single character. The string of characters a?c, for example, matches the following:

> abc
>
> adc
>
> aac
>
> afc
>
> a9c

Using careful naming conventions

The question mark and the asterisk can be helpful for identifying particular types of files, if you're careful about naming your files. For example, text editor files usually have the .txt extension, and Microsoft Word files have the .doc extension. Linux doesn't care what the name of a file is, but some programs work only with a particular type of file.

Suppose you followed the convention of naming all your text files with the .txt extension, and you want to see all the text files in a directory. You can use the ls command like this:

```
ls -l *.txt
```

The screen displays all the files in this directory with the .txt extension. Notice that we didn't say that the command shows you all text files or that it shows only text files. If you want to name a graphics file with a .txt extension, Linux happily obliges you. For your own sanity, however, be diligent in naming files. Some programs (such as those that create audio files or picture files) strictly enforce a naming convention on files they create, but Linux itself doesn't care.

What to do if you're not careful naming files

What do you do if the * is part of the filename you're trying to match? How can you tell the shell that you want only the file that contains *, and not all the other files? The backslash character prevents the shell from interpreting the * as a metacharacter and expanding it — in Linux terminology, the backslash *escapes* the meaning of the special character. For example, hi*est matches a file named *hightest,* but hi*est matches only the *hi*est* filename.

If you want to delete the file hi*est, then enter the command:

```
rm hi*est
```

The * expands to mean any character or characters (actually, * can also mean zero, or no characters) and the file is removed. You can also explicitly delete the file by using the following command:

```
rm hi\*est
```

The backslash tells the shell to treat the asterisk as a character and not to expand it to mean zero or more characters.

Although more regular expression characters are available, the ones listed in this section are enough for you to work with for a while.

Tweaking Linux Commands with Options

Most Linux commands are flexible and can be modified to perform special tasks. You can use two devices to alter a command: command options and standard input and standard output redirection. You find out about command options first.

You can use *command options* to fine-tune the actions of a Linux command. We introduce the ls command earlier in this chapter so that you can see the results of actions taken on the file system. To see how its options work, in the next example, try out the ls command several times, with different options.

Use the mkdir command to make a new directory called vacation and then use the cd command to change your working directory to that new directory:

```
[lidia@veracruz emptydirectory]$ mkdir vacation
[lidia@veracruz emptydirectory]$ cd vacation
```

At the Linux prompt, type ls as follows:

```
[lidia@veracruz vacation]$ ls
[lidia@veracruz vacation]$
```

That didn't do much, did it? It seems as if the account has no files. You may need an option. Try the -a option and see what happens:

```
[lidia@veracruz vacation]$ ls -a
.  ..
[lidia@veracruz vacation]$
```

Remember to type the commands and options exactly as shown. For example, the ls -a command has a space between the command and the option, and no space between the hyphen and the letter *a*.

Notice the two files (they're actually directories, but in Linux all directories are just files) that the ls command displayed. What? All you see are dots? Well, the single dot represents the directory you are in; the double dot represents the parent directory, which is typically the one above the directory you're in. (Linux creates these filenames and puts them into the directory for you. If you just installed your directory, all you have are files that begin with a period.)

Next, create a few additional files in the `vacation` directory, by using the `touch` command:

```
[lidia@veracruz vacation]$ touch file1
[lidia@veracruz vacation]$ touch .dotfile
```

Now if you use the same `ls` command (without the -a option), you see the following:

```
[lidia@veracruz vacation]$ ls
file1
[lidia@veracruz vacation]$
```

And if you redo the `ls` command with the -a option, you get this:

```
[lidia@veracruz vacation]$ ls -a
...  .dotfile   file1
[lidia@veracruz vacation]$
```

The `ls` command by default doesn't list files that begin with a period. By adding the -a option, you modify the action taken by `ls` to print every filename whether or not it begins with a dot.

The `ls` command has many options, and you can use more than one at a time. Want to see how? Modify the -a option by adding l (ell) to it. The command line becomes

```
[lidia@veracruz vacation]$ls -al
total 5
drwx------ 3 (user)(group)(size) Jul 04 14:33 ./
drwxr-xr-x 6 (user)(group)(filesize) Jul 04 22:15 ../
-rw-rw-r-- 1 (user)(group)(size) Jul 04 11:30 .dotfile
-rw-rw-r-- 1 (user)(group)(size) Jul 04 17:40 file1
```

As you can see, instead of just listing the filenames, the l option shows a more detailed listing of files. If long listings don't fit on a single line, Linux just wraps them to the next line.

 Most of the time, Linux doesn't care about what order you type the options and therefore considers `ls -al` and `ls -la` to be the same. Multiple option choices aren't available with all commands, though, and they work only with commands that have single letters to specify their options.

The `ls` command lists files in alphabetical order as the default, but you can tailor the output. For example, `ls -alt` displays the files in order by date and time, with the most recent first; `ls -altr` reverses that order.

Letting bash's Memory Make Your Life Easier

The bash shell has a good memory. By default, it remembers your last 500 commands. That function is very useful because it allows you to recycle your work. Several ways exist for recalling your past work, and this section describes how to do so.

Editing commands at the command line

One of the most useful bash features is *command-line editing,* which is the capability to change parts of a command line without having to retype the entire command. Suppose you type the following line and pressed Enter:

```
[lidia@veracruz lidia]$ ls -l * | more
```

but you actually meant to use the less command, not the more command.

Groan. You can press Ctrl+C to halt the command. But if you want to reexecute the command, changing *more* to *less*, without having to type the entire command, just type the following:

```
[lidia@veracruz lidia]$ ^more^less
```

This line resubmits the command to bash with more changed to less, as follows:

```
ls -l * | less
```

Output appears. If you have to stop the less command, type **q**.

The shell redisplays the first command with the change, and then the command is reexecuted. How does the shell know about the first command? History. bash remembers all the commands that you have typed (to a certain extent) and allows you to edit and resubmit them. Awesome.

We say "to a certain extent" because bash remembers only a certain number of commands, depending on a parameter in the environment. After bash holds that many previous commands, it throws away the oldest ones as you type in newer ones. Normally, this parameter is large (perhaps 1,000 commands), so bash essentially remembers every command that you enter. (We can't imagine ever wanting to be able to recall more than the last thousand commands that we entered.)

Bang-bang!

The fact that the shell remembers the command lines you type is useful for reexecuting commands at a later time. Simple *reexecution commands* are represented by exclamation points. In computerese, an exclamation point is called a *bang,* and two exclamation points are called — you guessed it — *bang-bang.*

Here are two key ways to use the exclamation point:

- ✔ !! reexecutes the last command.
- ✔ !*<partial command line>* reexecutes the command line that started with *<partial command line>.*

Here's an example. Type **!cat** on the command line as follows (*cat* is the *<partial command line>* mentioned in the preceding list):

```
[lidia@veracruz lidia]$ !cat
```

The bash shell searches backward through the previously executed commands in this session, looking for the first occurrence of a command line that starts with the letters *cat.* After the program locates the command, it is reexecuted.

Are you a little timid about doing this? Perhaps your memory of which command you typed and when is a little faulty. Add :p to the command line to see what history finds. The command looks like this:

```
[lidia@veracruz lidia]$ !cat:p
cat /etc/passwd
```

To run the command that !:p found, enter bang-bang, like this:

```
[lidia@veracruz lidia]$ !!
```

Don't use this type of command recall when logged in as root. It's too easy to mistakenly reexecute a command that causes unintentional problems.

While using history to find and reexecute command lines, you can also make additions to the command line. Starting from the beginning with our example, if you type the following

```
[lidia@veracruz lidia]$ cat /etc/passwd
```

then the file /etc/passwd is output to standard output, which in this case is the screen.

When you reexecute the preceding command by typing !!, you can also send the output to the sort command by using the pipe symbol:

```
[lidia@veracruz lidia]$ !! | sort
cat /etc/passwd |sort
[lidia@veracruz lidia]$
```

Linux pulls the /etc/passwd file from the disk and passes it to standard output, feeds it into the standard input of sort, and then outputs it to the screen in sorted fashion.

The bash shell also makes use of the up-arrow and down-arrow keys to reuse commands. The up-arrow key sequentially returns commands starting from the most recent. The down-arrow key, not surprisingly, goes forward in time. This is bash's most convenient feature.

This history command displays all the commands that you have used up to the Red Hat default of 1,000. You can use the history command to perform a sort of archaeological dig. For instance, if you want to see all the commands of a certain type that you have used, then you can pipe the output of the history command to the grep filter. To find all the times that you have entered the ls command, you can use the command history | grep ls.

Several shells (such as csh, bash, tcsh, and zsh) have this type of simple editing, but bash also has more elaborate editing.

Going back to the future

Linux offers a handy tool for rerunning long commands that you've already entered. Press Ctrl+P, and the display scrolls though the commands that you've entered, one command at a time in reverse order, showing the most recent command first. When the command you want appears on the screen, just press Enter to run it.

Recalling filenames

Suppose your mind has been wandering, and although you do remember that a file in /etc contains passwords, you can't remember whether the file is in /etc/passwd, /etc/password, or whatever. You may want the command interpreter to choose the proper spelling of the filename for you, rather than type what you think it may be.

You can first list the files in the /etc directory, and then use more to view the specific file you want to see (/etc/passwd):

```
[lidia@veracruz lidia]$ ls /etc/pass*
/etc/passwd
[lidia@veracruz lidia]$ more /etc/passwd
```

Or you can use a shortcut with bash by pressing the Tab key after you think you have a unique match:

```
[lidia@veracruz lidia]$ more /etc/pass<TAB>
```

The shell automatically expands the name of the file to /etc/passwd and then hesitates to see whether you want to accept the command:

```
[lidia@veracruz lidia]$ more /etc/passwd
```

When the shell automatically expands a filename and then hesitates, waiting for you to confirm a command by pressing the Enter key, this action is known as *command completion.* Now you can press the Enter key to execute the command.

But wait! What happens if you have two files, one /etc/passwd and the other /etc/password? When you press the Tab key, the system rings the bell, and the name doesn't expand. Press the Tab key a second time, and bash shows you all the possible expansions of that argument. If a huge number of expansions result, bash warns you:

```
#Press tab twice after typing the first line below.
[lidia@veracruz gifs]$ ls p
There are 255 possibilities. Do you really
wish to see them all? (y or n)
```

Chapter 16

Filing Your Life Away

· ·

In This Chapter

▶ Discovering the ins and outs of files and directories

▶ Finding your way through the Linux file system

▶ Moving around in the Linux file system

▶ Creating, moving, copying, and destroying directories and files

▶ Giving permissions and taking them away

· ·

*I*n this chapter, you take your first steps through the Linux file and directory structure. Don't worry, Linux may live a structured life, but it's still very flexible. With a little bit of introduction, you'll understand the Linux way of life.

We also introduce you to file types, subdirectories, and the root — which is not evil at all — directory. You're also shown the way home — to your home directory, that is. After you're oriented with the Linux files and directories structure, we show you how to make some changes, such as how to copy and move files and directories, as well as how to destroy them.

Getting Linux File Facts Straight

Linux files are similar to Unix, DOS, Windows, and Macintosh files. All operating systems use files to store information. Files allow you to organize your stuff and keep them separate. For instance, the text that makes up this chapter is stored in a file; all the other chapters are stored in their own files. Follow the bouncing prompt as we make short work of long files.

We use the command line interface (CLI) to examine file and file system basics in this chapter. Graphical User Interfaces, such as Nautilus, are great, and we use them extensively in this book. However, we believe that using a CLI is better for learning this subject. All the examples in this chapter use the Gnome Terminal Emulation Program to provide the CLI.

Storing files

We're going to go ahead and assume that you know that a *file* is a collection of information that is identified by a filename, and that Linux can store multiple files in directories as long as the files have different names. Linux stores files with the same name in different directories.

Each directory may contain only one file with the same name.

Wonderful or not, Linux filenames can be as long as 256 characters. They can contain uppercase and lowercase letters (also known as mixed case), numbers, and special characters, such as the underscore (_), the dot (.), and the hyphen (-). Because filenames can be made up of mixed case names, and each name is distinct, we call these names *case sensitive.* For example, the names *FILENAME, filename,* and *FiLeNaMe* are unique filenames of different files (such as Compaq's OpenVMS), but they are the same filename.

Although filenames technically can contain wildcard characters, such as the asterisk (*) and the question mark (?), using them is not a good idea. Various command interpreters, or *shells,* use wildcards to match several filenames at one time. If your filenames contain wildcard characters, you'll have trouble specifying only those files. We recommend that you create filenames that don't contain spaces or other characters that have meaning to shells. In this way, Linux filenames are different than DOS and Windows filenames.

Sorting through file types

Linux files can contain all sorts of information. In fact, Linux sees every device (disks, display, keyboard, and so on) except for network interfaces as a file. The following five categories of files will become the most familiar to you:

- ✓ **User data files** contain information you create. User data files, sometimes known as *flat files,* usually contain the simplest data, consisting of plain text and numbers. More complex user data files, such as graphics or spreadsheet files, must be interpreted and used by special programs. These files are mostly illegible if you look at them with a text editor, because the contents of these files are not always ASCII text. Changing these files generally affects only the user who owns the files.

- ✓ **System data files** are used by the system to keep track of users on the system, logins, passwords, and so on. As system administrator, you may be required to view or edit these files. As a regular user, you don't need to be concerned with system data files except, perhaps, the ones that you use as examples for your own private startup files.

✔ **Directory files** hold the names of files — and other directories — that belong to them. These files and directories are called *children*. Directories in Linux (and Unix) are just another type of file. If you're in a directory, the directory above you is called the *parent*. Isn't that homey?

When you list files with the `ls -l` command, it displays a list of files and directories. Directory files begin with the letter d. For example:

```
[lidia@veracruz lidia]$ ls -l
drwxr-xr-x 5 lidia lidia 1024 Oct 9 2001 Desktop
drwx------ 2 lidia lidia 1024 Oct 9 2001 nsmail
```

✔ **Special files** represent either hardware devices (such as a disk drive, a tape drive, or a keyboard) or some type of placeholder that the operating system uses. The `/dev` directory holds many of these special files. You can see this directory by running the following command at a command prompt:

```
ls -l /dev
```

✔ **Executable files** contain instructions (usually called *programs,* or *shell scripts*) for your computer. When you type the name of one of these files, you're telling the operating system to *execute* the instructions. Some executable files look like gibberish, and others look like long lists of computer commands. A lot of these executable files are located in `/bin`, `/usr/bin`, `/sbin`, **and** `/usr/sbin`.

Understanding files and directories

If you live in the Windows world, you can think of a Linux file system as one huge file folder that contains files and other file folders, which in turn contain files and other file folders, which in turn contain files and . . . well, you get the point. In fact, the Linux file system is generally organized this way. One big directory contains files and other directories, and all the other directories in turn contain files and directories.

Directories and subdirectories

A directory contained, or *nested,* in another directory is called a *subdirectory.* For example, the directory called `/mother` may contain a subdirectory called `/child`. The relationship between the two is referred to as parent and child. The full name of the subdirectory is `/mother/child`, which would make a good place to keep a file containing information about a family reunion called `/mother/child/reunion`.

The root directory

In the tree directory structure of Linux, DOS, and Unix, the big directory at the bottom of the tree is called the *root* directory. root is the parent of all other directories — the poor guy must be exhausted — and is represented by a single / symbol (pronounced slash). From the root directory, the whole directory structure grows like a tree, with directories and subdirectories branching off like limbs.

If you could turn the tree over so that the trunk is in the air and the branches are toward the ground, you would have an *inverted tree* — which is the way the Linux file system is normally drawn and represented (with the root at the top). If we were talking about Mother Nature, you'd soon have a dead tree. Because this is computer technology, however, you have something that looks like an ever-growing, upside-down tree.

What's in a name?

You name directories in the same way that you name files, following the same rules. Almost the only way that you can tell whether a name is a filename or a directory name is the way that the slash character (/) is used to show directories nest in other directories. For example, usr/local means that local is found in the usr directory. You know that usr is a directory because the trailing slash character tells you so; however, you don't know whether local is a file or a directory.

If you issue the ls command with the -f option, Linux lists directories with a slash character at the end, as in local/, so you would know that local is a directory.

The simplest way to tell whether the slash character indicates the root directory or separates directories, or directories and files, is to see whether anything appears before the slash character in the directory path specification. If nothing appears before the slash, you have the root directory. For example, you know that /usr is a subdirectory or a file in the root directory because it has only a single slash character before it.

Home again

Linux systems have a directory called /home, which contains the user's home directory, where he or she can

- ✔ Store files
- ✔ Create more subdirectories
- ✔ Move, delete, and modify subdirectories and files

Linux system files as well as files belonging to other users are never in a user's /home directory. Linux decides where the /home directory is placed, and that location can be changed only by a superuser, not by general users. Linux is this dictatorial because it has to maintain order and keep a handle on security.

Your /home directory is not safe from prying eyes. Be sure to maintain your privacy by locking your directory. (We tell you how in the "Owning Files and Granting Permissions" section later in this chapter.) But anyone logging in to your system as root (superuser) can see what's in your /home directory, even if you do lock it up.

Moving Around the File System with pwd and cd

You can navigate the Linux file system without a map or a GPS. All you need to know are two commands: pwd and cd. (These commands are run from the command line.) But you also need to know where you are to start with, hence the usefulness of the next section.

Figuring out where you are

Log in to your Red Hat Linux computer and open a Gnome Terminal Emulation Program. In this case, we log in as the example user lidia. To find out where you are in the Linux file system, simply type **pwd** at the command prompt as follows:

```
[lidia@veracruz lidia]$pwd
```

We receive the following response

```
/home/lidia
[lidia@veracruz lidia]$
```

indicating that we're logged in as lidia and are currently in the /home/lidia directory. Unless your alter ego is out there, you should be logged in as *yourself* and be in the /home/yourself directory, where *yourself* is your login name.

The pwd command stands for *print working directory*. Your *working directory* is the default directory where Linux commands perform their actions; the working directory is where you are in the file system when you type in a command. When you type the ls(1) command, for example, Linux shows you the files in your working directory. Any file actions on your part occur in your working directory unless you are root. For security reasons that we won't go into here, the root user is not configured by default to be able to work on the current working directory. You can change this, but in general, the root user must explicitly specify the current working directory. For example, if you are root and are in the /etc directory, and you want to indicate the hosts file, you must type **cat ./hosts** instead of just **cat hosts**.

Type this command:

```
ls -la
```

You see only the files that are in your working directory. If you want to specify a file that isn't in your working directory, you have to specify the name of the directory that contains the file, as well as the name of the file. For example, the following command lists the passwd file in the /etc directory:

```
ls -la /etc/passwd
```

Specifying the directory path

If the file you want to read is in a subdirectory of the directory that you're in, you can reach the file by typing a relative filename. *Relative filenames* specify the location of files relative to where you are.

In addition to what we tell you earlier in this chapter about specifying directory paths, you need to know these three additional rules:

- ✔ One dot (.) always stands for your current directory.
- ✔ Two dots (..) specify the parent directory of the directory you're currently in.
- ✔ All directory paths that include (.) or (..) are relative directory paths.

You can see these files by using the -a option of the ls(1) command. Without the -a option, the ls(1) command doesn't bother to list the . or .. files, or any filename beginning with a period. This may seem strange, but the creators of Unix thought that having some files that were normally hidden kept the directory structure cleaner. Therefore, filenames that are always there (. and ..) and special-purpose files are hidden. The types of files that should be hidden are those that the user normally does not need to see in every listing of the directory structure (files used to tailor applications to the user's preferences, for example).

Now specify a pathname relative to where you are. For example:

```
[lidia@veracruz lidia]$pwd
/home/lidia
[lidia@veracruz lidia]$ ls -la ../../etc/passwd
```

The last line indicates that to find the passwd file, you go up two directory levels (../../) and then down to /etc.

If you want to see the login accounts on your system, you can issue the following command from your home directory:

```
[lidia@veracruz lidia]$ ls -la ..
```

This command lists the parent directory. Because the parent directory (/home) has all the login directories of the people on your system, this command shows you the names of their login directories.

You've been looking at relative pathnames, which are relative to where you are in the file system. Filenames that are valid from anywhere in the file system are called *absolute filenames*. These filenames always begin with the slash character (/), which signifies root.

```
ls -la /etc/passwd
```

Changing your working directory

Sometimes, you may want to change your working directory. Why? Glad you asked. Because doing so allows you to work with shorter relative pathnames. To do so, you simply use the cd (for *change directory*) command.

To change from your current working directory to the /usr directory, for example, type the following:

```
cd /usr
```

Going home

If you type **cd** by itself, without any directory name, you return to your home directory. Just knowing that you can easily get back to familiar territory is comforting. There's no place like home.

You can also use cd with a *relative* specification. For example:

```
cd ..
```

If you are in the directory /usr/bin and type the preceding command, Linux takes you to the parent directory called /usr, as follows:

```
[lidia@veracruz lidia]$ cd /usr/bin
[lidia@veracruz bin]$ cd ..
[lidia@veracruz usr]$
```

Here are a couple of tricks: If you type **cd ~**, then you go to your home directory (the tilde ~ is synonymous with /home/username). If you type **cd ~<username>**, then you can go to that user's home directory. On very large systems, this command is useful because it eliminates the need for you to remember — and type — large directory specifications.

Creating and Adding to Files with cat

Unlike cats, the cat command is simple, easy to use, and one of the most useful Linux commands (sorry, Paul likes dogs and is allergic to cats). The name cat stands for *concatenate,* meaning *to add to the end of.* The cat command does exactly what you tell it to and takes your input (mostly from the keyboard) and outputs it to the screen. Real cats like to do what they want to do and will not help display the contents of Linux files.

Make sure that you are *not* logged in as root when you go through this section and the sections that follow. Wait until you are thoroughly familiar with this chapter before you ever log in as root. It's possible and fairly easy to delete any file or directory when you are root; you can even erase your entire disk by running the wrong command (rm -rf / — don't ever use this command unless you want to erase your entire disk). It's best not to run the examples that remove (using the rm command) and move files (the mv command) when you're logged in as root. You should exercise caution when you're logged in as a regular user too, because you can erase your own files accidentally. Linux (for the most part) doesn't have an *undo* function, although a change is in the works.

To find out what the cat command is all about, follow these steps:

1. **Make sure that you are in the /home directory.**

   To go home, click your heels . . . no, that's another book. Type **cd** at the prompt and then type **pwd**.

2. **Enter the cat command at the command prompt.**

   The cursor moves to the next line, but nothing else happens because cat is waiting for you to input something.

3. **Everything that you type will be repeated on the screen after you press Enter.**

   Big deal, you say? We explain why this is useful in a moment. For example, you could type the following:

   ```
   Hi
   Hey
   What?
   Huh?
   What!
   Whatever!
   ```

4. **To get out of the** `cat` **command, press Ctrl+D (if you're not at the beginning of a line, press Ctrl+D twice).**

Most Unix and Linux people write Ctrl+D as ^D, which means *end of file* (EOF) to Linux. When the `cat` command sees ^D, it assumes that it's finished with that line and moves to the next one. If ^D is on an empty line by itself, the `cat` command has no other input to move to and thus exits.

You can use the first two symbols shown below to save the output of the `cat` command to a file. The final symbol reads the content of a file and sends it to the `cat` command:

✔ > is known as *redirection of standard output.* When you use it, you tell the computer, "Capture the information that normally goes to the screen, create a file, and put the information into it."

✔ >> is known as *appending standard output.* When you use this symbol, you tell the computer, "Capture the information that would normally go to the screen and append the information to an existing file. If the file doesn't exist, create it."

✔ < is used to tell the computer, "Take the information from the specified file and feed it to *standard in* (also known as *standard input*), acting as though the information is coming from the keyboard."

In this example, you use the `cat` command to create a file by redirecting the output of the `cat` command from the screen to the filename you want:

1. **At the command line, type** cat > **followed by the name of your file. Then type your heart out.**

   Here's what we typed:

   ```
   [lidia@veracruz lidia]$ cat > dogs
   Hey again.
   Dogs make good friends!
   ```

   Everything is repeated to the file called `dog` rather than to the screen. Linux created `dog` for us because the filename didn't already exist.

2. **When you finish typing, just press** ^D **on an empty line.**

   You're right back at the Linux prompt.

Making Sure the cat Command Works

Are you wondering whether the `cat` command did what you wanted? You can check by using the `cat` command and the filename again (`cat` has nothing to do with cats):

```
[lidia@veracruz lidia]$ cat dogs
Hey again.
Dogs make good friends!
[lidia@veracruz lidia]$
```

This time the `cat` command took the file off the disk and put the output to *standard out* (also known as *standard output*), which in this case is your computer screen.

If you think of something else you want to add to the file, you can use the append symbol (>>) with the filename. Linux adds whatever you type to the end of the filename. Returning to `dogfile`:

```
[lidia@veracruz lidia]$ cat >> dogfile
Dogs don't listen very well, however.
```

Use the `cat` command to concatenate files or concatenate input to either the beginning or the end of the file. It is the only command created to do this. You can also use the >> symbol to add data to the *end* of a file.

You can use the >> symbol with many Linux commands. For example

```
cat file1 file2 file3 file4 >fileout
```

joins file1, file2, file3, and file4, putting the results in fileout. In the following

```
sort file1 >>file2
```

the `sort` command sorts the contents of file1 and appends it to a (perhaps already existing) file2. If file2 doesn't exist, the system creates file2 and then puts the sorted output into it.

When you finish, be sure to end the session with ^D.

Manipulating Files and Directories

Linux has many ways to create, move, copy, and delete files and directories. Some of these features are so easy to use that you need to be careful: Unlike other operating systems, Linux doesn't tell you that you're about to overwrite a file — it just follows your orders and overwrites!

We said it before, but we'll say it again: Make sure that you are *not* logged in as root when you go through these sections. You can unintentionally harm your computer when logged in as root. root — the superuser — can erase any file or directory no matter of what permissions are set. Be careful!

Creating directories

To create a new directory in Linux, you use the `mkdir` command (just like in DOS). The command looks like this:

```
[lidia@veracruz lidia]$mkdir newdirectory
```

This command creates a subdirectory under your current or working directory. If you want the subdirectory under another directory, change to that directory first and then create the new subdirectory.

Create a new directory called `cancun`. Go ahead, do it:

```
mkdir cancun
```

(Can you tell where we would rather be right now?)

Now create another directory called `vacation`:

```
mkdir vacation
```

And then change the directory to put yourself in the `cancun` directory:

```
cd cancun
```

Now create a file under `cancun` called `airfair`, by using the `cat` command (see the section, "Creating and Adding to Files with cat," earlier in this chapter):

```
cat >airfair
Not too bad.
^D
```

Now create another file:

```
cat >hotel
Pretty nice.
^D
```

And one more:

```
cat >plans
Vamos a Cancun!
^D
```

Now you have some files to work with.

Moving and copying files and directories

The commands for moving and copying directories and files are `mv` for move and `cp` for copy. If you want to rename a file, you can use the move command. No, you're not really moving the file, but in Linux (and Unix), the developers realized that renaming something was a lot like moving it. The format of the move command is

```
mv source destination
```

With your example files from the preceding section, you can move the file named `airfair` to a file named `newfair` by executing the following command:

```
mv airfair newfair
```

This command leaves the file in the same directory but changes its name to `newfair`. So you see the file was not really moved, but just renamed.

Now try moving the `newfair` file to the `vacation` directory. To do that, you have to first move the file up and then move it into the `vacation` directory. You can do it with one command:

```
mv newfair ../vacation
```

The destination file uses the .. (or parent directory) designation. This command tells Linux to go up one directory level and look for a directory called `vacation`, and then put the file into that directory with the name `newfair`, because you did not specify any other name. If you instead did this

```
mv newfair ../vacation/newplans
```

the `newfair` file would move to the `vacation` directory named `newplans`. Note that in both cases (with the file maintaining its name of `newfair` or taking the new name `newplans`), your current directory is still `cancun`, and all your filenames are relative to that directory.

Strictly speaking, the file still has not really moved. The data bits are still on the same part of the disk where they were originally. The *file specification* (the directory path plus the filename) that you use to talk about the file is different, so it appears to have moved.

In early versions of Unix, you were not allowed to use `mv` to move a file from one disk partition to another; you could only copy it by using the `cp` command. Linux allows you to use the `mv` command to move a file anywhere. Usually, `mv` leaves the data in place and just changes the file's name or the directory where the name is placed. But when the file is moved across disk partitions (for example, from `/usr` to `/home` in a lot of Linux systems), the data is copied to the new disk partition, the new name is put in place in that partition's directory structure, and the name and file's data are removed from the old disk partition.

Copying a file does move some data. The syntax is

```
cp source destination
```

Look familiar? It's the same syntax you use for the move command.

Now make two copies of the hotel file. Because you can't have two files of the same name in the same directory, you have to think of a new name, such as hotel2. (Hey, we're writing this early in the morning. How creative can we be?)

```
cp hotel hotel2
```

If you want a copy of a file but in a different directory, you can use the same filename. For example, suppose you want to copy a file called plans to the ../vacation directory. You can keep the name plans because its full pathname has vacation in it instead of cancun:

```
cp plans ../vacation
```

As you can see, the pathname specifications for files are similar from command to command, even though the file contents and commands are different.

Removing files

The command for removing, or deleting, a file is rm. If you've been following along in our little story, the handsome prince now has two beautiful princesses (hotel and hotel2) in the cancun directory. As most people know, this is probably one too many princesses, so get rid of the second one:

```
rm hotel2
```

You have removed the extra file from the current directory. To remove a file from another directory, you need to provide a relative filename or an absolute filename. For example, if you want to expunge plans from the vacation directory, you would type the following:

```
rm ../vacation/plans
```

You can use wildcards with rm, but please be careful if you do so! When files are removed in Linux, they are gone forever — kaput, vanished — and can't be recovered.

The following command removes *everything* in the current directory and all of the directories under it that you have permission to remove:

```
[lidia@veracruz lidia]$rm -r *
```

Don't do this as root (the superuser)!!! You should always be careful running any command as superuser, but be especially careful with commands that can erase entire directories and file systems.

To decrease the danger of removing a lot of files inadvertently when you use wildcards, be sure to use the -i option with rm, cp, mv, and various other commands. The -i option means *interactive,* and it lists each filename to be removed (with the rm command) or overwritten (with the mv or cp command). If you answer either y or Y to the question, the file is removed or overwritten, respectively. If you answer anything else, Linux leaves the file alone.

Removing directories

You can remove not only files but also directories. If you're still following along with the story about the handsome prince and his princess, you now have two directories in your home directory that are taking up a small amount of space. Because you're finished with them, you can delete them and recover that space for other tasks.

First, return to your home directory:

```
[lidia@veracruz lidia]$ cd
```

Now remove the cancun directory:

```
[lidia@veracruz lidia]$rm -rf cancun
```

Giving the rm command these options removes the cancun directory and all files and directories under it. (*Recursively* means to keep going down in the directory structure and remove files and directories as you find them. *Forcefully* means that the file should be removed if at all possible; ignore cases where rm may prompt the user for further information.)

Another command specifically for removing empty directories is called rmdir. With rmdir, the directory must be empty to be removed. If you attempt to remove the work directory without first deleting its files, the system displays the following message:

```
[lidia@veracruz lidia]$ rmdir vacation
rmdir: vacation: Directory not empty
[lidia@veracruz lidia]$ rm -rf vacation
```

Owning Files and Granting Permissions

All Linux files and directories have owners and are assigned a list of permissions. This system of *ownership* and *permissions* forms the basis for restricting and allowing users' access to files. File permissions can also be used to specify whether a file is executable as a command and to determine who can use the file or command.

Files and directories are owned by user accounts. User accounts are defined in the /etc/passwd file. For instance, you created the root (superuser) user account when you installed Red Hat Linux in Chapter 3 and the installation system created the superuser home directory — /root — plus several configuration files — for instance, .bashrc. The root user owns all those files and directories. If you created a regular user account — for instance, lidia — then that user's home directory and configuration files are all owned by lidia. Users can access and modify any files or directories that they own.

Files and directories all have group ownership in addition to user ownership. Groups are defined by the /etc/group file and provide a secondary level of access. For instance, you can assign group ownership to files that you own and allow other users who belong to the group to access those files.

Files and directories are assigned permissions that permit or deny read, write, and execute access. Permissions are assigned to the owner, group, and anyone of the file or directory. The owner, group, and anyone permissions are independent of each other.

Using the ls command with the -l option allows you to see the file's permissions, along with other relevant information, such as who owns the file, what group of people have permission to access or modify the file, the size of the file or directory, the last time the file was modified, and the name of the file.

First, create a file with the touch command. The Unix and Linux communities use the touch command for many things, one of which is to create a little zero-length file:

```
[lidia@veracruz lidia]$ touch vacationtime
[lidia@veracruz lidia]$ ls -l vacationtime
-rw-rw-r-- owner group 0 Oct 3  16:00 vacationtime
```

The -rw-rw-r-- are the permissions for the vacationtime file: The owner is you, and the group is probably you but may be someone or something else, depending on how your system is set up and administered.

You may be wondering how you can become an owner of a file. Well, you're automatically the owner of any file you create, which makes sense. As the owner, you can change the default file permissions — and even the ownership. If you change the file ownership, however, *you* lose ownership privileges.

To change the ownership of a file or a directory, use the chown command. (Get it? chown — change ownership.) In general, you have to be root to do this.

Suppose you've decided to settle down and lead a more contemplative life, one more in line with a new profession of haiku writing. Someone else will have to plan the weekend sprees and all-night bashes. So you give up ownership of the vacationtime file:

```
[lidia@veracruz lidia]$chown root vacationtime
```

This command changes the ownership of vacationtime to root. If you want to change it back, you can use the chown command, but you have to do it as root.

Files and users all belong to *groups*. In the vacationtime example, the group is users. Having groups enables you to give large numbers of users — but not all users — access to files. Group permissions and ownership are handy for making sure that the members of a special project or workgroup have access to files needed by the entire group.

To see which groups are available to you on your system, take a look at the /etc/group file. To do so, use the more command. You see a file that looks somewhat like this

```
root::0:root
bin::1:root,bin,daemon
...
nobody::99:
users::100:
floppy:x:19:
.....
your_user_name::500:your_user_name
```

where *your_user_name* is the login name you use for your account. Please remember that the file won't look exactly like this, just similar. The names at the beginning of the line are the group names. The names at the end of the line (such as root, bin, and daemon) are user-group names that can belong to the user-group list.

To change the group that the file belongs to, log in as root and use the chgrp command. Its syntax is the same as that of the chown command. For example, to change the group that vacationtime belongs to, you would issue the following command:

```
[lidia@veracruz lidia]$chgrp newgroupname vacationtime
```

TIP

Red Hat assigns a unique group to each user. For instance, when you add the first user to your system, that user gets the user ID and group ID of 500. The next user receives the user ID and group ID of 501, and so on. This gives you a lot of control over who gets what access to your files.

Making Your Own Rules

You, as the owner of a file, can specify permissions for reading, writing to, or executing a file. You can also determine who (yourself, a group of people, or everyone in general) can do these actions on a file. What do these permissions mean? Read on (you have our permission):

- **Read permission** for a file enables you to read the file. For a directory, read permission allows the ls command to list the names of the files in the directory. You must also have execute permission for the directory name to use the -l option of the ls command or to change to that directory.

- **Write permission** for a file means you can modify the file. For a directory, you can create or delete files inside that directory.

- **Execute permission** for a file means you can type the name of the file and execute it. You can't view or copy the file unless you also have read permission. This means that files containing executable Linux commands, called *shell scripts,* must be both executable and readable by the person executing them. Programs written in a compiled language such as C, however, must have only executable permissions, to protect them from being copied where they shouldn't be copied.

  For a directory, execute permission means that you can change to that directory (with cd). Unless you also have read permission for the directory, ls -l won't work. You can list directories and files in that directory, but you can't see additional information about the files or directories by just using an ls -l command. This may seem strange, but it's useful for security.

The first character of a file permission is a hyphen (-) if it is a file; the first character of a directory is d. The nine other characters are read, write, and execute positions for each of the three categories of file permissions:

- Owner (also known as the user)
- Group
- Others

Your vacationtime file, for example, may show the following permissions when listed with the ls -l vacationtime command:

```
-rw-rw-r--
```

The hyphen (-) in the first position indicates that it is a regular file (not a directory or other special file). The next characters (rw-) are the owner's permissions. The owner can read and write to the file but can't execute it.

The next three characters (rw-) are the group's permissions. The group also has read-write access to the file. The last three characters (r--) are the others' permissions, which are read-only.

[-][rw-][rw-][r--] illustrates the four parts of the permissions: the file type followed by three sets of triplets, indicating the read, write, and execute permissions for the owner, group, and *other* users of the file (meaning *everyone else*).

You can specify most file permissions by using only six letters:

- ✔ **ugo,** which stands for — no, not a car — user (or owner), group, and other
- ✔ **rwx,** which stands for read, write, and execute

These six letters, and some symbols such as = and commas, are put together into a specification of how you want to set the file's permissions.

The command for changing permissions is chmod. The syntax for the command is

```
chmod specification filename
```

Change the mode of vacationtime to give the user the ability to read, write, and execute the file:

```
chmod u=rwx vacationtime
```

That was easy enough, wasn't it? What if you want to give the group permission to only read and execute the file? You would execute the following command:

```
chmod g=rx vacationtime
```

Note that this last command does not affect the permissions for owner or other, just the group's permissions.

Now set all the permissions at once. Separate each group of characters with a comma:

```
chmod u=r,g=rw,o=rwx vacationtime
```

This command sets the user's permissions to just read, the group's permissions to read and write, and the other's permissions to read, write, and execute.

You can set the permission bits in other ways. But this way is so simple, why use any other?

Chapter 17

Becoming a Suit: Managing the Red Hat Linux File System

• •

In This Chapter

▶ Mounting a file system

▶ Using file system options

▶ Unmounting a file system

▶ Rehabilitating corrupted files

▶ Increasing disk space with a new drive

• •

Managing the Linux file system is not a complex job but it is an important one. You have the responsibility of managing the Red Hat Linux file system and ensuring that users (even if you're the only user) have access to secure, uncorrupted data. You are the manager — yes, a suit — of your file system.

This chapter introduces you to managing your Linux file system. Consider yourself a management trainee. When you're done reading this chapter, feel free to take a nice, long, expensive lunch.

Mounting and Unmounting

Red Hat Linux, and other Unix-like operating systems, use files in ways that are different from MS-DOS, Windows, and Macintosh operating systems. In Linux, *everything* is stored as files in predictable locations in the directory structure — Linux even stores commands as files. Like other modern operating systems, Linux has a tree-structured, hierarchical, directory organization called a *file system*.

All user-available disk space is combined in a single directory tree. The base of this system is the *root directory* (not to be confused with the root user), which is designated with a slash, /. A file system's contents are made available to Linux by using a process called mounting. Mounting a file system makes Linux aware of the files and directories that it contains. This is just like mounting a horse except that no horse is involved.

File systems can be mounted or unmounted, which means that file systems can be connected or disconnected to the directory tree. The exception is the *root file system,* which is always mounted on the root directory when the system is running and cannot be unmounted. Other file systems may be mounted as needed, such as ones contained on another hard drive, a floppy disk, Zip disks, USB disks, or a CD-ROM.

Check out Chapter 16 for more on the Linux file system.

Mounting Windows files from a floppy disk

Mounting provides a good example of the difference between Linux and MS-DOS/Windows. If you use a floppy or CD with Windows, you just insert it into the drive and immediately have access to it. With Linux, you must insert the floppy into the drive and then explicitly mount it. Sounds complicated? Not really.

You can mount a Windows disk (hard drive or floppy disk) on your Linux computer. You can then transfer files from one operating system to the other. We concentrate on mounting a Windows floppy disk in this section. The following steps show you how to mount such a disk.

1. **Insert a Windows MS-DOS formatted floppy (FAT or FAT32 but not NTFS) into the drive.**

2. **Click the Main Menu button and choose Programs⇨System⇨Disk Management.**

   The User Mount Tool window appears, as shown in Figure 17-1.

3. **Push the Floppy disk eject button on the floppy drive. Before you push it, the button should indicate the diskette is unmounted.**

   The floppy mounts, usually in only a few seconds.

   You know that the floppy has mounted when a floppy icon displays on the left of the screen.

4. **You can now read and write to the floppy (unless the read-only tab on the diskette is set).**

   See Chapter 16 for more on opening, reading, writing, changing, saving, and deleting files.

5. **Click the Exit button to leave the utility.**

Red Hat Linux and GNOME are configured to automatically start the process that mounts your floppy or CD when you insert it into the drive. We present the manual method here to show you how the process works.

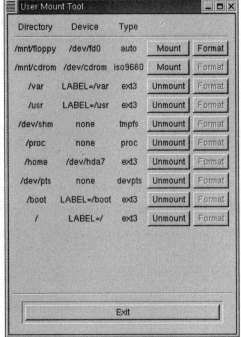

Directory	Device	Type		
/mnt/floppy	/dev/fd0	auto	Mount	Format
/mnt/cdrom	/dev/cdrom	iso9660	Mount	Format
/var	LABEL=/var	ext3	Unmount	Format
/usr	LABEL=/usr	ext3	Unmount	Format
/dev/shm	none	tmpfs	Unmount	Format
/proc	none	proc	Unmount	Format
/home	/dev/hda7	ext3	Unmount	Format
/dev/pts	none	devpts	Unmount	Format
/boot	LABEL=/boot	ext3	Unmount	Format
/	LABEL=/	ext3	Unmount	Format

Exit

Figure 17-1:
The User
Mount Tool
dialog box.

To manually mount the floppy in the command-line interface, log in as root, open the terminal window, and run the following command:

```
mount _t msdos /dev/fd0 /mnt/floppy
```

A directory that is used as a mount point is just like any other directory — it can store files and other directories. But you can't see or use any files or directories stored in a directory used as a mount point until the file system mounted on that directory is unmounted. (For more on unmounting files, see the "Unmounting file systems" section later in this chapter.)

Unmounting file systems

Unmounting a Linux file system is a little simpler than mounting one. Because the file system is already mounted, you don't have to specify any options or other information. You just have to tell the Red Hat Disk Management Druid to unmount the file system.

Be careful though. You never want to mount a hard drive-based file system like /, /usr, or /home. That sends your Red Hat Linux computer into never-never land. On the other hand, you have to unmount a removable drive, such as a CD-ROM or floppy drive, before removing it. You can also safely unmount a Windows partition because Red Hat Linux doesn't use it for any system-based purpose — you only mount a Windows partition when you're using that operating system.

To unmount a file system, follow these steps:

1. **Log in as root.**

2. **Click the Main Menu button and choose Programs⇨System⇨Disk Management utility.**

   The User Mount Tool window appears.

3. **Click the button to the right of the file system you're interested in.**

   The button indicates whether the file system is mounted or unmounted.

   After a few seconds, the button changes from Unmount to Mount to show that it's been unmounted.

4. **Click the Exit button to leave the utility.**

   The file system is unmounted. If the file system was a removable type, such as a floppy disk or CD, you can remove it. Otherwise, the file system is simply not available for use until you re-mount it.

You can run the `eject` command from a `bash` shell to eject a CD from its drive. You have to unmount the CD first, and then enter the `eject` command. Otherwise, to eject a CD, you must unmount it and then press the eject button on the CD-ROM drive. In either case, you can't eject the CD until you've unmounted it.

Sending Corrupted File Systems to Reform School

You can *corrupt* file systems by turning off your computer without properly shutting down Red Hat Linux. The result? The file doesn't open, or the data in the file's all scrambled up. Corruption can also occur via a driver error or a hardware crash. The type of corruption that occurs when you incorrectly turn off your computer is generally not serious. You shouldn't push fate, however, and avoid even mild corruption.

The `fsck` (File System ChecK) utility checks Linux file systems. The `fsck` utility reports errors and makes some repairs. Usually, the `fsck` program is called to duty automatically when your system boots. That way, if your system crashes, `fsck` checks out all the file systems that were mounted at the time of the system crash.

Understanding your Linux file systems permissions

Sections in this chapter explain how to mount and unmount a file system from a floppy. But those instructions assume that you're mounting a vanilla — your average PC — system. You can specify other options. Here's a short description of each option:

✔ **Read-only:** The file system is mounted as read-only. You can't write to the file system.

✔ **User mountable:** When set, any user in addition to root can mount the partition. This is useful when regular users must be able to mount devices such as CDs and floppy disks.

✔ **Mountable by device owner:** A regular user that owns the device file (for instance, /dev/fd0) can mount the file system.

✔ **Not mount at boot time:** Red Hat Linux does not automatically mount the file system when it boots.

✔ **No program allowed to execute:** A regular user is not allowed to execute files found on a file system. You may want to allow a regular user to mount a device (like a CD), but not execute programs on the device for security reasons.

✔ **No special device file support:** The device files found in the /dev directory are created with very specific permissions in order to enhance system security. This option prevents other, nonsecure device files from being used to mount a file system.

✔ **No setuid programs allowed:** This is a very important security feature. When an executable Linux file has its setuid bit set, it can be run by a regular user who belongs to the same group. If root owns the file, then whatever that file does is done with all the power of root. Files with setuid permission often present big security holes. Setting this option prevents any files found on the file system from exercising their setuid privileges.

✔ **User quota enabled:** This enables Linux quotas to be exercised. Quotas allow limits being set on what resources individual users can access.

✔ **Group quota enabled:** This enables quotas to be set for groups.

You can run fsck manually — as opposed to having the boot process run it automatically. In some cases, you must run it manually because it needs to prompt you during the process.

Unfortunately, fsck doesn't always do the trick. For example

✔ fsck can't find (let alone repair) corrupted data that's located in a structurally intact file.

✔ With the exception of the root file system, fsck runs on only unmounted file systems.

✔ You must make sure that the system is in single-user mode to use fsck on the root file system.

Here's the syntax you use to run the fsck command manually:

```
fsck (options) filesystem
```

The word filesystem here names the device driver (*block special file* in technical geek-speak) that connects Linux to the file system. If filesystem is omitted, the fsck utility checks all the file systems listed in the /etc/fstab file configuration file. If the fsck utility finds any errors, it prompts you for input on what to do about the errors. For the most part, you simply agree with whatever the program suggests. The fsck command has the following options:

Option	How You Use It
-p	Preen the file system. Perform automatic repairs that don't change the contents of files.
-n	Answer no to all prompts and only list problems; don't repair them.
-y	Answer yes to all prompts and repair damage regardless of how severe.
-f	Force a file system check.

Many people run the fsck command with the -y option. If you run fsck with the -p option, Linux performs some steps automatically, placing lost files in the lost+found directory, deleting zero-length files, and placing missing blocks back on the list of *free blocks*.(Free blocks are blocks still available for filling with data, among other things.)

It is possible for fsck to cause problems with your disk. The best way to ensure that fsck does not cause damage is to run it when your computer is operating in single user mode. Change the state of your computer to single user mode by running the init -s command.

Increasing Drive Space

Sooner or later, you're likely to want to add more hard drive storage to your Linux system to hold more programs and data or to enable more users to log in. You can increase drive storage by adding one or more disk drives.

The first step to increasing your drive space is to add a new disk drive. The following tasks are required to add a drive to your system (regardless of whether the drive is SCSI or IDE) and make it accessible to users:

- ✔ Physically attach the disk drive to your computer system. Be careful to turn off the power to your computer and monitor. Disconnect the power cable. Be careful not to cut yourself when reaching into the computer. You should also use the antistatic strap that comes with the hard drive; follow the instructions included with the strap.

- ✔ Provide a suitable device driver for the drive's controller in Linux.

- ✔ Define at least one partition (see the following section).

- ✔ Create the block special files for the partition(s).

- ✔ Create a Linux file system(s) on any partition(s) to be used for user files.

- ✔ Enter the new file systems into /etc/fstab, the configuration file.

- ✔ Mount the file systems (you may have to make a directory for a mount point).

The following sections guide you through the process of creating a drive partition and configuring a hard drive, a floppy drive, and a CD-ROM drive after they are physically installed.

Creating a drive partition

You have to partition your new hard drive after you've added it to your Linux computer. The drive partition is Linux's basic file storage unit. Here are the general steps you follow to create a drive partition:

1. **Create the file systems on the drive partitions.**

2. **Combine the file systems to form a single directory tree structure.**

   The directory tree structure can be on one drive or spread across many.

3. **Define the drive partitions.**

   You can define drive partitions when adding a new drive or sometime later.

   In most cases, Linux defines drive partitions during the original Linux installation. You may divide a drive into one, two, four, or more partitions, each of which may contain a file system or may be used as a swap partition. *Swap* partitions allow very large programs or many small programs to run even if they take up more memory than you have as RAM in your computer. The total of all your swap partitions and RAM is called *virtual memory*.

4. **Create a file system.**

   The file system occupies a single space on the drive that has a unique block special file (device) name. This unique name accesses the file system regardless of whether the data is stored on all or only part of a physical drive or is an aggregation of multiple physical drives.

Adding and configuring a hard drive

The business of adding a hard drive to your microcomputer can be broken down into two steps:

- ✔ Physically adding the hard drive
- ✔ Logically making Linux aware of it

The first step is beyond the scope of this book, because your drive may be either IDE or SCSI, and the setup of the physical drive is dependent on the rest of the hardware in the system. We suggest that you consult the hardware manual that came with your system or have a computer reseller install your new hard drive. The Linux system is complicated by the fact that several operating systems — such as DOS, Linux, and SCO Unix — may share the same hard drive.

To complete all the steps necessary to install and configure your new drive, you must know the total formatted drive capacity and the number of heads and cylinders, among other details. You can usually find this information in the documentation, from the manufacturer, or from the computer's BIOS.

You may want to keep a record of the data from the partition table (as displayed by fdisk), such as

- ✔ Partition numbers
- ✔ Type
- ✔ Size
- ✔ Starting and ending blocks

Installing a drive

After the drive is attached to the system, Linux should recognize it when you boot. To review the booting messages in a slower fashion than they're displayed, use the dmesg command.

Here's what to look for:

- ✔ If you added a new IDE drive, look for the mention of a new hdx drive, where the *x* is replaced with the letter *b, c, d,* or *e.* This information tells you that your kernel saw the new hard drive as it booted, and rebuilding the kernel is not necessary in order to add this drive.

    The messages for an IDE drive may look like this:

    ```
    hdb: HITACHI_DK227A-50, 4789MB w/512KB
               Cache,CHS=610/255/63
    ```

And sometime later, a message appears that looks like the following, which describes the existing partitions on the new drive (if any):

```
hdb: hdb1 hdb2 < hdb5 hdb6 hdb7 hdb8 >
```

✔ If you're adding a new SCSI disk drive, you see a boot message indicating a new disk drive that has the designation sdx, where the *x* is a letter. In the IDE or SCSI case, you may see other messages with additional information.

A SCSI disk drive has messages that look like this:

```
SCSI device sdb: hdwr device= .......
  sdb: sdb1
```

If you see these messages, the kernel has seen your new drive, and you don't have to rebuild the kernel to use the new drive.

The Linux distribution on the companion CD-ROMs features block special files for each of eight IDE disks (had – hdh) with nine partitions each (1 – 9). Linux also has block special files for seven SCSI hard drives (sda – sdg), which can have eight partitions each (1 – 8). In addition, Linux has a block special file for a SCSI CD-ROM (scd) with eight partitions (0 – 7). If you have lots of drives, or if your Linux distribution doesn't have enough block special files for your drive, you may have to create one or more additional block special files for the device, like this:

```
cd /dev; makedev sdg
```

This command creates the device driver (called a block special file) for SCSI drive 7. Note that in both IDE and SCSI drives, the letters and drive numbers correspond: *a* is for the first disk, *b* is for the second disk, and so on.

If you add a SCSI disk drive with a lower ID number than one you already have, the new disk drive takes on that number. Suppose you have SCSI disk drives with hardware ID numbers of 0, 2, and 3. Linux gives these drives the names sda, sdb, and sdc, respectively. You make your partitions and your file systems, and create your entries in /etc/fstab to show where you want the file systems mounted. Now you get a new disk drive and set the hardware ID number to 1. When you reboot, the new disk drive gets the sdb designation and the disk drives with ID numbers of 2 and 3 are renamed to sdc and sdd, respectively. You must now, at the very least, change your /etc/fstab table. For this reason, we recommend adding SCSI disk drives to your system, starting with ID 0 and working up the number chain, with no gaps in the numbering.

Partitioning a drive

You can use fdisk to partition the drive after you've added it to your computer. You need to partition a disk before formatting it (adding a file system). For example, if you want to invoke `fdisk` for partitioning the first IDE drive, you type the following command:

```
fdisk /dev/hda
```

Using `fdisk` is not too difficult; you can partition the drive fairly easily. We don't discuss it in this book though.

Making the file system

Every drive partition is simply an empty space with a beginning and an end. Unless the partition is being used for swap space, you have to put some type of file system on the partition before it can become useful. The `mkfs` (for make file system) command is used to create the file system on the partition. Normally, the file system is a native Linux file system, which at this time is called `ext3`. The Linux version of `mkfs` has been nicely streamlined and requires hardly any input.

To create a file system on the disk drive partition `sda1`, for example, you type the following command:

```
mkfs -t ext3 /dev/sda1
```

Or, for an IDE drive, type this command:

```
mkfs -t ext3 /dev/hda1
```

If you want to create an MS-DOS file system on the drive partition, you use this command:

```
mkfs -t msdos /dev/sda2
```

Be careful to type these commands precisely. You can easily format the entire disk if you make a mistake. For instance, typing in **mkfs -t ext /dev/sda** formats the whole disk. The difference is that `sda2` specifies a single partition, while `sda` means the whole disk.

You can continue to execute `mkfs` commands to create file systems for every partition on your new drive. Or you can leave some partitions without file systems (for future use), as long as you remember to perform the `mkfs` command on them before trying to attach them to your file system by using the `mount` command or the `/etc/fstab` table.

Congratulations! Your drive has been physically added to your system and partitioned, and you've added file systems to it. Now the drive is ready to join the rest of the file system — simply use either the `mount` command or the `/etc/fstab` file, which we describe earlier in this chapter.

Chapter 18

Revving Up RPM

● ●

In This Chapter

▶ Introducing RPM

▶ Finding out what RPM does

▶ Installing, updating, removing, querying, and verifying software with `gnorpm`

▶ Comparing RPM to `tar`

● ●

*T*his chapter introduces the Red Hat Package Manager (RPM). Red Hat, Inc. developed RPM in conjunction with another Linux distributor, Caldera Systems. RPM makes a grand effort to reduce the amount of work you have to do when you install software. In other words, RPM makes installing, updating, and removing software an automatic process. Woo hoo!

As of this writing, RPM is the most popular system for installing, modifying, and transporting Linux software, and without RPM, Linux would be not be where it is today. This handy-dandy tool is a big reason why Red Hat is the de facto Linux distribution leader. Motor through this chapter to find out everything you need to know about RPM.

Introducing RPM

One of the primary reasons that the Red Hat Linux distribution became popular was that it added value for its customers with technologies like Red Hat Package Manager (RPM).

All the software that was installed during the Red Hat installation process is stored in RPM's giving format, called *packages*. Packages are a collection of individual software — applications, libraries, documentation, and so on — contained in one file.

The package-management concept has been around for quite a while, with all the major Unix vendors supplying their own systems. The idea is to distribute software in a single file and have a package manager do the work of installing or uninstalling, and managing the individual files. The Linux world has benefited greatly from this system that simplifies the distribution and use of software.

You *could* install software without RPM, but we're not sure why you would — the RPM package contains everything you need to install and run an application. For instance, if you didn't have the RPM package, installing Mozilla would work a little something like this. You'd have to install the individual pieces that make up the Mozilla system; that can require dozens or more steps. You can also install, update, or uninstall RPM software. (See the "Taking a Look at What RPM Does" section for more details.)

We remember, back in the day, when we used the Linux system professionally for the first time. We had to install all the software using the dreaded tape archive system (tar). Trust us, tar was a bear to modify. RPM, on the other hand, accelerates like crazy as you wind out its engine. And yet, it's quite easy to manage.

The /mnt/cdrom/RedHat/RPMS directory contains all the RPM packages.

Taking a Look at What RPM Does

RPM performs three basic functions: installing, upgrading, and removing packages. In addition to these functions, it also can find out all sorts of information about installed and yet-to-be-installed packages. (All this and it washes windows, too.) Here's a brief rundown of each function:

- ✔ **Installing packages:** RPM installs software. Software systems such as Mozilla have files of all types that must be put into certain locations in order to work properly. For example, under Red Hat, some (but not all) the Mozilla files need to go into the /usr/bin directory. RPM does that organizational stuff automatically without any fuss or muss.

Not only does RPM install files into their proper directories, but it also does such things as create the directories and run scripts to do the things that need to be done. Such a tidy and organized little scamp.

- ✔ **Upgrading packages:** Gone are the days when updating a system was worse than going to the dentist. RPM acts like the personal Linux assistant you wish you had, updating existing software packages for you. RPM also keeps track — in a database of its own — of all the packages that you've got installed. When you upgrade a package, RPM does all of the bookkeeping chores and replaces only the files that need to be replaced. It also saves the configuration files that it replaces.

- ✔ **Removing packages:** The package database that the RPM keeps is also useful in removing packages. To put it simply, RPM takes out the trash. (Housekeeping was never so easy.) RPM goes to each file and uninstalls it. Directories belonging to the package are also removed when no files from other packages occupy them.

✔ **Querying packages and files:** RPM can also give you a great deal of information about a package and its files. You can use the query function to find out the function of a package and what files belong to it. It can also work on the RPM packages themselves, regardless of whether they have been installed.

✔ **Verifying packages:** RPM can validate an installed package against a checksum (a computer fingerprint) to see if and how it has been changed. This feature is very useful for security reasons. If you suspect that a file or system has been hacked, you can use RPM to find out how it has changed.

RPM often adds or modifies system files when it installs a package. If you erase an RPM package, those files and changes are removed too. This is what Martha Stewart would definitely call a "good thing" because it helps keep your system running reliably and avoids the problems that Windows users encounter when old system files compete with newer ones.

Using GNOME RPM

Red Hat Linux provides a great tool called GNOME RPM for working with RPM packages. GNOME RPM, also called gnorpm, is a graphical tool that provides all the functions for managing RPMs. It's like putting automatic transmission on a car — GNOME RPM does the shifting for you.

Okay, GNOME RPM does the shifting for you, but you still have to drive it. But enough car talk. GNOME RPM provides easy access to RPM functions such as install, upgrade, uninstall, query, and verify. The following sections describe how to use GNOME RPM to rev up your RPM.

Starting GNOME RPM

To start GNOME RPM, click the Main Menu button and choose Programs⇨System⇨GNOME RPM. If you're not logged in as root, then you can either type the root password when prompted in the Input window (see Figure 18-1) or run it in unprivileged mode. If you run in nonprivileged mode, you can use the query and verify functions but you can't install, upgrade, or uninstall packages. Typing the root password causes the GNOME RPM window to appear as shown in Figure 18-2.

GNOME RPM displays all the Red Hat RPMs that are installed by default on your system. The individual packages are organized into groups such as Amusements, Applications, and so on. Click the plus [+] sign to the left of each group folder icon to see the contents of the packages. For example, if you click Applications⇨Multimedia, you see all the multimedia packages on your system, as shown in Figure 18-3.

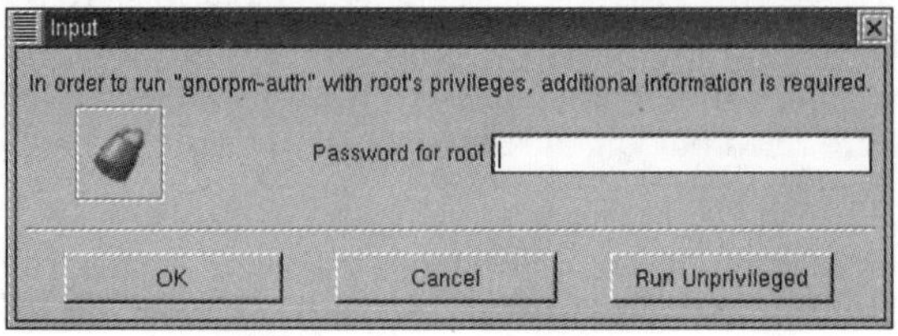

Figure 18-1:
The Input
window
prompts you
for the root
password.

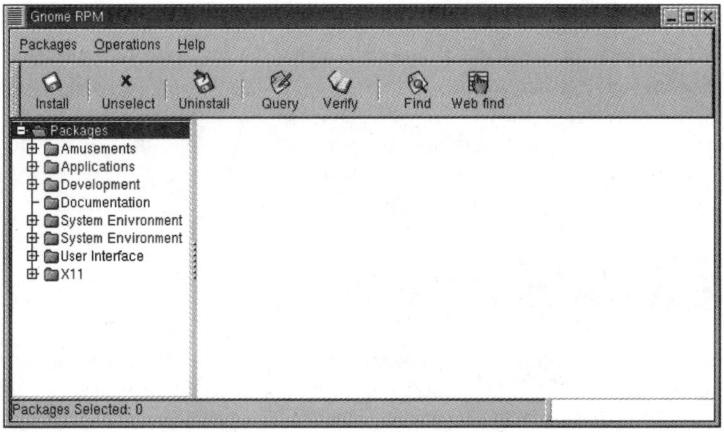

Input	☒

In order to run "gnorpm-auth" with root's privileges, additional information is required.

Password for root |

OK	Cancel	Run Unprivileged

Figure 18-2:
The GNOME
RPM main
window.

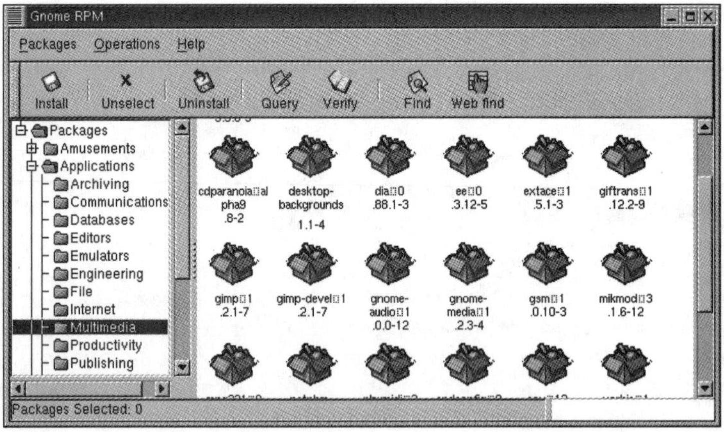

Gnome RPM

Packages   Operations   Help

Install   Unselect   Uninstall   Query   Verify   Find   Web find

- Packages
  - Amusements
  - Applications
  - Development
  - Documentation
  - System Enivronment
  - System Environment
  - User Interface
  - X11

Packages Selected: 0

Figure 18-3:
The
Multimedia
group
packages
window.

Gnome RPM

Packages   Operations   Help

Install   Unselect   Uninstall   Query   Verify   Find   Web find

- Packages
  - Amusements
  - Applications
    - Archiving
    - Communications
    - Databases
    - Editors
    - Emulators
    - Engineering
    - File
    - Internet
    - Multimedia
    - Productivity
    - Publishing

cdparanoia-al   desktop-   dia-0   ee-0   extace-1   giftrans-1
pha9   backgrounds   .88.1-3   .3.12-5   .5.1-3   .12.2-9
.8-2   1.1-4

gimp-1   gimp-devel-1   gnome-   gnome-   gsm-1   mikmod-3
.2.1-7   .2.1-7   audio-1   media-1   .0.10-3   .1.6-12
.0.0-12   .2.3-4

Packages Selected: 0

This may be a *For Dummies* book but you, of course, are no dummy. It's obvious what the GNOME RPM buttons, displayed along the top of the GNOME RPM window are used for. The following sections describe how to use them for their intended function.

Installing an RPM package from a CD-ROM

When you install your Red Hat Linux system, all the software that is copied to your hard drive from the CD-ROM comes from RPM packages. When you want to add additional software from the companion CD-ROM or an RPM repository such as www.freshmeat.net, or Red Hat itself at www.redhat.com, you can do so by using the Install button. To install an RPM package from a CD-ROM, follow these steps:

1. **Insert CD1 that came with this book in the CD-ROM drive.**

2. **Start GNOME RPM by clicking the Main Menu button and choosing Programs⇨System⇨GnoRPM.**

   If you're logged in as root, skip to Step 4.

   If you're not logged in as the root user, then you're prompted to enter the root password in the Input dialog box that pops up (refer to Figure 18-1). Only root can install RPM packages.

3. **Type the root password into the dialog box and click OK.**

   The GNOME RPM window appears.

4. **Click the Install button.**

   GNOME RPM reads the CD-ROM and displays the RPMs, organized by group. By default, GNOME RPM displays uninstalled packages.

5. **If you want to display other types of packages, you can click the Filter button at the top of the Install window and change to another option.**

   For example, you can display all the RPM packages on CD1 by selecting the All Packages option, as shown in Figure 18-4.

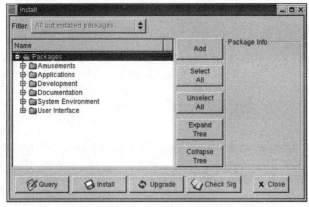

Figure 18-4:
The Install window with the All Packages filter selected.

6. **Select a package or packages from the groups.**

   For example, you can click Applications, click Communications, and then click the `pilot-link` package (which reads the digital audio directly from a CD), as shown in Figure 18-5. (If you double-click a package that is not yet installed, then it is automatically installed.)

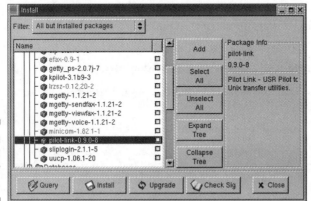

Figure 18-5:
Selecting a package for installation.

7. **The Installing window appears to provide the status of the process while it occurs.**

   After the package finishes installing, you can connect your PalmPilot and download/upload address books, calendars, and submarine games to your heart's content (Chapter 12 describes the process in detail).

Installing an RPM package from the Internet

What happens if you want to install a package that is not on one of this book's CD-ROMs? GNOME RPM automatically searches the Internet for RPM packages to install. This is a pretty cool addition because in the old days (say, 1999), in order to use RPM to install downloaded software, you would have had to manually search the Internet with your browser, sort through myriad search results for the package that matched what you actually wanted, download the file(s), and then use the `rpm` command (the manual version of `gnorpm` described later in this chapter) to install the software. That process takes almost as long as it takes to read the previous sentence.

To install an RPM package from the Internet in a greatly-simplified way, follow these steps:

1. **Insert the Red Hat Linux CD1 disc in the CD-ROM drive.**

   Be sure you're logged on to the Internet.

2. **Click the Main Menu button and choose Programs⇨System⇨GnoRPM.**

   The GNOME RPM starts.

   If you're not logged in as the superuser, then you're prompted to enter the root password in the dialog box that pops up. Only root can install RPM packages.

3. **Type the root password and click OK.**

4. **Click the Web Find button.**

   GNOME RPM goes out onto the Web and downloads a file from www. redhat.com/RDF. This file stores a list of all the RPM packages that Red Hat knows about. The Rpmfind window appears, as shown in Figure 18-6.

5. **Scroll up and down the list of available packages and click the package that you want to install.**

   Alternatively, you can enter a word in the text box at the top of the screen and click the Search button. Rpmfind finds the package (if it exists, of course) for you.

6. **Click a specific package you're interested in.**

   Information about the package appears in the subwindow on the right side of the screen, as shown in Figure 18-7.

   Check out the rplay package, for example. This is a streaming audio package being developed under the GNU Public License — anyone can use the package and redistribute it as long as they don't put any additional restrictions on it. rplay isn't quite ready for prime time yet, but we expect it to be useful in the future. Clicking rplay causes its various versions to appear.

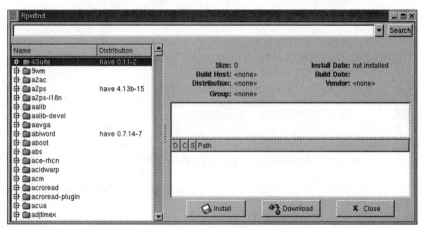

Figure 18-6:
The Rpmfind
window.

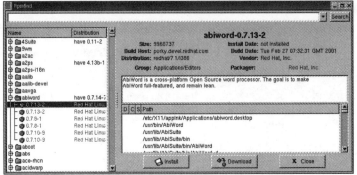

7. **To install automatically, click the Install button.**

The `gnorpm` command does the work for you; it also provides a progress screen along the way.

Alternatively, you can download the package and install it later by clicking the Download button. Install at your leisure.

8. **When you finish installing packages, click the Close button to exit the window.**

You can play around with your package after installation. It's as simple as that — almost as great as your birthday!

You can upgrade a package that already has been installed on your system. Follow the instructions in the previous sections that describe installing RPMs from a CD-ROM and the Internet. Click the Upgrade button instead of the Install button and the existing package is upgraded.

Removing an RPM package

You may want to remove an RPM package. For instance, say you wanted to experiment with the Abiware word processor but you decided you no longer want to use it; go ahead — remove it. Or maybe you want to save disk space.

Removing packages that you don't use is a good, simple trick; RPM packages are good residents on your computer because they lend themselves to easy removal. The `gnorpm` command permits you to remove packages via the `uninstall` function.

To remove an RPM package, follow these steps:

1. **Click the Main Menu button and choose Programs⇨System⇨GnoRPM.**

GNOME RPM starts.

2. **If you're not logged in as the root user, the Input dialog box pops up and you're prompted to enter the root password, which you should do, and click OK.**

   The GNOME RPM window opens up.

3. **Click any of the package groups and then any of the subgroups.**

   The individual packages are displayed.

4. **Click on the package that you want to remove — like that in Figure 18-8 — to select it.**

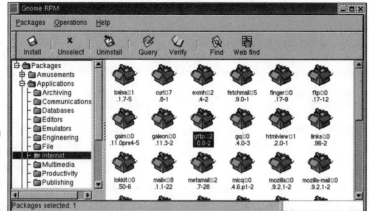

Figure 18-8: Selecting a package to remove.

5. **Click the Uninstall button.**

   The Continue Removal window appears to confirm the removal process.

6. **Click Yes to remove the package.**

   Clicking No simply returns you to the main GNOME RPM window with no harm done.

   You may encounter problems if you've modified the files that the package installed. But then again, you shouldn't have any reason to modify the files unless you like to mess around with configuration files. If you're *that* sort, you don't need us to tell you about the ramification of any changes you make. (If you're not *that* sort, don't mess with configuration files.)

7. **When you finish removing packages, click the Close button to exit the window.**

If you remove a package and realize that you didn't want to, then you have — in most cases — done very little harm. The beauty of installing everything on your Red Hat Linux computer from RPM packages is that you can easily reinstall any package.

The masochistic way: Rolling your own

If you like to roll your own, you can use the rpm command to install packages. The -i parameter indicates that an installation is to take place. You can also have rpm run in verbose (a lot of information) mode by using the -v option. (Note that you can combine options into a single group — for example -i -v can become -iv). To add the package, type the following command from a CLI:

```
rpm -iv /mnt/cdrom/RedHat/
     RPMS/pilot-link*
```

You can manually remove packages by running RPM from the GNOME terminal emulation window. For example, the following command removes the Samba software:

```
rpm -e samba
```

Sometimes, however, other package files occupy the same directories of the package that you want to delete. In these cases, you get a message saying that the directory cannot be deleted because it is not empty.

Getting information about an RPM package

After installing a package — for example, pilot-link — you can find out information about the contents of the package by using the gnorpm query function. To use this function, follow these steps:

1. **Click the Main Menu button and choose Programs⇨System⇨GnoRPM.**

   GNOME RPM starts.

   You do not have to enter the root password when prompted in the Input window. GNOME RPM allows the non-root user to query packages.

2. **Click the Run Unprivileged button if you don't intend to install, upgrade, or uninstall a package.**

   Sometimes it's necessary to click the button three times before it understands that you're trying to get its attention.

   The RPM package groups appear on the left side of the window.

3. **Click the group folder icon on the left side of the window.**

   The icon expands to show you the subgroups that contain the individual packages.

4. **Click a subgroup and then the package to be queried.**

   For example, choose Applications⇨Communications⇨Pilot-link.

   You can also use the Find button at the top of the page to locate packages to be queried. If you want to query uninstalled packages that reside on the CD-ROM, then insert the disc and wait for it to be mounted.

5. **After you select a package, click the Query button at the top of the window.**

   Information appears about when and where the package was created, what it does, and what files it contains, as shown in Figure 18-9.

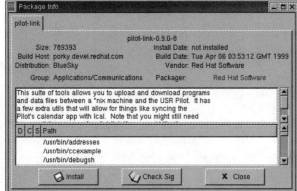

Figure 18-9:
The GNOME
RPM
Package
Info
window.

You can perform a query manually from the GNOME terminal emulation window. The `rpm` query command displays information about an RPM package. You can use the command to display information about an installed package as follows:

```
rpm -qi howto-html
```

By varying the query options, you can also list the files in the package, list all installed packages, and so on. Consult the RPM man page for more information.

Verifying RPM packages

You may need to verify that an installed package is what it says it is. You may, for example, think that a package isn't working correctly. Whatever your reason, `gnorpm` provides a `verify` function. To use this function, follow these steps:

1. **Click the Main Menu button and choose Programs⇨System⇨GnoRPM.**

   GNOME RPM starts.

   You do not have to enter the root password when prompted in the Input window.

   GNOME RPM allows the non-root user to query packages.

2. **Click the Run Unprivileged button if you don't intend to install, upgrade, or uninstall a package.**

   You may have to click the button a few times before it understands what you want.

   RPM package groups are shown in the left half of the gnorpm window.

3. **Click the group folder icon and then the subgroup icon.**

   The individual packages icons are displayed.

4. **Click the package to be verified and click the Verify button at the top of the screen.**

   GNOME RPM checks the fingerprint of every file that belongs to the package against a known copy. Progress appears in the Verifying Packages window. When the program finishes, it displays information about what — if any — differences between the known and existing fingerprints exist. Figure 18-10 shows a sample window.

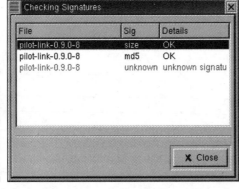

Figure 18-10:
The GNOME
RPM
Verifying
Packages
window.

The Verifying Packages window tells you if any files in a package have been changed or don't exist. It lists any changes in the files that belong to the package. For example, the first time that you add or delete a user account, the /etc/passwd file is modified.

8000

The `rpm` command can also verify information about installed packages and their files. This is a very useful system administration tool. For example, if you're in doubt about the configuration file — suppose you accidentally removed the `/usr/bin/pilot-clip` file, then you can run this command:

```
rpm -V pilot-link
```

The pilot-link RPM package keeps a `checksum` and compares the state of the installed files against it. The command returns

```
missing     /usr/bin/pilot-clip
```

which shows you that the `pilot-clip` file has been removed.

Modifying GNOME RPM defaults

You can modify the GNOME RPM defaults by choosing Operations⇨ Preferences from the GNOME RPM window as shown in Figure 18-11. The following list shows some of the primary functions that you can alter:

- ✔ Behavior
- ✔ Package listing
- ✔ Install window
- ✔ Network
- ✔ Rpmfind
- ✔ Distributions

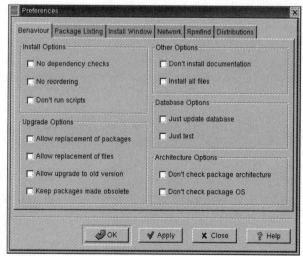

Figure 18-11: The Preferences window.

The following sections describe some of the more interesting and useful functions in each of the main systems.

Behavior

The individual files that make up an RPM package often can simply be copied to their respective directories. Sometimes, however, more work is required. For example, some RPM packages require that a script be run after the files are copied to complete the installation. The following options are available in the GNOME RPM Behavior section of the Preferences window (refer to Figure 18-11):

- ✔ **No dependency checks on installations:** To work correctly, some packages require that other packages be installed. RPM normally checks to see if all such packages — dependencies — exist before installing. You can turn off that check if you want to, though.

- ✔ **Don't run scripts:** RPM runs scripts, when they exist, after installing the software contained in a package. You can turn that off by selecting this option.

- ✔ **Don't reorder packages:** Sometimes you need to change the order that packages are installed. Another package may need to be installed first to satisfy a dependency.

- ✔ **Upgrade Options defaults:** You should never need to change these options.

- ✔ **Don't install documentation:** You can choose not to install README, docs, and other files by selecting this option.

- ✔ **Install all files:** Clicking this option installs all the files in a package.

- ✔ **Just update database:** This option updates the RPM database file but does not install any files.

- ✔ **Just test:** This option sees if the package can be installed. When you use this option and select a package to be installed, for example, then the process is started but nothing is installed.

- ✔ **Don't check package architecture:** Most RPM packages are dependent on the type of processor that your computer uses. For example, the packages on the Red Hat installation CDs shipped with this book can be used on Intel-based computers only.

- ✔ **Don't check package OS:** GNOME RPM does not check the operating system (OS) that the package is set to use.

Package listing

This is a really difficult set of options to understand. You can display packages as icons or as a list. Decisions, decisions.

Install window

GNOME RPM color-codes the packages that it displays based on their status. Older packages are gray, current ones green, and new ones blue. You can change those colors to your taste.

GNOME RPM automatically looks to your CD-ROM drive to find packages. The default directory is /mnt/cdrom/RedHat/RPMS. You can change that by clicking the Install Window tab in the Preferences window and editing the Default File Selection Dialog Path text box shown in Figure 18-12.

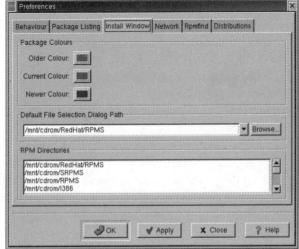

Figure 18-12:
The Default
File
Selection
Dialog Path
text box.

GNOME RPM also has a list of secondary directories to search when the Red Hat installation CD is not mounted. The secondary paths are listed in the RPM Directories window. The first entries show common CD-ROM directories, while the last ones point to your hard drive. You can change those entries to point to other locations.

Network

If your Red Hat Linux workstation is on a network that uses a proxying firewall, then you have to configure GNOME RPM to work with it. (A proxying firewall is a device that prevents unauthorized people from connecting to your network.) You can configure GNOME RPM to use a proxying firewall by choosing Operations⇨Preference. When the Preferences window opens, click the Network tab and the window shown in Figure 18-13 appears.

You must type the host name of the proxy in the HTTP Proxy field. The host name looks something like myproxy.mynet.com, as shown in Figure 18-14. Sometimes packages are downloaded by FTP, and you may need to type the host name of the FTP proxy in the corresponding field. If your proxying firewall requires a username and password, then type them in the Proxy User and Proxy Password fields.

GNOME RPM keeps a cache of download sites that you've accessed. You can change the length of time that it saves this information by changing the cache expire entry. Finally, GNOME RPM lists your local hostname in the field by that name. You rarely need to change your hostname.

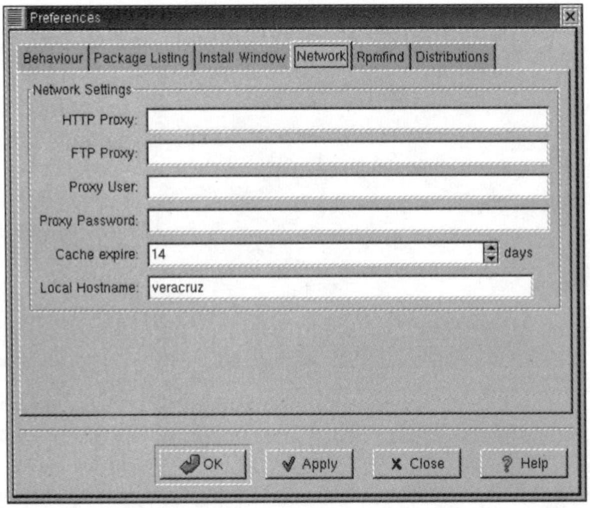

Figure 18-13:
The GNOME
RPM
Network
Preferences
window.

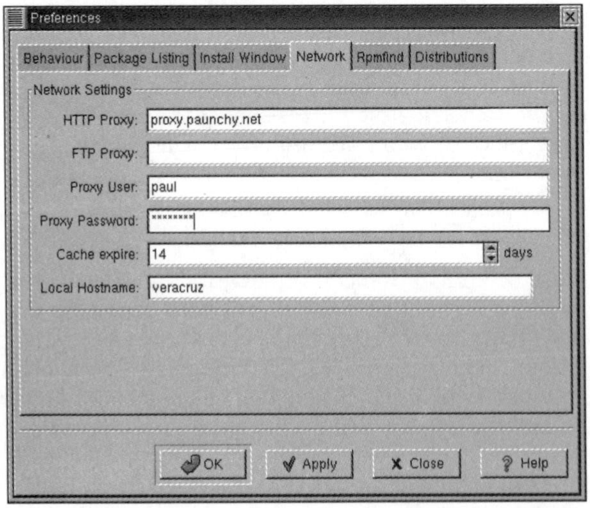

Figure 18-14:
The RPM
Network
Preferences
window
showing the
firewall
proxy.

Rpmfind

The Rpmfind window, shown in Figure 18-15, controls RPM find and download capabilities. The default server is located on Red Hat's Web site. This may change over time or other (better?) servers may pop up. Well, you have the power to change it here by changing the location to which your downloads are saved. One common location to save RPM packages is the /usr/local/src directory.

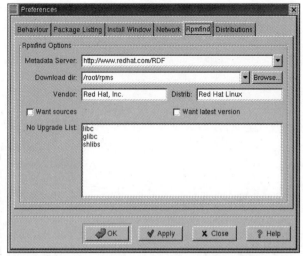

Figure 18-15:
The Rpmfind
tab of
Preferences
window.

Until the advent of the RPM (and the Debian package manager on Debian Linux systems), Linux software was only distributed by tar archives, which are sometimes referred to as tarballs or more descriptively, hairballs. The tar file storage mechanism stores one or more files in a single file in a tar format. A tar file has the file suffix of .tar; if the tar file is compressed, it has a suffix like .tgz or .tar.gz. Using the tar-based distribution system is sufficient if your software does not change often and you are young. But when you need to upgrade or change software, or work with complex software systems, it becomes quite difficult to work with. Rather than spending your life spitting up hairballs, systems like RPM greatly simplify your life.

Chapter 19

Bringing In the Red Hat Repairman: Troubleshooting Your Network

In This Chapter

▶ Understanding the philosophy of troubleshooting

▶ Gardening with the fault tree

▶ Diagnosing network problems

*T*his book is perfect, and there's no way that anything described in it can ever go wrong. You'll be as lonely as the Maytag repairman if you expect trouble (the trouble is trouble never happens). Errata (corrections) are as outdated as a brick and mortar bookstore. This book makes setting up computers and networks so easy that you'll wonder why other people have so many problems! Blah, blah, blah, yada, yada, yada.

Well, maybe not. This guy named Murphy hangs out in both virtual and real bookstores. He's always jumping in just when things are starting to go well. The guy just can't keep his nose out of other people's business. This chapter is meant to smooth things out between you and Murphy in case he catches up with you.

It's the Tree's Fault, Not Mine!

Troubleshooting is, as they say, more of an art than a science. Sometimes it's easy to see what the problem is and how to fix it. Other times it's not. The difficulty that you have fixing problems depends, of course, on how hard the problem is and how well you know your stuff. Obviously, the better acquainted you are with computers and Linux, the better you'll be at troubleshooting.

The blind leading the blind

Paul's colleague, Ken Hatfield, once said, "One of the side benefits from lots of troubleshooting comes from what I call the value of blind alleys. Most often in troubleshooting, you go down blind alleys, or in your tree example, the wrong branches of the solution tree. But in doing so, you learn something. In the future, when you encounter a different problem down the road, that previous blind alley may be the road to the solution." Well said.

Here's an example: Paul recently had a server that was having a lot of problems. The /var

file system had filled up, which caused some programs that used it to fail. When space on /var was freed up, most of the programs started to do their job again. But one program didn't work. Paul spent a long time trying to figure out why it didn't work even after the problem was fixed. As it turned out, this particular program's real problem was that its license had expired. He had not only walked down a blind alley but bumped into a wall and kept trying to go forward. D'oh!

Every problem has a solution. Computers are cause-and-effect-based machines. When something breaks, or doesn't work, there's always a reason. The reason may not be easy to find, but it exists.

But how do you find the cause? That's a million-dollar question. Getting a million bucks isn't easy unless you're willing to grind your teeth, plot against your fellow contestants for months on a desert island, purchase ten million Power Ball tickets, or — believe it or not — work hard and work smart. Some people are willing to eat rats for the chance or are lucky enough to win the lottery, but most just have to work hard. Oh well.

Working hard is easy, but how do you work smart? That's where the idea of the fault tree comes in. The fault tree looks like an upside-down tree. The trunk of the tree represents the fault, or problem. The ends, or leaves, of the branches represent all the possible causes. The fault tree is a conceptual aid that helps you to eliminate all but the cause of your problem. After that's done, solving the problem is virtually assured.

For example, Figure 19-1 shows part of a fault tree that points out what major subsystems you should look at. To find the solution to a problem, you need to systematically identify what's working. You work your way to what's not working, and then when you find it, you usually solve your problem. The fault tree concept helps to formalize the process.

Following are some of the possible faults:

✔ The first branch on the left involves problems with the physical connection: Do you have a network adapter? Is the cable connected properly to the adapter? If so, do you have a break in the cable? If so, then you have to fix or replace the cable.

✔ The second branch deals with the network interface configuration: Have you configured the IP address for your Ethernet adapter correctly? If so, is the netmask correct?

✔ The third branch helps decide if the problem exists with the network routing. Can your network packets be directed towards the correct network?

The fault tree helps you break down any big problem into simpler ones. By eliminating each simple problem one-by-one, you should eventually locate the root cause. The fault tree is a simple method for thinking a problem through.

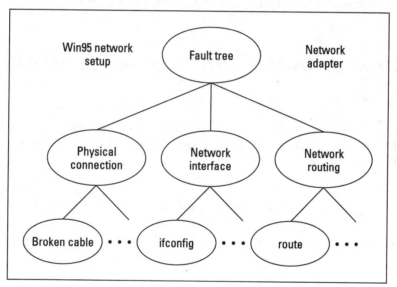

Figure 19-1:
The fault
tree.

The Fix Is In: Troubleshooting Your Network

One common problem involves getting your Red Hat Linux computer to work on a network. Not that you're having such problems after working through Chapter 6, but if the impossible happens and Murphy comes to visit, then this section should help out.

Your Red Hat Linux machine is the foundation of your network and must be set up correctly for anything to run. If it isn't working, or if you have an unusual setup (or Murphy is in a bad mood), you can check for several different causes.

We use the Red Hat Linux network as the troubleshooting example in this chapter. The Red Hat Linux network is one of the more difficult things to set up correctly because it not only depends on your Linux computer, but other computers as well. Suppose that your Red Hat Linux network is not working. Use the following sections as a simple fault tree that you can follow to troubleshoot your network.

Please see The Part of Tens chapters for insights into other problems. Chapter 21 describes how to find information about your Red Hat Linux computer; it also points out where you can get help. Chapter 22 discusses some of the simple, frequently encountered problems that people have with Red Hat Linux. Chapter 23 describes ten security fixes.

Ticking through Your Linux Networking Checklist

We describe the most likely problems in order from most simple to most complex. After cataloging the problems, we look at one of the branches of the fault tree to solve a problem.

Is the power turned on? Check

First verify that you turned on the power. Sounds simple, but hey, sometimes the simplest things go wrong.

I is an enganeer

An experienced electrical engineer and Linux author once got really angry with a cable TV company. His cable service went dead in the middle of a Philadelphia Eagles game. They were losing, but the Eagles don't appear on TV much in Albuquerque. The cable company was called immediately. Blah! Blah! Blah! My connection . . . Blah! Blah! Well, the nice support person guided the poor engineer step-by-step through his own fault tree. First step: Is your VCR/TV turned on? "Yes, of course." Step two: Is the VCR button on your VCR toggled on? "Of course, ah, woops, no it isn't. Ah yes, it works now, thank you very much. Goodbye." D'oh! What was five years of electrical engineering school good for?

Is your network cable broken? Nope

Make sure that your network cables are not broken or cut. Check the connectors to make sure that they're okay. You should also make sure that you are using the correct network cable, which should be category 5 (8-wire) straight-through cable.

Is your Ethernet hub or switch working? Check

Your Ethernet hub or switch should also be turned on. Ensure that the network cables are also connected securely.

If you're stuck in the Middle Ages (with me!) and are using that coaxial network cable called Thinnet — or 10base2 for geeks — then you don't have to check an Ethernet hub/switch because there is none. Thinnet connects each NIC (computer, printer, and so on) to every other NIC on the subnet. In other words, each computer that is on a Thinnet cable is connected electrically to all the other computers in the network. Each computer sees all the network traffic on that cable. If any part of that bus is compromised, all traffic ceases. For example, if you disconnect the terminator at either end of the cable, all communication ends. The best way to troubleshoot that type of problem is to start at one end and work your way down the line. Try to get just two computers working together, then three, and so on. Eventually you'll find the problem.

Determining whether your network cable has been compromised requires addressing the following issues:

- ✔ If you're using Thinnet, make sure the BNCs (Bayonet Nut Connectors) are securely attached.

- ✔ Look at the interface between the cable and Ethernet switch/hub — or the BNC connector if you are using Thinnet — to make sure they are in good physical contact. Sometimes the cable can pull out a little bit and break the connection.

- ✔ Look at the cable itself and make sure it hasn't been cut or crushed.

- ✔ If you're using Thinnet, make sure that each end of the cable has a 50ohm terminator attached to it. Thinnet must be terminated or else it won't work right, just as it won't work right if the cable is broken. The reason for this is that the radio frequency (RF) signal reflects from the unterminated end and interferes with the incoming signals. If you have a cable that you know is good, try substituting it. The idea is to eliminate as many segments that you are unsure about as possible. If you have just two computers in close proximity and you suspect a problem with the cable you are using, all you can do is try another cable. If the computers are far apart and rely on several segments or a long cable, try moving them closer together and using one short segment. If you have three or more computers, try getting just two of them working together. Then try adding another one. Proceed until you find the faulty segment.

Is your Ethernet adapter inserted correctly? Yup

You have to have an Ethernet adapter to be connected to an Ethernet network. Make sure that your Ethernet adapter is plugged into your computer's system board — also known as a motherboard — snugly. Sometimes it's necessary to pull it out and then reinsert it. That process of pulling out an adapter and then plugging it back in is called *reseating*.

Is your network adapter configured correctly? Roger

Sometimes a startup script is misconfigured, which causes the startup screen to go by without you seeing an error message. If that happens, log in as root and from the shell prompt, type the command:

```
ifconfig
```

You see a listing of two different interfaces, as shown in the following code, or three interfaces if you have PPP configured. The program ifconfig tells the Linux kernel that you have a network adapter and gives it an IP address and network mask. This is the first step in connecting your Linux computer to your network.

```
lo        Link encap:Local Loopback
          inet addr:127.0.0.1  Bcast:127.255.255.255
          Mask:255.0.0.0
          UP BROADCAST LOOPBACK RUNNING  MTU:3584  Metric:1
          RX packets:115 errors:0 dropped:0 overruns:0
          TX packets:115 errors:0 dropped:0 overruns:0

eth0      Link encap:10Mbps Ethernet  HWaddr 00:A0:24:2F:30:69
          inet addr:192.168.1.1 Bcast:192.168.1.255
Mask:255.255.255.0
          UP BROADCAST RUNNING MULTICAST  MTU:1500  Metric:1
          RX packets:16010 errors:18 dropped:18 overruns:23
          TX packets:7075 errors:0 dropped:0 overruns:0
          Interrupt:10 Base address:0x300
```

The physical connections aren't set up right

If you don't see the line containing lo, which is the loopback interface, or eth0, which is your network adapter, then your physical network connections aren't set up right. The loopback interface is not a physical device; it's used for the network software's internal workings. The loopback interface must be present for the network adapter to be configured.

If the loopback interface is not present, type the following command:

```
ifconfig lo 127.0.0.1
```

If the network adapter — generally an Ethernet card — is not present, type the following command:

```
ifconfig eth0 192.168.1.1
```

Because this is a class C network address, ifconfig automatically defaults to the 255.255.255.0 netmask. If you have an unusual netmask, which you shouldn't, type the following command:

```
ifconfig eth0 192.168.1.1 netmask 255.255.255.0
```

Type **ifconfig** and you should see your network adapter displayed correctly. If it's not, examine the manual page on ifconfig. You display this manual page by typing the following command and then pressing Enter.

```
man ifconfig
```

You can page through the document by pressing Enter to go line-by-line, pressing the spacebar to go forward one page at a time, pressing Ctrl+B to page backward, or pressing Q to quit. The ifconfig man page shows a great deal of information on what and how ifconfig works. If you're still having problems, look at the Linux startup information by running the following command:

```
dmesg | more
```

Note that we pipe (use the | symbol) the output from dmesg to the more command. Linux pipes are used to transmit the output command to the input of another. After you run the preceding command, you see the information that was displayed during the boot process. The more command shows one page of information at a time; use the spacebar to display each subsequent page. Look for your Ethernet NIC, which should appear after the Adding Swap line in the following code:

```
Freeing unused kernel memory: 60k freed
Adding Swap: 13651k swap-space (priority ?1)
Eth0:  3c509 at 0x310 tag1, BNC port, address ... aa,IRQ 11.
3c509.c:1.16 (2.2) 2/3/98
becker@cesdis.gsfc.nasa.govbecker@cesdis.gsfc.nasa.gov.
```

Or maybe you have a hardware problem

If you don't see your Ethernet adapter, then you may have a hardware problem. Check your adapter. Reseat it (take it out and put it back in) and see if it works. If not, then you probably need a new NIC. If you do see the NIC, then look inside the Linux kernel and see which devices it has. Type the following command to change to a special directory called /proc where process information is located:

```
cat /proc/devices
```

You should see a line with your network adapter listed. If you don't, then Linux doesn't know that it exists. If the NIC is Plug and Play (PnP) compatible, then that is often the problem. Linux frequently has problems working with PnP NICs. It's best to turn PnP off. Run the following program to see if you have a PnP NIC:

```
pnpprobe
```

If you see that your Ethernet NIC is PnP, then you can use the isapnp program to reconfigure it. isapnp is a difficult program to use — it's best to use the configuration program that comes with the NIC. In this case the 3c5x9cfg.exe, which runs under DOS, is used for configuring the 3Com 3c509 NIC. Use your NIC's configuration program and turn off PnP.

Try to run your Ethernet NIC again. If it still doesn't run, then you need to find out more information.

Maybe you have an interrupt or address conflict

You may have an interrupt or address conflict. Look at the list of interrupts and then the IO addresses of all the devices that the kernel knows about by typing the following commands:

```
cat /proc/interrupts
cat /proc/ioports
```

The IO address is the actual location in memory where the device — such as the network adapter — is accessed by the microprocessor (for instance, your Pentium chip). The interrupt is a way that the microprocessor is informed that it should stop whatever it's doing in order to process information that has arrived at the device that is sending the interrupt.

When your Ethernet adapter receives a packet, it sends an interrupt to the microprocessor to say an event has occurred. Your Pentium stops what it's doing and processes the new information. Actually, the microprocessor interacts with Linux to do the processing.

Type **cat /proc/interrupts** to show both the interrupts and the IO addresses with which Red Hat Linux is familiar. The output should look like that in the following code:

```
 0:      378425    timer
 1:        1120    keyboard
 2:           0    cascade
10:       16077    3c509
13:           1    math error
14:       63652 +  ide0
```

Typing **cat /proc/ioports** shows the input/output ports that are used by Red Hat Linux to interact with the computer's devices. The following output shows the I/O ports used on this computer:

```
0000-001f : dma1
0020-003f : pic1
0040-005f : timer
0060-006f : keyboard
0080-009f : dma page reg
00a0-00bf : pic2
00c0-00df : dma2
00f0-00ff : npu
01f0-01f7 : ide0
0300-030f : 3c509
03c0-03df : vga+
03f0-03f5 : floppy
03f6-03f6 : ide0
03f7-03f7 : floppy DIR
```

Look for your network adapter. In this case, it's the 3c509. If the adapter is working, there are no conflicts. If a conflict exists, you have to reconfigure the adapter. Run your Ethernet NIC configuration program and set the adapter's parameters in its EEPROM. Older adapters may have jumpers or little switches called DIP switches to set. If you think you have to do this, remember to write down all the other devices' interrupts and IO addresses so you don't end up conflicting with something else.

Or perhaps you've got a funky kernel

You also may be using a kernel that does not have networking installed. (This is unlikely in the newer versions of Red Hat Linux because the Linux kernel automatically loads networking — and other modules — on demand. But it's still informative to go ahead and look at these files in order to gain an understanding of how Linux works.)

Display the networking devices by typing the following command:

```
cat /proc/net/devices
```

The following output shows that the kernel is configured for loopback (lo) and Ethernet interfaces (eth0). The loopback interface is used only for internal networking. If you don't see the Ethernet interface, you may have an unsupported network adapter or a defective or misconfigured one. The Red Hat Linux kernel, by default, automatically loads modules as they are needed. You can look back at the results of your boot process by using the dmesg command. Look for a message that says delaying eth0 configuration. That most likely means that Linux was not able to load the network adapter module or the adapter isn't working.

Display the information about your devices by using the cat /proc/net/dev command:

```
Inter-|    Receive                              |   Transmit
 face |packets errs drop fifo frame|packets errs drop fifo
               colls carrier
    lo: 116    0  0  0        116      0     0   0    0 0
  eth0: 16292 19 19 23 19    7245      0     0   0   54 0
```

Sometimes a network adapter works only if you compile its driver directly into the kernel.

The next step is to make sure that your network routing is configured correctly. This is also a very easy thing to get confused. You don't need to set up routing outside your LAN yet, but Linux needs to know where to send packets on its own network. Look at your routing table by typing the following command:

```
netstat -nr
```

You see a listing of your routing table similar to the following code:

```
Kernel IP routing table
Destination     Gateway          Genmask         Flags   MSS
          Window  irtt Iface
192.168.1.0     0.0.0.0          255.255.255.0   U         0 0
          0 eth0
127.0.0.0       0.0.0.0          255.0.0.0       U         0 0
          0 lo
0.0.0.0         192.168.1.254    0.0.0.0         UG        0 0
          0 eth0
```

The destination is the location — IP address — that you want to send packets to; for example, the address 192.168.1.0 refers to my local network. The gateway is the address (computer or router) where the packets need to be sent so that they can find their way to their destination. In the case where the destination is the local network, then the 0.0.0.0 means no gateway.

The *genmask* is used to separate the parts of the IP address that are used for the network address from the host number. The flags are used to indicate things like U for up and G for gateway. The metric is used as a measure of how far a packet has to travel to its destination (a number greater than 32 is considered to be infinite). The next two flags — Ref and Use — are not important for this discussion.

The Iface field shows what network interface is being used (etho refers to an Internet adapter and lo for the loopback interface; the loopback interface is used internally by the Linux kernel and you should not have any need to use it directly). The information about each interface — the routing table — is displayed below the headings. For example, the first line tells Linux to send packets destined for addresses of 192.168.1.0 through 192.168.1.255 to the Ethernet adapter (eth0). The second line deals with the kernel's internal loopback interface. The third and last line, with the address of 0.0.0.0, is known as the default route. It defines where to send all packets that are not covered by a specific route.

Defining a route to the loopback interface

You must have a route to the loopback interface (also referred to as lo), which is the127.0.0.0 address. If you're missing either or both parameters, you must set them. To set the loopback device — which must be set for the network adapter to work — type the following command:

```
route add -net 127.0.0.0
```

To set the route for the network adapter and your local network, type the following command:

```
route add -net 192.168.1.0
```

This route is assigned automatically to your network adapter. But if you want to assign it explicitly, type the command as follows:

```
route add -net 192.168.1.0 dev eth0
```

Type **netstat -r -n** to see your routing table. You should see entries for the loopback and the Ethernet. If you don't see a route to your network interface, try repeating the preceding steps. You may have to delete a route. To delete a route, type the following command:

```
route del 192.168.1.0
```

Note that we use the network address instead of a host address here. The zero (0) designates the class C network address of 192.168.1.

Doing the ping thing

If the network adapter is configured correctly and the routing is correct, check the network. The best way to do this is to ping the loopback interface first and then the other computer. Type the following command, let it run for a few seconds (one ping occurs per second), and stop it by pressing Ctrl+C:

```
ping 127.0.0.1
```

You should see a response like the one shown in the following code:

```
PING 127.0.0.1 (127.0.0.1): 56 data bytes
64 bytes from 127.0.0.1: icmp_seq=0 ttl=64 time=2.0 ms
64 bytes from 127.0.0.1: icmp_seq=1 ttl=64 time=1.2 ms
64 bytes from 127.0.0.1: icmp_seq=2 ttl=64 time=1.1 ms
64 bytes from 127.0.0.1: icmp_seq=3 ttl=64 time=1.1 ms
?
--- 127.0.0.1 ping statistics ---
4 packets transmitted, 4 packets received, 0% packet loss
          round-trip min/avg/max = 1.1/1.8/4.6 ms
```

Each line shows the number of bytes returned from the loopback interface, the sequence, and the round-trip time. The last lines are the summary, which shows if any packets did not make the trip. This is a working system, but if you don't see any returned packet, something is wrong with your setup and you should review the steps outlined in the preceding paragraphs.

Next try pinging your Ethernet interface by typing:

```
ping 192.168.1.1
```

You should see a response like the following code:

```
PING 192.168.1.1 (198.168.1.1): 56 data bytes
64 bytes from 198.168.1.1: icmp_seq=0 ttl=64 time=2.0 ms
64 bytes from 198.168.1.1: icmp_seq=1 ttl=64 time=1.2 ms
64 bytes from 198.168.1.1: icmp_seq=2 ttl=64 time=1.1 ms
64 bytes from 198.168.1.1: icmp_seq=3 ttl=64 time=1.1 ms
?
--- 198.168.1.1 ping statistics ---
4 packets transmitted, 4 packets received, 0% packet loss
          round-trip min/avg/max = 1.1/1.8/4.6 ms
```

Is there another computer or device to talk to? Uh-huh

Try to ping another computer — if one exists — on your network. Type the following command, let it run for 10 to 15 seconds, and stop it by pressing Ctrl+C:

```
ping 192.168.1.2
```

You should see a response like the following code:

```
PING 192.168.1.2 (192.168.1.2): 56 data bytes
64 bytes from 192.168.1.2: icmp_seq=0 ttl=32 time=3.1 ms
64 bytes from 192.168.1.2: icmp_seq=1 ttl=32 time=2.3 ms
64 bytes from 192.168.1.2: icmp_seq=2 ttl=32 time=2.5 ms
64 bytes from 192.168.1.2: icmp_seq=3 ttl=32 time=2.4 ms

--- 192.168.1.2 ping statistics ---
4 packets transmitted, 4 packets received, 0% packet loss
              round-trip min/avg/max = 2.3/2.5/3.1 ms
```

If you get a continuous stream of returned packets and the packet loss is zero or very near zero, your network is working. If not, the problem may be in the other machine. Review the troubleshooting steps again in this chapter. Note that the ICMP is taking about 1 full millisecond (ms) longer to travel to the external computer than to the loopback device. That is because the loopback is completely internal to the Linux computer.

If you can't locate the problem and you're using a PPP connection to an Internet service provider (ISP), establish a PPP connection and try to ping the computer where you have your account. It's considered a security breach to continuously ping someone else's computer — and at least bad manners — so don't leave it running. Also, the ISP's firewall may not allow the Internet Control Message Protocol (ICMP) packets that ping uses. ICMP packets are the simplest type of packet defined in the Internet Protocol. They're used for doing simple things like a ping.

Chapter 20

Configuring X

∙∙∙

In This Chapter

▶ Uncovering details about your video controller, monitor, and mouse

▶ Configuring the X Window System

▶ Finding help if the X Window System still doesn't work

▶ Paying attention to Xtermination etiquette

∙∙∙

Did you receive an error message during the installation, informing you that the X Window System (what we'll call X from now on) was not installed properly and that you had to install it later? Or was your video card or monitor not included in the supported hardware in Chapter 3. Perhaps you simply skipped configuring X in the first place. If so, this chapter is for you. Take solace in the fact that X is one of the trickiest parts of the Linux system to get working properly.

X was invented at the Massachusetts Institute of Technology (MIT). MIT designed X to display graphical applications across a wide range of machines. It was originally built to run on Unix platforms but has been adapted to Linux, Windows, and other platforms.

Discovering Your Hardware's True Identity

Before you start X, you need to find out information about your video controller card, monitor, mouse, and keyboard.

For your video controller card, you need to find out:

▸ The model number (and perhaps the video chip used)

▸ The amount of video RAM it has

You should be able to find this information in your system's documentation or by using Windows, as described in Chapter 3. The Xconfigurator utiltity is also good at probing and discovering details about your video equipment.

Next you need to know the following about your mouse:

- The model number and manufacturer
- Whether it's a PS/2 bus mouse or a serial mouse

Again, your system's documentation should tell you, and often the bottom of the mouse offers some basic information.

A PS/2 mouse usually has a round connector on the end of its wire, or tail. A serial mouse has an oblong connector with nine holes. All varieties of PS/2 bus mice look the same to Linux. Different serial mice, however, have different characteristics. If you have a serial mouse, you need to know its model number and manufacturer, or whether it emulates some other well-known mouse.

Three-button mice work best with Linux, but you can get by with a two-button mouse. To X, holding down both buttons at the same time on a two-button mouse is equivalent to holding down the middle button of a three-button mouse, but only if the system is configured correctly. You can find out how to configure the mouse in Chapter 3.

Finally, you need to know about your monitor. Most monitor manuals have a table at the back with such information as:

- Horizontal sync range
- Vertical sync range
- Resolution
- Whether it is *multiscanning,* which means your monitor can run at several resolution rates

Older monitors, particularly VGA monitors that came with older systems, often aren't multiscanning. These monitors can be damaged if you try to use them at a higher resolution than VGA, which is 640 x 480 and 60 Hz.

Horizontal and vertical sync range numbers help X determine how to place the dots on the screen. The resolution number tells X how many dots can be on the screen horizontally and vertically. The 640 x 480 resolution is usually considered to be the worst, and 1,280 x 1,024 is usually considered to be the best for normal use. Strive for 800 x 600 resolution as a minimum and 1,024 x 768 as an ideal for most systems.

Higher video resolution uses more video memory (which is on the video card and therefore separate from the system memory), allows fewer simultaneous colors on the screen (for a given amount of video memory), and typically shrinks text on the screen, making it harder to see. On the other hand, using a higher resolution means that more information can be visible on the screen at one time for the same size monitor (even though the writing may be so small that you can't read it without new glasses). Some video cards can be upgraded to add more video memory, and some cannot.

Most newer monitors have built-in protection mechanisms to keep them from burning up in what is known as *overdriving,* but older monitors do not. Older monitors can literally catch on fire. Try to find the specifications for your monitor from the manual, from a dealer, or from the manufacturer's Web page.

If you hear noise from your monitor or smell burning components, turn off your computer immediately. If you think that the screen doesn't look right, press Ctrl+Alt+Backspace right away to stop X Server and then try a lower resolution. Otherwise, you can easily damage the monitor.

Running Xconfigurator

After you find out all about your video hardware, you're ready to start configuring X. We assume that you don't have X up and running. If it is up and running, you can skip the rest of this chapter.

The next step is to use a program called Xconfigurator. This program asks you a series of questions, such as the type of mouse, the type of graphics card, and the amount of video memory in your system. As you supply the answers, Xconfigurator builds a file called .xinitrc that X Server uses later to communicate with your mouse, the video card, and the rest of the system. (Xconfigurator is the same program that the Red Hat installation system uses.)

Xconfigurator also tries to obtain information by probing the hardware. Sometimes the program is accurate, but it can make a mistake, particularly in older PCs, with older video cards, or with serial mice. Therefore, you may have to supply information to the program. As Linux becomes more sophisticated in the methods, it uses to probe hardware, and as hardware becomes more sophisticated in the information it can return to the operating system, fewer questions need to be asked. For now, though, you have Xconfigurator.

To run the Xconfigurator program, follow these steps:

1. **Log in as root and open a Terminal window by clicking the GNOME Terminal icon on the GNOME panel at the bottom of the screen (it looks like a monitor).**

   Before you modify your current X Window settings, you should save the configuration file.

2. **Type the following command to make a backup copy of XFree86 configuration file (/etc/X11/XF86config):**

   ```
   cp /etc/X11/XF86config /etc/X11/XF86config.bak
   ```

The XF86config file stores the X Window System configuration information.

3. Run the configuration program by entering the following command at the command prompt:

```
Xconfigurator
```

4. When the Welcome screen shown in Figure 20-1 appears, press the Enter key to continue.

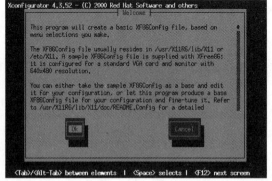

Figure 20-1: Selecting your graphics controller card.

5. The PCI Probe screen opens, as shown in Figure 20-2.

Xconfigurator is able to detect most PCI-based video controllers. In fact, you have very little choice other than to select the given PCI card when Xconfigurator does detect it. But that's not a problem because there's no reason why you'd want to use any other controller.

Figure 20-2: The PCI Probe screen.

The Custom/Generic monitor options

Xconfigurator gives you several generic monitor choices. You can use a generic monitor if your particular monitor is not found in the list of monitors. The following are descriptions of each setting:

✔ **Standard VGA:** This is the most basic resolution that you can use. It works in more circumstances than any other resolution but isn't so useful for getting work done. If you have trouble with the higher resolutions, then try this one — if only to find a starting point for getting to a higher one. Standard VGA is your safest bet.

✔ **Super VGA:** This is an intermediate resolution. It has a high enough density to get a reasonable-looking screen with which you can get work done. The resolution is also low enough to work on a large number of systems.

✔ **Generic Monitor that can do:** These selections describe monitors that can display resolutions up to the given value.

✔ **8514 Compatible:** This setup is a leftover from ancient times. We rarely run into these monitors, but they may still exist in some numbers. If you have one, try it. Otherwise, don't bother.

✔ **Super VGA, 1024 x 768:** This is the highest resolution that you can get from the Custom setup. If your video card can handle it, you'll pack a lot of information onto your screen. Otherwise, try a lower resolution.

6. **If Xconfigurator detected your video controller, press the Enter key to continue and skip to Step 8. Otherwise, continue to Step 7 (and do not pass go, and do not collect $200!).**

7. **If you're using an older video controller, and Xconfigurator doesn't detect it, you're shown a list of manufacturers and models; choose your graphics card, tab over to the OK button, and press Enter.**

   Use the arrow keys to maneuver through the list. If you can't find a match, try the Generic VGA Compatible option as an alternative until you can find out more about your card. You can also select the Unlisted Card option, which appears at the end of the list. You are then asked whether you want different types of servers based on different chip sets. Not all video cards are specifically supported, and therefore, they utilize their chip sets to give them support.

   If you select the Unlisted Card option, VGA16 or SVGA is a good guess for most cards. The cards may not run at their maximum capacity, but at least they'll work. (Note, however, that older cards are prone to locking up and misbehave when pushed beyond their limits.)

   The Monitor Setup window appears, as shown in Figure 20-3. It shows all of the monitors that Xconfigurator knows about.

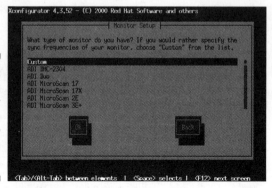

Figure 20-3:
Selecting
your monitor
from the
Monitor
Setup
window.

8. **Use the cursor keys to maneuver through the list and select your monitor; if you find it, tab to the OK button and press Enter.**

If the make and model isn't listed, then there are several generic options to select from. Use the PgDn key to jump down several pages to where the generic monitors are shown. The list starts with three generic LCD monitors, as shown in Figure 20-4; if you are using a laptop or a flatpanel LCD display, then select from these.

Make your selection from the various monitor resolutions. In general, the higher the resolution that you can drive your monitor, the better your graphics look. If you choose one that doesn't work, don't worry; you can always come back to this menu and make another selection.

After you select your monitor, the Video Memory screen opens, and you are prompted to enter the amount of video memory available for X, as shown in Figure 20-5.

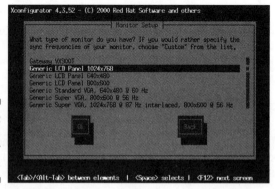

Figure 20-4:
The generic
monitor
settings.

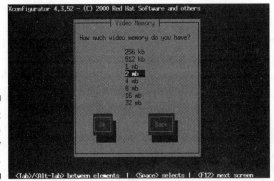

Figure 20-5:
The Video
Memory
screen.

9. **Xconfigurator highlights the memory value that it detects.**

The amount of video memory that your video adapter has determines the resolution and number of colors that your monitor can display. Resolution is the density of pixels — the dots of light that make up your display — on your screen. The number of colors is the number of colors that each pixel can display.

If you don't know the amount of video memory in your video card, enter less rather than more in order to get X working. The less memory you tell X you have, however, the fewer colors at any given resolution you have available. After you get X working, you can go back and increase the memory.

10. **Select your memory amount, tab down to the OK button, and press the Enter key.**

The Clockchip Configuration screen, shown in Figure 20-6, appears.

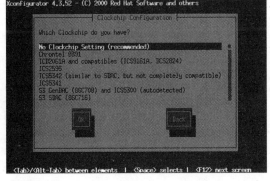

Figure 20-6:
The
Clockchip
Configura-
tion screen.

11. **The No Clockchip Setting (Recommended) is selected by default, and because you don't need to enter any other value unless you know you have a reason to do so, tab down to the OK button and press the Enter key.**

This is another leftover from the early days of video cards. When you're here, the Select Video Modes screen appears, as shown in Figure 20-7.

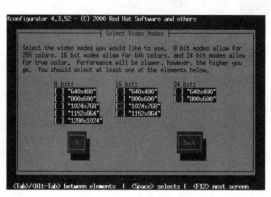

Figure 20-7: Selecting your resolution and colors in the Select Video Modes screen.

12. **In the Select Video Modes screen, select your monitor resolution.**

You have the choice of one or more screen resolutions with 8, 16, or 24 bits of color. The higher the value of bits you select, the more colors you can see. But the number of colors takes up the memory on your video card. More memory is used as you go up in resolution, too.

The lowest (8-bit) allows only 256 colors on the screen at one time. The 16-bit option allows for 65,535 colors, and 24-bit allows for over 16 million colors (also known as *true color*).

To select the different resolutions, use the Tab and arrow keys to move among the choices, and use the spacebar to select and deselect entries. Select a reasonably high resolution/colors setting, and if it doesn't work, then back off to a lower setting until you find your maximum setting. (Alternatively, start low and work your way up.)

If you select more than one resolution at any one mode, you can switch between them after starting X Server by pressing Ctrl+Alt+Plus and Ctrl+Alt+Minus. If you have only one resolution at any one mode, pressing Ctrl+Alt+Plus does nothing.

13. **When you're done selecting resolutions, Tab down to the OK button and press the Return key.**

The Starting X screen, shown in Figure 20-8, appears.

Figure 20-8:
You are prompted to test the X configuration in the Start X screen.

14. **Select the OK button and press Enter to test your X configuration. If you select the Skip button, then no test is performed, and you are prompted to finish the configuration.**

    If X Server has been configured correctly, then a graphical — X — screen appears that asks if you can see it. If you can see it, then everything is cool, and you should click the Yes button. You then see a screen asking you whether you want to have X start up when you boot your system. Select Yes if you want to do so. Finally, an informational screen appears; click the OK button.

    The final You're Done screen is shown in Figure 20-9.

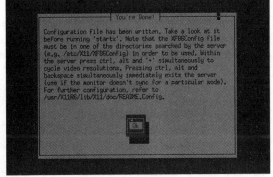

Figure 20-9:
The You're Done screen.

15. **Press the Enter key and you return to the shell prompt.**

    If you still have problems, then start the entire Xconfiguration system again. You can also consult the HOWTO documents in the /usr/doc/HOWTO/ XFree86-HOWTO documents for more help.

Starting Your Xengine

Now you're ready to try out your new X configuration.

If you're already running X — have reconfigured it — then you can either reboot your computer or restart X. It's generally better and easier to simply restart it. To do this, press the Ctrl+Alt+Backspace keys at the same time. The screen goes black, flashes, takes a breath, flashes some more, and — if all goes well — returns with the new configuration.

If you're not running X, you can start it by entering the startx command at the command prompt.

If your new configuration doesn't work for some reason and the screen reverts to some unusable display, then something has gone wrong. It may be that you specified the video card incorrectly or that you answered some other question incorrectly. If you run into trouble, you can do several things:

- ✔ Rerun Xconfigurator. Hopefully, you can zero in on the correct configuration.
- ✔ Find out more detailed information about your video card and monitor by consulting manuals, documents, or Web sites.
- ✔ Find a newer version of XFree86 code from Red Hat at www.redhat.com or the XFree organization itself at www.xfree86.org.
- ✔ Find an experienced Red Hat Linux guru to help you.
- ✔ Purchase another video adapter or monitor.
- ✔ Take a cruise to Fiji, where at the University of the South Pacific, they have a really good computer science department in which everyone uses Linux.

If you try these solutions and still don't have X running, look around for a Red Hat Linux users' group at a local college or high school. Or perhaps a group of computer professionals in your area may help. If you call the local college computer science department, the folks there probably can help you find a student or staff member who uses Linux, has installed it on several types of machines, and can help you either figure out why your graphics system is not working or get a newer version of XFree86 that may support your video card. You may also consider purchasing a better video adapter. Even high-end cards are not terribly expensive and can give you a much better display.

If you feel strange going to these people to ask them for help, remember that they were once new to Linux, too, and probably had to struggle through an even more difficult installation. When you do go, remember to take *all* the accumulated information about your system that you have detected. It will save both you and them time and energy.

Delving deep into color depth

Color depth, the number of colors your system can have active on the screen at any one time, is loosely a function of both the amount of video memory your system has and the screen resolution.

If your system has a small amount of memory (such as 1MB), your screen can have a resolution of 1,024 x 768 pixels (dots) with 256 colors (8 bits) on the screen at one time. If your system has 2MB, you can have 64K colors (16 bits) on the screen at the same time at the same resolution. If you have an older video board with a small amount of video memory but some additional video memory sockets, you may be able to upgrade the amount of video memory on the video card.

If you have only 1MB and want to see 64K colors on the screen at one time, you can reduce your resolution from 1,024 x 768 to 800 x 600 pixels. If you want true color (24 bits), you can set your resolution to 640 x 480 pixels. The picture that you're viewing will take up more of the screen, but color depth versus resolution is a trade-off that you can make by choosing the right options.

When you want to display an image and the color depth is not correct, nothing drastic happens. The picture may look a little lackluster or not quite normal. X has an interesting capability to have virtual color maps, which allow the active window to utilize all the colors of the bits of color depth, even if other windows are using different colors. When this option is turned on (as it is with the Red Hat distribution on this book's companion CDs), the various windows turn odd colors as your mouse moves from window to window, but the window that your mouse activates is shown in the best color available. With newer video cards and larger video memories, which allow for true color at high resolutions in every window, this option is less useful.

Finally, if your hardware is too new or proprietary, or if you have a notebook computer, you may want to buy a commercial X Server from Metrolink (www.metrolink.com) or Xi Graphics (www.xigraphics.com). Sometimes their codes work when XFree86 does not. Plus, if you buy an X Server, you can call the company's technical support line if you can't get it installed.

If you knew all the issues involved in working with PC video hardware, you'd think it's fantastic that XFree86 developers can get it working at all (for more on XFree86, see the nearby sidebar). Even though XFree86 is freely distributable, you may want to make a donation to its development fund, which is listed at www.XFree86.org.

If your X Server is working and you want it to stop, press Ctrl+Alt+Backspace. You can then log off the root account. If you want to start X working again, log in to an account and type **startx**. X Server starts in a few moments. (Note that you can use the xdb utility to create a graphical login screen that doesn't exit by default to the command line.)

Finding out how X drivers are born

Your X programs come from code that was contributed to X project, which was first connected with Project Athena at the Massachusetts Institute of Technology. Later, the project became the main focus of the XConsortium, a nonprofit group established to develop Xtechnology.

Because the source code was freely distributable, a group of programmers from all over the world formed to give support to X Window code on low-end PC systems. They called themselves XFree86 based on the fact that their code was free and directed toward PCs, which were largely based on Intel x86 compatible processors.

Over time, they ported their code to freely distributable operating systems on other architectures. They did this — and continue to do this — for the

love of programming. The XFree86 team of programmers tries to give support to new video controllers as they come out. Unfortunately, giving this support is often difficult for several reasons:

- They have no relationship with the video controller manufacturer.

- The video controller manufacturer thinks that keeping the programming interface secret gives it an edge against its competitors.

- The video board is built into a larger system board.

- The video controller is simply too new.

Until support for new hardware is available, most people rely on SVGA compatibility mode to get the card to work.

Xterminating X

If you're accustomed to a Windows computer, having a section on shutting down the graphical interface may seem strange. After all, the Windows graphical interface is Windows — the GUI and the operating system are symbiotic. You can't run one without the other.

Red Hat Linux can run without running X. All you have to do is change the run level. The following steps show you how to do that:

1. **Log in as root.**

2. **Open a terminal emulator window.**

3. **Type** init 3 **at the command prompt and press Enter.**

   X stops and you are returned to the command prompt.

You can also stop X in emergencies (say, if it freaks out) by pressing Ctrl+Alt+Backspace.

Part V
The Part of Tens

The 5th Wave   By Rich Tennant

"When we started the company, we weren't going to call it 'Red Hat'. But eventually we decided it sounded better than 'Beard of Bees Linux'."

In this part . . .

Ah, the part you find in every *For Dummies* book: The Part of Tens. Here's where we get to rummage around and come up with ten of this and ten of that.

In Chapter 21, we list ten important places to find help. You can use some of these sources also to enhance and widen your knowledge of Linux. There's no end to the things you can find out about Linux.

The ten most frequently encountered problems after people have installed Red Hat Linux are described in Chapter 22. If you have trouble that's not described in Chapter 19 — the network troubleshooting chapter — turn here first.

Unfortunately, the world is still a dangerous place. Chapter 23 outlines the top ten computer security threats. We describe how to be a little safer in the wild west otherwise known as the Internet.

Chapter 21

Ten Sources of Help

In This Chapter

▶ Read, read, read

▶ Check out the Linux HOWTOs

▶ Go back to Linux school

▶ Become a Linux newshound

▶ Become a Linux groupie

▶ Pay for Linux support

▶ Go the commercial route

▶ Visit Linux-oriented Web sites

▶ Attend Linux vacations, er, conferences

▶ Try to help others

*B*y now, you're probably wondering whether any end exists to the amount of information and knowledge needed to run a Red Hat Linux system. The answer is yes; there is an end to the knowledge that you *need* to run a system well. But there's no end to the learning process if you want to understand how things work and interact. In this chapter, we suggest several ways to get additional training and support.

Books and More Books

When we started working with computers many years ago, the number of computer books about computers could fill one bookshelf, and they were mostly about the electronics of the hardware itself. Networking texts described the probability of two Ethernet packets colliding. We hardly ever saw books on computers in the popular press bookstores. Today, thousands of books on computers are available; most describe the software and its interactions, with the hardware taking a back seat. Books like the *For Dummies* series aren't just for bookstores any more. You can find them in mass-market venues like Wal-Mart, for instance.

Perhaps you looked at other books before you bought this one and were intimidated by their use of technical terms. Or you thought them too general for what you wanted to do, and you wanted something more task-oriented. You may want to look over those books again because your knowledge level will be higher after reading this book. TCP/IP networking, compiler design, operating system theory, formal language theory, computer graphics, and systems administration training are all topics that you can study in greater depth when you've got a Linux computer at your disposal.

Lots of books specifically about the Unix operating system are partially or completely applicable to Linux, such as books on Perl, a comprehensive interpreter. By getting one (or more) books on Perl and sitting down with your Linux system, you have both a new tool for doing your work and a new appreciation for a complete programming language. If you want to find out how to write Perl, you can just view the source code.

Linux HOWTOs

Don't forget about the Linux HOWTOs, which come on the commercial version of Red Hat Linux. You can obtain the disc at www.redhat.com. These excellent guides to Linux are covered under the Linux Documentation Project — LDP — copyleft, which means you can print them.

School Days

Another way to find out more information about Unix and Linux is to take a course, perhaps at a local community college. Many colleges offer courses on Unix, and some have started using Linux to teach the Unix courses. You can do your homework on your system at home, or if you have a notebook (laptop computer), you can work anywhere. (Jon typed text for the first edition of this book in a hotel in Auckland, New Zealand, and updated text for the second edition in the United Airlines lounge in Chicago.) What we would have given during college for the chance to do computer projects sitting in the comfort of our own pub . . . er, dorm rooms. Instead, we had to sit in a room with a bunch of punch-card machines . . . well, never mind. We would have been much more comfortable and productive with a Linux system.

In the News

You can obtain additional information about the Linux operating system from the Internet. A facility called *Netnews* has tens of thousands of newsgroups, and each newsgroup covers a special topic. More than 30 newsgroups are devoted to Linux topics. You can search for newsgroups at www.dejanews.com and www.mailgate.org.

An ISP (Internet service provider) usually provides access to Netnews. You can use a text newsreader (such as trn, tin, or pine) or one of several Web browsers (such as the Mozilla browser included on the CDs that come with this book) to read Netnews.

User Groups

User groups are springing up all over the country. Some are more active than others, but most hold meetings at least once a month. Some groups are Linux only; others are connected to a larger computer group — either Unix or a more general computer users association. User groups are a great opportunity to ask questions. User groups also tend to stimulate new ideas and ways of doing things.

You can find out if a Linux user group is in your area by checking with GLUE (Groups of Linux Users Everywhere), which is a service run by SSC (the publishers of the *Linux Journal*). GLUE is an automated map of user groups, and you can find it at the following address:

```
www.ssc.com
```

When you arrive at the site, click the <u>Resources</u> link, which takes you to the Linux Journal site. Then check out the Resources area there to find out where the user group closest to you meets.

No user group in your area? Then post a message at your local university or community college saying that you want to start one; other people in your area may decide to join you. Terrified at the thought of trying to start a user group? User group leaders often are not the most technically knowledgeable members but are simply good planners. They organize the meeting space, find (hound) speakers, send out meeting notices, locate sponsors, arrange refreshments (beer), and perform other organizational tasks. Sometimes being the leader seems like a thankless job, but when a meeting goes really well, it makes all the work worthwhile. So, as a newbie to Linux, you may not know a grep from an awk, but you still may make a very good chairperson.

Bring in the Cavalry

Some people want to be able to hire people to manage or fix their systems. This is what the commercial computer world calls *support*. Often, the place where you bought your computer, — whether it's a store, a value-added reseller (VAR), or the manufacturer — provides the support.

Linux is criticized for not providing that same level of support. Although the number of hardware vendors that offers support is low, more and more people are well-versed in using Linux and are willing to offer some level of support, whether it be by e-mail, telephone, or on-site services.

The first group of people that offers support is the distribution makers. Red Hat Software, Inc. sells support contracts to their customers. These contracts range from e-mail support to telephone support. Red Hat, for example, recently introduced round-the-clock (24/7) support for a reasonable fee. Check out the Red Hat Web page (www.redhat.com) for more details.

Another group of people offering support is resellers of Linux systems. These people typically install Linux on hardware that you purchase from them. They will repair your system when it breaks, and help you with knotty problems (all for a fee).

The final group of people who offer support is the independent consultants who have learned about Linux and are now in the business of offering support for the system. You can find a list of consultants in a document called the Consultants HOWTO, which is available at the following address:

```
www.cyrius.com/tbm/usr/doc/HOWTO/Consultants-HOWTO
```

Once you become familiar with the resources that Red Hat Linux offers, you'll realize that it offers better support than most other proprietary systems. We find that consulting the HOWTOs or Usenet groups to solve problems and answer questions is easier than going through the traditional Help Desk route.

Commercial Applications

Many Linux users are frugal (we prefer that term to *cheap*) and often want or need to use only freely distributable software. And in many cases, the freely distributable software is very good and does exactly what you want it to do. Other times, though, the software you want is available only as a commercial application.

Some Red Hat Linux users buy the latest and greatest hardware and want the same commercial applications on Linux that they've got on their other operating systems, no matter what the price.

For commercial application vendors everywhere who may be reading this, we cannot stress enough that you should look at Linux just like *any other operating system.* You can sell your applications to a market that is not only appreciative but also believes, for various reasons, that its operating system should be *open.*

An example of functionality in the commercial world is Applixware Office by Applix, Inc. This office suite includes a word processor, a spreadsheet, a presentation package, a mail front end, an HTML authoring program, a graphical program for drawing pictures (usually to include in your presentation or paper), an application building program, and a scripting language that allows you to tie these and other programs together.

We wrote this book using Applixware Words and Sun Microsystems StarOffice. We chose to use these word processors instead of Microsoft Word because we could easily cut examples of code from the screen of our Red Hat Linux systems and paste them into the text of the book. We can also run the applications used as examples on the same machine. After finishing a chapter, we saved the chapter file in Rich Text Format (RTF) and e-mailed it to our editors. They used Microsoft Word and had no problem reading the material. Hey, the two worlds can get along.

Likewise, we use Applixware Presentation Editor to make presentations about Linux on Linux. When we talk about Linux at a show or a convention, we can demonstrate how to use X Window System while we have the presentation slides on the screen. If we used Microsoft PowerPoint, we would have to reboot the system into Linux to do the demo, an awkward approach at best. Applixware has many of the same functions as Microsoft products. Recent versions of Applixware Office can read and create PowerPoint output, and now we can run our systems truly FAT-free. (FAT file system free that is).

Visit Web Sites

A variety of Web sites are available for help. Some of these sites provide technical information, some provide news about the Linux community, and others furnish a bandstand for the Linux community to voice its opinions. Here are some sites that you may want to check out:

- **Linux International:** www.li.org
- **Linux Org:** www.linux.org
- **LinuxHQ:** www.linuxhq.com
- **Linux Today:** www.linuxtoday.com

- ✔ **Linux Documentation Project:** www.metalab.unc.edu/LDP/
- ✔ **Linux Now:** www.linuxnow.com
- ✔ *Linux Journal, Linux Gazette, Linux Resources:* www.ssc.com
- ✔ **Linux Focus:** www.linuxfocus.org
- ✔ *Linux Weekly News:* www.lwn.net
- ✔ **Slashdot:** www.slashdot.org
- ✔ **Freshmeat:** www.freshmeat.net
- ✔ **Sourceforge:** www.sourceforge.net

This list is not exhaustive. You can find links to many more sites in some of the Web sites mentioned here.

Some of the lists offer opinions that are for mature audiences only. Most of the lists are moderated, and most of the opinions are mature, but people sometimes get carried away.

Attend Conferences

You can attend a number of conferences and trade shows to find out more information on Linux. All these shows are accurate as of the time we're writing this, but events may change. Where possible, we listed the more general Web addresses for these events.

You may have to do a little Web surfing to find the next upcoming event. If you get stuck, try the Linux International Web site (www.li.org), which has an Events page that lists new events.

Linux Kongress

Linux Kongress is the oldest Linux event. Held in Germany every year, it's a technical conference with a small trade show. The Web site is www.linux-kongress.de.

Linux Expo

Linux Expo is held every spring in the Raleigh/Durham area in North Carolina. It's a technical conference, trade show, and all-in-all good time. In 1998, more than 2,000 attendees and numerous vendors attended. The Web site is www.linuxexpo.net.

USENIX/FREENIX

USENIX, a technical organization that has long supported Unix users, holds several technical conferences and small trade shows each year on various topics. A few years ago, a separate set of presentations, called FREENIX, was created for freely distributed operating systems such as Linux. If you're interested in a good technical conference that attracts Unix giants (such as Dennis Ritchie) or if you are a Linux developer, you may want to take a look at www.usenix.org.

CeBIT

CeBIT, the largest computer trade show in the world, is held yearly in Hannover, Germany. It often draws more than 600,000 people. Last year, Linux International (www.li.org) had a booth along with several other Linux vendors and drew more than 3,000 people. CeBIT is mostly a trade show, with very little (if any) conference sessions on Linux. To find out more about CeBIT, check out www.messe.de.

Comdex

For the past four years, Comdex has held a Linux Pavilion, made up of an ever-growing group of vendors who try to explain Linux to over 200,000 resellers, distributors, and other vendors. Comdex is held in the spring and fall in different U.S. cities. You can check out its Web site at www.key3media.com.

IDG's Linux World

Linux World is a new show with conferences that provides a venue for many commercial vendors. Its Web site is at www.linuxworldexpo.com.

Try to Help Others

After you've exhausted all avenues of help (or maybe even before), you should just try to figure it out yourself. Often, you'll find that the pieces fit together or that the software is not as difficult as you thought. Here are some tips:

- ✔ **If you are investigating a large software package, scan the documentation one time and then concentrate on the necessary topics.** Jon still remembers the first time he tried to learn groff, which is a powerful text-processing system. The documentation was daunting, and he thought he would never learn the package. It turns out he was right — he never learned it. But he did learn enough to do a few simple things and that was all he needed to know. With those "few simple things" (less than 2 percent of the power of the package), he could write letters, create overhead slides, and do the necessary text processing. When he needed another command, he'd look it up in a reference book.

- ✔ **Create a small sample of what you want to do.** If you're working with a new command or part of Linux, create a small example of the one part of the command or software that you don't know, and see how that works.

- ✔ **Keep it small.** A friend of Jon's named Mike Gancarz wrote a book called *The Philosophy of Unix*. In this book, he talks about how Unix systems were created and programmed in the early days, utilizing lots of the small, cryptic (we prefer the word *terse*) commands that lurk below the glossy interface of X Window System. With these commands, you can create powerful programs called shell scripts or just use the commands one at a time to transform your data. The main tenet of his book is to keep things small, simple, and modular.

- ✔ **Remember that Linux is only a piece of code and your computer is only a machine.** So what if you make a mistake? You're probably running Linux on a machine that has only one user, you. That's the great thing about Linux: It runs on such inexpensive machinery that you can buy an old 486 computer with enough hard drive and memory in it to run Linux as a practice system, all for under $50. (Jon bought such a machine at a Ham Fest. It runs Linux very nicely.) So even if you have to reinstall your system due to some mistake you made, it won't disturb anyone else on your practice machine. You now know how to install Linux, so no one but you has to know when something goes wrong.

Our other suggestion is to help someone else. "What?" you say. "How can I help someone? I'm just a beginner in this field!"

We all started that way. No one is born with a knowledge of computer science. We all pick it up over time. The way to cement a thought or an idea, however, is to explain it clearly to someone else. Helping others install Linux on their PCs helps cement some of the concepts you've discovered. Another idea is to attend a Linux Install Fest, where lots of people go (with their machines) to install Linux. Here, not only do you get to help someone else, but you can also probably find out something from other attendees.

A main tenet of Linux is the word *open.* Linux is open and is best when shared.

Chapter 22

Ten Problem Areas and Solutions

. . . .

In This Chapter

▶ I can't boot Linux anymore

▶ My hard drive numbers have changed since installation

▶ My CD-ROM isn't detected

▶ I don't know how to remove LILO and restore my MBR

▶ I can't use LILO to boot

▶ The ls command doesn't show files in color

▶ Linux can't find a shell script (or a program)

▶ When I start X Window System, I see a gray screen

▶ I don't know how to make X Window System start at boot time

▶ I never seem to have the correct time

. . . .

*I*n any complex, technical situation, people end up having problems and issues that they need help with. The problems in this chapter were taken from a database of questions and answers created after hundreds of people installed the CD-ROMs. We answer some of these questions in the rest of the book, but because they still generate "what happened" questions, we repeat the information here.

I Can't Boot Red Hat Linux Anymore

Problem: You've installed Linux and everything is fine (naturally). Then one day you make a change to your Windows or Windows NT system, and Linux stops working. You no longer see the lilo boot prompt, so you can no longer specify that you want to boot Linux.

Solution: Various operating systems tend to think that they're the only operating system on the hard drive or on the system. So when they're installed or updated, they write things to an area of the system called the

Master Boot Record (MBR). This process overlays the Linux boot loader (called LILO) and stops you from booting Linux. The best correction requires an ounce of prevention: Make an emergency boot disk, as we instruct you to do during installation. Keep this disk handy when you update your system (or during any other significant system event, such as repartitioning hard drives or rebuilding your kernel). Then if you make a mistake, you can boot the floppy, which enables you to reboot your Linux operating system. When you've rebooted your system by using the boot disk, just log in as root and type **lilo** on the command line. This repairs the MBR by reinstalling LILO.

If you install multiple operating systems on a new machine, do yourself a favor and install Linux last. Otherwise, you have to keep reinstalling LILO.

My Hard Drive Numbers Have Changed Since Installation

Problem: Linux numbers hard drives each time it boots, calling SCSI hard drives names like sda, sdb, sdc, and sdd. Suppose that sda holds your Microsoft operating system, sdb holds the bulk of Linux, sdc holds your user files, and sdd holds your swap space. Now you add another hard drive and your user files are on sdd and your swap space is on sde. The new hard drive is called sdc but has nothing on it. What happened?

Solution: SCSI hard drives are lettered according to the SCSI IDs set on each hard drive. Linux names the hard drives by using this ordering scheme. If you insert a new hard drive into the SCSI bus with a SCSI ID that is lower than an existing hard drive, you rename all hard drives with a SCSI ID number above the one you just installed. It's best to start installing your SCSI hard drives with a SCSI ID of 0, 1, 2, and so on; then put other SCSI devices at the other end of the SCSI bus (SCSI IDs 6, 5, 4, and so on).

Most SCSI controllers are set to SCSI ID 7 by default.

IDE hard drives are numbered according to the IDE controller they're on and whether they're a master or a slave on that controller. For this reason, adding a new hard drive to a set of IDE controllers won't change the existing names, as shown in the following two tables:

Controller	Hard Drive	Linux Name
ide0	master	hda
ide0	slave	hdb
ide1	master	hdc

Controller	Hard Drive	Linux Name
ide1	slave	hdd
ide2	master	hde
ide2	slave	hdf
ide3	master	hdg
ide3	slave	hdh

Controller Designation	Controller Priority
ide0	primary controller
ide1	secondary controller
ide2	third controller
ide3	fourth controller

My CD-ROM Isn't Detected

Problem: You're installing Linux, but it doesn't find your CD-ROM.

Solution: Most newer CD-ROMs are either EIDE (ATAPI) or SCSI, and most newer computer systems have enough support to see either the ATAPI CD-ROMs or the SCSI CD-ROMs, so CD-ROM support is not quite so much an issue as in the early days. In addition, some older systems and CD-ROMs are now supported.

Some early CD-ROMs pretended to be other devices (such as tape drives or floppies) to fool the computer system into using them, but these CD-ROMs were hidden from the detection system. If your system is one of these, don't despair: You can supply information to help Linux find your CD-ROM.

First look at the preceding section about hard drive numbering. This enables you to figure out the name that Linux would call your CD-ROM if Linux knew about it. If you have an EIDE/ATAPI CD-ROM, type the following line whenever you see the boot or lilo prompt while booting or installing your system:

```
linux hdX=cdrom
```

where *X* is the number your CD-ROM would have if it could be detected.

I Don't Know How to Remove LILO and Restore My MBR

Problem: You don't know how to replace the boot record that was on your system before you started installing Linux.

Solution: You can log in to Linux as root, and then type the following command:

```
lilo _u
```

Another solution is to boot MS-DOS or Windows 95, 98, NT/2000 and XP to an MS-DOS prompt and type the following:

```
fdisk /mbr
```

I Can't Use LILO to Boot

Problem: You need to put Linux on a hard drive or a partition that is beyond the 1023rd cylinder, the second IDE hard drive, or the second SCSI ID number, or you need to do something else to make it difficult for Linux to boot using LILO. Can you boot Linux in another way?

Solution: You can use a program called LOADLIN to boot from your MS-DOS or Windows system:

1. **Copy your configured Linux kernel to the C drive of your MS-DOS or Windows system.**

   The easiest way to do this is to install Linux, log in as root, and type the following:
   ```
   grep image /etc/lilo.conf
   ```
   A line similar to the following appears:
   ```
   image=/boot/vmlinuz-2.2.16-21
   ```
   This points to your compressed kernel, which in this example is located at `/boot/vmlinuz-2.2.10-3`.

2. **Copy the compressed kernel to a floppy disk, as follows:**
   ```
   mcopy /boot/vmlinuz-2.2.16-21 a:\vmlinux.gz
   ```
   The kernel name `vmlinuz-2.2.16-21` refers to a specific version of the Linux kernel. Except for the `/boot/vmlinuz-` part, which remains constant, the name may be slightly different on your system.

   A copy of `LOADLIN` is on the CDs that come with this book.

3. **Boot MS-DOS or Windows and put the CD in your CD-ROM drive.**

4. **Go to the DOSUTILS directory and copy** `LOADLIN.EXE` **to your C drive.**

   If you're using MS-DOS or Windows 3.1, copy the `LOADLIN16` file, which is the 16-bit version of the program.

5. **Copy the kernel image you just made on the floppy disk to your C drive.**

Now you can exit Windows and get to the MS-DOS prompt. You can then type the following (assuming your root partition is on partition `/dev/hda5`) to boot Linux:

```
C:\> loadlin vmlinux.gz root=/dev/hda5 ro
```

The ls Command Doesn't Show Files in Color

Problem: When running the `ls` command to show files in color, the command doesn't display files in color.

Solution: You have to edit the `bashrc` file in your home directory to add the following line to the end of the file:

```
alias ls='ls _-color=auto'
```

Log off and then back in to reexecute your `bashrc` file (assuming that you're using the `bash` shell), and `ls` shows different file types in different colors.

Linux Can't Find a Shell Script (Or a Program)

Problem: You type a command name, but Linux can't find the command, even if it's in the current directory.

Solution: When you type a shell or binary command name, Linux looks for the name in specific places and in a specific order. To find out what directories Linux looks in, and in what order, type the following command:

```
echo $PATH
```

You see a stream similar to the following:

```
/bin:/usr/bin:/usr/local/bin
```

Linux looks in these directories to find the command, program, or shell you want to execute. You may see more directories depending on your distribution or how your system administrator (if you have one) set up your system.

Now suppose you create a shell or a program called flobnob and want to execute it (and assuming that you've set the permission bits to make flobnob executable by you). You've got a couple of choices (well, you've got more than two choices, but I'm listing the safest ones). One choice is to type the following on the command line:

```
./flobnob
```

This tells Linux to look in this directory (./) and execute flobnob.

Your second choice is to move flobnob to one of the directories shown in the PATH variable, such as /usr/local/bin.

When I Start X Window System, I See a Gray Screen

Problem: You configured the X Window System, but when you log in as a general user (that is, not as root) and type **startx**, all you get is a gray screen with a big X in the middle. You wait a long time, but nothing happens.

Solution: First recognize that you may have to wait a long time for a slow CPU with a small amount of main memory (about 8MB). Some machines with small amounts of memory take as long as 6 minutes to start X. But assuming that you start X on a machine with a faster CPU and more memory, you may have problems with permissions on your home directory. This is particularly true if X works when you're logged in as root (that is, as superuser) but not when you're logged in as a general user.

To correct this problem, log in as root and go to the home directory of the user who is having problems. For this example, suppose that the login name of the user is lupe. After you're in the user's home directory, issue the ls -ld command to see who owns that directory and what the directory's permissions are:

```
cd ~lupe
ls _ld .
drwxrwx-- root bin 1024 Aug 31 16:00 .
```

In this example, the directory is owned by root and the group ownership is bin, which doesn't allow lupe access to the directory structure inside the directory. Because the shells and terminal emulators that X needs require access to that directory structure, X can't fully work.

To correct this problem, use the chown and chgrp commands to change the ownership of the /lupe home directory to lupe and to change the group ownership of the lupe home directory to users:

```
chown lupe ~lupe
chgrp users ~lupe
```

Make sure you replace the lupe login name that we use in this example with the login name you're having difficulty with.

I Don't Know How to Make the X Window System Start at Boot Time

Problem: You don't want to log in to a command-line mode (such as DOS) and then type **startx**. Instead, you want to log in through X Window System.

Solution: We set up our machines so that they start in nongraphical mode and then allow us to switch to X. (Many times, we only want to make a simple edit or look at something on the system, and logging in without X is simply faster.) If you like to see a graphical interface from the beginning, though, do the following. In the /etc/inittab file, change this line:

```
id:3:initdefault:
```

to this:

```
id:5:initdefault:
```

Save your changes and reboot. X starts at the end of the boot process, and you can then log in through the graphical interface. To go back to the old way of booting, change the line in the /etc/inittab file back to the following:

```
id:3:initdefault:
```

and reboot the machine.

I Never Seem to Have the Correct Time

Problem: When you boot Linux, the time is wrong, so you set it with the date command. Then you boot Windows and its time is wrong, so you reset it. When you reboot Linux, its time is wrong again.

Solution: Most Unix systems keep their time by using Universal Time (also known as Greenwich Mean Time, or GMT), but Microsoft systems keep their time as local time. When you set the time in either system, you set the CPU clock to that version of the time. Then when you boot the other system, it interprets what is in the CPU clock differently and reports a different time.

Linux enables you to store and think of the clock as either GMT or local time. You make this choice when you install the system. To change your choice, follow these steps:

1. **Log in as root.**

2. **Type** timeconfig.

   The Configure Timezones dialog box appears. Set your system clock to GMT (Greenwich Mean Time) by selecting the Hardware Clock Set To GMT option at the top of the screen.

3. **Deselect the Hardware Clock Set To GMT option.**

   Highlight the option by pressing the tab key, if necessary. (Actually, you should be there when you activate the `timeconfig` command.)

4. **Press the spacebar to deselect the option. Press the tab key until you reach the OK button, and then press Enter.**

5. **Reset the time to the proper value by using the** `date` **command if you reboot Linux or through the Windows system if you boot Windows.**

Chapter 23

Ten Security Vulnerabilities

In This Chapter

▶ Simplifying your system

▶ Encrypting your communications

▶ Using firewalls

▶ Updating your software

▶ Backing up your data

▶ Introducing buffer overflows

▶ Getting social

▶ Using good passwords

▶ Scanning the horizon

▶ Keeping track of your logs

*T*hey're here! The monster is under the bed. There are Greeks in that horse. Here's Johnny! Come into the light. One thing's for sure, the bad guys are out to get you.

Well, do you want the good or bad news first? The good news: The Internet has changed the world for the better and continues to do so in more and unforeseen ways. And the speed of change will only accelerate. The bad news: Because the Internet is constantly changing, the number of ways that someone can use the Internet to hurt you is always growing. This chapter outlines some of the more dangerous spooks that lurk out on that darkly lit electronic street.

Our purpose in this chapter is to point you in the right direction so you can gain a general awareness of computer security. Computer security is, unfortunately, a complex subject. Because it is complex we cannot hope to do any more than touch on some important aspects here. We'll give you some specific instructions for adding security to your new Red Hat Linux computer. More importantly, we'll point out some of the most important areas that you should be aware of. This chapter introduces ten important security topics. You can use them as a starting point to increase your computer security.

How Many Daemons Can Dance on the Head of the Linux Process Table?

Every commercial operating system vendor wants to make their operating systems easy to install and use. Operating systems are inherently complex animals and Linux is no exception. (Of course, we're not biased when we say that Linux is an overall simpler system than Windows whether you measure simplicity by the number of lines of code or the transparency of its design.) Vendors walk the tightrope of making the systems easy to use so that they are used while making them reasonably secure.

Ease of use and security often do not coexist very well. Your operating system will be much easier to use, for instance, if you install and activate every software package and option. On the other hand, running every software package means that you have more potential vulnerabilities. If you install 10 doors and 20 windows in your home, you can certainly enter and leave as you please but it also provides burglars with more opportunities to do you harm. The same thing with your operating system. The more software you install, the more chances someone has of getting inside your computer.

We can't think of a cure-all for this dilemma. The best answer from a security viewpoint is to not provide intruders with any openings: place your computer in a locked room with no network or external connections and turn it off. You'll have a really safe system that holds the floor from hitting the ceiling.

As with most things in life the real answer is to use your best judgment and balance security with ease of use. Run only the services you need. For instance, don't run the Samba file system service if you don't want to use your Red Hat Linux computer as a file system server. Don't run the text-based gpm service if you use the graphical X Window mode on your computer. The list is endless and beyond the scope of this book to discuss in detail. You can find more info with the following sources:

- ✔ **Web sites:** www.sans.org and www.usenix.org both deal with security issues.
- ✔ **HOWTOs:** www.redhat.com/docs/manuals/linux/RHL-7.2-Manual/custom-guide/ch-gnomelokkit.html and www.redhat.com/docs/manuals/linux/RHL-7.2-Manual/custom-guide/openssh.html both are written for Red Hat 7.2 but still provide valid advice.
- ✔ **Books covering security:** Browse through your local bookstore to find Linux books that discuss reducing services. Some good books are: *Red Hat Linux Security and Optimization* and *Linux Security Toolkit*.

Open the Encrypt

It's hard to trust communication media that you do not completely control — such as university LANs, wireless home networks, and the Internet. Our point: Trust no one!

Any public network is potentially dangerous, especially the Internet. One way to protect yourself is to use encryption for all communication. You use encryption when you conduct credit card transactions or read remote e-mail. Secure Socket Layer (SSL) communication is the standard encryption mechanism for secure Internet browsing and e-commerce transactions.

The Secure Shell (SSH) protocol is used to conduct encrypted CLI terminal sessions and file transfers. Red Hat bundles the open source version of SSH called OpenSSH with its distributions. When you install Red Hat Linux, you automatically get the OpenSSH client. You can use OpenSSH from a terminal session by entering the command ssh destination. The destination is the computer that you want to communicate with.

Using encryption is essential when you use wireless networking. WIFI (also known as 802.11b) wireless networks come with the ability to use built-in encryption based on the WEP protocol. WEP does *have* some significant security vulnerabilities, though. The only long-term answer is to either wait until the next standard comes along to fix the problem or else use OpenSSH to provide your own encryption. You'll be much safer if you use OpenSSH and SSL for as much of your communication as possible.

Aaha, No Firewall. Very, Very Good.

Broadband connections give you a quantum leap in speed and convenience when connecting to the Internet. The two choices for a broadband connection are DSL and cable modems. Once you start using them, you'll never go back to slow, Stone Age telephone-based modems.

But every silver lining has a dark cloud. Broadband connections not only give you fast Internet connections but also continuous ones. With a telephone-based modem, a hacker can only attack your home computer and private network while connected to the Internet. Using a 24/7 broadband connection means that every hacker on the Internet — that means every hacker in the world — can constantly bang on your computer and private network. That's a lot of vulnerability.

Firewalls provide you with your number one protection from Internet based attacks. The modern Netfilter/iptables packet filtering firewall system gives you excellent protection when properly configured. Chapter 8 describes how to configure Netfilter/iptables for the three Internet connection paths that we use in this book. You should never, ever connect to the Internet without first configuring your personal firewall.

We don't mean to imply that you are invulnerable to attack if you use a telephone-based modem to connect to the Internet. Traditional modem connections are just as vulnerable as continuous broadband connections when they are active. What we mean is that a modem that isn't connected to the Internet is a safe modem.

Keeping Up with the Joneses

Nobody's perfect and that goes for operating system vendors. Even open source Linux developers and great companies like Red Hat make mistakes. Vulnerabilities are found in software systems all the time and have to be fixed.

Well, Red Hat provides a way to keep up to date with current problem and security fixes through its Web site. Go to www.redhat.com/updates to find the newest and safest versions of all your systems RPM packages. You can also find out how to configure your Red Hat Linux system to update itself automatically.

Backups? I Don't Need No Stinking Backups!

If you don't regularly make backups of your computer, you face security vulnerability, plain and simple. You may lose some or all of your valuable information if your computer is compromised. You should back up your data as frequently as possible.

You can use one of many techniques and software for making backups, but that's stuff we couldn't possibly begin to cover — there's too much to say. We wouldn't be able to cover Red Hat Linux if we even began to go into detail.

So we'll keep it simple: Archiving your home directory and copying it to another location is a simple and effective backup mechanism.

For instance, the following commands use the ubiquitous Linux tape archive (tar) command to create an archive of your home directory. You can then use the OpenSSH scp command to securely copy the archive to another location, such as your ISP account or another computer that you have access to. Follow these steps to create an archive of your home directory.

1. **Log in to your user account.**

2. **Run the following** `tar` **command.**

```
tar czf myusername.tgz .
```

   In this case, the "c" option means to use `tar` to copy the specified files and directories. The "z" option tells `tar` to compress the data. The "f" option defines the text that follows it — myusername.tgz — as the file to copy the files to. The single dot "." says to copy all the files in the current working directory to the archive.

3. **Use OpenSSH to copy the** `tar` **archive to another location.**

```
scp myusername.tgz myloginaccount@myisp.com
```

   This command securely copies the `tar` archive to the account myloginaccount at the myisp.com ISP.

My Buffer Overflow-eth

The most popular way hackers use to break into computers is with buffer overflows. The buffer overflow technique attempts to feed crazy streams of data to programs in order to make them behave in ways that their designers never intended. (It is beyond the scope of this book to describe what a queue does in detail. Suffice it to say that Linux uses a queue to store instructions and addresses for later use.) The end result of the buffer overflow is that sometimes the program will provide the hacker with a shell or other open door when it fails.

The unintended shell is an open door to your computer. Sometimes the shell has root — superuser — privileges and then the hacker owns your system.

Here are some simple techniques that you can use to minimize buffer overflows:

✔ **Minimize the number of services that you run.** You run zero risk of compromise from a buffer overflow vulnerability in service A if you do not run that service.

   For instance, the Lion worm wrecked havoc in the spring of 2001. Lion exercised vulnerability in the Linux sendmail and lpd printer services. Computers that did not run those services were not vulnerable to the Lion worm.

✔ **Update your Red Hat Linux computer as often as possible.** Red Hat posts package updates that fix vulnerabilities as they become available. Buffer overflow fixes comprise many of the package updates. Updating your system will fix many buffer overflow vulnerabilities.

Social Engineering 1010101010

Okay, you've exercised the security measures discussed in this chapter so you assume that your computer is reasonably safe. What does a poor hacker in these security aware times have to do to break into your system? Hackers have families too (well, maybe not).

Some hacker techniques don't rely on technological means at all. One such technique is social engineering, which is a fancy way of saying "I'm going to trick you or your associates into giving information to use against you."

Social engineering can be as simple as a hacker calling you to see if you're at home or in the office. If you're not physically present, then the hacker or burglar can break in and steal the computer or its disks. It's pretty much a trivial process to break into a computer if you posses it. Another social engineering technique hackers employ is to call a corporation's help desk and pretend to be a VIP. The poor minimum wage slave can often be bullied or cajoled into giving out a password or other important information.

The moral of the story is to exercise good security hygiene and be careful of strangers. Don't give out information unless it is essential and you can verify the authenticity of the request.

Bad Passwords

Probably the most easy to avoid, and most often abused, vulnerability is poor or non-existent passwords. Passwords are your number one line of defense. If your password is guessable or even worse, blank, then you will be broken into.

Bad passwords are easy to fix. Start by assigning a password to every account you create — especially root. Then make it a habit to use "good" passwords. Passwords can be cracked by brute force because computers have become very fast. Because you connect to the Internet, it is quite possible for hackers to steal your /etc/passwd file that contains the encrypted version of your text-based passwords and use a computer to crack them.

You should use passwords that do not use any word that can be found in a dictionary. For instance, don't use the password "redhat73". Instead, change the "e" in "red" to "3" and the "a" in "hat" to "@". Your password becomes ""r3dh@t73, which means that the cracking software will have to use brute force to discover it instead of a mere dictionary search.

Scan Me

Information is king when it comes to people hacking into systems and keeping them out. Hackers use knowledge about your computer and network to break into your systems. One common power tool for gaining information about what type of operating system you have and the services that it runs is nmap. Nmap is a port-scanning tool that can discover a wealth of information about individual computers and networks.

For instance, once you connect your computer to the Internet you can log in to your ISP account and scan your own connection. If your firewall is running correctly, then the scan will show little or nothing. That's good. If the scan displays information about your computer and network, either your firewall isn't running correctly or isn't running at all.

You can use that information to your advantage. Seeing what the hackers see gives you the ability of plugging your security holes.

I Know Where You Logged In Last Summer

Linux is very good at keeping a diary. Red Hat configures installation to keep logs of every user login and other technical information. Examining logs is more of an art than a science, however. We don't have any explicit techniques for determining if your system is being attacked or has been broken into. Sorry.

Experience counts for a lot when examining logs for discrepancies. The more you keep track of your system the more you'll recognize its idiosyncrasies and general behavior. Red Hat checks its general purpose logs in the /var/log directory. Check your logs frequently.

Part VI
The Appendixes

The 5th Wave — By Rich Tennant

"Drive carefully, remember your lunch, and always make a backup of your directory tree before modifying your hard disk partition file."

In this part . . .

This is the part of every book where you find things that just didn't fit into the flow of the chapters. This part includes the fun and exciting appendixes.

Appendix A shows you how to figure out what stuff your computer is made of. Appendix B describes how to install Red Hat Linux without using a mouse. The two make a good pair, because sometimes it is necessary to obtain information about your hardware in order to make the installation easier, or even just to make it work at all. Appendix B describes a method that does not require a graphics card to work. The text-based method works on more machines than the standard graphical one described in Chapter 3. It's included here as a fall-back mechanism in case the one described in Chapter 3 doesn't work for you.

The venerable, but still highly useful, vi editor is described in Appendix C. vi is a text-based (non-graphical) text editor. It has been around for decades and is widely used by system administrators around the world to get their work done. Knowing at least a little about vi is useful because it's included on nearly every Linux computer.

Appendix D provides information on Linux man pages. Man pages are the most basic way of distributing information in Linux (and UNIX). They're simple to use, too!

Finally, the contents of the companion CD-ROMs are described in Appendix E. The basic layout of the directory tree is described in that appendix.

Appendix A

Discovering Your Hardware

• •

In This Appendix

▶ Figuring out which resources Red Hat Linux requires

▶ Identifying your hardware and its function

• •

This appendix helps you determine what kind of hardware you have on your system. If you have problems installing Red Hat Linux in Chapter 3, or just want to do some extra preparation, then this appendix can help you. By determining what hardware subsystems you have on your computer, you are better able to install Linux.

Generally, Linux runs on any Intel processor that is a 386 or newer, as well as on various Digital Equipment Corporation (DEC) Alpha, Sun SPARC, Motorola, MIPS, PowerPC, and HP/PA platforms.

Knowing if Your Hardware Can Handle Red Hat Linux

Linux supports *symmetric multiprocessing (SMP),* which means you can have more than one CPU per computer. In fact, Linux supports several processors per system. If your system has more than one CPU, Linux can utilize those CPUs also, either by speeding up a specific program written to take advantage of multiple CPUs or by allowing more programs to execute at one time. (If you have an SMP system, would you care to trade with us?)

The Intel processor should have the following amount of RAM (main memory):

▸ Without graphics, Linux runs (er, walks) with 4MB.

▸ With graphics, Linux runs at a minimum with 8MB; with 16MB, the graphics get much faster.

✔ With 32MB, Linux screams and the speed of the application (particularly a graphics-oriented program) increases dramatically.

✔ Some Linux developers have 128MB in the systems because they tend to run many programs at a time, and each program takes up a certain amount of RAM when running.

Some early CD-ROM drives are not IDE; they attach directly to sound cards and other devices. Red Hat Linux can try to detect and use these. If you don't have an IDE/ATAPI or SCSI CD-ROM drive, you need to know the make and model number of your CD-ROM drive and what type of controller (perhaps a specific sound card) the CD-ROM drive is attached to. To do this, you have to open up your system and look for the make and model number of the CD-ROM on the physical drive.

You can install Linux on a notebook (laptop computer) by using the notebook's built-in CD-ROM drive (if it has one), or a CD-ROM drive attached to the notebook's docking station, or a SCSI CD-ROM drive attached to a PCMCIA SCSI controller. If you don't have any of these, you can try to get a PCMCIA Ethernet controller and do a network installation, given that another Linux system on the network has a CD-ROM drive installed. If that is the course you take, then consult Red Hat's installation documentation at `www.redhat.com/support`.

You also need a keyboard, a mouse, and a video card. Linux supports a wide range of video cards. Even if your card is not supported directly, Linux may support it as a generic VGA, XGA, SVGA, or other graphical hardware, standard video card. Most video cards that have been available for a while are supported.

Finding Out What You Have

One of the most important preliminary steps for a successful installation of Linux is finding out the type of hardware you have. You can find most of this information in the manuals that came with your computer. The manuals won't be much help, however, if:

✔ You threw the manuals out

✔ You lost the manuals

✔ You bought your computer secondhand from someone who threw away or lost the documentation

✔ You bought your PC with Windows already installed

The last reason is the most insidious because it means the people you bought the PC from did not bother to buy the documentation for each part of the PC when they assembled it for you. That would have cost them more money.

Instead, it used OEM parts (read that "sans documentation and colorful box"), and bought only one copy of the documentation for their use. With Windows already installed, the company reasoned that an end user wouldn't need any documentation about the system.

Contact the place where you bought your system. Perhaps you can obtain a copy of the documentation from the dealer.

If that doesn't work, open up your system and look at the components. For instance, a source of information about your hard drive is the label on top of the disk drive. If you don't feel comfortable opening up your system, you may want to take it back to where you bought it — assuming you didn't buy it by mail order — and perhaps the dealer can open it up and tell you what you have.

You can also look to the World Wide Web for information. Many vendors use their Web site to provide technical data about their devices. For that, you need to know your equipment's manufacturer, make, and model number.

Another source of information is Windows itself. Step-by-step instructions in the following sections show you exactly how to use these operating systems to get all the information you need.

If you don't have any literature about your system, and you don't have Windows on your system (perhaps you like to run FAT-free), and no dealer is within hundreds of miles, don't give up hope. Red Hat Linux is good at sniffing out and identifying hardware during the installation.

Talking to Your Computer (And Knowing What You Should Ask)

Knowing how your computer is constructed can help you when you install Red Hat Linux. Your computer is built from several primary groups of equipment. The following list shows what the groups are:

- **Hard drive controllers.** How many do you have, and what are their types (IDE, SCSI)? Which hard drives are connected to which controllers? If a SCSI controller is installed in your machine, what's its make and model number?

- **Hard drives.** How many hard drives do you have? For each drive, what is its size and order (which one is first, second, and so on)?

- **CD-ROM.** What is the interface type? Is it an IDE drive, a SCSI drive, or some other type? For CD-ROM drives other than IDE (ATAPI) or SCSI, what is the make and model number?

✔ **RAM.** How much RAM is installed on the computer?

✔ **Mouse.** What type of mouse do you have — a bus mouse, a PS/2 mouse, or a serial mouse? How many buttons does it have? If you have a serial mouse, which COM port is it attached to and what protocol does it use (such as Microsoft or Logitech)?

✔ **Monitor.** What is the make and model of the monitor? What are its vertical and horizontal refresh rates? You need this information only if you will be using the graphical portion of Linux, called X Window System.

✔ **Video card.** What is the make and model number of the video card or video chip set and the amount of video RAM?

✔ **Network interface card (NIC).** If you have a network connection, what is the make and model number of the network interface card?

✔ **Network information.** If you have a network connection, what is your IP address, netmask, gateway IP address, name server IP addresses, and host and domain names? If you need help, contact your network administrator or Internet service provider (ISP).

To install Red Hat Linux, you need to answer the questions in the preceding list. Now that you know what you should be looking for, the next section delves a bit more into how to locate and capture that information.

Linux displays a lot of information about your computer while it's starting up. You'll see information about your computer's memory, disk drives, network adapters and so on. Unless you are very fast at taking notes, or have Superman's X-Ray vision, you can use the Linux dmesg utility after you system has started. Run the **dmesg | more** command from a terminal emulator screen to replay the start-up information. (Chapter 4 shows how to start a terminal emulator and run Linux commands.)

Hard drive controllers

The two main types of hard drives are IDE and SCSI, and each type has its own controller. IDE is more common in PCs, and newer PCs usually have two IDE controllers rather than one. For each IDE controller, your system can have only two hard drives: a master and a slave. Therefore, a PC with two IDE controllers can have up to four hard drives. You should know which hard drive is which. Also, if you have a Windows system that you want to pre-serve, you should know which hard drive it resides on. The following is the normal configuration on a Windows system:

✔ The first controller's master drive is called C.

✔ The next hard drive is called D and is the slave drive on the first controller.

   ✔ The next hard drive is E and is the master drive on the second controller.

   ✔ The last hard drive is F and is the slave drive on the second controller.

Normally, Windows is located on your C drive, and data is on your other drives. This lettering scheme is just one possibility; your hard drives may be set up differently and may even include CD-ROMs as drives on your IDE controllers.

Some high-end PCs have a SCSI controller on the motherboard or on a separate SCSI controller board, either in addition to or instead of the IDE controllers. Older SCSI controllers can have up to eight devices on them, numbered 0_7, including the controller. Newer SCSI controllers (known as *wide controllers*) can have up to 16 devices, including the controller itself.

If all you have is a SCSI hard drive, usually drive 0 or drive 1 is your C drive, and others follow in order.

If you have a mixture of IDE and SCSI controllers, your C drive could be on any of them. The sections later in this chapter — "Getting Information from Windows" and "Getting Information from MS-DOS" — show you how to identify how many hard drives you have, what type they are, and the controllers to which they are attached.

Old systems and new hard drives

Hard drives are made up of cylinders of information, which in turn are made up of tracks of information, which in turn are made up of blocks of information. Newer hard drives have more cylinders than older computer systems can handle easily. Therefore, a method called *logical block addressing,* or LBA, was created so that older computer systems can work with newer hard drives, which have more than 1,023 cylinders.

The BIOS setup under hard drives typically specifies whether your computer system is capable of LBA. Your hard drive may already be accessed as an LBA hard drive. Some BIOS systems do this automatically the first time a hard drive with a large number of cylinders is accessed. Note, however, that changing your hard drive to an LBA specification, if it is not LBA already, will make the data on the hard drive inaccessible. Therefore, before changing your hard drive to LBA, you should back it up if it contains any data. (You may decide that adding another hard drive is not such a bad idea as an expansion strategy.)

Different hardware systems have different ways to enter the BIOS setup. Usually, you can enter the BIOS setup when you turn on the power and start to boot; when you press the Reset button on the front of the system and start to reboot; or when you go through the normal shutdown of your Windows system, and ask to reboot. As your computer starts, it displays a message telling you what key to press in order to enter the BIOS menu. The key is generally the Delete or F1 key, but can also be F2 or F10.

Introducing hard drives

You need to decide whether you want to put Linux on a separate hard drive from MS-DOS and Windows or whether you want the two operating systems to share one hard drive.

From here on, unless we mention a particular system, consider MS-DOS and Windows as the same thing.

We strongly recommend that you put Linux on a separate hard drive. First, you can now find 2GB hard drives for less than $100 (U.S.). Second, the task of shrinking MS-DOS and Windows small enough to allow Linux to reside in its full glory on an existing hard drive is difficult at best and impossible at worst. And although splitting the Red Hat Linux distribution across hard drives is possible, doing so will make updating the distribution difficult.

If you do purchase another hard drive, install it as the second hard drive on the first IDE controller or as drive 1 on your SCSI controller (assuming that your existing Windows hard drive is either the first hard drive on your IDE controller or ID 0 on your SCSI controller). Adding hard drives is a hardware thing; the store where you buy the hard drive should be able to add it to your system for you. And while the system is there, you can ask the store folks to tell you the details on the other hardware in your system.

While installing Red Hat Linux on your hard drive, you may be asked to supply the number of drive heads (or tracks), the number of cylinders, and the number of sectors per track. Most modern hard drives provide this information on a paper label on the outside of the drive. Some modern hard drives are set up for Windows, and Linux can access the number of drive heads, cylinders, and sectors.

If you have your computer apart looking for other information (a pox on manufacturers who don't supply such useful information), you may as well write down all the hard drive information you can find. You should look for the number of heads, cylinders, and sectors. This information is used to tell the operating system where to put data with respect to the beginning of the hard drive. If you have trouble, check out the "Getting Information from Windows 95/98" and "Getting Information from MS-DOS" sections. SCSI hard drive users don't have to supply this information because the SCSI controller and device drivers calculate it on the fly. SCSI hard drive owners should, however, know the size of their hard drives, which is printed on the hard drive or is available through the sections just mentioned.

Getting Information from Windows

If you have Windows 95, 98 or ME, but not Windows 2000/XP, you can use the msd program in MS-DOS mode as described in the next section to find out about the hardware in your system. Much more information is available, however, through the Control Panel in Windows.

With pencil and paper handy, it's time to get to the Control Panel and all that information. Follow along with these steps:

1. **Click the Start button and choose Settings⇨Control Panel.**

2. **Double-click the System icon, and then click the Device Manager tab.**

3. **At the top of the screen, select the View Devices by Connection option.**

   This shows all components and how they relate to each other.

   If you have a printer attached to your system, at this point you can click the Print button. Then, in the Print dialog box that appears, select the All Devices and System Summary option. Click OK. This procedure prints a full report about your system. You may not have all the information you need, such as which hard drive goes with which controller, but you will save yourself a lot of writing.

4. **In the list, on the Device Manager tab, click Computer.**

5. **Click the Properties button.**

   The Computer Properties dialog box appears.

6. **Select the Interrupt Request (IRQ) option and write down the displayed information.**

   The Setting column, at left, lists interrupt requests. The hardware using a particular IRQ is listed in the right column. Note that no two devices can use the same IRQ.

7. **Select the Direct Memory Access (DMA) option and write down the displayed information.**

8. **Select the Input/Output (I/O) option and write down the pertinent information.**

   Look for and write down entries regarding a sound card (if you have one) and a parallel port (LPT).

9. **Click Cancel.**

   You return to the Device Manager tab of the System Properties dialog box.

Now you need to find out about the other devices in your system. This process takes some time, so you may want to pause here and grab something to drink, fix something to eat, and put on some tunes before following these steps:

1. **On the Device Manager tab (from the control panel) of the System Properties dialog box, select the View Devices by Type option.**

   In the list, notice how a plus or minus sign precedes some icons. A plus sign indicates that the entry is collapsed. A minus sign indicates the entry is expanded to show all subentries.

2. **In the list, make sure that all items are expanded.**

   Expanded simply means that a minus sign precedes the icon. If a plus sign is there instead, click it and it changes to a minus sign. As you expand some entries, you may see more plus signs. Click each plus sign to expand it. You may need to use the scroll bar to the right of the window to bring additional items into view.

3. **Look through the list for Standard IDE/ESDI Hard Disk Controller or SCSI Host Adapter.**

   Write down the complete label, which tells you what type of drive controller you are currently investigating.

4. **Look at the first subentry under that hard drive controller, if any. Write down the type of drive. Now double-click that drive entry.**

   The General tab of the Properties dialog box for that device appears.

   If the controller has no entries, do not despair. Some systems have extra hard drive controllers (particularly if you are using SCSI hard drives) that are not connected to any hard drives. Also, be aware that the first controller may have some other type of device connected to it, such as a tape drive or a CD-ROM. If no drives are attached to this controller, just go on to the next controller.

5. **Click the Settings tab, write down the drive type, and then click Cancel.**

   The screen returns to the Device Manager tab of the System Properties dialog box.

6. **Write down the highlighted information, which is the type of hard drive controller.**

7. **For each disk subentry for that controller, repeat Steps 4 to 6.**

8. **Follow the same general steps for any other hard drive controller entries.**

9. **For the Display adapters entry, simply write down each subentry.**

   Don't bother clicking Properties because it won't supply you with any information that is useful for installing Linux.

10. **For the Keyboard entry, write down each subentry.**

11. **Likewise for the Monitor entry.**

12. **Like-likewise, for the Mouse entry.**

13. **Like-like-likewise, for the Ports (Com & LPT) entry.**

14. **Finally, for the Sound, Video, and Game Controllers entry, copy information on both the General tab and the Resources tab.**

    Double-click the first subentry, and the General tab appears (as usual). Write down the information. Then, instead of clicking Cancel, click Resources at the top of the screen to display the Resources tab. Write down the information, and then click Cancel.

15. **Back at the Device Manager tab, click Cancel.**

    The screen returns to the Control Panel.

Whew. That was a lot of copying, but you aren't finished yet. Follow these steps for fascinating facts about your monitor:

1. **Make sure that the Control Panel is displayed.**

   If it isn't, click the Start button and choose Settings⇨Control Panel.

2. **Double-click the Display icon.**

   The Display Properties dialog box appears.

3. **Click the Settings tab.**

   The screen displays your monitor's settings.

4. **Copy the information under Color Palette and Desktop Area.**

   The Color Palette information is 16 color, 256 color, High Color (16 bit), or True Color (24 bit). The Desktop Area information is 640 by 480 pixels, 800 by 600 pixels, 1,024 by 768 pixels, or some higher numbers.

5. **Click Cancel.**

   You are returned to the Control Panel.

And now, it's time to check the time:

1. **From the Control Panel, click the Date/Time icon.**

   The Date/Time Properties dialog box appears.

2. **Click the Time Zone tab, if necessary, so that it appears on top of the Date & Time tab.**

3. **Copy the text at the top of the screen.**

   The text begins with *GMT,* which stands for Greenwich Mean Time, which is the world standard. The number after GMT indicates the difference between your time and the GMT. Be sure to copy the words that indicate your time zone, such as Eastern Time (U.S. and Canada).

4. **Click Cancel.**

Tired of this yet? You're almost finished. Next you discover delightful details about your printer:

1. **From the Control Panel, double-click the Printers icon.**

2. **Double-click to select the first non-networked Printer icon (one without a wire underneath it).**

   Another window appears. This new window has the same name as the printer you double-clicked. Don't click the icon labeled Add Printer.

3. **In the menu bar at the top of the window, choose Printer⇨Properties and then click the Details tab.**

4. **Copy the make and model and the communications port the printer is attached to.**

   The make and model appears at the top of the screen, next to the printer icon. The communications port is listed after `Print to the Following Port`.

5. **Click Cancel.**

6. **Double-click the next Printer icon, and repeat Steps 3 through 5.**

7. **Close any open windows by clicking the Close button.**

   The Close button is the one with the X, in the upper-right corner of a window.

The following, we promise, is the last set of steps. Here's how you get the hard facts about your hard drives:

1. **Double-click the My Computer icon on the Windows 95/98 desktop.**

2. **Select the first hard drive by clicking its icon. Copy down the capacity and the free space left.**

3. **Repeat Step 2 for all other hard drives.**

This information will be useful later as you make decisions about how much space to leave for Windows 95 or Windows 98 (if any) and how much space you have for Linux on each hard drive.

Getting Information from MS-DOS

If you're running MS-DOS or Windows 3.1 — egads! — you have a program on your system called Microsoft Diagnostics, or msd. This program will tell you information about the hardware on your system, which you can then use to determine how to set up Linux.

If you have a printer attached to your system, you're in luck. You can avoid writer's cramp by following these steps:

1. **Make sure your system is in DOS or MS-DOS mode.**

   If you have just booted, you may be in MS-DOS mode. The screen will mostly be black with a prompt like this c:\>.

   If you have booted and are in Microsoft Windows 3.1, press Alt+F+X, which exits Windows and returns you to DOS. Then you will see the c:\> prompt.

2. **Type** msd **to start the program.**

   The main screen appears, with categories such as computer and memory.

3. **Press Alt+F+P.**

4. **Press the spacebar and choose Report All.**

5. **Press the Tab key until the cursor is in the Print To section.**

6. **Use the up- and down-arrow keys on the keyboard to select the port your printer is attached to or to create a file to hold the information.**

7. **Press Tab until the cursor is on the OK button.**

8. **Press the Enter key.**

9. **Fill in the Customer Information, if you want.**

10. **Press the Tab key until the cursor is on the OK button.**

11. **Press the Enter key to print the report or create the file.**

   If you're creating a file, you may want to press the Tab key to move to the text box that contains the name of the file that will be holding the report, and change the file extension to txt, so that the file will be easier to print later from Windows.

Although you may not get all the information you need from this printout, you will get a great deal of it, and it will probably be more accurate than information you write by hand.

If you don't have a printer, get some paper and a pen and prepare to copy some information:

1. **Make sure your system is in DOS or MS-DOS mode.**

   See Step 1 in the preceding set of steps for more information.

2. **Type** msd **to start the program.**

   The main screen appears, with categories such as computer and memory.

3. **Press P (for processor) and copy the information on the screen.**

   The screen displays the type of processor in your system (usually a 386, 486, or some other type of Intel chip).

4. **Press Enter to return to the main screen.**

5. **Press V (for video screen) and copy the displayed information.**

   You see your system's video adapter type (usually VGA, XGA, or SVGA). Also look for the display type (such as VGA Color or SVGA Color), manufacturer, and video BIOS version. Pay particular attention to the video BIOS version because it may also list the computer chip set used to make the video controller, which in turn will be used to set up the graphical part of Linux.

6. **Press Enter to return to the main screen.**

7. **Press N (for network) and copy the displayed information.**

   If your system has no networking capability or none that msd knows about, you may see a message that says `no network`.

8. **Press Enter.**

9. **Press U (for mouse) and copy the displayed information.**

   Look for entries for mouse hardware, the driver manufacturer, the DOS driver type, and the number of mouse buttons. Well, you don't really need to refer to the screen to figure out that last one.

10. **Press Enter.**

11. **Press D (for disk drives) and copy the pertinent information.**

    Now it gets interesting. Copy your floppy drive's capacity and number of cylinders. (For a floppy drive, these values are usually 1.44MB and 80 cylinders, respectively.) Then look for your hard drives, usually designated as C, D, E, and so on. Each one should have a Total Size entry and a number such as 400M, which stands for 400 megabytes. You should also see an entry such as CMOS Fixed Disk Parameters, followed by something like 731 Cylinders, 13 heads, 26 sectors/track. This information is useful in setting up your disks for Linux.

12. **Press Enter.**

13. **Press L (for parallel ports) and write down the pertinent information.**

    The screen displays entries such as LPT1 and LPT2. Linux usually finds out about these all by itself. In case it doesn't, write down the port address, which is usually a number such as 0378H.

14. **Press Enter.**

15. **Press C (for the COM ports) and write down the pertinent information.**

    The COM ports are your serial ports, which are typically used for a modem, a serial printer, and other interesting gadgets. Copy the port address, baud rate, parity, data bits, stop bits, and UART chip used. Usually, you don't need any of this information for Linux, but it's useful to have a complete record of your system.

16. **Press Enter.**

17. **Press Q (for IRQ list) and copy the information.**

    The different hardware pieces use IRQ, which stands for *interrupt request,* to signal the main CPU that they have some data that has to be processed.

    No two devices can have the same IRQ. Copying the information in these columns for all 16 IRQs (0_15) is important for later sanity.

18. **Press Enter to go back to the main screen, and then press F3 to end the msd program.**

Leaving a Trail of Bread Crumbs

This next step is very important: Back up your system! It's beyond the scope of this book to describe how to back up Windows computers. You should consult the Microsoft Web site at www.microsoft.com to investigate what back-up utilities are available to you.

Appendix B

Installing Red Hat Linux in Text Mode (The Ugly Way)

● ●

*R*ed Hat Linux gives you two installation interface choices: a graphical and a menu-based one. The graphical system simplifies the process by grouping similar configuration choices together. (We cover this option in Chapter 3.)

The menu-based option takes you step-by-step through the entire installation and works on more computers than the graphical one. The graphical system doesn't work on all video cards.

Stage 1: Starting the Installation

To begin the menu-based installation, follow these steps:

1. **Insert the CD into your CD-ROM drive (and your boot floppy disk if you can't boot from CD) and boot or reboot your computer.**

In Chapter 2 we show you how to test and see if you can boot from CD-ROM and, if you can't, how to create a boot floppy disk with Windows, MS-DOS, or Linux.

The Welcome to Red Hat Linux screen appears along with the `boot:` prompt.

During the installation, you and Red Hat Linux talk to each other by using — what else — dialog boxes. To maneuver between highlighted options in a dialog box and make your choices, use the following keys (note that *cursor* means the cursor or the highlight): Table B-1 gives you the lowdown on how to maneuver through those text boxes like a pro.

Table B-1	Installation Keyboard Shortcuts
Key	**What It Does**
Tab	Moves the cursor to the next section in the screen
Alt+Tab	Moves the cursor to the previous section in the screen
Left arrow	Moves the cursor backward through a list of options
Right arrow	Moves the cursor forward through a list of options
Up arrow	Moves the cursor up through a list of options
Down arrow	Moves the cursor down through a list of options
Spacebar	Selects an item from a list of options
Enter	Selects the highlighted item
F12	Accepts the values you chose and displays the next screen

2. **Type in** text **at the boot prompt and press Enter (the graphical installation process will begin after 60 seconds if you don't enter anything).**

   The Linux kernel loads and shows you a couple of pages of hardware and system information, indicating whether your hardware is being detected by the Linux kernel. From here on you can use the keyboard shortcuts described in Table B-1 to manuever through the dialog boxes.

   If the hardware isn't being detected, you can get more installation information from Red Hat's online installation manual — in HTML format — located on the CDs in the `/mnt/cdrom/doc/rhmanual/manual` directory. You can mount the CDs on another Linux or Windows system and view the document with Netscape. Most of the time, thankfully, and particularly with newer systems, Linux detects all your computer's basic hardware.

   If you want to stop the installation process, simply eject the boot disk, remove the CD from the drive, and reboot or shut down your machine.

3. **The Red Hat Linux informational screen appears. Select OK.**

4. **In the Language Selection dialog box, select the language that you speak and select OK.**

   You can choose from several languages, but by all means, pick one that you — hopefully — understand.

5. **In the Keyboard Selection dialog box, select the keyboard that you want to use and select OK.**

6. **The Mouse Selection screen appears. Red Hat does a good job at detecting your mouse so you should be able to select OK and proceed to the steps that determine what software you install.**

Red Hat provides a complete and detailed Red Hat Linux installation guide at www.redhat.com/docs/manuals. You can find additional Red Hat Linux resources at ftp.redhat.com and www.redhat.com/apps/support. Or check out the Red Hat Linux 7.3 Bible by Christopher Negus and published by your good friends and buddies at Hungry Minds, Inc., for more detailed information about using Red Hat Linux.

If you have access to another computer — Linux or Windows — you can mount the Red Hat Linux CD-ROM on that computer and look at the manual with Netscape or another browser. If you have another Linux computer, then open the /mnt/cdrom/doc/rhmanual/manual/index.htm file. On a Windows computer, you will want to look at D:\doc\rhmanu\manual\index.htm, assuming that your CD-ROM drive is the D: drive.

7. **In the Installation Type dialog box, select OK.**

The Workstation option is selected by default in the Installation Type window. We base this book on the software that the Workstation installation type installs. The Laptop type is similar to the Workstation. The Laptop type is optimized for laptops, of course, and includes extra software for systems like PCMCIA cards. You can choose the Laptop installation type if necessary and it should work with the examples in this book.

Red Hat provides several installation methods: workstation, laptop, server and upgrade. The Server class installs software that provides services; Custom starts with a minimal workstation and allows you to select most of your software; Upgrade will simply start with a current Red Hat installation and install a new version of every package.

Linux asks next if you want to let the Red Hat Linux installation system automatically partition your disk or if you will do so manually. The next several steps describe how to partition your computer.

8. **In the Disk Partitioning Setup screen, select Autopartition and OK.**

You are also given the choice of using Red Hat's Disk Druid utility and the old standby fdisk. Disk Druid is a good system for manually partitioning your disk. Fdisk does not provide the support that Disk Druid provides. You should not have to use either one. If you do, please be careful because you can overwrite a partition that you might not want to.

9. **In the Automatic Partitioning dialog box, select OK.**

You get three choices in this step: Remove All Linux Partitions on This System, Remove All Partitions on This System, and Keep All Partitions and Use Existing Free Space. The first — default — option will take any existing Linux file systems and combine them into three: /boot, / and swap; the second will use the entire disk and create /boot, / and swap. The last option will only use free space.

Use the second option if you have a Windows PC and want to recycle it as a Linux-only computer. You should use the third option if your disk has extra space and you want to save everything that is already stored on it.

This book uses the automatic method because it provides the most straightforward installation process for you with by far the least hassle. The manual method can be quite difficult to perform, and unless you have a compelling reason to do so, there isn't much point.

The automatic partitioning process removes all the data from any existing Linux partitions that are on your hard drive. Your Windows partitions will not be affected if you have any.

10. **A Warning screen pops up. You are informed that all the data on your Linux partitions will be erased if you proceed. Select Yes to continue — and erase your Linux data.**

Selecting No returns control to the Automatic Partitioning screen in Step 9.

Eventually the Network Configuration dialog box appears. The next section shows you how to connect your network from this dialog box.

11. **The Partitioning dialog box, showing the partitions and their mount points, opens. The default automatic partitioning scheme uses three partitions: /boot, / (root) and swap. These partitions should work well for you. Tab down and select OK to continue.**

12. **You are given two choices on the Boot Loader Configuration screen. Select LILO and then OK.**

LILO and GRUB perform the same function, allowing you to choose between one or more operation systems (Linux and Windows for instance). GRUB is a new system that is designed for hard-core Linux users. GRUB provides lots of options and flexibility. Most users do not need those options so we suggest using LILO. LILO is also installed on the master boot record (MBR) of your disk and is more robust in our opinion.

13. **A second Boot Loader Configuration dialog box starts. You should not have to enter any information (any options you would enter are for very old computers or advanced Linux administrators) so select OK to continue.**

14. **The third Boot Loader Configuration screen opens up. You will see only the information for starting your Linux computer unless you are configuring a dual-boot system (Linux and Windows for instance). Select OK to continue.**

15. **Next, you'll see the fourth, and final — no kidding — Boot Loader Configuration screen. Select OK and the boot loader for your Linux workstation will be installed on the MBR of your hard disk.**

As you fill in the dialog boxes, you may find that Red Hat Linux guesses what information is needed and fills in some sections automatically. If Linux has guessed incorrectly, simply change the information.

Stage 2: Configuring Your Network

If you have an Ethernet adapter and are connected to a Local Area Network (LAN), and you chose to configure your Red Hat Linux computer network connection, this section is for you. If you skipped the network nonsense, you can skip this section.

The following steps describe how to configure your Red Hat Linux computer network connection:

1. **In the Hostname Configuration dialog box, type the name of your Linux computer.**

   For example, type the name **veracruz** at the prompt, select the OK button, and press Enter.

   Press the Tab key to get to the OK button and press Enter.

2. **(Optional) If Red Hat can't detect your Ethernet (or wireless) adapter, the Load Module dialog box will start. Select the type of network adapter that you have.**

   You are given a list of Ethernet adapters to choose from. You must select the manufacturer and model of your adapter. Note that Ethernet adapters are often referred to as network interface connectors (NIC).

3. **(Optional) Configure your Ethernet adapter.**

   Red Hat can attempt to find the configuration information about your adapter. If you select the Autoprobe option and your Ethernet adapter is less than a few years old, then Red Hat Linux most likely will detect the information. Otherwise, use the Specify Options and enter the information yourself.

4. **Choose whether to enter your IP address manually or to have a BOOTP or a DHCP server hand you a dynamic IP.**

   The latter two options — BOOTP and DHCP — are not frequently used in home or small networks. This book uses, and you should select, the Static IP address option.

5. **Enter your IP Address, Netmask, Default Gateway (IP), and Primary Nameserver.**

   The following list gives a brief description of the four parameters. But describing the Internet Protocol (IP) is beyond the scope of this book. Please consult the various networking HOWTOs.

- **IP address.** This is the numeric network address of your Linux computer and is what your computer is known as on your local network and — in many cases — the Internet. If you haven't registered your private network's (also known as local networks or LANs) address space with the InterNic (the organization that is in charge of distributing IP addresses), then you can use the public address space that goes from 192.168.1.1 to 192.168.254.254.

- **Netmask.** Private networks based on the Internet Protocol (IP) are divided into subnetworks. The netmask determines how the network is divided. For addresses such as the one in the preceding bullet (192.168.1.1, and so on), the most common netmask is 255.255.255.0.

- **Default gateway (IP).** This is the numeric IP address of the computer that connects your private network to the Internet (or another private network). Red Hat guesses the address of 192. 168.1.254, for example, if you choose an address of 192.168.1.{1-254} for the IP address. You can accept this address, but leaving it blank is a better option, unless that address is your actual gateway. Chapter 15 describes how to configure your Linux computer to connect to the Internet via a telephone connection. If you do that, then setting a default route now can interfere with your connection.

- **Primary nameserver.** The Internet Protocol uses a system called Domain Name Service (DNS) to convert names such as `www. redhat.com` into numeric IPs. Red Hat Linux again makes a guess based on the IP address and netmask that you use. We suggest, however, leaving this box blank, unless you are on a private network with a nameserver or will be connected to the Internet (your ISP will supply a DNS). When you designate a nonexistent nameserver, then many networking programs work very slowly as they wait in vain for the absent server.

- **Secondary and Tertiary nameservers (IPs).** These are the IP addresses of the second and third DNS servers that your computer will use. They are generally the addresses of your ISP nameservers.

6. **When you finish with this dialog box, select the OK button and press Enter.**

   The Hostname Configuration dialog box appears.

7. **Enter the host, or FQDN, name for your computer. The host name consists of your machine's alias and domain name. For instance, if you want to call your computer "veracruz" and your domain name is "paunchy.net", then your FQDN is veracruz.paunchy.net. (You can also use just your computer name — veracruz — if you want. The FQDN is more descriptive however.)**

8. **When you finish filling in this dialog box, select the OK button and press Enter.**

9. **In the Firewall Configuration menu, select the No Firewall option and then the OK button.**

   Red Hat creates a firewall using the ipchains system by default. There are two levels — medium and high — available to you. However, we describe several methods for constructing a firewall using the newer and more advanced Netfilter/iptables system in Chapter 8. Those firewalls are customized to the methods we use to connect your computer to the Internet (analog modem and broadband) and a LAN.

10. **Select your language in — you guessed it — the Language Support menu. Select the OK button to continue.**

11. **Select your time zone in the Time Zone Selection dialog box. Click OK.**

12. **In the Root Password dialog box, type a password to use for logging in to your Linux system for the first time, and then type your password again and select OK.**

   The password is for the *root user,* also known as the *superuser,* who has access to the entire system.

13. **In the Add User dialog box, type the account name and password that you want to use for yourself.**

   For instance, if you're Joe Sixpack, then you can enter a Linux user name like *j6pack* in the User ID box. You can optionally enter your full name in the (guess what?) Full Name box. Finally, you must enter your password twice just like for root. Using a good password as you did for root is important. You don't want Joe Blow to be able to look at your valuable information.

14. **In the User Account Setup dialog box, enter any or all of the people who you want to be able to log in to your Linux computer.**

   Your new user name is displayed. This screen allows you to add, delete, and edit new or old users. Don't worry about getting everyone added at this point because you can do so at any time after you've installed Linux.

Stage 3: Entering the Point of No Return

Now you have chosen what software to install and how to configure your soon-to-be Red Hat Linux computer. You are now at the point where your hard drive needs to be formatted and the Red Hat Linux software installed on your computer. To put it as dramatically as possible, you are at the point of no return.

1. **The Package Selection menu appears. The Gnome graphical desktop system is selected by default. You can choose the KDE desktop if you want. You can select the Software Development and Games groups if you want extra compilers and games. This book works fine by just using the default configuration. Select OK to continue.**

   You can also choose the Individual Packages option. In that case, you'll be allowed to select any or all of the packages that come on your companion CD-ROMs.

2. **The Installation to Begin dialog box opens.**

3. **If you want to install Red Hat Linux on your computer now, select OK.**

   Your hard drive partitions — which are selected automatically by the installation process when the Workstation option is used — are formatted and the Red Hat Linux software is installed.

   If you do not want to continue, then select Back. You return to the last step of the previous section. You can continue going back one step at a time.

   After the installation has finished (it can take at least 15 minutes or so, depending on your computer), the Create a Bootdisk dialog box opens.

4. **Insert a blank DOS-formatted floppy disk and select OK.**

   Creating a boot disk is a good idea, just in case something happens to the boot partition on your disk. Microsoft products, for example, have a bad habit of overwriting the Master Boot Record (MBR) — and therefore your Linux booting system — when they are installed or even updated. If you think that nothing will ever happen to your MBR, select No, press Enter, and then listen while we tell you about a bridge we have for sale in New York City. . . .

   The Red Hat installation process is ready to start writing software to your hard drive.

Configuring X

Phew. You're almost to the finish line. Really.

One of the last things that you need to do is install X Server so that you can use the X Window System graphical user interface (GUI) to interact with Linux. Configuring an X Server means you specify the video card and monitor for your system, including how much video memory it has, what speed it runs at, and a series of other options. Sometimes — particularly with newer systems and newer graphics cards — most of this information is provided automatically by the system.

1. **After configuring your network (or not configuring it, either way), the Red Hat Linux installation system attempts to detect your video card.**

   If Linux finds your card, press the Enter key and skip to Step 3. If the system can't detect your video card it displays the Select a Video Card window containing a long list of video cards, and you can continue on to Step 2.

2. **Use the arrow keys to move through the list and select your video card; then press the Tab key to move to the OK button and press Enter.**

   If you don't see your video card but you see a previous model by the same manufacturer, then select that. If you don't see a video card that matches your equipment or an older model, then you have the following choices:

   - **Unlisted Card:** This is the very last option in the menu. You can select it to use a generic driver. One negative aspect to this option is that if you select a generic driver, then your graphical display runs slower. The positive aspect is that you have a graphical display that works.

   - **Generic VGA:** If you choose this option, then the points made in the Unlisted Card option apply here too. The only difference is that Generic VGA can't supply as high a resolution as some of the options available under the Unlisted Card option.

   If none of these options work, then we strongly suggest that you consider purchasing a modern video card if you want to see Red Hat Linux in its GUI glory!

   After you select the video card, Red Hat installs the RPM video driver package from the CD. The Monitor Setup dialog box then appears with a list of monitors to select from.

3. **Select a monitor that fits your own.**

   Older monitors can't handle resolution rates and scan frequencies higher than what they were designed for. A monitor designed for a 640 x 480 resolution (and a low scan frequency) can't display a 2,048 x 1,024 resolution (and a high scan frequency). More importantly, if you try to make the monitor display that high of a frequency, it may burst into flames. (Some don't believe this until they see a monitor start smoking.) Modern monitors, called multiscanning, can automatically match themselves to a series of scan frequencies and resolutions. Some of these monitors are even smart enough to turn themselves off if the frequencies become too high, instead of bursting into flames. Finding the documentation and matching your vertical and horizontal frequencies properly is the best way to go (particularly with older monitors). Lacking this information, try a lower resolution (VGA or SVGA) first, just to get X running.

4. **In the Screen Configuration dialog box, specify whether you want to probe to find out the configuration of your video card.**

   To probe or not to probe? Probing tries to determine the configuration of your video card. If the probe is successful, then you don't have to make any guesses about your hardware.

   Some computers can *hang up* — that is, stop responding to your keyboard — as the result of probing. If that happens, you must restart the installation process.

   If you decide not to probe, then the next screen asks you to specify the amount of video memory that you have.

5. **Specify the amount of memory on your video card. After you select the memory amount, press the Tab key to select OK and then press Enter.**

   Note that this memory is different than the amount of main memory. Most modern cards have 1, 2, 8MB or more of video memory. Use your arrow keys to move down the list.

   If you don't know how much video memory your card has, try 1MB (the 1 Meg option). Although this setting limits the resolution of your screen, you will probably be able to get X going. Later, you can experiment with the Xconfigurator program (described in Chapter 19) to figure out the best values for how much video memory you have.

6. **Specify your video clockchip.**

   This specification is a vestige of older systems and older video boards. We recommend that you select the No Clockchip Setting option. After you make your selection, use the Tab key to select the OK button and then press Enter.

   Note that this dialog box doesn't appear if the probe was successful.

7. **Select the video mode that you want to use.**

   You are asked to select the combination of screen resolution and the number of colors. You need to make the choice because the memory in your video card must be used for both purposes. The fewer color bits that you use mean the fewer shades of color that your display will use. The higher resolutions pack more detail onto your screen.

   Make a reasonable choice. If you're already running Windows on your system, you can look at the Display dialog box in the Control Panel to see how it's set up and then use that configuration as your starting point for Linux.

8. **In the Starting X dialog box, select OK.**

   Red Hat now tests your new X configuration.

   If you configured X correctly, this message appears: `Can you see this message?`. You have 10 seconds to either select Yes or press the Enter key.

9. **If you want to start X automatically at boot time, choose Yes; otherwise, choose No.**

   You have the option of starting X every time you boot or reboot your computer. This book assumes that you choose that option, and X is the default environment used in all further discussions.

   If you choose No, then your system will start up in character-cell or text mode. You can always manually start X with the `startx` command or modify the `/etc/inittab` to automatically start X. The line `id:3:initdefault` should be changed to `id:5:initdefault` in the `inittab` file to do that.

   After you make your choice, an informational screen appears, telling you where the configuration file can be found. It also points you to the `X README.Config` file for more information.

   If you have a problem with your X configuration, then you are regretfully informed about the situation. You have the option of quitting or going back and starting over. If you're game, go back and try, try again.

   If, for some reason, you can't get X working at this point, you can always try finishing the configuration of X later by running the Xconfigurator program.

Restarting Your System

Ta Da! You're finished with the installation. Not surprisingly, the Done dialog box appears.

Follow these steps to start your system:

1. **All that's left to do is select OK.**

   Before the system reboots, remove the CD and the floppy disk. Otherwise, you'll be faced with going through the entire installation process again. There's no need to groan — you can always re-reboot and remove the pesky critters.

   Your system reboots, and you can start Linux.

2. **When you see the `LILO boot:` prompt, press the Tab key.**

   You see a list of operating system names that you chose to represent your different systems to LILO. Type the name that represents Linux and then press Enter. Watch the next glorious event: Your Linux system boots! Pass out the champagne.

3. **After the startup messages stop and the `login:` prompt appears, type root and then press Enter. Then enter the root password.**

   You are now logged in as superuser, also known as root. Chapter 4 can help you get up to speed with your new Linux system.

If you did not give your computer a name and domain name during the network configuration process, then it's now referred to as `localhost.localdomain`. Otherwise, the welcome screen refers to whatever name you gave it, for example:

```
Welcome to veracruz.paunchy.net.
```

Appendix C

vi Me

● ●

*E*veryone who manages a Linux computer needs a good editor. Whether you're an administrator for a star-struck dot-com or a single, lonely Red Hat Linux computer, you need to edit simple text files. The ubiquitous vi editor fits the bill. vi is lean, fast, and an effective editor that's found on all Linux distributions.

Comprehending Text Editors

A text editor is an essential tool for Linux. It enables you to create and modify an array of text files, including the following:

- ✔ User files, such as the login file
- ✔ System configuration files, such as /etc/fstab, /etc/inittab, and /etc/lilo.conf
- ✔ C and C++ programs
- ✔ Shell programs
- ✔ Mail messages

Red Hat Linux comes with not one but two text editors: ed and vi. The ed editor is a line-oriented text editor. It was one of the first editors for Unix systems and traditionally is included with every Unix and Linux system. It's also a small editor, so small distributions of Unix and Linux can include it. You can always count on ed being there.

The second editor that comes with Linux is vi; it's included with almost every Linux distribution (some specialized distributions such as Trinux don't necessarily include it). This full-screen editor also supports the command set of a line-oriented editor named ex. The third major text editor for Linux is emacs; some people prefer to use this editor for most of their work.

In Red Hat Linux, ex and vi are emulated by another text editor named vim. The commands for vi work just fine with vim. In addition, vim has more capability than vi. For instance, vim makes editing easier by allowing you to switch from command to insert mode and still move around the file with the cursor keys. On the other hand, vi forces you to continually toggle between the two modes in order to insert text and move around the file. Therefore, vi isn't included as a separate program with Linux systems. When you type **vi**, you're really using vim, but this fact is invisible to you.

Getting Friendly with vi

The vi editor on your Red Hat Linux system is really the vim editor. With a little vim and vigor, you can invoke it by using vi, because a symbolic link exists between vi and vim.

Like the ed editor, the vi editor has two modes of operation and the same type of single-letter commands. To start vi, you type **vi** at the command line. The screen clears, and the left-most column displays tildes (~). You are looking at an empty, unnamed buffer in memory, into which you can enter text until you save the text to a named file.

You can start the vi editor in a number of ways, with different options, but the most common way is to start vi with only a filename as the argument, like this:

```
vi /etc/hosts
```

where /etc/hosts is the name of either an existing file that you want to edit or a new file that you want to create.

The vi editor has three modes of operation:

- ✔ Visual command mode
- ✔ Colon command mode
- ✔ Text mode

When you invoke vi with a filename, the editor screen appears. At the bottom-left corner is the following line:

```
"filename" [New File]
```

This status line tells you what the editor is doing. In this case, the editor has opened a buffer, and the save and quit option saves the contents of the buffer to the filename file. If you did indeed invoke vi with the following command:

```
vi /etc/hosts
```

the bottom-left corner would display the following line:

```
"/etc/hosts" [readonly]
```

When you first invoke vi, you are in visual command mode, which is the default. You can use four special commands to either locate text or transition to more complex commands:

/	Forward search
?	Backward search
n	Continue the search in whichever direction you were currently going
:	ex command (ex is the line editor included in vi)

In command mode, the characters you type are used as commands, not as input into the file. To use commands, type the character on the command line. For the first two search commands (/ and ?), the cursor moves to the bottom of the screen, where you then type the string that you're searching for. After you press Enter, the search begins. If you want to search for an additional string, you can just press the lowercase n key to reexecute the search; to search backwards, press the uppercase N key.

When you type the : command, the cursor moves to the bottom of the screen and waits for you to enter a command or a command string. You must press the Enter key to execute the command.

Given that characters you type are interpreted as commands in command mode, how do you get from command mode to text mode? Simple. Enter a command to do something in text mode, and vi takes you there. Here are some commands that you can use to switch from command mode to text mode:

i	Insert text before the cursor
a	Insert text after the cursor
I	Insert text at the beginning of the current line
A	Insert text at the end of the current line

As soon as you type any of these commands, Linux puts you in text input mode. Do not press Enter after entering the command. Any text you type after you invoke the command is placed in a buffer and echoed to the screen.

You may be asking yourself (because the directions are skimpy or you have no one else to ask), "How do I get out of text mode and back to command mode?" Again the answer is simple. If you want out, just press the Escape (Esc) key, and you're immediately whisked back to command mode. That's pretty easy, isn't it?

If you don't know whether you're in command mode, just press Esc a few times.

Moving around in a file

After you know how to open a file in vi, you're ready to find out how to move around in it. The commands in Table C-1 move the cursor around. First, make sure that you're in command mode; otherwise, Linux places these keys in your file just like any other data.

Table C-1	Moving Around in vi
Command	*What It Does*
j	Move one line down
k	Move one line up
h	Move one character to the left
l	Move one character to the right
Ctrl+f	Scroll down a full screen
Ctrl+b	Scroll up a full screen

If you want to go to a specific line number, you use a colon command. Type a colon (:), and it appears at the bottom of the screen. Next, type the line number where you want to be. Here's an example:

```
:12
```

When you press Enter, the cursor moves to the beginning of line 12.

Deleting and moving text in vi

This section describes how to delete and move text in vi. The vi editor has several commands for deleting. You can delete characters, words, or lines. The command for deleting a word is dw; this command deletes the word to the right of the cursor. You can delete more words at once by prefacing the dw command with the number of words you want deleted from the cursor position. For example, the command 6dw deletes the next six words following the cursor. Table C-2 lists additional deletion commands.

Table C-2	Deleting in vi
Command	*What It Does*
D	Deletes up to the end of the current line
dd	Deletes the current line
x	Deletes the character under the cursor (4x, 5x, and so on)

A handy command to remember is u, which is the undo command. You can immediately undo edits with this command, in the unlikely event that you make a mistake.

The business of moving text around in the file usually requires the following general steps:

1. **Position the cursor at the beginning of the first line you want to move or copy.**

2. **Type** ma, **marking that position with the letter** *a.*

3. **Position the cursor at the beginning of the last line that you want to move or copy.**

4. **Type** mb, **marking that position with the letter** *b.*

5. **Position the cursor at the line where you want to insert the text.**

6. **Type** `a, bm. **if you want to move the text, or** `a,bt. **if you want to copy the text.**

   Note that the single quotation marks and period are required.

Controlling your editing environment

You can control your editing environment in vi by setting options with the :set command. Table C-3 lists some common :set command options.

Table C-3	Everyday :set Options
Command	*What It Does*
all	Displays a list of all :set commands and their status
errorbells	Sounds the terminal bell when errors occur
ignorecase	Makes searches case insensitive

(continued)

Table C-3 *(continued)*

Command	What It Does
number	Displays line numbers in the leftmost column on the screen
showmode	Displays an indicator at the bottom-right of the screen, indicating which mode you are in: input mode, change mode, replace mode, and so on

Note: You can turn off `:set` command options by prefixing the command with `no`, as in

```
:set nonumber
```

This turns line numbering off.

Checking out common vi commands

Table C-4 summarizes common `vi` commands. We describe some of these commands elsewhere in the book; others are new.

Table C-4	Everyday vi Commands
Command	What It Does
a	Inserts text after the cursor
A	Inserts text at the end of the current line
I	Inserts text at the beginning of the current line
i	Inserts text before the cursor
o	Opens a line below the current line
O	Opens a line above the current line
C	Changes up to the end of the current line
Cc	Changes the current line
cw	Changes the word
J	Joins the current line with the next one
rx	Replaces the character under the cursor with x (x is any character)

Command	What It Does
~	Changes the character under the cursor to the opposite case
$	Moves to the end of the current line
^	Moves to the beginning of the current line
mx	Marks the current location with the letter x
Ctrl+l	Redraws the screen
:e filename	Edits the file
:N	Moves to line N (N is a number)
:q	Quits the editor
:q!	Quits the editor without saving any changes
:r filename	Reads the file and inserts after the current line
:w filename	Writes the buffer to a file
:wq	Saves changes and exits the editor
/string	Searches forward for string
?string	Searches backward for string
n	Finds the next string
u	Undoes the last command
Esc	Ends input mode and enters visual command mode

Don't worry about the sheer large number of options and commands. We've used vi now for 20 years and have never learned — or used — more than 20 percent of them. vi is our workhorse for system administration, and it works quite well with one hand tied behind your back!

Appendix D

Diggin' Them Linux Man Pages

• •

In This Appendix

▶ Starting the `man` command

▶ Reading the man pages

▶ Finding commands

• •

*U*nix and Linux systems are largely made up of small, terse commands executed on the command line. Typically, each command is associated with at least one man page. The Linux man pages have nothing to do with gender: The *man* stands for *manual*.

At one time, the man pages were the only documentation that came with Unix systems. Somewhere, we still have the thin book we received as first-time Unix users and system administrators. All that it contained was the man pages, and from that, we were supposed to install a Unix system. Many years later, we still look at the man pages first to get a quick idea of what a command should do, and what arguments to use on the command line or what values to set.

This appendix shows you how to use the `man` command, how to read and understand the man pages, and how to locate other man pages that may help you understand the Linux command you're investigating. Man pages are essentially help files.

Checking Out How the Man Pages Are Organized

You can find the man pages in several directories throughout the system:

▸ `/usr/man`

▸ `/usr/local/man`

▸ `/usr/X11/man`

▸ `/usr/lib/perl5/man`

Each directory is broken up into subdirectories (referred to as sections) of the manual. See Table D-1.

Table D-1:	Man Sections and Where to Find Them	
Man Section	*What the Section Covers*	*Available in This Directory*
Man 1	User commands	/usr/share/man/man1
Man 2	System calls	/usr/share/man/man2
Man 3	Library functions	/usr/share/man/man3
Man 4	Special files	/usr/share/man/man4
Man 5	File formats	/usr/share/man/man5
Man 6	Games (look at everyone going to that section!)	/usr/share/man/man6
Man 7	Miscellany	/usr/share/man/man7
Man 8	System administration commands	/usr/share/man/man8
Man 9 (mann)	nroff, troff, and groff (and now tk) macros	/usr/share/man/man9

Most directories have more than one section. Two sections may have entries for a command of the same name. For example, man section 1 has an open command, and man section 2 has an open system call. To make sure that you're reading about the right command, you can specify the command on the man command line. For example: [paul@veracruz paul]$ man 2 open

Most sections of the man sections (which are basically databases of information) have two parts:

✔ An intro page represented by a file called intro.n, where the *n* is a number that corresponds to the section number.

✔ All commands, calls, library names, and filenames, represented by files with the name command.n, where *n* is the section number name.

If you use cd to change to the /usr/man/man1 directory and issue the ls command, you see files such as cat.1 and grep.1. Oddly, you don't find a file called cd.1, because the cd command is built into the different shells, and its documentation is covered in the bash.1 file, or the csh.1 file.

If you're using `bash` as a shell, you can get information about the rest of the built-ins as follows:

```
[paul@veracruz paul]$ help
```

The intro page briefly describes that section of the manual and indicates whether you need to know anything special about that section. Printing an intro page is simple. For example:

```
[paul@veracruz paul]$ man 2 intro
```

or

```
[paul@veracruz paul]$ man 3 intro
```

Using the Man Command

Okay, if you didn't get the pun in the heading, you need to watch more cartoons.

To get started using the man pages, follow these steps:

1. **With Linux up and running, log in as a user (either a general user or root).**

2. **Type the** `man` **command.**

   The system asks what manual page you want. The syntax of the `man` command (like many other commands) requires at least one argument.

3. **Supply an argument by typing** `man ls`.

   The first `man` is the command name, and the second `man` tells Linux that you want information on the manual program itself. The system may tell you to wait a moment while it formats the page to your screen, and then it displays the reference page for the `man` command. Please read Chapter 15 for more information about how commands are organized.

4. **If a colon (:) appears at the bottom of the screen, press the spacebar to see the next page, or use the arrow keys to maneuver around the pages.**

5. **To quit the man program, press the q key.**

Checking Out Topics in the Man Pages

Each man page is made up of several sections. Here, we list the sections that we think are most important in your quest to figure out how to read man pages. Note that some man pages don't contain all these sections, and other pages contain more sections than those outlined here.

Name

The name is usually the command name, followed by a hyphen, followed by a one-line description of the command's functionality; this is usually what you see if you execute a man -k command or an apropos command. Either of these commands, when followed by a word, lists the name field from every manual page that contains that word. Type the following:

```
[paul@veracruz paul]$ apropos cat
```

 Your apropos command may produce few or no commands. Perhaps no one has generated the database made up of command names and descriptions. To do this, either you or your system's administrator has to become superuser or root and then execute the following command line:

```
/usr/sbin/makewhatis
```

Synopsis

The synopsis is a shorthand way to describe what the command is looking for in terms of an argument list. For example:

```
lpq [-l] [-Pprinter] [job # ...] [user ...]
```

is the synopsis for the lpq command (whose job is to show what is in the print queue). The command name (lpq) is first, followed by a series of bracketed arguments. If an argument is enclosed in square brackets, the argument is optional, meaning the lpq command needs no arguments. If you type

```
[paul@veracruz paul]$ lpq
```

you probably get a no entries message — which means nothing is waiting to be printed — or a list of people's jobs waiting to be printed on the default printer.

If you want to see what's waiting to be printed on another printer, you use the optional argument -p followed by the name of the printer. For example:

```
[paul@veracruz paul]$ lpq -Pzklpsa
```

Now if you type this command, you probably get a message like `lpq: zklpsa: unknown printer`, indicating that your system does not know about a printer named `zklpsa`. If you get something else, please let us know because that may explain where our print jobs are going . . . no, no, just kidding.

If, however, you have a printer called hp5l, then you can enter the following command to find out its status:

```
[paul@veracruz paul]$ lpq -Php5l
```

In any case, the purpose of this section is not to show you all the functionality of the `lpq` command. Rather, the synopsis section shows in a shorthand way how you should use the command, including which arguments are optional.

Another confusing thing you may see is the . . . notation. Looking back at the `lpq` command synopsis, you see it twice, once following the `job #` argument, and once following the `user` argument. This notation tells you that you can list as many job numbers on the line as you want, separated by spaces, and as many user names as you want, separated by spaces.

Sometimes you see a command argument that begins with one hyphen (-) or two - -. These notations are technically known as *options,* whereas `job #` and `user` of the `lpq` command are *arguments.* Options tell the command how to manipulate arguments. You may see an option line that looks like this:

```
cat    [-benstuvAET]
```

or even

```
ls [-abcdfgiklmnpqrstuxABCFGLNQRSUX1]
```

Don't be overwhelmed. If you deal with the options one at a time, you'll be able to understand how the command works. Take heart in the fact that most of the time, most people use only one or two options.

If you use the `man ls` command, you see that `ls` has many more options. That's why `ls` has been described as "a command that went bad with good intentions."

Description

The description section is a brief introduction to the command's functionality, which is then expanded on by what the options specify the command to do. A good example of a description is the manual page for man itself.

Options

The options section tells how the command treats data in the arguments. Each option modifies the command's actions, drastically or subtly. The options can also pass information to the command about where to find files. The three types of options are:

✔ No argument

✔ Attached argument

✔ Positional argument

No argument means the option has a hyphen, followed by one or more single-character options. For example:

```
[paul@veracruz paul]$ ps -ax
```

The a and the x do not have any other values that they have to look at. But in the following command:

```
[paul@veracruz paul]$ lpq -Pzklpsa
```

the -P option needs you to supply an argument, in this example, zklpsa.

Environmental variables

Sometimes, to cut down on the information you have to give the command, you can set an *environmental variable*. Each shell (or command interpreter) has an *environment* that it works in. This environment (when it is created) consists of certain files that are open, some memory, and almost always some environmental variables.

Using the bash shell, type the following (if you're not sure that you're using the bash shell, type bash at the command prompt and then continue with the example):

```
[paul@veracruz paul]$ printenv
```

You see something like this:

```
USERNAME=
COLORTERM=gnome-terminal
HISTSIZE=1000
HOSTNAME=veracruz.paunchy.net
LOGNAME=paul
HISTFILESIZE=1000
INIT_VERSION=sysvinit-2.74
MAIL=/var/spool/mail/paul
LD_LIBRARY_PATH=/usr/local/applixware/axdata/axshlib/lib
TERM=xterm
HOSTTYPE=i386
PATH=/usr/bin:/usr/bin:/usr/local/bin:/usr/X11R6/bin:/bin:
  /usr/X11R6/bin:/usr/local/netscape:
  /home/paul/bin:/usr/X11R6/bin:
  /usr/local/netscape:/home/paul/bin
CONSOLE=/dev/console
KDEDIR=/usr
HOME=/home/paul
INPUTRC=/etc/inputrc
PREVLEVEL=N
RUNLEVEL=5
SHELL=/bin/bash
XAUTHORITY=/home/paul/.Xauthority
USER=paul
PGDATA=/var/lib/pgsql
BASH_ENV=/home/paul/.bashrc
BOOT_IMAGE=linux
DISPLAY=:0
SESSION_MANAGER=local/atlas.paunchy.net:/tmp/.ICE-
            unix/7376,tcp/atlas.paunchy.net:1371
OSTYPE=Linux
WINDOWID=62914566
GDMSESSION=Default
LD_PRELOAD=/usr/local/lib/open.so
SHLVL=3
_=/usr/bin/printenv
```

This list includes lots of environmental variables, but we don't have the space to describe them all. So, here are the most important ones:

- ✔ **PATH** tells the shell all the places to look for commands.
- ✔ **HOME** tells cd where to go when you don't supply any arguments.
- ✔ **OSTYPE** tells the shell and programs what operating system they're on.

Different shells have different ways to set these variables (and create and set others) to tell the commands what to do.

A variable not being set to some value (null) is different than a variable that doesn't exist (unset), and these differences vary from command to command. For example, in the preceding listing, the first variable, USERNAME, is set to NULL. The fact that it's there at all is significant. The fact that it is set to NULL instead of some other value is also significant to various programs.

Diagnostics

Error messages or exit codes indicate that something has gone wrong in the program or the shell. Normally, Unix error messages are terse. Sometimes things may seem to be wrong when they really are okay. For example, most new Unix users think that when they issue an ls command in an empty directory, they should get an error message such as directory empty or file not found. The problem? The command ls by itself can display the filenames in any order (as opposed to ls *, which displays the files in alphabetical order). So if you have a directory with three files in it named *file, not,* and *found* — which happen to print in that order — you can't determine whether the directory is empty or not. We admit that this example is a bit contrived, but the developers of Unix thought that less was better than more (we're not talking about the command names less and more), and that silence is golden (which means something if you've ever heard those old, noisy, hard-copy terminals).

Most programs display an *exit code,* which you normally don't see unless it's a non-zero code, which means the program ended unsuccessfully. If you're a programmer, you can test for this, and if you do programming or shell-script writing, we encourage you to set and test exit codes.

Bugs/deficiencies

Yes, all programs have bugs, and most Linux people are good about correcting them. But some bugs are so arcane that they affect only one in a million people, and to try and correct them would mean redesigning the entire program. This type of bug is regarded as a deficiency or a limitation and is listed in the man page.

Compatibility issues

When a new version of a command or a program comes out, it may work slightly differently than the old command or program. This modification can cause a *compatibility issue* with shell scripts that have been written to use the old command or program. If the author of the command or program thinks a problem may occur, it should be documented here.

Caveats

Caveats are warnings that the programmer wants to give to the user of the command or program. Caveats may include things to think about before executing the command or program, security issues, or how much file system space the program uses on large applications.

Disclaimers

Disclaimers are usually legal statements included at the insistence of the author's employer or the employer's lawyers, telling you that if you use this program and it harms someone, don't come back to them. All programs in all operating systems have disclaimers someplace.

Authors

The authors are simply the people who wrote the command or program that the manual page is describing. Often, this section also explains how to report bugs or discuss new features you may want to see.

Acknowledgments

The acknowledgments section, which is much more pleasant than the disclaimers section, recognizes the previous work put into a program that the author has built on. Allowing and encouraging people to build on the work of others is the essence of Linux and the GNU Public License.

Debugging options

Some programs, such as sendmail, have the capability to diagnose problems. If the manual page has a debugging options section, you can find information on setting and using these options to debug the program.

Configuration files

Along with options and environmental variables, another way to determine what program the manual page is describing how to operate is through *configuration files,* sometimes known as *startup files.* These files may be in your home directory, a systemwide directory, or a sitewide directory.

Often, Linux looks for them in a certain order: Sitewide files have the strongest influence, and systemwide files and local user (your startup) files have the second and third strongest influence, respectively. The systems administrator can use those files to set policies across companies and systems, while allowing you to tailor the program to your needs.

Two examples of startup files are the `.bashrc` file, which is probably in your home directory, and the `/etc/bashrc` file in the `/etc` directory. Note that the file in your home directory starts with a period. This type of file is called a *hidden,* or *dot,* file. You don't normally see hidden files when you list your directory, unless you issue the `ls -a` or `ls .*` command.

Copyrights

Many people mistakenly believe that Linux code or other freeware code is not copyrighted. This is typically not true. The authors of the code often take great care to copyright their code because they want to receive credit for their work.

Copying permissions/distribution policy

The copyright holder gives away most Linux code through the GNU Public License, or what is commonly called *copyleft.* The copyleft stipulates that those holding a copy of the code can use it for whatever purpose they want, as long as they make the code freely available to anyone who wants it. If they change the code, they must make the changed code (including the source code) freely available to those who want it.

Sometimes, other copying and distribution policies are associated with the command or program that the manual page is describing. These policies can include the following types of permissions, where you may:

- ✔ Use but not redistribute the code
- ✔ Use the code, but no source code is available
- ✔ Use and distribute the code as shareware, by paying a fee for continued use
- ✔ Have limited use, such as educational or personal (but not commercial) use
- ✔ Use the code on one machine only

If you bought the operating system, or a *layered product distribution* (a distribution that includes both the operating system and a commercial application), or both from a CD-ROM vendor, then the overall distribution policy on the CD-ROM is usually the most strict (that is, you're limited to installing it on one machine because of its licensed software). You don't have to worry as long as you follow its overall licensing.

POSIX compatibility/standards conformance

In the dark days of computer science, each vendor went off to develop its own operating system, with its own set of commands and programming interfaces. This way of thinking created a Tower of Babel (not to be confused with the Tower of Hanoi, which is a puzzle game) among computer users and programmers. When Unix systems first appeared, however, they were portable across different types of hardware, and you could have the same operating system, commands, and programming interfaces whether you were programming a Digital Equipment Corporation system, a Sun Microsystems computer, an IBM computer, or others. Unfortunately, this approach lasted about ten minutes in the scope of Unix's life, because as Unix escaped from Bell Labs, it went to the University of California, Berkeley, and *poof:* Two different Unix systems were now in existence!

A little later, vendors started introducing their versions of Unix, some using System V as a basis, others using BSD (as the Berkeley version was called). Some vendors, such as Sun Microsystems, started out with BSD and then switched to System V (to the chagrin of its users).

In 1988, the IEEE developed the POSIX standard for operating systems. The IEEE is a great organization, and probably the best thing that it did was to build on Unix rather than start over from scratch. It took the interfaces from the existing System V and Berkeley versions of Unix.

Other places to look for help

You can find help in several other places on the system. One place is the /usr/doc directory, which contains the documentation that comes with the individual software packages. For instance, the nmap network security package described in Chapter 5 installs documentation about what it does and how to use it in the /usr/doc/nmap directory.

Note: Some system administrators conserve disk space by not loading /usr/doc on their systems. With the abundance of inexpensive disks, this is usually penny wise, pound foolish. Documentation, such as that found in /usr/doc, can be put on one system and then made available to everyone through the magic of the Network File System (NFS). Tell your system administrator to do that. If you are your own system administrator, go into a closet and give yourself a lecture!

If an operating system is POSIX- compatible and a program is written to POSIX standards, the program should run on the operating system with no problems, and users should be able to use that operating system with little or no retraining from the last POSIX operating system they learned.

Although much work still has to be accomplished both in defining what POSIX is and in vendors implementing POSIX, POSIX compliance and certification are worthy goals.

Other standards should be implemented and met by manufacturers, distribution makers, and developers (not necessarily in that order) — standards for network communication, for the way data is put on the CD-ROM, and so on. Both formal standards and informal defacto standards exist, both of which help your system work better with the next system.

Linux was built with POSIX compatibility as a goal, and it follows many of the other standards. This makes it easy to port code from one set of POSIX-compatible interfaces to another and from one POSIX-compatible operating system to another. It also allows Linux to interoperate with other operating systems. Many Linux people are active in standards bodies, and the movement toward standards is generally supported in the Linux community.

Files

In addition to the startup or configuration files mentioned previously, sometimes the command or program that the manual page is describing uses other files in the system and temporary files for holding intermediate work. Such files are listed in this section of the man page. If a command does not work, perhaps one of these files is missing, has the wrong file permissions (or the directories they are in have the wrong permissions), is owned by the wrong person, or has corrupt data.

Future work

The future work section lists the author's plans for the command or program that the manual page is describing, often in an attempt to generate interest and help from other people.

See also/related software

The see also/related software section lists programs associated with the command or program that the manual page is describing. Often, several programs make up a system of programs to do a particular task. Some programs have similar capabilities, but are not quite the same. Some programs are the antithesis of the program you're looking at (for example, cut and paste). The *see also* often gives you an overall picture of what the program is supposed to do or leads you to the right program for the job.

Finding the Right Man Page

If you don't know what command you're looking for, use the apropos command followed by the word you're interested in. The apropos command searches all the man pages looking for that word, and lists the man command names along with one-line descriptions of all the commands that contain that word. You should probably pipe the output of the apropos command into the more command:

```
[paul@veracruz paul]$ apropos print | more
```

The apropos command can match partial words (called *strings*), which is why we suggested print instead of printer. The shorter your *keyword*, the more matches the command finds.

After you have the pages you want to look at, execute the man command for each one. From the one-line description, you can probably decide which commands fit your needs.

Look at the description field, which gives you a better idea of what the command can do. If you're still not sure about the command's basic functionality, look at the see also section, to see whether any other commands fit the bill.

After that, skip the synopsis section — it's usually a reminder of how to type the command — and go directly to the options section. Read through the options section, trying to apply the options to the basic description of the command.

After you've read several man pages, you'll notice that the same options appear for similar commands.

This is all pretty much passive work. To find out what a command really does, you should try it out. Create a small test file by using an editor, or use an existing file, such as the /etc/passwd file, as input. (It's better not to practice while logged in as root as you could accidentally damage a file or directory.)

From time to time, we read all the man pages in the system, concentrating on the command descriptions. We do this because we want to become familiar with new commands. Also, our memories aren't what they used to be. But to be fair to our failing memories, the system does have close to 1,200 general-user commands and about 260 system administration commands.

Appendix E

About the CD-ROMs

● ●

*T*he CD-ROMs that come with this book contain the full GNU Public License distribution of Red Hat Linux 7.3.

System Requirements

Make sure that your computer meets the minimum system requirements listed here. If your computer doesn't match up to most of these requirements, you may have problems using the contents of the CDs:

✔ A Pentium class PC with a 200MHZ or faster processor recommended. Actually, you can run Linux on 386 and 486 computers but the graphics run slowly. (Older 386 and 486 computers make for great Linux servers. Linux servers very often do not use graphical interfaces and the slower processors still handle functions like firewalls, personal Web servers, and such very well.)

✔ At least 32MB of total RAM installed on your computer. For the best performance, we recommend that people who want to use X Window System have at least 64MB and preferably 96MB of main memory.

✔ At least 800MB of hard drive space available to install all the software from the CDs. You'll need less space if you don't install every program. 2.5GB recommended for full installation.

✔ A CD-ROM drive.

✔ A 3¼-inch floppy disk drive and a blank 3¼-inch disk.

✔ A monitor capable of displaying at least 256 colors or grayscale.

✔ An IDE or a SCSI hard drive.

✔ A keyboard and a mouse.

✔ A modem with a speed of at least 28,800 bps if you want to go online. (Older, slower modems will work but will unnecessarily make your hair gray from the frustration of waiting through Web page downloads.)

Using the CDs

You receive the Publisher's Edition of Red Hat Linux on the companion CDs. The instructions for installing the Red Hat Linux operating system from the CDs are detailed in Part I. After you install the software, return the CDs to their plastic jacket, or other appropriate place, for safekeeping.

What You'll Find

The CD does not contain the freely distributable parts (or source code) of Red Hat Linux, but you can visit

```
ftp.redhat.com
```

All the packages included in this release of Red Hat Linux are available for download there.

You can obtain the Red Hat Linux installation manual from Red Hat's Web site

```
www.redhat.com.
```

We also recommend that you take a look at the official Red Hat Linux installation guide, available from the Red Hat Web site at

```
www.redhat.com/docs/manuals/linux
```

Because the CD-ROMs have a full implementation of Linux, to list all the accompanying tools and utilities would take too much room. Briefly, the CDs includes most of the software you need to access the Internet; write programs in several computer languages; create and manipulate images; create, manipulate, and play back sounds (if you have a sound board); play certain games; and work with electrical design.

For information about Red Hat Linux agreements and installation, see the pages at the end of this book, following the index.

If You Have Problems (Of the CD Kind)

We tried our best to test various computers with the minimum system requirements. Alas, your computer may differ, and Linux may not install or work as stated.

The two likeliest problems are that you don't have enough RAM for the programs you want to use, or you have some hardware that Linux doesn't support. Luckily, the latter problem occurs less frequently each day as more hardware is supported under Linux.

You may also have SCSI hard drives that use a controller not supported by Linux or a controller that is simply too new for the Linux development team to have given it the proper support at the time these CDs were pressed.

If you have trouble with corrupt files on the CDs, please call the Hungry Minds Customer Care phone number: 800-762-2974 (outside the United States: 317-572-3393). Customer service won't be able to help with complications relating to the program or how it works. Please see the Installation Instructions in Part I.

Index

Symbols

\> (appending standard output), 243, 244
* (asterisk), 226–227
\ (backslash), 227
! (bang), 231–232
!! (bang-bang), 231–232
[] (brackets), 218
.. (destination or parent directory), 246
$ (dollar sign), 218
^D (end of file), 243
- (hyphen), 251
| (pipe symbol), 224–225
prompt, 218
? (question mark), 226–227
\> (redirecting standard output), 243
/ (slash), 51, 52, 238
< (standard input), 243

• A •

AbiWord word processor, 15, 213–214
About to Install window, 50
absolute filename, 241
access and permission, 249–250
access point, 100–101
Account Configuration window, 44
Account Wizard (your e-mail browser),
    130, 131
Accounts tab (Internet Connection window),
    69, 70
Add a Printer Entry window (printtool), 211
Add New Launcher function (Panel), 150–152
adding
  file, 242–243
  hard drive, 260
  new account, 56–59
Address Book (Mozilla), 137
address conflict, 288–289
ad-hoc connection, 100–101
ADSL (asymmetrical DSL), 87, 90.
    See also DSL

• B •

aliasing command, 219–220
AOL Spinner, 189–190
Appearance menu (Sawfish), 155
appending standard output (>), 243, 244
Apple and Linux, 184
applications Web site, 214
Applixware (VistaSource), 199, 201
Applixware Office (Applix, Inc.), 313
apropos command, 381
archives, video, finding, 103
asterisk (*), 226–227
.asx file, 190
asymmetrical DSL. See ADSL
AT&T WorldNet, 64
Attach File dialog box (Mozilla), 136, 138
attachment to e-mail, sending, 136, 138
automatic partitioning at installation, 37–40
Automatic Partitioning window, 38
automating firewall, 121–124
awesfx, 173

background, changing, 154
backing up
  file before working on hard drive, 23
  importance of, 330–331, 347
  PDA database to computer, 166–167
backslash (\), 227
Backspace key, 225
backups. See backing up
bandwidth, 77, 78
bang (!), 231–232
bang-bang (!!), 231–232
bash shell
  command-line editing feature, 230
  commands and, 220
  as default, 55, 58
  history of, 221
  memory of, 230
  overview of, 217–220
  recalling filename, 232–233
  reexecution commands, 231–232
  syntax for commands, 221–224
Beowulf clusters, 14

BIOS (Basic Input/Output Settings), 19, 339
black hat, 76
blind alley, value of, 282
Blue Screen of Death, 13
Bookmark⊅Add (Nautilus), 163
bookmarking, 163
boot disk, creating
  at installation, 48
  before installation, 18
  Linux, 21–22
  Windows or MS-DOS, 20–21
Boot Loader Configuration window, 40
boot window, 53
booting. *See also* boot disk, creating
  from CD-ROM, 18–20
  definition of, 31, 52
  initial, steps for, 52–54
  into MS-DOS mode, 27
  troubleshooting, 317–318, 320–321
border for window, changing, 155
Bourne shell, 220, 221
brackets ([]), 218
bridge, 101
broadband connection. *See also*
    cable modem; DSL
  description of, 77
  network and, 63
  security issues, 329–330
  video clips and, 193
browser. *See also* Mozilla
  on CD-ROM, 15
  Galeon, 162
  Nautilus as, 162–163
  your e-mail, 130–133
buffer overflow, 329–330
bump, 190
burning CD, 178–181
buying
  cable modem, 81
  commercial X Server, 307
  dial-up modem, 65
  StarOffice, 203

● *C* ●

C shell, 221
cable modem
  buying, 81
  connecting via, 79–80
  description of, 77
  DOCSIS standard and, 81, 86
  down sides to, 79

Internet protocols, setting up, 82–86
  provider, finding, 80–81
  registering with ICP, 86
cable of network, checking, 285–286
cable programming, finding, 194
cable television (CATV), 78
Calc (StarOffice), 200
case sensitivity of filename, 236
cat command, 242–244
category 5 cable, 80
CATV (cable television), 78
cd command, 228, 241–242
cdparanoia, 177–178
cdrecord, 179, 180–181
CD-ROM. *See also* CD-ROM drive;
    CD-ROM, files on
  booting from, 18–20
  burning, 178–181
  converting to MP3, 184
  dismounting, 22
  ejecting from drive, 256
  installing RPM package from, 267–268
  mounting, 22
  playing with xmms, 170–171
  ripping, 177–178
  system requirements for, 383
  troubleshooting, 384
  uses for, 5
CD-ROM, files on
  block special files, 261
  installation guide, 32
  LOADLIN program, 320–321
  Mozilla, 128
  Netfilter/iptables, 16
  networking information, 97
  overview of, 383–384
  Publisher's edition operating system, 13
  rawrite.exe, 20
  window managers, 144
CD-ROM drive
  determining make and model, 336
  forcing system to use, 33
  troubleshooting, 321
central office (CO), 78
CERT Web site, 126
chain, 125
Change Connection Status window, 76
chgrp command, 250
children, 224, 237
chmod command, 252
Choose Hardware Device Type window, 102
Choose window, 75

chown command, 250
Cisco 675 or 678 DSL modem
 configuring, 93–95
 connecting, 89–92
CLI. *See* command line interface
Clockchip Configuration screen
 (Xconfigurator), 300–301
Close option, 148
closing window, 148
coaxial connector, 80
code
 open source, 12, 316
 typing, 2–3
color depth, 305
command line, deleting text from, 225
command-line editing feature
 (bash shell), 230
command line interface (CLI)
 graphical user interface compared to, 55–56
 Linux and, 141
 overview of, 235
 shell as, 217, 220–221
commands
 aliasing, 219–220
 apropos, 381
 bash shell and, 220
 cat, 242–244
 cd, 228, 241–242
 chgrp, 250
 chmod, 252
 chown, 250
 cp, 246–247
 date, 142
 dmesg, 260, 290, 338
 eject, 256
 history, 232
 less, 225–226
 ls, 220, 221–224, 228–229, 321
 ls -l, 249
 man, 371
 mkdir, 228, 245
 mkfs, 262
 more, 223–226, 287
 mount, 220
 mv, 219–220, 246–247
 options, 228–229
 pwd, 239–240
 reexecution, 231–232
 regular expressions, 226–227
 rm, 219–220, 247–248
 rmdir, 248
 rpm, 272, 273, 275

sort, 232, 244
startx, 50, 145, 304
su(1), 218
syntax for, 3, 221–224
tar, 328–329
touch, 229, 249
vi text editor, 365–367
which, 219
Community Supported RealPlayer Download
 Page (Real Network), 185
competition within cable industry, 80
Compose window (Mozilla), 136, 137
Composer function (Mozilla), 137
CompuServe, 64
computer
 laptop, 20, 65, 336
 name of, 2, 42
 running inside another computer, 168
conferences about Linux, 313–314
configuration utility, 16
Configure Filter window (printtool), 212
configuring
 Cisco DSL modem, 89–95
 DNS, 111–112
 Ethernet NIC, 101–107
 hard drive, 260
 host name, 110–111
 Internet connection, 66–73
 Mozilla, 128–133
 network at installation, 40–43, 353–354
 printer, 211–213
 RealPlayer, 195–196
 sound card, 173–181
 system at installation, 44–47
 wireless NIC, 101–103, 107–110
 X Server, 48
 X Windows System, 298–305
 your e-mail browser, 130–133
confirmation behavior of functions,
 changing, 160
connecting to Internet, 75–76
Consultants HOWTO document, 312
copying
 file or directory, 159–160, 246–247
 music, 177–178, 181
 window or screen, 163
Corel Corporation Web site, 199
corrupting file system, 256
cp command, 246–247
Create a New Internet Connection
 window, 66, 67
Create Launcher Applet window, 150–151, 207

Create New User window, 57
Create the Account window, 68, 70
cursor (GMIX Mixer), 172
Custom installation, 36, 38
Custom view, 161

• D •

^D (end of file), 243
Data Over Cable Service Interface
    Specification (DOCSIS), 81, 86
date command, 142
Default File Selection Dialog Path text box
    (GNOME RPM), 277
default operating system, 53, 54
default shell. *See* bash shell
defragmenting hard drive, 24–26
deleting
  e-mail message, 136
  file or directory, 160
  text from command line, 225
  text with vi, 364–365
  user account, 59
Desk Guide button, 152
desktop
  overview of, 146
  Sawfish window manager, 142, 143–144,
    155–156
  shortcut icon, creating on, 152, 162, 189,
    207–208
  StarOffice, 208–210
  switching between, 153
  virtual, 152–153
Desktop⇨Background, 154
desktop manager, 46. *See also* GNOME
desktop productivity tools, 15, 165–167. *See
    also* StarOffice
Desktop⇨Screensaver⇨Xjack, 154
destination directory (..), 246
Destroy option, 148
destructive repartitioning, 23
/dev directory, 237
device file, 71
Devices screen check, 82, 83
Devices tab (Network Configuration window),
    102, 103
DHCP (Dynamic Host Configuration Protocol)
  cable modem and, 82
  network, configuring system for, 41
  wireless network and, 107–108
dial-up modem, 63, 77. *See also* modem

Digital Subscriber Lines. *See* DSL
dip dial-up program, 72–73
directory. *See also* files
  copying, 159–160, 246–247
  creating, 160, 245
  deleting, 160
  file and, 236
  /home, 238–239, 241–242
  home, typing name of, 2–3
  man pages, 369–371
  as mount point, 255
  moving, 159, 246–247
  naming, 238
  overview of, 237
  ownership of, 249–250
  /proc, 288
  removing, 248
  subdirectory and, 237
  /usr/doc, 379
  viewing, 160–161
  working, 239, 241
directory path, specifying, 240
disabling Ethernet adapter, 109
disk drive, adding, 258–259
Disk Partitioning Setup window, 37
dismounting CD, 22
displaying firewall rules, 124–125
dmesg command, 260, 290, 338
DNS (Domain Name Server)
  configuring, 111–112
  IP address and, 43
  setting up, 73–75
DNS tab (Network Configuration
    window), 74, 75
documents and StarOffice, 209–210
dollar sign ($), 218
domain name, 112
Domain Name Server. *See* DNS
down arrow key, 225, 232
Download Community Supported Player Page
    (Real Network), 185
downloading
  RealPlayer, 184–188
  StarOffice, 201–203
Draw (StarOffice), 200
drive space, increasing, 258–262
Druid, 98. *See also* Network Configuration
    Druid; Service Configuration Druid
DSL
  Cisco modem, configuring, 93–95
  Cisco modem, connecting, 89–92

configuration overview, 87–88
description of, 77, 78, 86–87
equipment for, availability of, 81
provider, finding, 88–89
types of, 90–91
dual-boot system, 22
Dynamic Host Configuration Protocol.
    See DHCP
dynamic IP address, 126

• *E* •

Earthlink, 64
`ed` editor, 361, 362
Edge Flipping, turning on, 153
Edit⇨Changes (StarOffice), 209
Edit Local Printer Entry window
    (`printtool`), 212
Edit menu (StarOffice), 209
editing command at command line, 230
`eject` command, 256
`emacs` text editor, 361
e-mail
  getting, 135–136
  sending, 136–138
e-mail client (StarOffice), 200
emulating three-button mouse, 36,
    172–173, 296
encryption, 327
encryption key, 110
end of file (^D), 243
ending session, 59–60
Enter a Modem window, 66–67, 68
environment of shell, 222–223
`/etc/init.d/iptables` script, 122
`/etc/passwd` file, 58
`/etc/re.d/init.d/network` script, 114
Ethernet adapter. *See also* network
    interface card
  cable modem and, 82
  configuring, 101–110, 104–107
  disabling, 109
  LAN and, 97
  reseating, 286
Ethernet Device General window, 82, 84
Ethernet Device Protocol window, 84
Ethernet Device window, 104
Ethernet hub or switch, checking, 285–286
Ethernet or Wireless Device window, 102, 103
Evolution, 165–167
Evolution Configuration wizard, 167

`ex` line-oriented editor, 361–362
executable file, 237
execute permission, 251–252
exiting graphical boot menu, 53
expanding filename, 222
exporting file, 213
external modem, 65, 71
Extreme Linux system, 14

• *F* •

FAT or FAT32 partitions, 24, 26
FAT16 partitions, 26
fault tree, 282–283
`fdisk`, 261–262
file address, 51–52
File⇨Exit, 148
file manager, 209. *See also* Nautilus
File Manager menu (Nautilus), 159
File menu (StarOffice), 209
File⇨New⇨Directory (Nautilus), 160
File⇨Open Location (RealPlayer), 190
File⇨Open Web Location (Mozilla), 133
file permission, changing, 203
File⇨Print (StarOffice), 213
File⇨Quit, 148
file sharing, 14
file specification, 246
file system
  corrupting, 256
  making, 262
  mounting, 253–255
  overview of, 51–52, 253
  `pwd` command and, 239–240
  repairing, 256–258
  unmounting, 255–256
filename
  absolute, 241
  case sensitivity of, 236
  expanding, 222
  Linux, 236
  recalling, 232–233
  regular expressions for, 226–227
  relative, 240
files. *See also* directory
  .asx, 190
  backing up, 23, 328–329, 347
  copying, 159–160, 246–247
  creating and adding, 242–243
  deleting, 160
  `/etc/passwd`, 58

files *(continued)*
    importing and exporting, 213
    large, support for, 13
    moving, 159, 246–247
    .m3u, 192
    naming conventions, 227
    overview of, 235
    ownership of, 249–252
    PDF, reading, 164–165
    .ram, .ra, and .rm, 190
    removing, 247–248
    saving to /usr/local/src
        directory, 186, 187
files *(continued)*
    .sdw, 209
    storing, 236
    types of, 236–237
    viewing, 160–161
filtering rules
    displaying, 124–125
    permissive versus restrictive, 118
    saving to script, 121–122
    setting up, 118–121
Find and Replace feature (StarOffice), 209
finding
    radio stations, 189–190
    video clips, 192–194
fips utility, 23–24, 26–29
firewall. *See also* iptables
    automating, 121–124
    description of, 16, 115
    displaying rules, 124–125
    DSL and, 95
    filtering rules, 118–122
    getting RealPlayer through, 194–196
    importance of, 116, 327–328
    proxying, 196–198
    testing, 125–126
    turning off and on, 122–124
    using RealPlayer with, 196–198
flat file, 236
Focus Behavior menu (Sawfish), 155
focusing on window, 155
forcefully, 248
forcing system to use CD-ROM drive, 33
forwarding e-mail message, 136
frame style, 155
free block, 258
free distribution of Linux, 12
free software for Linux, 14–15, 200
fsck utility, 256–258
FTP (File Transfer Protocol) client, 16
FTP sites, Red Hat software, 16

fully protected multitasking, 13
functions and shells, 221
Fvwm, 144

• **G** •

Galeon, 162
gateway, 42, 106
general application, 145
generic monitor, 297
genmask, 291
Get StarOffice page (Sun Microsystems), 202
gEyes, 150
Ghost (Norton), 23, 24
Gimp, The, graphics manipulation program,
    15, 153, 163
G.Lite, 90
GLUE (Groups of Linux Users
    Everywhere), 313
GMIX Mixer, 171–173
GNOME (desktop manager)
    application running inside, 146–147
    closing window, 148
    as default, 46, 141
    focus of window, getting, 147
    logging out, 154
    login screen, 54
    maximizing window, 149
    minimizing window, 148, 149
    moving window, 147
    Nautilus and, 154–155, 157–162
    overview of, 13, 145–146
    resizing window, 148
    Sawfish window manager and, 143–144
    screen lock, 154
    shell, starting from within, 55–56
    starting automatically at boot time, 50
    terminal emulator, 144, 218
    virtual desktop, 152–153
    Workstation installation and, 31
GNOME File Manager, 146
GNOME Hint screen, 145
GNOME login window, 145, 146
GNOME Main Menu button, 59, 66
GNOME Panel
    Add New Launcher function, 150–152
    icons on, 149
    launching RealPlayer from, 188–189
    Main Menu button, 150, 152
    overview of, 119, 141, 146
    Panel submenu, 150
    Programs submenu, 150

GNOME RPM
  getting information about package, 272–273
  installing package, 267–270
  modifying defaults, 275–279
  overview of, 265
  removing package, 270–272
  starting, 265–266
  verifying package, 273–275
GNOME RPM window, 265, 266
gnorpm. *See* GNOME RPM
GNU, 221
Gnumeric, 163–164
Google and Nautilus, 162
GPL license, 200
graphical interface, 141, 143. *See also*
    X Window System
graphical manipulator, 163
graphical method of installation, 32
graphical user interface (GUI). *See also*
    GNOME; Nautilus; X Window System
  command-line interface compared to, 55–56
  OK button, 3
  Windows operating system and, 143
graphics library, 142
graphics program, 200
graphics server of X, 142
groff, 318
Gross, Terri, 191
group, 249, 250
GRUB, 40
gtv player, 183
GUI. *See* graphical user interface

• *H* •

Halt button, 60
halting computer, 154
hanging machine, 297–298
hard drive
  adding and configuring, 260
  backing up files before working on, 23
  defragmenting, 24–26
  free space on, 17
  increasing space on, 258–262
  installing, 260–261
  installing Linux on separate, 340
  logical block addressing, 339
  nondestructive repartitioning, 23–29
  number change since installation, 318–319
  partitioning, 261–262
  partitions of, 22, 259
  preparing, 18

space needed for Linux system, 28
space needed for StarOffice, 203, 205
types of, 339–340
hardware. *See also specific devices*
  determining make and model of, 336–337
  MS-DOS, getting information from, 344–347
  requirements for, 335–336
  types of, 337–338
  Windows, getting information from, 341–344
Hardware Device tab (Wireless Device
    Configuration window), 109
Hardware tab (Network Configuration
    window), 102, 103
Hatfield, Ken, 282
HDSL, 90
help. *See* HOWTO documents; man pages;
    training and support; troubleshooting
Help Agent window (StarOffice), 210
Help menu (StarOffice), 210
helping other user, 318
high availability, 14
high bit-rate DSL, 90
high-speed connection. *See*
    broadband connection
history command, 232
history of Red Hat Linux, 11–12
/home directory, 238–239, 241–242
home directory, typing name of, 2–3
hostname
  configuring, 110–111
  entering, 85
Hosts tab (Network Configuration
    window), 111
HOWTO documents, 303, 310, 326
HTML editor (StarOffice), 200
HTTP protocol and RealPlayer, 195, 196
hyphen (-), 251

• *I* •

-i option, 248
ICMP (Internet Control Message Protocol)
    packet, 293
icon, creating on desktop,
    152, 162, 189, 207–208
icon bar, 144
iconifying window, 148
Icons view, 161
ICP (Internet cable provider), 79, 80–81, 86
IDE device, 180, 260–261, 318–319, 338–339
IDSL, 90
IEEE 802.11b standard, 99, 327

IMAP, 130
importing file, 213
Impress (StarOffice), 200
improvements and open source code, 12
Incoming Server window (your e-mail browser), 130, 132
increasing drive space, 258–262
infrastructure, 100–101
initial boot, steps for, 52–54
input, 224–225
Input screen, 82
Input window, 265, 266
Insert menu (StarOffice), 210
Insert⇨Tables (StarOffice), 210
inserting table into document, 210
Install Options window, 36
Install window (GNOME RPM), 267–268
installing. *See also* menu-based installation
  About to Install window, 50
  Account Configuration window, 44
  Automatic Partitioning window, 38
  Boot Loader Configuration window, 40
  CD-ROM writing utility, 179
  Disk Partitioning Setup window, 37
  documentation on, 383
  first screen, 33
  graphical versus text-based methods, 32
  hard drive, 260–261
  information needed prior to, 31–32
  Install Options window, 36
  installation guide, 32
  Installing Packages window, 48
  Keyboard Configuration window, 34, 35
  Language Selection window, 34
  Linux on separate hard drive, 340
  Mouse Configuration window, 34, 35
  network, 40–43
  Network Configuration window, 40, 41
  package, 264, 272
  point of no return, 47–48
  RealPlayer, 184–188
  RPM package from CD-ROM, 267–268
  RPM package from Internet, 268–270
  Selecting Package Groups window, 46
  StarOffice, 203–206
  starting process, 33–36
  stopping process, 32, 47
  system, configuring, 44–47
  Time Zone Selection window, 43
  types of installations, 36–37
  Workstation installation, 31, 36–40
  X Configuration window, 46–47, 49
  X Server, 48–50

Installing Packages window, 48
Institute of Electrical and Electronic Engineers (IEEE), 99
integrated product, 13
internal modem, 65, 71–72
Internet. *See also* broadband connection
  accessing, 15–16
  black hat and, 76
  connecting to, 75–76
  installing RPM package from, 268–270
  Mozilla, navigating with, 133–135
  Nautilus, navigating with, 162–163
Internet cable provider. *See* ICP
Internet Connection window, 66, 67, 69, 70
Internet integration manager. *See* Nautilus
Internet Protocol. *See* IP
Internet service provider. *See* ISP
interrupt conflict, 288–289
intranet, accessing, 15–16
IO address, 288–289
IP (Internet Protocol)
  Domain Name Service and, 42
  netmask and, 41
  network address classes, 106
  port and, 117
IP address
  description of, 41
  DNS and, 73
  gateway and, 42
  genmask, 291
  public versus private, 105
  routable versus non-routable, 88
IP packet, 117
ipchains, 117
ipconfig program, 286–287
iptables
  overview of, 117–118
  preventing automatic start of script, 124
  setting up, 118–121
iptables-save utility, 121–122
isapnp program, 288
ISDN, 65
ISDN Digital Subscriber Loop (IDSL), 90
ISP (Internet service provider)
  backup DNS server address, 112
  configuring connection, 66–70
  finding, 64–66
  ICP and, 80

• J •

journaled file system, 14

• K •

K Desktop Environment (KDE)
  choosing, 46
  overview of, 13, 141, 144
  Red Hat User Manager and, 56
kernel, 12, 289–291. *See also* Linux
    operating system
kernel module, 106–107
Keyboard Configuration window, 34, 35
keyboard focus, 155
keyboard shortcuts
  Ctrl+Alt+Backspace (shut down session),
    60, 154, 306
  Ctrl+Alt+Delete (reboot), 29, 47
  Ctrl+Alt+Minus (switch resolution), 302
  Ctrl+Alt+Plus (switch resolution), 302
  Ctrl+C (halt command), 230
  Ctrl+D (exit cat command), 243
  Ctrl+P (rerun entered command), 232
  Ctrl+U (delete text from command
    line), 225
  Ctrl+X (exit graphical boot menu), 53
keystrokes, 3
Kill App option, 148
Korn, David, 221
Korn shell, 221
kudzu utility, 71

• L •

LAN (local area network). *See also*
    Network Configuration Druid
  ad-hoc or infrastructure, choosing, 100–101
  configuring Ethernet or wireless NIC,
    101–110
  connecting to, 97
  creating, 98
  firewall and, 116
  preparing to configure wireless NIC, 99–100
Language Selection window, 34
laptop, 20, 65, 336
Laptop installation, 36, 37
large file support, 13
launching. *See* starting
left arrow key, 225
less command, 225–226
LILO (Linux Loader)
  Custom installation and, 39
  Master Boot Record and, 317–318
  purpose of, 53
  removing, 320

selecting as boot loader at installation, 40
  troubleshooting boot failure, 320–321
links text-based Web browser, 15
Linux International Web site, 313, 314, 315
Linux Journal, 199
Linux Loader. *See* LILO
Linux operating system
  Apple and, 184
  boot disk, creating with, 21–22
  distribution of, 13
  file system, 51–52
  free software for, 14–15
  future of, 7
  hard drive space required for, 28
  history of, 11–12
  interfaces for, 141
  TCP/IP networking and, 98
  Web sites related to, 133, 313–314
Linux User Group, 64
List view, 161
LOADLIN program, 320–321
local area network. *See* LAN
localhost.localdomain, 42
locating modem
  with Linux, 71–72
  with Windows, 73
logging in, 45, 54–55, 219–220
logging off, 59–60
logging out, 154
logical block addressing, 339
login account, 80
login name, 68. *See also* user name
login screen, 54
logs, checking, 331
loopback interface, 119, 287, 290, 291
Loudness control (GMIX Mixer), 172
ls command
  options, 228–229, 249
  troubleshooting, 321
  uses of, 220, 221–224
lynx text-based Web browser, 15

• M •

MAC address, 86
Main Menu button (Panel), 150
man command, 371
man pages
  apropos command and, 381
  overview of, 369–371, 382
  topics in, 372–381
Master Boot Record (MBR), 48, 317–318, 322

maximizing window, 149
memory
  non-volatile, 93
  video, 49, 336
menu bar (StarOffice), 209–210
menu-based installation
  network, configuring, 353–355
  point of no return, 355–356
  restarting system, 359–360
  starting, 349–353
  X, configuring, 356–359
Metrolink, 305
MHz (Megahertz), 87
Microsoft. *See also* Windows
    operating system
  NTFS file system, 23, 24
  Windows Media Player, 184, 190
  Word Track Changes feature, 201
MIME (Multipurpose Internet Mail Extension)
    types, 162
minicom terminal emulator, 91–92
minimizing window, 148, 149
Miscellaneous section (Sawfish), 156
mkdir command, 228, 245
mkfs command, 262
mkisofs utility, 179
modem. *See also* cable modem; DSL; ISP
  analog, 78
  buying, 65
  configuring, 66–73
  dial-up, 63, 77
  dip dial-up program and, 72–73
  external, 65, 71
  internal, 65, 71–72
  locating with Linux, 71–72
  locating with Windows, 73
  transmission of data packets by, 86
Modems tab (Internet Connection window),
    69, 70
modifying
  GNOME properties, 154–155
  GNOME RPM defaults, 275–279
  modem settings, 67
  user account, 59
monitor
  choosing at installation, 49
  finding information about, 296
  resolution and, 49, 296–297, 299
  Xconfigurator options, 297

Monitor Setup window (Xconfigurator),
    299, 300
more command, 223–226, 287
mount command, 220
mount point, 52
mounting
  CD, 22
  file system, 253–255, 257
mouse
  emulating three-button, 36, 172–173, 296
  finding information about, 296
  keyboard focus and, 155
  selecting, 35–36
Mouse Configuration window, 34, 35
movie trailers, finding, 193
moving
  file or directory, 159, 246–247
  text in vi, 364–365
  window, 147
Mozilla (Web browser)
  Address Book, 137
  AOL Spinner and, 189–190
  Composer function, 137
  configuring, 128–133
  getting e-mail, 135–136
  history settings, 128–130
  home page, picking, 128, 130
  MP3 and, 192
  navigating with, 133–135
  release of, 127
  sending e-mail, 136–138
  speed and, 15
  StarOffice e-mail client compared to, 200
  your e-mail browser, configuring, 130–133
Mozilla INBOX window, 135
MP3, 171, 191–192
MS-DOS
  boot disk, creating with, 20–21
  defragmenting hard drive in, 26
  fips utility, 23–24, 26–29
  getting hardware information from, 344–347
.m3u file, 192
Multimedia group packages window, 265, 266
Multipurpose Internet Mail Extension (MIME)
    types, 162
multiscanning monitor, 49, 296
multitasking
  fully protected, 13
  security issues with, 76, 116

music. *See also* RealPlayer (Real Network)
  copying, 177–178, 181
  radio stations, finding, 189–190
  video clips, finding, 103
mv command, 219–220, 246–247

• *N* •

naming conventions, 227
naming directory, 238
naming file. *See* filename
NAT (network address translation), 88
NAT (network address translation)
    rules, 119
Nautilus
  copying file or directory, 159–160
  creating directory, 160
  deleting file or directory, 160
  moving file or directory, 159
  navigating Internet with, 162–163
  overview of, 157
  RealPlayer 8 icon in, 187
  running programs and scripts, 161–162
  setting preferences with, 154–155
  starting manually, 158
  viewing file or directory, 160–161
Nautilus window, 203, 204
navigating Internet
  with Mozilla, 133–135
  with Nautilus, 162–163
Net. *See* Internet
Netfilter/iptables. *See also* iptables
  overview of, 16, 117–118, 327–328
  starting, 122
netmask, 41, 106
Netnews, 310–311
Netscape. *See also* Mozilla
  Communicator 4.78, 15, 127, 128
  Navigator, 127
network. *See also* LAN
  boot disk, creating for, 20–21
  broadband connection and, 63
  configuring at installation, 40–43, 353–355
  encryption and, 327
  flexibility of with file sharing, 14
  GNOME RPM and, 277–278
  manually starting and stopping, 113–114
  RealPlayer and, 198
  restarting, 85
  troubleshooting, steps for, 283–293

wireless, 98, 101
network address translation (NAT), 88
network address translation (NAT)
    rules, 119
network bridge, 81
Network Configuration Druid
  overview of, 98–99, 100
  starting, 102–104
  troubleshooting, 113
Network Configuration window
  configuring system at installation, 40, 41
  Devices tab, 102, 103
  DNS tab, 74, 75
  Hardware tab, 102, 103
  Hosts tab, 111
network interface card (NIC). *See also*
    Ethernet adapter
  ad-hoc or infrastructure, choosing, 100–101
  cost of, 98
  Ethernet, configuring, 101–107
  PnP (Plug and Play) type, 288
  preparing to configure, 99–100
  wireless, configuring, 101–104, 107–110
Network Preferences window
    (GNOME RPM), 278
news clips, finding, 193–194
newsgroups, 310–311
NIC. *See* network interface card
nmap, 331, 379
nondestructive repartitioning, 23–29
non-routable address, 88
non-volatile memory, 93
notebook computer, 20, 65, 336
NT boot record (Windows), 39
NTFS file system (Microsoft), 23, 24

• *O* •

office suites, 15, 315. *See also* StarOffice
OK button, clicking, 3
online distribution of Linux, 12
Open File dialog box (Mozilla), 134
Open Location window (RealPlayer), 190–191
Open Page dialog box (Mozilla), 133–134
Open Secure Shell. *See* OpenSSH
open source code, 12, 318
open source software, 127
opening Web page, 133
OpenSSH, 16, 101, 327

operating system. *See also* Linux operating
     system; Windows operating system
   coexistence of, 17
   default, 53, 54
   kernel, 12, 289–291
   security vulnerability and, 326
   separating command interface from,
     220–221
   standalone versus dual-boot, 22
   tweaking, 12
   UNIX, 12
organizing bookmarks, 163
Other Options window, 68, 69
output, 224–225
overdriving, 297
owned by hacker, 116
ownership of file, 249–252

• P •

package. *See also* RPM (Red Hat
     Package Manager)
   description of, 263
   getting information about, 272–273
   installing, 267–270, 272
   modifying default settings, 275–279
   removing, 270–272
   verifying, 273–275
Package Info window (GNOME RPM), 273
pager applet, 152
Panel. *See* GNOME Panel
Panel submenu (Panel), 150
parallel port, 211
parent, 224, 237
parent directory (...), 246
partition. *See also* partitioning
   description of, 22
   modifying default, 39
   mount point, 52
partitioning
   automatic at installation, 37
   hard drive, 259, 261–262
   nondestructive repartitioning, 23–29
password
   Cisco modem, 93
   DSL modem, 88
   etiquette for, 45
   mistake in, making, 54
   Pluggable Authentication Module (PAM)
     and, 58
   PPP compared to login, 68

root user, 45
   security and, 330
   typing, 58
PATH variable, 222
PC, virtual, creating, 168
PCI Probe Results dialog box
     (sndconfig), 174
PCI Probe screen (Xconfigurator), 298
PCMCIA card, 20, 65
PDA, Evolution and, 165–167
PDF file, reading, 164–165
penguin logo, 11, 12, 134
permission
   changing, 203, 252
   granting, 249–250
   mounting or unmounting file
     system and, 257
   specifying, 251–252
Permissions tab (Nautilus Properties
     window), 203, 204
personal firewall, 116
personal workstation, boosting, 14–15
pine text-based e-mail reader, 15
pinging, 292–293
pipe symbol (|), 224–225
piping, 224–225
plain old telephone service (POTS),
     77, 86–87
playmidi, 173
Pluggable Authentication Module
     (PAM), 58
PNA protocol, 195, 198
PnP (Plug and Play) NIC, 288
point-to-point protocol (PPP), 64
POP, 130
port, 117
porting, 14
PPP (point-to-point protocol), 64
PPP account name and password, 68
PPP connection, 293
PPP connection status window, 76
Preferences⇨Sawfish, 155
Preferences window
   GNOME RPM, 275–279
   Mozilla, 128, 129–130
   RealPlayer, 195, 196
preparing hard drive, 18
primary DNS, 42
printer, configuring, 211–213
printing with StarOffice, 213
printtool configuration tool, 211–213
Prism Access, 64

Prism2 (Intersil), 99
private IP address, 105
private network. *See* LAN
/proc directory, 288
proc file system, 175
/proc/sound file, 175
program, running, 161–162
Programs⇨Applications⇨AbiWord, 214
Programs⇨Applications⇨Gnumeric, 163
Programs⇨Applications⇨Nautilus, 158
Programs⇨Applications⇨xpdf, 164
Programs⇨Graphics⇨The Gimp, 163
Programs⇨Multimedia⇨Audio Mixer, 171–173
Programs⇨Multimedia⇨gtv, 183
Programs⇨Multimedia⇨xmms, 192
Programs⇨Multimedia⇨XMMX, 170
Programs submenu (Panel), 150
Programs⇨System⇨GNOME RPM, 265
prompt (#), 218
Properties window (Nautilus), 203, 204
proprietary software, 12
Proxy Server text box (RealPlayer), 197
proxying firewall, 196–198, 277–278
PS/2 bus mouse, 296
public IP address, 105
Putty, 16
pwd command, 239–240

• *Q* •

querying package, 265
question mark (?), 226–227
QuickTime (Apple), 184
Qwest, 89

• *R* •

radio stations, finding, 189–190
.ram, .ra, and .rm files, 190
read permission, 251–252
reading PDF file, 164–165
read-only permission, 257
Real Audio, Inc., 190, 192–193
RealAudio connection and firewall, 115
RealJukebox (RealAudio), 184
Really log out? window, 59–60
RealPlayer (Real Network)
    downloading and installing, 184–188
    firewall and, 115, 194–198
    launching from GNOME Panel, 188–189

overview of, 15
support for, 184
using, 190–191
video clips and, 192–194
Web site, 190
RealPlayer8 Welcome window, 188
real-time programming, 14
reboot
    Ctrl+Alt+Delete, 29, 47
    definition of, 31, 52
Reboot button, 60
recalling filename, 232–233
recursively, 248
Red Hat Dialup Configuration utility, 66–70
Red Hat Linux
    features of, 13–14
    future of, 7
    history of, 11–12
    as integrated product, 13
    Web site, 126, 312, 328
Red Hat Network configuration window,
        82, 83
Red Hat Package Manager. *See*
        GNOME RPM; RPM
Red Hat PPP dialer utility, 75–76
Red Hat User Manager, 56–59
redirecting standard output (>), 243
reexecution commands, 231–232
registering cable modem with ICP, 86
regular expressions, 226–227
relative filename, 240
Remove All Partitions on This System option
        (Automatic Partitioning window), 38
removing
    directory, 248
    file, 247–248
    LILO, 320
    package, 264
    RPM package, 270–272
    repairing file system, 256–258
repartitioning, 23–29
replying to e-mail, 136
requirements
    hard drive space for Linux, 28
    hard drive space for StarOffice, 203, 205
    system for CD-ROM, 383
Rescan function (Nautilus), 158
reseating Ethernet adapter, 286
resizing
    partitions, 23–24, 26–29
    window, 148

resolution
  color depth and, 305
  description of, 302
  monitor and, 49, 296–297, 299
resources. *See* training and support;
    Web sites
Restart button (Service Configuration
    window), 123
restarting network, 85
restoring Master Boot Record, 320
restrictive filtering rules, 118
revision marks, 201
RG45 connector, 80
RG78 coaxial port, 80
right arrow key, 225
ripping CD, 177–178
Ritchie, Dennis, 220
`rm` command, 219–220, 247–248
`rmdir` command, 248
root directory, 51, 237–238, 253
root file system, 254
root partition, 52
root user
  `cat` command and, 242
  logging in as, 55
  password for, 45
  reexecution commands and, 231
routable address, 88
router, 101
`rplay` package, 269
RPM (Red Hat Package Manager), 263–265.
    See also GNOME RPM
`rpm` command, 272, 273, 275
RPM package. *See* package
Rpmfind window (GNOME RPM), 269, 278
RTSP protocol, 195, 198

• S •

Sans Web site, 126, 326
satellite connection, 65
saving file to `/usr/local/src`
    directory, 186, 187
Sawfish window manager
  overview of, 143–144
  properties, setting with, 155–156
  X Window System and, 142
scalability, 14
ScanDisk, 29
Schedule (StarOffice), 200
screen lock, 154

screensaver, changing, 154
script, running, 161–162
SCSI drive, 180, 261, 318, 338–339
SDSL, 91
.sdw file, 209
search function (Nautilus), 162
secondary nameserver, 43
Secure Shell, 16, 329
Secure Socket Layer (SSL), 101, 327
security measures. *See also* firewall; security
    vulnerabilities
  ad-hoc connection and, 100
  backups, 328–329
  DSL and, 95
  DSL modem, 88
  encryption, 327
  logging in and, 54
  logs, checking, 331
  nmap, 331, 379
  screen lock, 154
  Web sites, 126
  wireless network and, 98, 101
security vulnerabilities. *See also*
    security measures
  broadband connection, 327–328
  buffer overflow, 329–330
  overview of, 325–326
  password, 330
  social engineering, 330
Select Installation Type window
    (StarOffice), 205
Select Video Modes screen (Xconfigurator),
    301, 302
Selecting Package Groups window, 46
sending e-mail, 136–138
serial mouse, 296
serial ports, 35–36, 71
Service Configuration Druid, 122–124
Service Configuration window, 113, 122, 123
session
  ending, 59–60
  starting, 54–55
shell. *See also* `bash` shell
  command options, 228–229
  environment of, 222–223
  history of, 220–221
  overview of, 55, 217
  regular expressions, 226–227
  wildcards, 236
shell script, 251, 321–322
shortcut icon, creating on desktop, 152, 162,
    189, 207–208

Show Properties menu, 189
shut down session (Ctrl+Alt+Backspace),
       60, 154
single-line DSL (SDSL), 91
sizing. *See* resizing
slash (/), 51, 52, 238
slice number, 180
slider (GMIX Mixer), 172
Small Computer System Interface
       (SCSI), 180, 261, 320, 338–339
sndconfig utility, 173–181
social engineering, 330
software
   free, for Linux, 14–15, 200
   GNU, 221
   Netfilter/iptables filtering,
       16, 117–118, 122
   open source, 127
   proprietary, 12
   RPM (Red Hat Package Manager), 263–265
   security vulnerability and, 326
   tar (tape archive system) and, 279
sort command, 232, 244
sound, transmitting through Web, 135
sound card
   setting up and testing, 173–181
   volume, controlling, 171–173
Sound Card Test screen (sndconfig), 176
Sound Configuration Introduction screen
       (sndconfig), 173–174
sound system. *See also* sound card
   GMIX Mixer, 171–173
   xmms, 170–171
sox, 173
special file, 237
splitterless ADSL, 90
spreadsheet program, 163–164, 200
SprintLink, 64
SSC, 311
SSL (Secure Socket Layer), 101, 327
standalone system, 22
standard input, 222, 223
standard output, 222, 223
standard VGA, 297
StarOffice (Sun Microsystems)
   adding launcher applet for, 150–152
   advantages of, 206
   availability of, 15
   desktop, 208–210
   downloading, 201–203
   Find and Replace feature, 209

importing and exporting files, 213
installing, 203–206
Microsoft Word compared to, 168
overview of, 14, 200–201
printing, 211–213
starting, 207–208
Track Changes feature, 201, 209
version 6.0 compared to version 5.2, 206
StarOffice desktop window, 208
Start button (Service Configuration
       window), 123
Start Here window (GNOME Nautilus control
       utility), 154, 155
starting
   Gimp, 163
   GNOME RPM, 265–266
   Gnumeric, 163
   installation, 33–36
   Nautilus, 158
   Netfilter/iptables, 122
   network manually, 113–114
   RealPlayer from Panel, 188–189
   session, 54–55
   StarOffice, 207–208
   terminal emulator program, 218
   vi editor, 362
   X, 145, 306, 325
   X Server at boot, 49–50
   xmms MP3 player, 192
   xpdf, 164
Starting X screen (Xconfigurator), 303, 304
startx command, 50, 145, 306
stateful filtering, 117, 118
Stereo Spearation control
       (GMIX Mixer), 172
stopping
   installation process, 32, 47
   network manually, 113–114
   X Window System, 154, 308
storing file, 236
streaming MP3, 191
streaming multimedia player, 15
streaming technology, 183
streaming video, 192
subdirectory, 51, 237
Sun Microsystems. *See* StarOffice
super VGA, 297
superuser
   logging in as, 219–220
   password for, 45
   su(1) command and, 218

support. *See* training and support
swap space partition, 52
switching
  between desktops, 153
  between resolutions, 301
Symmetric DSL, 91
symmetric multiprocessing, 14, 333
syntax for commands, 3, 221–224
system, configuring at installation, 44–47
system administration tools. *See also*
      Network Configuration Druid
  network, 74–75
  Red Hat User Manager, 56–59
  rpm command, 272, 273, 275
system data file, 236

• T •

Tab key, 3, 233
tar (tape archive system), 264, 279, 328–329
TCP transport protocol, 195
TCP/IP Settings window
  Ethernet NIC, 83, 84, 104, 105, 106
  wireless NIC, 107, 108, 109
telephone network system, 78
telephone service and Internet
      connection, 65
Telnet, 16, 126
temporary IP address, 126
terminal emulation window, 119, 145, 218, 219
terminal emulator
  bash shell and, 217–218
  creating user account from, 59
  minicom, 91–92
  X Window System and, 143, 144–145
terminal session, 55–56
tertiary nameserver, 43
testing
  boot from CD-ROM, 19
  firewall, 125–126
  sound card, 173–181
text, deleting from command line, 225
text editor
  overview of, 361–362
  vi, 361–367
  xedit, 145
text-based installation, 32
text-based system, 55
text-based Web browser, 15
Thinnet, 285
Thompson, Ken, 220
three-button emulation, 36, 172–173, 296

time, setting, 323–324
Time Zone Selection window, 43
Tools menu (StarOffice), 210
Torvalds, Linus, 12, 176, 191
Toshiba Libretto laptop, 20
touch command, 229, 249
Track Changes feature, 201, 209
training and support. *See also*
      troubleshooting
  books, 309–310
  college courses, 310
  commercial applications, 312–313
  conferences, 314–315
  Consultants HOWTO, 312
  distribution makers, 312
  Netnews, 310–311
  resellers, 312
  user group, 304, 311
  Web sites, 313–314
troubleshooting. *See also* training
      and support
  boot failure, 19–20, 317–318, 320–321
  cable modem and, 79
  CD-ROM, 386
  CD-ROM drive not detected, 319
  fault tree, 282–283
  hard drive number change, 318–319
  HOWTO documents, 301, 310
  ls command, 321
  modems, 72–73
  network, steps for, 283–293
  overview of, 281–282
  RealPlayer and firewall, 198
  restoring Master Boot Record, 320
  shell script loss, 321–322
  tips for, 315–316
  wrong time, 323–324
  X Window System, 304, 322–323
true color, 301
turning firewall off and on, 122–124, 198
turning on Edge Flipping, 153
Tux, 12
tweaking operating system, 12
typing
  code, 2–3
  URL into browser, 133

• U •

Universal DSL, 90
UNIX operating system, 12, 220–221
unmounting file system, 255–256, 257

up arrow key, 225, 232
Up One Level button (StarOffice), 209
upgrading package, 264, 270
URL, typing into browser, 133
USENIX Web site, 126, 314, 326
user account
  creating, 45–46, 56–59
  ownership and, 249–250
user data file, 236
user group, 64, 304, 311
user ID, 250
User Manager help window, 56–57
User Mount Tool window, 254, 255
user name, 2, 58
User Name and Password window, 68, 69
user-level program, 142
/usr/doc directory, 379
/usr/doc/HOWTO directory, 97
/usr/local/src directory, 186, 187
utilities. *See also* Nautilus; Network
    Configuration Druid
  cdrecord, 179, 180–181
  CD-ROM writing, 179
  configuration, 16
  fips, 23–24, 26–29
  fsck, 256–258
  GNOME Nautilus control, 154–155
  iptables, 117–121, 124
  iptables-save, 121–122
  kudzu, 71
  mkisofs, 179
  Netfilter/iptables, 327–328
  network system administrative tool, 74
  printtool configuration tool, 211–213
  Red Hat Dialup Configuration, 66–70
  Red Hat PPP dialer, 75–76
  sndconfig, 173–181
  xdb, 307

• **_V_** •

VDSL, 91
verifying package, 265, 273–275
Verifying Packages window
    (GNOME RPM), 274
very high bit-rate DSL (VDSL), 91
vi text editor, 361–367
video card and video memory, 49, 338
video clips, finding, 192–194
video controller card, 295–296, 305
video memory, 297, 303

Video Memory screen (Xconfigurator),
    299, 300
video streaming, 183
View as List button (Nautilus), 160–161
View menu (StarOffice), 210
View⇨Statistics (RealPlayer), 191
viewing
  file or directory, 160–161
  Web page, 162
vim text editor, 362
virtual desktop, 152–153
virtual PC, creating, 168
viruses, 54
VistaSource Web site, 199
VMwareWorkstation (VMware, Inc.), 168

• **_W_** •

war driving, 100
Wavelan (Lucent Technologies), 99
Web browser. *See also* browser; Mozilla
Web page
  creating, 137
  HTML editor and, 200
  opening, 133
  viewing, 162
Web sites
  conferences, 313–314
  Consultants HOWTO document, 312
  drivers for Prism2, 99
  GNOME applications, 165
  GPL license, 200
  Linux International, 313, 314, 315
  Linux Journal, 199
  Linux User Groups, 64
  Linux-related, 133, 214
  Metrolink, 305
  MP3, 191–192
  newsgroups, 310–311
  Norton, 24
  Putty, 16
  Real Audio, 192–193
  Real Network, 184
  RealPlayer, 190
  Red Hat Linux, 126, 312, 328
  Sans, 326
  security issues, 126, 326
  SSC, 311
  Sun Microsystems, 201
  training and support, 313–314
  USENIX, 314
  video clips, 192, 193

Web sites *(continued)*
  VistaSource, 199
  VMWare, Inc., 168
  WRTI, 191
  XFree, 304
  XFree86, 305
  Xi Graphics, 305
Welcome screen (Xconfigurator), 298
Welcome to the Installation window
    (StarOffice), 204, 205
Welcome to Red Hat Linux screen (Mozilla),
    128, 129
which command, 219
WIFI, 101
wildcards, 226–227, 236
window, working with, 147–149
window manager program, 142, 143–144,
    155–156. *See also* GNOME; StarOffice
Window menu (StarOffice), 210
Windows Media Player (Microsoft),
    184, 190
Windows operating system
  Blue Screen of Death, 13
  boot disk, creating with, 20–21
  coexistence with, 17
  defragmenting hard drive in, 24–25
  getting hardware information from, 341–344
  GUI and, 143
  installation process and, 38, 39
  installing on virtual PC, 168
  locating modem with, 73
  mounting files from floppy disk, 254–255
  NT boot record, 39
  partitioning and, 24
WinModem, 65
Wireless Device Configuration window,
    107, 109
wireless equivalent privacy, 101
wireless network, 98, 99, 101
wireless NIC, configuring, 107–110
Wireless Settings window, 109–110
word processor
  AbiWord, 15, 213–214
  StarOffice, 200
  Track Changes feature, 201
  WordPerfect 8, 199
WordPerfect Office (Corel), 199
working directory, 239, 241
workstation, boosting personal, 14–15
Workstation installation
  overview of, 31
  partitions and, 52
  steps of, 36–40
  xmms and, 170

write permission, 251–252
Writer (StarOffice), 200
WRTI Web site, 191

X Configuration window, 46–47, 49
X Server
  buying commercial, 305
  installing, 48–50
  overview of, 142
  starting automatically at boot time, 49–50
X Window System
  configuring, 298–303, 356–359
  general applications and, 145
  overview of, 13, 141
  parts of, 142
  programs that interact with, 143
  purpose of, 295
  starting, 145, 304, 323
  stopping, 154, 306
  terminal emulator and, 144–145
  troubleshooting, 304, 322–323
  virtual color map capability, 303
  window manager and, 143–144
Xconfigurator program, 298–303
xdb utility, 305
xDSL, 91
xedit, 145
XF86config file, 297
xfig, 145
XFree86 team, 305
XFree Web site, 304
Xi Graphics, 305
Ximian Evolution, 165–167
.xinitrc file, 298
xmms MP3 player, 15, 170–171, 192
xpaint, 145
xpdf, 164–165
Xterm. *See* terminal emulator

your e-mail browser, configuring, 130–133
You're Done screen (Xconfigurator),
    301, 303

• Z •

zip data-compression program, 15

redhat®

www.redhat.com

[more information available at http://www.gnu.org/copyleft/gpl.html]

GNU GENERAL PUBLIC LICENSE

Version 2, June 1991
Copyright © 1989, 1991 Free Software Foundation, Inc.
59 Temple Place, Suite 330, Boston, MA 02111-1307, USA

Preamble

The licenses for most software are designed to take away your freedom to share and change it. By contrast, the GNU General Public License is intended to guarantee your freedom to share and change free software — to make sure the software is free for all its users. This General Public License applies to most of the Free Software Foundation's software and to any other program whose authors commit to using it. (Some other Free Software Foundation software is covered by the GNU Library General Public License instead.) You can apply it to your programs, too.

When we speak of free software, we are referring to freedom, not price. Our General Public Licenses are designed to make sure that you have the freedom to distribute copies of free software (and charge for this service if you wish), that you receive source code or can get it if you want it, that you can change the software or use pieces of it in new free programs; and that you know you can do these things.

To protect your rights, we need to make restrictions that forbid anyone to deny you these rights or to ask you to surrender the rights. These restrictions translate to certain responsibilities for you if you distribute copies of the software, or if you modify it.

For example, if you distribute copies of such a program, whether gratis or for a fee, you must give the recipients all the rights that you have. You must make sure that they, too, receive or can get the source code. And you must show them these terms so they know their rights.

We protect your rights with two steps: (1) copyright the software, and (2) offer you this license which gives you legal permission to copy, distribute and/or modify the software.

Also, for each author's protection and ours, we want to make certain that everyone understands that there is no warranty for this free software. If the software is modified by someone else and passed on, we want its recipients to know that what they have is not the original, so that any problems introduced by others will not reflect on the original authors' reputations.

Finally, any free program is threatened constantly by software patents. We wish to avoid the danger that redistributors of a free program will individually obtain patent licenses, in effect making the program proprietary. To prevent this, we have made it clear that any patent must be licensed for everyone's free use or not licensed at all.

The precise terms and conditions for copying, distribution and modification follow.

TERMS AND CONDITIONS FOR COPYING, DISTRIBUTION, AND MODIFICATION

0. This License applies to any program or other work which contains a notice placed by the copyright holder saying it may be distributed under the terms of this General Public License. The "Program", below, refers to any such program or work, and a "work based on the Program" means either the Program or any derivative work under copyright law: that is to say, a work containing the Program or a portion of it, either verbatim or with modifications and/or translated into another language. (Hereinafter, translation is included without limitation in the term "modification".) Each licensee is addressed as "you".

   Activities other than copying, distribution and modification are not covered by this License; they are outside its scope. The act of running the Program is not restricted, and the output from the Program is covered only if its contents constitute a work based on the Program (independent of having been made by running the Program). Whether that is true depends on what the Program does.

1. You may copy and distribute verbatim copies of the Program's source code as you receive it, in any medium, provided that you conspicuously and appropriately publish on each copy an appropriate copyright notice and disclaimer of warranty; keep intact all the notices that refer to this License and to the absence of any warranty; and give any other recipients of the Program a copy of this License along with the Program.

   You may charge a fee for the physical act of transferring a copy, and you may at your option offer warranty protection in exchange for a fee.

2. You may modify your copy or copies of the Program or any portion of it, thus forming a work based on the Program, and copy and distribute such modifications or work under the terms of Section 1 above, provided that you also meet all of these conditions:

   a) You must cause the modified files to carry prominent notices stating that you changed the files and the date of any change.

   b) You must cause any work that you distribute or publish, that in whole or in part contains or is derived from the Program or any part thereof, to be licensed as a whole at no charge to all third parties under the terms of this License.

   c) If the modified program normally reads commands interactively when run, you must cause it, when started running for such interactive use in the most ordinary way, to print or display an announcement including an appropriate copyright notice and a notice that there is no warranty (or else, saying that you provide a warranty) and that users may redistribute the program under these conditions, and telling the user how to view a copy of this License. (Exception: if the Program itself is interactive but does not normally print such an announcement, your work based on the Program is not required to print an announcement.)

   These requirements apply to the modified work as a whole. If identifiable sections of that work are not derived from the Program, and can be reasonably considered independent and separate works in themselves, then this License, and its terms, do not apply to those sections when you distribute them as separate works. But when you distribute the same sections as part of a whole which is a work based on the Program, the distribution of the whole must be on the terms of this License, whose permissions for other licensees extend to the entire whole, and thus to each and every part regardless of who wrote it.

Thus, it is not the intent of this section to claim rights or contest your rights to work written entirely by you; rather, the intent is to exercise the right to control the distribution of derivative or collective works based on the Program. In addition, mere aggregation of another work not based on the Program with the Program (or with a work based on the Program) on a volume of a storage or distribution medium does not bring the other work under the scope of this License.

3. You may copy and distribute the Program (or a work based on it, under Section 2) in object code or executable form under the terms of Sections 1 and 2 above provided that you also do one of the following:

   a) Accompany it with the complete corresponding machine-readable source code, which must be distributed under the terms of Sections 1 and 2 above on a medium customarily used for software interchange; or,

   b) Accompany it with a written offer, valid for at least three years, to give any third party, for a charge no more than your cost of physically performing source distribution, a complete machine-readable copy of the corresponding source code, to be distributed under the terms of Sections 1 and 2 above on a medium customarily used for software interchange; or,

   c) Accompany it with the information you received as to the offer to distribute corresponding source code. (This alternative is allowed only for noncommercial distribution and only if you received the program in object code or executable form with such an offer, in accord with Subsection b above.)

The source code for a work means the preferred form of the work for making modifications to it. For an executable work, complete source code means all the source code for all modules it contains, plus any associated interface definition files, plus the scripts used to control compilation and installation of the executable. However, as a special exception, the source code distributed need not include anything that is normally distributed (in either source or binary form) with the major components (compiler, kernel, and so on) of the operating system on which the executable runs, unless that component itself accompanies the executable.

If distribution of executable or object code is made by offering access to copy from a designated place, then offering equivalent access to copy the source code from the same place counts as distribution of the source code, even though third parties are not compelled to copy the source along with the object code.

4. You may not copy, modify, sublicense, or distribute the Program except as expressly provided under this License. Any attempt otherwise to copy, modify, sublicense or distribute the Program is void, and will automatically terminate your rights under this License. However, parties who have received copies, or rights, from you under this License will not have their licenses terminated so long as such parties remain in full compliance.

5. You are not required to accept this License, since you have not signed it. However, nothing else grants you permission to modify or distribute the Program or its derivative works. These actions are prohibited by law if you do not accept this License. Therefore, by modifying or distributing the Program (or any work based on the Program), you indicate your acceptance of this License to do so, and all its terms and conditions for copying, distributing or modifying the Program or works based on it.

6. Each time you redistribute the Program (or any work based on the Program), the recipient automatically receives a license from the original licensor to copy, distribute or modify the Program subject to these terms and conditions. You may not impose any further restrictions on the recipients' exercise of the rights granted herein. You are not responsible for enforcing compliance by third parties to this License.

7. If, as a consequence of a court judgment or allegation of patent infringement or for any other reason (not limited to patent issues), conditions are imposed on you (whether by court order, agreement or otherwise) that contradict the conditions of this License, they do not excuse you from the conditions of this License. If you cannot distribute so as to satisfy simultaneously your obligations under this License and any other pertinent obligations, then as a consequence you may not distribute the Program at all. For example, if a patent license would not permit royalty-free redistribution of the Program by all those who receive copies directly or indirectly through you, then the only way you could satisfy both it and this License would be to refrain entirely from distribution of the Program.

   If any portion of this section is held invalid or unenforceable under any particular circumstance, the balance of the section is intended to apply and the section as a whole is intended to apply in other circumstances.

   It is not the purpose of this section to induce you to infringe any patents or other property right claims or to contest validity of any such claims; this section has the sole purpose of protecting the integrity of the free software distribution system, which is implemented by public license practices. Many people have made generous contributions to the wide range of software distributed through that system in reliance on consistent application of that system; it is up to the author/donor to decide if he or she is willing to distribute software through any other system and a licensee cannot impose that choice.

   This section is intended to make thoroughly clear what is believed to be a consequence of the rest of this License.

8. If the distribution and/or use of the Program is restricted in certain countries either by patents or by copyrighted interfaces, the original copyright holder who places the Program under this License may add an explicit geographical distribution limitation excluding those countries, so that distribution is permitted only in or among countries not thus excluded. In such case, this License incorporates the limitation as if written in the body of this License.

9. The Free Software Foundation may publish revised and/or new versions of the General Public License from time to time. Such new versions will be similar in spirit to the present version, but may differ in detail to address new problems or concerns.

   Each version is given a distinguishing version number. If the Program specifies a version number of this License which applies to it and "any later version", you have the option of following the terms and conditions either of that version or of any later version published by the Free Software Foundation. If the Program does not specify a version number of this License, you may choose any version ever published by the Free Software Foundation.

10. If you wish to incorporate parts of the Program into other free programs whose distribution conditions are different, write to the author to ask for permission. For software which is copyrighted by the Free Software Foundation, write to the Free Software Foundation; we sometimes make exceptions for this. Our decision will be guided by the two goals of preserving the free status of all derivatives of our free software and of promoting the sharing and reuse of software generally.

NO WARRANTY

11. BECAUSE THE PROGRAM IS LICENSED FREE OF CHARGE, THERE IS NO WARRANTY FOR THE PROGRAM, TO THE EXTENT PERMITTED BY APPLICABLE LAW. EXCEPT WHEN OTHERWISE STATED IN WRITING THE COPYRIGHT HOLDERS AND/OR OTHER PARTIES PROVIDE THE PROGRAM "AS IS" WITHOUT WARRANTY OF ANY KIND, EITHER EXPRESSED OR IMPLIED, INCLUDING, BUT NOT LIMITED TO, THE IMPLIED WARRANTIES OF MERCHANTABILITY AND FITNESS FOR A PARTICULAR PURPOSE. THE ENTIRE RISK AS TO THE QUALITY AND PERFORMANCE OF THE PROGRAM IS WITH YOU. SHOULD THE PROGRAM PROVE DEFECTIVE, YOU ASSUME THE COST OF ALL NECESSARY SERVICING, REPAIR OR CORRECTION.

12. IN NO EVENT UNLESS REQUIRED BY APPLICABLE LAW OR AGREED TO IN WRITING WILL ANY COPYRIGHT HOLDER, OR ANY OTHER PARTY WHO MAY MODIFY AND/OR REDISTRIBUTE THE PROGRAM AS PERMITTED ABOVE, BE LIABLE TO YOU FOR DAMAGES, INCLUDING ANY GENERAL, SPECIAL, INCIDENTAL OR CONSEQUENTIAL DAMAGES ARISING OUT OF THE USE OR INABILITY TO USE THE PROGRAM (INCLUDING BUT NOT LIMITED TO LOSS OF DATA OR DATA BEING RENDERED INACCURATE OR LOSSES SUSTAINED BY YOU OR THIRD PARTIES OR A FAILURE OF THE PROGRAM TO OPERATE WITH ANY OTHER PROGRAMS), EVEN IF SUCH HOLDER OR OTHER PARTY HAS BEEN ADVISED OF THE POSSIBILITY OF SUCH DAMAGES.

END OF TERMS AND CONDITIONS

Installation Instructions

To install Red Hat Linux from the CDs to your hard drive, check out Chapter 3.

The book includes a copy of the Publisher's Edition of Red Hat Linux from Red Hat, Inc., which you may use in accordance with the license agreements accompanying the software. The Official Red Hat Linux, which you may purchase from Red Hat, includes the complete Official Red Hat Linux distribution, Red Hat's documentation, and may include technical support for Official Red Hat Linux. You also may purchase technical support from Red Hat. You may purchase Official Red Hat Linux and technical support from Red Hat through the company's Web site (www.redhat.com) or its toll-free number, 1 (888) REDHAT1.

Limited Warranty. (a) WPI warrants that the Software and Software Media are free from defects in materials and workmanship under normal use for a period of sixty (60) days from the date of purchase of this Book. If WPI receives notification within the warranty period of defects in materials or workmanship, WPI will replace the defective Software Media. (b) WPI AND THE AUTHOR OF THE BOOK DISCLAIM ALL OTHER WARRANTIES, EXPRESS OR IMPLIED, INCLUDING WITHOUT LIMITATION IMPLIED WARRANTIES OF MERCHANTABILITY AND FITNESS FOR A PARTICULAR PURPOSE, WITH RESPECT TO THE SOFTWARE, THE PROGRAMS, THE SOURCE CODE CONTAINED THEREIN, AND/OR THE TECHNIQUES DESCRIBED IN THIS BOOK. WPI DOES NOT WARRANT THAT THE FUNCTIONS CONTAINED IN THE SOFTWARE WILL MEET YOUR REQUIREMENTS OR THAT THE OPERATION OF THE SOFTWARE WILL BE ERROR FREE. (c) This limited warranty gives you specific legal rights, and you may have other rights that vary from jurisdiction to jurisdiction.